SUNY COLLEGE AT OSWEGO
Its Second Century Unfolds

Dr. Edward Austin Sheldon,
founder and principal, 1861–1897.

Dr. Virginia L. Radley,
president of the college since 1978.

SUNY COLLEGE AT OSWEGO

Its Second Century Unfolds

Dorothy Rogers

SUNY College at Oswego

Copyright © 1988 by Auxiliary Services,
State University College at Oswego, Inc.

All Rights Reserved

FIRST EDITION

Manufactured in the United States of America

Contents

Foreword: Dr. Virginia L. Radley	vii
Preface	ix
1. Building a Proud Tradition—Then a Hiatus	1
2. The Darkest Years	24
3. Years of Transition	45
4. The Curtain Rises on a New Era	70
5. Dramatic Changes in Faculty and Curriculum	89
6. A Turbulent Era of Student Activists	104
7. Campus Life: Some New Directions	120
8. A New Mission: The Pursuit of Excellence	144
9. A Faculty of Distinction: Its Mission and President	171
10. The Roles Faculty Members Play	191
11. Crafting a Curriculum: Basic Issues and The Liberal Arts	203
12. Professional Studies and Special Programs	224
13. Student Life in the 1980s	239
14. More About Students of the 1980s	261
15. Beyond the Horizon	283
Appendix: State University's First Family	301
Notes	303
Index	315

Dr. Dorothy Rogers

Foreword

THE author, Dr. Dorothy Rogers, was born in 1914, one of five children of a prominent Ashburn, Georgia, family. Her ancestors and relatives were lawyers, teachers, doctors, college professors, college presidents, and businessmen and women—all deeply committed to the efficacy of education in molding the *vir bonus*, the good citizen.

Dr. Rogers, a graduate of the University of Georgia with a Ph.D. from Duke University, came to Oswego in 1946. Over the years, as professor of psychology, Dr. Rogers taught hundreds of Oswego graduates, until her death on January 7, 1986. It was said that if her classes were scheduled at midnight, they would be closed out within an hour.

In 1978, she was designated Distinguished Service Professor and in 1983 was elected vice-president of the National Women's Party.

With a list of twenty-five publications to her credit, this remarkable woman, despite an incredibly busy schedule, managed to travel extensively throughout North and South America, Europe, Asia, Africa, the Middle East, India, Australia, New Zealand, and sundry other points in this world—over eighty countries in all. Reflective of these experiences were her best-selling travel books *Jeopardy and a Jeep* and *Highways Across the Horizon*.

Her numerous texts in child, adolescent, adult, and developmental psychology are widely used in colleges and universities across the United States, three of them repeatedly hitting the top of the lists in sales nationwide.

Dr. Rogers was classically educated and no stranger to Latin, Greek, modern foreign languages, and literature, yet her interests ranged widely to embrace feminist issues and concerns, alternate life styles, financial trends on Wall Street, and, above all, student mores and modes of behavior. Perhaps her greatest contribution will emerge from the longitudinal research she did on the students in her own classroom over a forty-year period, much of it still waiting to be mined.

No description of her accomplishments can possible recreate her living person. The College at Oswego is fortunate to have had for almost forty years a master teacher, a Renaissance mind, and a stellar person in Dr. Dorothy Rogers.

Virginia L. Radley
President
State University of New York
College at Oswego

Preface

THIS book briefly reviews and extensively updates the centennial history, *Oswego: Fountainhead of Teacher Education, A Century in the Sheldon Tradition*, written by Dorothy Rogers and published by Appleton-Century-Crofts in 1961. It pays tribute to the thousands of students and faculty members who identify with this college, since 1948 renamed the State University of New York, Oswego. Recorded in this book are the outstanding accomplishments over the years of the college, a source of real and deserved pride. The final chapter, concerning the current era, constitutes perhaps the most comprehensive portrait of a college done to date. Finally, this volume provides perspective, telling us where we've been, where we are, and where we may be going.

Because of the key role played by institutional leaders, the content is organized by administrations from Edward Austin Sheldon to Virginia L. Radley. Each administration, in turn, is discussed in terms of four topics: general developments, faculty, curriculum, and students. All are viewed against the backdrop of the environment and the times, because each college generation has its distinctive values and way of life. Nevertheless, at any one time—despite their overall common themes—campuses differ from each other almost as much as they do by eras.

In certain respects this volume differs from most college histories in that it is more encompassing. The majority of such books focus mainly on academic matters. Here the total operation is surveyed, including campus life. This book also provides an in-depth study of a contemporary college operation. The final chapter focuses on the future, in recognition of the fact that colleges are ever-changing rather than static and underscoring the need for planning. Paths into the future never follow a straight line, but zig and zag as unforeseen developments occur—for example, the advent of the computer.

The reader may wonder why certain items are treated as they are. For example, the college is sometimes called SUNYCO because it is often thus designated and its formal name is so long (State University of New York College of Arts and Science at Oswego). Some individuals are quoted relatively often because, for one reason or another, they spent much time reminiscing. Students' graduation dates are given except when the quest to locate them proved too elusive.

The writing of college histories has not, to date, won its spurs as an academic enterprise, although James R. Chumney of Memphis State says that this specialty is "becoming an increasingly sophisticated field." At one time, notes Lawrence O. Christensen, co-author of the history of the University of Missouri at Rolla, it was thought that researchers should deal only with big issues in their research, and local studies were judged "antiquarian or provincial." James R. Chumney calls history writing a serious professional risk; and Clifford S. Griffin, who wrote the history of the University of Kansas, declares that "the problems of writing an institutional history made me sure I didn't want to write one again."[1]

Among the problems college historians often encounter are the unwillingness of many institutions to put money into the research, the lack of adequate archival materials, or the keeping of college records "under lock and key." Some institutional records simply do not exist. In addition, it is difficult to know what to reject or to include. Writing recent history also involves "passing judgment on those in power" and on current colleagues. Sometimes a history's publication has been held up because officials or faculty members disapproved of its contents.[2]

Feelings about college histories, including those of their authors, have been ambiguous at best. However, university historians are beginning to become more visible partly because officials want some help in attempting to "figure out how they got to where they are now—and they want professionals to do the task." Also, there is growing interest in local institutions and the role they play in their communities.[3]

This writer, too, has encountered her share of problems. A call for memoirs, published in the *Alumni Bulletin,* netted one medium-length letter and three or four notes. Sifting through masses of college data proved a prodigious and rarely exciting task. It has also proved impossible, within the scope of this book, even to mention more than a fraction of the persons who really deserve recognition. Mainly, those mentioned happened to be involved in matters under discussion. Considerable space is accorded President Radley because she is SUNY's first woman president, the first out of sixty-four presidents; she not only plays the key role in SUNYCO's current destiny, but also is widely known in higher education and is a colorful, dynamic personality as well.

This book could hardly have appeared had it not been for the assistance of persons too numerous to mention. Contributors include many alumni (identified by date of graduation when available), current students, and individuals unless otherwise identified, who are present or former faculty members. A large debt is also due the *Oswegonian* (the student newspaper), past and present, and to librarians supervising the college archives: Judith Wellman, Lois Stolp, and Nancy Osborne. Those who read portions of the manuscript to check for accuracy were Elizabeth Moody, Frederick Ratzeburg, Barbara Gerber, Richard Wheeler, Nancy Osborne, Thomas Gooding, Linda Syrell, and Ruth Everett. Others to whom special credit is due include Virginia Radley, Donald Mathieu, David King, Alexander Beattie, George Pitluga, Margaret Lowery, Celia Sgroi, Mary Brown, Lori Smolinski, Cherie Blanchard, Ann Hoefer, Suzanne Boshart, Lisa Potter, and Mary Furnari. Dorothy P. Heindel was the general editor.

1

*Building a Proud Tradition— Then a Hiatus**

EVERY college has its setting. That of our college is steeped in historic lore, and every student who studies here is exposed to the rich heritage of the Oswego area.

Although the Iroquois Indians had lived here, no one knows for how long. Samuel Champlain, perhaps the first white man to come to this area, arrived about 1615. Father Simon LeMoyne, a Jesuit missionary, came in 1654 recognizing it as a fine place for trade. Dutch and English traders had pushed as far as Oswego by the 1680s, and the English built their first fort in 1727 making Fort Oswego the first English stronghold on the Great Lakes. During the Colonial period, Oswego became one of several frontier posts on the major waterways into the interior of British North America, an important fresh-water port where soldiers, missionaries, traders, and Indians stopped to trade, fish, or camp.

During the period 1750 to 1755, the fur trade peaked, causing the British to judge Oswego one of the most important places on the continent and the French to look on it as one which must be destroyed. During the French and Indian War (1754–63) between the English and their allies on one side, and the French and their Indian allies on the other, the French under Montcalm in 1756 destroyed three of the forts the English had constructed at Oswego. The French King Louis XV struck a silver medal to commemorate this event. Only two copies of this medal are known to be in existence; one is in the Louvre in Paris, the other in the Oswego Historical Society's collection.

After rebuilding Oswego in 1759, the English continued to use it as a naval base. During the American Revolution, it was a military outpost controlling a significant gateway of communication to Canada and the West.

---

*The years of Principals Edward Austin Sheldon, the founder, 1861–97, and his successor, Isaac B. Poucher, 1897–13.

Around 1796, after the post was turned over to the United States, the westward migration of traders and settlers favoring the Northern water route began to pass through the area in growing numbers. Oswego's first modern business—the forwarding of goods—began in 1796.

The first attempts to structure the area formally were made around 1797, when a state surveyor laid out a 100-acre tract on the west side of the river into streets, to be called "forever thereafter by the name of Oswego." The word "Oswego" is a variation of the Indian name Osh-we-geh, which means "pouring-out place." Thus, Oswego's name reflects its function as a watershed for over 5,000 square miles, which includes more than a tenth of the area of New York State.

Oswego had become a United States naval base by 1808, and that same year the brig *Oneida* (which was built here) became the first United States naval vessel on Lake Ontario. Four years later, during the War of 1812, Oswego became an important base for naval construction and a depot for naval supplies. Sir James Yeo captured Oswego in May 1814 but found that most of the supplies had been either removed or destroyed.

After the war, in the 1820s, many people were attracted by Oswego's water power. Incorporated as a village in 1828, Oswego grew as the railroad and other industries thrived. In 1848, when the population numbered 12,000, the legislature named it a city; by 1865 the population had grown to 20,000. Meanwhile, the Erie Canal had been connected with the harbor via the Oswego Switch Canal, thus enabling the Oswego route to compete with the Erie Canal route from Buffalo. Ships were lined up so closely together that it was possible to walk across the river's mouth on their bows.

Later, Oswego attracted many immigrant groups, including English, Scots, Irish, German and French Canadian settlers. In the early nineteenth century its culture was predominantly controled by Protestant churches. Among visitors to Oswego in the nineteenth century were "Fanny Wright, a radical unspeakable of sorts; Buffalo Bill Cody; and even Harry Houdini, the magician."[1]

Of significance to the college's beginnings was the status of higher education in those times. After the American Revolution, rapid growth in the nation occurred, shared somewhat by the colleges and, until the Civil War, stories were those of individual institutions. All tried to adjust to their nation's new needs, but they disagreed about the best course of action. There was much debate about such matters as admissions, curricula, goals, and what college life should be like.

The present collegiate system began about the 1860s, when the first steps were taken toward modernizing the curriculum. After the Civil War, an academic revolution began: the curriculum opened up to science, electives became popular, and career preparation became a major goal. Coeducation made progress in the collegiate culture and was endorsed as a part of students' informal education.

The social and economic changes which occurred between the Civil War and World War I left their mark. A more democratic philosophy prevailed, along with a recognition of the right to higher education for working-class children. Except for brief periods, the times were generally prosperous due to scientific, agricultural, and industrial advances. College attendance became the route to social mobility.

Against this background, Edward Austin Sheldon founded the Oswego Normal School in 1861. Born in 1823, Sheldon attended Hamilton College for over a year, then became a junior partner in a garden nursery, which subsequently failed. Having no further employment, he set out to investigate the plight of the poor of Oswego. Finding 1,500 people who could neither read nor write, he formed the Orphan and Free School Association to provide a home for orphans and free schooling for the poor, similar to the "ragged schools" that existed in England. However, after a few years, the money contributed by prominent citizens gave out and the school closed.

In 1849 he married Frances Stiles and, that same year, opened a private school, the Oswego Seminary. This venture also failed and, in 1851, he accepted the position of superintendent of Syracuse Schools, a post he held until 1853. During that period, he consolidated and graded the Syracuse elementary schools and assembled the books that formed the core of the new Syracuse public library.

Sheldon returned to Oswego in 1853 as the first superintendent of city schools, making his home in the United States Hotel. In 1856 he purchased the tract now known as Shady Shore, and the home he constructed in 1857 serves today as the home of the college's president. In the first location Sheldon selected for his home, a large tree stump about two feet in diameter "mastered him." Unable to remove it, he chose the present site. Depending upon the season, Sheldon drove to the school in a cutter or buggy drawn by a small, dark pony.

In 1859 he instituted a system of ungraded classes called arithmetic schools for "uncouth, untutored, rough, overgrown boys." Sheldon said, as far as he knew, this unclassified school for making up deficiencies was a new feature, not only of Oswego but also of any system of graded schools. Sheldon taught these children in an old stone building, donated by the owner, which Sheldon himself cleaned and repaired.

During a trip to Toronto in 1859, Sheldon discovered materials in the National Museum representing an adaptation of Pestalozzian objective teaching; these materials had been used in the Home and Colonial School in London, England, a training School for teachers. Sheldon purchased the exhibit for $300 (a third of his year's salary). Using these trophies, in fall 1859 he introduced his version of objective teaching, which he called "object teaching." City teachers were required to attend meetings every Saturday for grounding in Sheldon's version of the Pestalozzian method.

Realizing their preparation would improve under the tutelage of someone who had first-hand acquaintance with Pestalozzian techniques, he lured from the London Home and Colonial School a Pestalozzian expert, Margaret E. M. Jones, who spent the 1861–62 year teaching a class of Oswego city teachers, including Sheldon. When she returned to London at the end of the year, Sheldon assumed charge of the school, by then supported by the city.

The original class taught by Jones met in a cloakroom of a wooden building on the west side of West Fourth near Bridge Street. In 1865 the school moved to the former United States Hotel on West Seneca between Sixth and Seventh Streets. Remodeled by the city, it served as housing for the teachers-in-training, as well as the five-hundred children who constituted the practice school.

The Board of Education, by an 1864 legislative act, placed the training school under the control of the state superintendent; the state gave $50 for the instruction of each student for up to fifty students. In 1865 the state legislature assumed support of the training class and named it the Oswego State Normal and Training School. In 1866 the Board of Education bought the United States Hotel building, headquarters of the Oswego State Normal School. That same year, 1866, the state provided for six normal schools, including Oswego, each to be governed by local boards appointed by the state superintendent of instruction.

Meanwhile, Sheldon's object teaching had not gone unchallenged. At the New York State Teachers Convention of 1862, a Dr. H. B. Wilbur, superintendent of the New York State Idiot Asylum, branded Oswego's object teaching "vicious." However, the fallout from this onslaught proved quite benign. A committee of the National Teachers Association, chaired by a Professor Greene from Brown University, came to Oswego to test and report on its methods. Greene's report in 1865 was so favorable that Oswego's fame spread abroad. In 1869, Sheldon resigned as superintendent of Oswego City Schools and secretary of the Board of Education to devote full time to the Normal School. A second major challenge arose in 1870; local critics took aim at object teaching, and object lessons were discontinued. However, at least locally, Sheldon won out, and object teaching revived until Herbartianism swept through American education. Its more scientific approach stressed the organization of subject matter around meaning and the rejection of faculty psychology in favor of unity of mental activity. On the less favorable side, it brought slavish submission to the so-called formal steps of instruction, rigid organization of subject matter, and a subject-centered curriculum. Yet the prevailing winds of its popularity blurred educators' vision and obscured its flaws.

Sheldon and the school continued to win honors, adding a glow to an already bright image. Sheldon never earned a college degree but was awarded two honorary degrees; the first an honorary master's by Hamilton College in 1869, and the second in 1875, an honorary doctorate by resolution of the Board of Regents. At the 1893 World's Fair, in Chicago, Sheldon became president of the Department of Professional Training and Teachers, the highest honor in his field. At the close of the Fair, the Oswego Normal School was awarded a medal of honor.

Sheldon's wife died in 1896, a terrible blow to him; nevertheless, in 1897, at the age of 74, he enrolled as a student in a summer-school course in Chicago to learn more about the Spear methods of teaching arithmetic. In the very next month, August, Sheldon died. But his work survived him, with his signature clearly stamped on it.

The Sheldon years deserve a detailed review, beginning with Sheldon. His appearance matched his disposition—pleasant, warm, fatherly. His gray locks fell in long curls almost to his shoulders; in 1877 he adopted a shorter hair cut with a small curl at the back of his head and a curl above his forehead.

Sheldon could be extremely firm about matters of principle, a characteristic both friends and critics came to respect. When the Normal trustees asked him to modify certain policies, his daughter, Mary, said he brought his hand down on the table with great force and said, "I would resign from this school and lose my salary before I would give up that which I know is right." Like the current president, Virginia L. Radley, he was unwavering in maintaining a secure academic beachhead on campus.

He was also a strict disciplinarian with students. While carpentry work was being done on the building, he watched carefully that the students marched to and from classes in an orderly way, keeping time with music. On one occasion he came upon a well-done drawing of a man hanging from a hangman's gallows. He asked that the artist come forward, but no one ever did, presumably for fear of being disciplined. Another time, when about twenty students were studying in the corridor, several of them began throwing notes around. Sheldon arrived at that moment and herded them all into his office. He was severe with them, possibly because some were previous offenders. Several were expelled and some suspended.[2] Despite occasional incidents of this sort, he was perceived as merely doing what he believed right. Mary E. Laing (1874) said of him: "As an antagonist he never antagonized, bcause the man was so completely merged in the cause." His favorite hymn was "Calm Me, My God."[3]

Most often students recalled Sheldon's responding to them warmly. It was believed he never forgot a student no matter where he met one, and he frequently went out of his way to treat them kindly. When student Lillie Herrick first entered the Normal, for example, Sheldon personally helped her find her classrooms; since there were no lockers in which this early commuter could leave her books, he let her keep them in a corner of his private desk.

Every year Sheldon entertained the students at his own expense, either taking them on an excursion or, more frequently, asking them to a "lick" or sugar party at his home. Since it was too far for students to walk, he provided conveyances for all. On one particular Saturday, four hundred students arrived. Sheldon and his wife took their places near a large iron kettle filled with maple syrup and helped serve everyone. The maple syrup was in the form of a glaze on cracked ice obtained from drifting pieces in the lake or stirred to soft sugar and eaten with crackers and lemonade. These parties at his home, now Shady Shore, were held amid a lovely grove of trees on grounds sprinkled wilth wildflowers.

Sheldon, Hermann Krusi, Jr., Isaac Poucher, and Matilda Cooper were often called the Big Four of the early Normal School. Krusi, next in importance to Sheldon, was with the Normal from 1862 to 1887. He had studied and worked with his father, Herman Krusi, Sr., who had been an aide to Pestalozzi. Krusi, Jr., taught in London's Home Colonial School, where he first met Margaret E. M. Jones, a leading exponent of Pestalozzianism.

Krusi moved from London to a Normal School in Massachusetts; from there Sheldon lured him to Oswego. Krusi was brilliant, with a gift for sorting the ersatz from the real. In many ways he was ahead of his time, stressing that one perceives first the whole and then the parts, a psychological principle considered a discovery years later. Philosophically, he was the main interpreter of Pestalozzianism at Oswego. Sheldon said that Hermann Krusi was the only living man who had linked together the significant educational movements of the past with those of the present.

Krusi was well liked and close to Sheldon. Though he was a language professor, English was his second language, making him difficult to understand. He encouraged students not to rely solely on books for ideas; in his geometry class, Krusi did not use a textbook but instead required original solutions and proofs of propositions. His approach to subject matter encouraged "the determination of facts, independent thinking and reasoned out conclusions."[4] Leaving the Normal School in 1887, he moved on to harbor and municipal improvement in Manila, the Philippines.

The third member of the Big Four, Isaac Buchanan Poucher, taught mathematics at the Normal from 1865 to 1897, serving also as principal from 1897 until his retirement in 1913. He was a superb mathematics teacher but less than successful as principal. Small, nervous, and quick in movement, he always seemed to be in a hurry.

The fourth member of the Big Four was Matilda S. Cooper. Later married to I. B. Poucher, she was considered the best demonstrator of Pestalozzian techniques. Always she wore a gold ring set with small rubies and diamonds Margaret Jones had sent her from London.

Mary V. Lee, remarkable for her personality, intellect, and teaching abilities, joined the staff several years later in 1874. Holder of a medical degree from the University of Michigan, the first earned there by a woman, she later studied at Cambridge. At Oswego she taught and published in the areas of zoology and physical culture. Isabel Lawrence (1873) observed that during the second half of the nineteenth century, the world became "a ferment, caused by the works of Darwin, Huxley and other scientists." Mary V. Lee, noted for her work in science, was chief interpreter of this movement at Oswego. She readily dismissed as fraud any departures from scientific principle.

Mary V. Lee, like Oswego's famous Dr. Mary E. Walker of Civil War vintage, sharply disapproved of conventional women's attire. She asked, "Why should I go around with dragging skirts gathering up dust and filth and germs?" Replying to her own question, she cut off four inches from the bottom of her trailing skirts, so that her heels showed as she walked around Oswego. In consequence she was seen as "shockingly immodest." Then she said, "God gave me a proper skeleton to support my flesh and to protect my organs; why, therefore, should I try to impose over this another artificial skeleton?" Her own answer was to take off her corset and to go everywhere without stays. Then, noted one observer, "to cap the climax it seems that Dr. Lee next developed the audacity to appear with her hair bobbed short." Later, in the 1950s, someone said that "she merely lived before her time, as she dressed pretty much the same as the State Teachers College girls of this day all do."

Sheldon's daughter, Mary, who later married Oswego alumnus Earl Barnes, taught at Oswego from 1874 to 1876 and again from 1878 to 1884. Moving with her husband to California in 1891, he to become a professor of education at Stanford University, Mary Sheldon Barnes was named an assistant professor of history, the first woman on the Stanford faculty. Throughout her career she applied the scientific method to the teaching of history. She died in Rome, and it was said her ashes were scattered over its seven hills. However, the *Vocationist* indicated that Mary Sheldon Barnes died in London on August 27, 1898. Her body was cremated, and her ashes were buried in the cemetery in Rome, just outside the old Aurelian Wall. The gravestone reads simply, "Born in Oswego, New York." Alumnus Uldrick Thompson (1880) wished that the first account were correct because it was more in keeping with Mary Sheldon's character.[5]

Lillie Herrick recalls other instructors, among them Henry Straight, who taught the natural and physical sciences in 1878. He employed various classroom techniques quite innovative for that period, such as dissection in biology and experimental laboratory work. Another, and perhaps best-loved, faculty member was Ardie (Ordelia) Lester, who taught rhetoric, English, spelling, and vocal music.[6]

Certain alumni memoirs indicate that some of the instructors were quite innovative in their teaching methods. Students were encouraged to think, not to parrot any local "party line." George B. Ransom, a Rear Admiral in the United States Navy in 1913, recalled that he had been taught at the Normal School forty-two years before (1871) the principles involved in wireless telegraphy. He added, "Possibly, if we'd only had an electrical laboratory, the invention of this apparatus might have been made then."

From 1861 to 1865 the training course lasted just one year and was purely pedagogical; however, academic training was added in 1865, and the four-year classical course in 1867. In 1865 two courses were offered: the elementary preparatory and training course and an advance preparatory course, consisting mostly of methods in practice teaching. The four-year classical course included the identical requirements of other courses in addition to Latin, Greek, and German. Regardless of the course taken, the final year was devoted to professional work. Because of criticism that the work was too elementary, the Elementary English course was abolished in 1891, and a year was added to the advanced English course in 1893. Manual training was added in 1892 and, in 1893, a four-year scientific course was instituted.

Sheldon and most of his staff practiced object teaching, essentially a Sheldon creation, which focused on first-hand knowledge of objects. Objective teaching emphasized understanding, but the difference was mainly one of emphasis and not fundamental aim. Sheldon developed ideas, in addition to those of Pestalozzi, which were quite advanced for that day. He stressed the importance of children's curiosity, focused on their needs, and insisted on variety and change of pace. The heart of the program, practice teaching, had been adopted by Normals throughout the country. However, no basic changes were to be made in Oswego's program until the 1930s. Indeed, residues of those early features persisted until the Campus School closed its doors in 1981.

What Sheldon called the Big Fight came in 1872, a challenge to his famous object teaching. On January 26, 1872, four members of the Board of Education moved that object teaching be discontinued in Oswego's junior schools and that Cornell's primary geography and Appleton's elementary arithmetic be substituted. The motion was tabled, but the controversy dragged on for several months. Parents' chief complaint was that object teaching resulted in poor records on state regents' examinations and treated "unimportant" subjects such as science and nature study, while more basic information, especially geography, was neglected. Two school-board members actually came to blows over the issue, one attacking the other with a pick axe; however, others intervened, and no real harm was done. A letter to the newspaper argued that gymnastics and object teaching should be sent out of doors. Children don't need to "to go school to write about colors, about light and heavy, about rough and smooth," argued this critic. A child can learn more about these matters in just an hour's play "in the yard or in the gutter, than a month in a schoolroom." Object teaching was reinstated a year or so later.[7]

Oswego also played an important pioneering role in manual training, transplanted from Europe. Manual training was part of the regular curriculum from 1862 to 1886. In the first year, 1862, the drawing course included stick laying, weaving, paper cutting, color, form, and inventive drawing. In fall 1886 a workshop of sorts was established in the school basement, forerunner of the current industrial arts department. In 1893 a regular course in manual training was organized by Richard Piez, a graduate of Baltimore Polytechnic Institute. The shop was thoroughly remodeled in 1894 and included twenty double benches and a full complement of tools. All students enrolled in the shop course did their practice teaching in that area. This experience and Oswego's reputation made its graduates sought throughout the nation as shop teachers.

Just as Oswego had become famous as a center for training elementary school teachers, it became well known as a source for manual training instructors. It might be said that Oswego helped pave the way for manual training through selling Pestalozzianism to American educators; Pestalozzi is called the father of manual training. Sheldon's broad concept of manual training resembled the manual arts of later times as he applied manual training to various modes of expression: drawing, penmanship, and painting.

Oswego cannot claim to have offered the first manual training course in America; this distinction belongs to the Massachusetts Institute of Technology. However, Oswego was the first Normal School to offer such training, and was among the first, if not the first, in 1896, to organize a shop for training teachers to make their own classroom equipment, and among the first to introduce a shop course in the elementary school.

Nineteenth-century students in America, and particularly in Oswego, dressed to meet style and weather conditons. Male students of the 1880s wore mustaches, often "drooping and dispirited looking," with a "pensive melancholy effect which was considered very distinguished and intriguing." They might wax the ends into points—although some girls objected that they tickled—or form them into handlebars. In the winter they wore wrist-length undershirts and ankle-length "drawers," often of thick flannel. Shirttails were tucked inside the drawers, which were so heavy that suspenders were passed through loops of tape attached to the waistband to keep them from slipping. This "arctic outfit" often was supplemented with mufflers, cardigan jackets, and knit wristlets. If a man had a sore throat, he might try to cure it by wrapping his neck in a stocking. In the spring the young men donned underwear of cotton material called balbriggan, also of wrist and ankle length. Before the 1880s men fastened their socks to their drawers with safety pins, or let them hang down, leaving gray flannels showing, but after that date garters were the fashion. In winter they wore derbys, and in summer, boaters of rough straw with wide brims and bands.

Young women's garb was far more cumbersome and confining, especially for formal wear. The women wore stockings supported above the knee with ribboned garters and four linen petticoats edged with lace or embroidery, the three outer ones starched to hold out the skirt. A whalebone and steel corset clasped around their middles shaped them into an "hourglass." The result was bulging hips and bosom, the standard for beauty. The women were so tightly squeezed together they could hardly breathe, one reason they were inclined to faint. Indeed, as someone remarked, "corseting a woman was like cinching up a pack horse." Over the women's petticoats was fixed a bustle and finally a tight bodice. Women often took with them an extra handkerchief, hairpins, and smelling salts, but no rouge, powder, or lipstick; the latter would have damaged their reputation. Their dresses, often of strange color combinations such as pink and brown, yellow and purple, was a bewildering confusion of tucks, flounces and trimmings. Sleeves, tight in the beginning of the 1880s came to assume the contours of hams displayed in butcher shops. On the street, women wore simpler clothing: fewer petticoats, black cotton stockings, and high-buttoned shoes, which reached a third of the way to the knee.

Women would braid their long hair into a plait behind and place "the front locks into curling papers or horrible contrivances of brown kid which looked like large angle worms." The women's bustle of the 1880s sometimes was "a cagelike affair of coiled wire; in others a thick pad of hair, held in place by tapes around the waist. . . ." After 1889 the somewhat diminished bustle was transferred to the front and called a rat. Girls were not supposed to show their ankles, and gentlemen were not supposed to suspect that women had legs until after the wedding.[8]

The typical Normal student of Sheldon's time was a girl, or young woman, mostly of the lower-middle or middle-middle class; some came with teaching experience. In the early days, most students came from surrounding towns and farms, but as Oswego became well known, a considerable number began coming from other states. Once arrived, girl students were largely insulated from the world outside the school. Some lived in the Welland or in the Little Welland annex, where they prepared their own food. Others lived in approved clubs or boarding houses in town.

The students had to budget money carefully, although things cost little by today's standards. In the 1890s a pair of buckskin-lined mittens cost about 40¢, a calico dress $1.00, four pairs of black stockings 54¢, a money order 5¢, soap 5¢, and rubbers 50¢. For a picnic or a treat, students could buy a dozen bananas for 15¢ and half a watermelon for 10¢.

While the boys were given complete freedom, the girls were severely restricted and expected to behave like ladies, which meant they were hostages to etiquette and rules. All contacts with males were strictly supervised. They could go out only with boys to whom they were related or engaged; otherwise they must entertain them at the Welland. Even by 1865 student government was making some headway at boys' schools, but in primarily female schools, such as Oswego, the *in loco parentis* policy prevailed. That is, faculty members acted in place of parents; and female students, like children, were expected to obey without question. There is no record of any rules applying to boys.

Considerable attention was paid to the physical well-being of students. Illnesses were not uncommon. Girls had no dieting problems because curves were fashionable; also, they lacked money for snacks. For common ailments, students would usually use home remedies: for swelling, a bread and milk poultice; for coughing, horseradish; for a sore eye, salt and water or milk and peppermint. Toothaches were treated in a variety of ways. Dentists used a "turnkey" which consisted of a hardwood handle with a steel rod attached at right angles with the handle, and tipped with a strong hook, somewhat like a fish hook. Laughing gas was used for pain when extracting teeth. A tank of gas would be brought in, the inhaler adjusted on the patient, and the gas turned on.[9]

Today's students would have found campus activities limited indeed. The only significant school-sponsored, extracurricular activity in Sheldon's time was the literary society; there were three at Oswego. Meetings and get-togethers of these societies were held every Wednesday afternoon. Each society chose a subject for study for a certain number of weeks, and its members read papers on phases of the topic. They apparently studied a surprising amount—there were few outside distractions. There were church socials and recreation such as sleighing, and occasional parties, which included imitations of the faculty. On the Fourth of July it was popular to ride in the trolley car out to the lake, where at times there were carnivals and balloon ascensions.[10]

Recorded escapades for those days are rare, at least at the Normal. However, once some upper-class young men, at home on vacation from Yale, Cornell, and elsewhere, broke into the Normal School and painted the statuary, including various goddesses and gods, not with paint, but with charcoal and removable materials, giving them a grotesque appearance. Faculties in those days surveyed such escapades with faces carved in stone.

Getting to school could be a problem, especially in winter. Hacks were driven around town, but girls lacked money for them and struggled instead through the snow, collectively imprinting it with surrealistic patterns. Student Lillie Herrick had to walk a mile and a half each way to and from school—hence, Sheldon excused her from attending assembly exercises. Often she walked through unbroken snowdrifts covering sidewalks.

Other personal glimpses may be obtained from students' own memoirs. Lillie Herrick's reflect the priority given filial obligations in those times. In 1880 Sheldon told her that she would be graduated the next January; however, she did not return after vacation because her mother was ill, and she had made Lillie promise never to leave her again. Later her mother died, but Lillie could not return. It was not unusual in those days for filial duty to result in termination of a daughter's career.

Uldrick Thompson (1880) recorded a pleasant experience. He was so impressed by a woman, six years his senior, who had studied at Oswego that he decided he would attend too. In this particular fall, uncertain whether his acquaintance was going to attend Oswego or the Albany Normal, he asked about her destination at the railway ticket office. Learning she had gone to Oswego, he said, "Give me a ticket there." He later met and married Oswego student Alice Haviland, daughter of Robert Haviland, one of the original importers of Haviland porcelain.

Sheldon often said, "A school is honored and great in its graduates, in what they do rather than what the school does." In other words, the "bottom line" is how a school's alumni turn out. On this score, the Oswego Normal of Sheldon's time rates well, partly because its graduates were inspired to continue their education.[11] Helen Williams (1869) was the first woman to receive a Bachelor of Arts degree from the University of Michigan in 1871. Mary Sheldon (1868) also earned a University of Michigan degree in 1871. Another alumna, who took graduate work at Cornell, established a scholarship available only to graduates of the Oswego State Normal and Training School, in memory of Edward Austin Sheldon.

Many Oswego alumni achieved distinction in fields other than teaching. Eliza Taylor (1891) became a teacher in Boston and an outstanding physician. Lena H. Severance is credited with clearing passage of the pension bill for teachers in the normal schools and other New York State institutions. A student of the late 1880s was George Fitz (1883), whose father made telescopes and built the refracting telescope now in use in the Mt. Hamilton Observatory.

Elizabeth Farrell (1895) presided for twenty-five years in the Henry Street settlement on Manhattan's Lower East Side, which offered community services for the poor. She developed a plan of education called ungraded classes and selected chronic truants for the first such class. In 1906 she was appointed to a position created especially for her: Inspector of Ungraded Classes.

In 1906 another Oswego alumna founded and organized the Boston Girls'

High School of Practical Arts for students with aptitude in manual rather than scholastic activities. It allowed special training in tasks leading to millinery and dressmaking on the one hand and, on the other, in basic skills in all arts applied to making a home. Also, the School provided training in skills which might serve as a basis for learning a trade.

Lottie (Charlotte) Blair-Parker (1872) was one of the first women playwrights in America. She authored several plays including *Way Down East*, a melodrama that played from 1898 to 1935, and a novel, *Homespun*. Theater Professor John Kingston directed a revival of the play at Sheldon Hall during the 1961 centennial. In her best-known play, written in the 1890s, Blair-Parker had subtly challenged the double standard sexual morality for women and men.

Most Oswego graduates, however, went into teaching, often under circumstances that would appall today's teachers. Here are instructions given teachers by local school boards in 1872:[12]

> Teachers each day should fill lamps, clean chimneys and trim wicks. Each teacher should bring a bucket of water and a scuttle of coal for the day's session. You should make pens carefully; you may whittle nibs to the individual taste of the pupil. Men teachers may take an evening each week for courting purposes or two evenings a week, if they go to church regularly. After ten hours in school, teachers should spend the remaining time reading the Bible or other good books. Women teachers who marry or engage in unseemly conduct shall be dismissed. . . . Any teacher who smokes, uses liquor in any form, frequents pool or public halls or gets shaved in a barber shop, will give good reason to suspect his worth, intentions, integrity and honesty. The teacher who performs his labors faithfully and without fault for five years will be given an increase of 25¢ per week in his pay, providing the Board of Education approves.

Oswego alumni fared somewhat better than the average, at least economically. By 1880, 98.5 percent of them were teaching in twenty-nine states and territories, including Japan, the Sandwich Islands, Nova Scotia, and Argentina, and at considerably higher than average pay, because of Oswego's reputation.

Alumnus Uldrick Thompson left an account of several alumni. He credited his teaching ability with what he learned in his two and a half years at the Oswego Normal where, he said, he had mastered the art of teaching. In 1881 he went to teach in the Hoboken Academy, where six other graduates of the Normal were also employed. John Babcock (1880) became a physician and surgeon; another graduate, archaeologist Eugene P. Andrews (1887), deciphered and translated the inscriptions on the East Architrave of the Parthenon. At Cornell, Andrews invented the mechanism by which all chimemasters are trained. Another Oswego alumnus at the Academy, Arthur Hoight, made a fortune from waste material used "to the last drop in the sugar industry in Hawaii." It was Hoight who organized the Oswego boys into the Oswego Alumni Association and was the leader in raising funds to build Sheldon Hall.[13]

Frequently, alumni undertook unenviable jobs because they were especially challenging. Harriet Daily (1897) taught mountaineers in remote parts of Tennessee and North Carolina, first in a small shack, twelve by twenty-four feet. One woman brought her two girls to one of the mission schools, saying, "I've brought you my girls and I want you to put a face on them." She referred to the impression that the school had made in changing expressions of pupils' faces. One mountain woman, on noting Daily's modest library of about fifteen volumes, asked: "Don't it hurt your head to read so many books?"

Perhaps the most significant achievement of the early alumni was the establishment of new Normal schools and city training schools during a period of enormous growth for such institutions. Most of them were founded and staffed by persons from such Normal schools as Bridgewater, Albany, Illinois, and Oswego, with Oswegonians playing the larger part. Oswego alumni founded twelve state and many city normals throughout the country, several in foreign countries, and helped in the founding of others. In 1886, A. B. Mayo declared that as far as he knew, every normal school, whether city or state, was organized on the Oswego plan. Joseph E. Deupree, historian, often says that Ferris State College in Michigan was "born in pre-revolutionary France and is a spin-off of the State University of New York."[14] He has arranged a shelf of books in the college museum that contains copies of Russo's *Emile, Pestalozzi: His Life Works and Influence,* which Hermann Krusi wrote after he left Oswego; this author's *Oswego: Fountainhead of Teacher Education;* and his own *Century of Opportunity.* "I think W. N. Ferris, founder of Ferris State, must be one of your most illustrious alumni," wrote Deupree to the author (Dorothy Rogers). "After all, what other one has been a governor, a U.S. senator, a college president, a bank president, and a prophet, all in the same suit of clothes."

Alumni achievements abroad were focused mainly in Mexico, Argentina, and Japan. The Presbyterian mission in Mexico was in charge of two normal schools; one of these, the Mexico City Normal School, was directed from 1881 to 1896 by Oswego alumnae.[15] Also contributing importantly to this school was the Philadelphia Womens' Board or Society. The senior Presbyterian missionary in Mexico City was E. Milton Greene from Staten Island. Beginning in 1881, Oswego's Frances Snow was the first director of the new Mexico City Normal, which displaced the girls' school operated by the mission. She had taken a ship to Vera Cruz and from there a railroad trip to Mexico City, which was interrupted by a train wreck caused by ranchers whose cattle had been killed. In protest, they had placed rails across the track in large numbers and displaced two rails; as a result, the engine was thrown off the track, end to end.

From the first, Reverend Greene was impressed greatly by Frances Snow's competency, calling her superior to any other teacher in Mexico City. He had visited her classes and knew her methods, "undoubtedly those object methods instilled in her by E. A. Sheldon and his colleagues." Six years later Frances Snow became engaged to Reverend Hiram Hamilton, agent in Mexico for the American Bible Society, and resigned. She was replaced, at her own recommendation, by Ella DeBaun, who was judged highly competent.

The three Oswegonians and six other Americans who founded and directed normal schools in Argentina, with just one exception, were experienced prior to their arrival. In Argentina the idea was to establish a public Normal school system in which Americans were employed by the Argentine government; in Mexico, Americans were employed by the American Presbyterian Board of Foreign Missions.

In 1964 Alice H. Luiggi authored a volume, *65 Valiants*, the enlarged edition of a Spanish language book published in Buenos Aires. It tells of sixty-five American educators; all but three were women, who, between 1870 and 1900, founded and directed Normal schools in Argentina. Certainly, the five Oswego graduates—Clara Armstrong (1868), Jeannette Stevens (1875), Mary MacMillan (1876), Alcinda Morrow (1868), and Anna Rice Roberts (1872)—were highly significant in the schools' development.

Since the publication of Oswego's centennial edition, Alexander Beattie, Oswego alumnus and librarian, has established that five instead of four Oswego alumnae founded, directed, or taught in Argentine normals in the late nineteenth century.[16] The fifth individual was Anna Rice Roberts, who taught just two years, from 1874 to 1876. She was the first Oswego alumna to serve in the first Normal school founded in the northeastern city of Paraná. She had married the vice principal, George Roberts, from Rochester, and these two were the trailblazers for other Americans who established a national network of Normal schools in Argentina. The school at Paraná was the model on which the other Argentine normals were established, just as Oswego was the model for many Normal schools throughout the United States. Also, as with Sheldon in this country, Anna Rice and George Robertses' work may be considered "the key ingredient in Argentine primary teacher preparation."

A century after the American educators went to Argentina, Oswego alumna continued to receive recognition in Argentine journals and history books. One writer, E. Guevara, referred to Anna Rice Roberts as one of the group that proved to be the "seed plant" for Argentine educators. Guevara also referred to two other Oswego alumnae, Clara Armstrong and Jeannette Stevens, to whom he devoted an entire chapter in his 1960 book.

These alumnae continue to receive recognition. A reference book, *Historical Dictionary of Argentina*, 1978, describes the work of Clara Armstrong and that of her sister, Frances Armstrong (1906). In *Sarmiento's Daughters*,

1980, Edmundo Coreas identifies Clara Armstrong as the first woman to found a Normal school in South America. Both Mary MacMillan and Clara Armstrong are discussed in *Un Siglo de Educación en Catamarca*, 1981, by E. Ahumada de Del Pino. This volume includes an entire chapter about Armstrong's founding and directing of the Maestras de Catamarca, renamed in 1928 the Escuela Normal Clara J. Armstrong, in memory of its founder. The chapter concludes with a summary of a speech by a student, paying homage to Clara Armstrong upon her resignation.

Japan credits the United States with having had the greatest external influence on its education system. The basis of that influence was the Oswego movement as interpreted by Hideo Takamine (1877), for whom Oswego's Takamine Drive is named. Sent by the Japanese government in 1875 to study at the Normal, he became vice-principal of the Tokyo Normal School soon after his return to Japan. In 1881 he became principal of the school. In 1891 the Tokyo Normal became the Tokyo Higher Normal School with Hideo Takamine its principal. He resigned from this school in 1893 but remained actively involved in the field of education as a member of the National Textbook Council and of the Board of Trustees of the Imperial Museum. In 1897 he was appointed principal of the Higher Normal School for Women and in 1885–86 wrote a series of four volumes titled *New Principles of Education*.[17]

While principal of the Tokyo Normal School, Hideo Takamine introduced a new era in Japanese education by advocating developmental teaching methods based on Pestalozzianism and the Oswego movement. His school became the model for later Japanese teachers' colleges. Emma Dickerman Straight, another early graduate of Oswego (1871) taught several years in a normal school in Tokyo.[18]

These alumni were remarkably adaptable; they could teach almost anything, and did. Versatility was their speciality, supported by the broadly based education obtained from the remarkable Sheldon faculty.

The earliest alumni frequently had informal gatherings to celebrate special occasions. In 1875 Sheldon arranged an alumni excursion up the Saguenay by chartered steamer. Fifty-eight faculty members and alumni spent two weeks on this trip, at a total cost of $25 per person. The first alumni meeting was held at Normal Hall on July 9, 1867, and the Oswego Normal School Alumni Association was established in 1886, with 108 members. The first branch of the Alumni Association was organized on Long Island in 1891; the second, the Oswego Boys Club in New York City, held a dinner each year on the last Saturday evening in February, beginning in 1901. By the time of Oswego's fifty-year celebration, the affair had become as settled an institution as Washington's birthday.

Education historian Carter Good calls Sheldon "one of three persons who contributed most to improving the quality of elementary education in the nineteenth century"; the others were Horace Mann and Francis Parker. Sheldon accounted for a number of firsts in teacher training. He instituted the first training class for teachers-in-service; he organized the first city training classes, which later were to spread across the country; and he founded the school which became the pattern for all normals in New York State and for a majority throughout the country. Sheldon's emphasis on child study was also new; he paved the way for the ultimate unification of educational control in New York State, finally achieved in 1904. The State Superintendents' Council in 1897 declared that future historians, in treating progress in primary education and training teachers, would portray Edward Austin Sheldon as standing alone—"the Pestalozzi of the new world."

Although Sheldon was not the first individual to bring Pestalozzian ideas to America, Oswego put them in a form that could be adopted by the Normals of that day. Of special significance was the way Oswego related object teaching to the individual pupil for the first time in American education. In this regard Herbartianism proved a step backward, since it focused instead on subject matter and learning process. Sheldon's own creation was securely rooted in a healthy blend of theory and pragmatism.

Oswego was the first normal school in New York State to establish a practice or training school worthy of the name; the first to introduce general method and teach the pedagogy of particular subjects; the first to establish a free public kindergarten; and the first to purchase grounds for a school garden. Oswego was probably the first institution to combine educational theory with practice and to use practice schools efficiently for that purpose. The Oswego Normal was also the first such school to use a genuine laboratory approach, systematically testing theories and ideas. In addition, it was the first among the Normals to insist on physical examinations of students and on adapting exercises to individual needs.

Meanwhile, both the Oswego staff and alumni did much to build a professional literature of pedagogy; Sheldon, members of his staff, and alumni wrote prolifically. They were pioneers in education methods. Oswego was also significant in the history of manual training and critic work, winning recognition for these areas across the country. It was the first Normal to organize a manual training course, the first to recognize manual training as general education, and the first to have a well-defined course in kindergarten methods. Significantly, it initiated a Normal school tradition, corresponding to the centuries of tradition surrounding liberal arts institutions.

Oswego alumni had tremendous influence on teacher education nationally. They did much to disseminate educational ideas, for both Sheldon and his staff took an active part in professional meetings across the country. By 1886 over half the alumni had taught outside New York, including every state, the District of Columbia, and six foreign countries. By 1900 there was hardly a Normal school in America that did not have one or more Oswego alumni among its best teachers. Oswego truly earned the title "Mother of Normal Schools."

Oswego's own faculty members, past and present, have been among the most appreciative of the Sheldon tradition. Richard Piez wrote: "I like to think of Dr. E. A. Sheldon as we think of his contemporary, Abraham Lincoln, who goes down in history as a great emancipator. Lincoln freed the Negro from slavery; Sheldon emancipated childhood from the thralldom of mechanized memoriter learning." Mary E. Laing (1874) wrote that, in its educational philosophy, "Oswego has not represented an idea so much as an attitude of mind . . . characterized by liberality, reverence and large receptivity toward life. The school has trained its students to be learners. It has made its teachers learners with its students. . . . Oswego graduates have no single characteristic so conspicuous as this spirit of open-mindedness and essential progressiveness. It is the life of the school." Ralph Spencer, provost from 1978 to 1985, concludes that the significant part of the Sheldon heritage is Oswego's continuing effort to relate formal education to practical matters of life. Although Sheldon was "gentle and forgiving," he was intolerant of learning that could not be translated into practical concerns.

Isaac Poucher's principalship, which followed Sheldon's, was distinguished by many events. Among these was Oswego's award of a gold medal and diploma of honor at the Paris International Exposition in 1900, a testimony to Sheldon's achievements and their so-called halo effect. A second event was Brines' creation in Paris of a sculpture of Sheldon instructing a young boy (see photograph in center section) which remained in the capitol at Albany for two decades and was then brought to Oswego. A lesser event, in 1908, was the reopening of the Sheldon residence. Abandoned and in poor condition, it had been broken into. Outside, the top of a tree had been sawed off and carried away. Charles Sheldon, Edward's son, was allowed to live in the house rent-free, but the fruit from the trees was reserved by the local board. The next year Sheldon was allowed to continue living there, paying $5 a month, but the fruit was still reserved by the board.

A major event in those years was the acquisition of a new site and building for the school, a project Sheldon had advocated. Among reasons given for a new building was the City Board of Health's declaration that ten rooms in the current building were "unfit to be occupied by human beings, and the children have no place but the streets for recreation." Consequently, the state legislature appropriated $25,000 to purchase a new site. In 1907 a prolonged and heated debate ensued over the site choice. The Commissioner of Education wanted the Sheldon site of twenty-seven acres and his old homestead, but the board unanimously rejected this choice. Alternatives were the Orphan Asylum, Fitzhugh Park, the Merrick Orchard, or properties belonging to Gerritt Miller and Dr. W. H. Kidder.

In 1908 the board wrote to the commissioner expressing its views.[19] A Mr.

Stolwell rejected certain sites because they were in almost full view of the railroad tracks. In addition, there was a "large turbulent hoodlum element in that vicinity." The Merrick Orchard site was rejected because it was close to the Army post and constituted a potential hazard to the Normal's young ladies. A Mr. Coon supported the Kidder site on East Seventh Street because "few people from that locality are found in the police courts." It was "pleasant and safe for young ladies to pass through, either in the daytime or in the evening, to attend lectures, concerts, etc." Commissioner Draper, whose view ultimately prevailed, continued to insist on the Sheldon site because it was ample in size, had landscape possibilities, and alone commanded views of Lake Ontario. With regard to the distance from the city, he said (as it turned out, prophetically), "It must not be forgotten that such things are bound to follow the flag," and future generations would be disposed to say "it was the best thing that came our way to do for the Oswego Normal School."

In 1911 the semicentennial celebration was held in the Normal School and described in the volume *First Half Century: State Normal and Training School, Oswego, N.Y.*, of detailed interest mainly to alumni. At this time, the pupils, as they were called, numbered three hundred. The faculty had grown from fifteen to twenty-one since 1887, and annual appropriations for the school had grown from $18,000 to $40,000. Alumni from all over made the pilgrimage to their alma mater for this event, and heroic efforts were made to attach names to faces. In his commencement address at the Normal that year, Thomas E. Finnegan, third Assistant Commissioner of Education, made a recommendation that was later followed in principle. He observed that not all of New York's ten state Normals should offer all courses of study needed for training teachers, for each school "is so organized and located as to possess special advantages for doing the work of some of these courses." For each Normal to conduct all these courses would involve unnecessary duplication of faculty and equipment. Finnegan cited as an example that "the Oswego institution has been the pioneer normal school for our state in manual training work and has been authorized to give a special manual training course."

Another feature of the semicentennial celebration was a reception for the alumni at the new State Armory. The reception committee received guests in the drill room, and the officers' quarters and smaller rooms were used as dressing and restrooms for the 1,100 people who attended. The local papers called it "the largest and most brilliant reception ever." On this occasion, Isabel Lawrence spoke of the Oswego Normal as "having a soul." Also at this time it was moved that October 4, Sheldon's birthday, become Founder's Day. Founder's Day remains a tradition, celebrated each fall, although not necessarily on the anniversary of Sheldon's birth. The climax of the celebration came on July 1, 1911, when the cornerstone of the new building was laid in the presence of many people, including children of the training school, who sang "America" and "Columbia, the Gem of the Ocean." In the cornerstone is a sealed copper box which contains a Bible, copies of the Oswego *Palladium* and the Oswego *Daily Times*, an address by the Honorable P. W. Cullinan, a catalog of the Oswego Normal and Training School, a small American flag, a copy of *Redbook* presented by a Mr. Frederick Clark, and a program of the semicentennial exercises. One visitor, William C. Bagley, one-time Oswego Normal teacher and later a famous educator at Columbia University, commented upon the "magnificent building being erected to house this school." The legislature had appropriated $340,000 for its construction, and the building was formally dedicated two years later.[20]

In a sense, Isaac Poucher's 1897 to 1913 administration was mainly a postscript to the Sheldon era and a holding operation. Poucher did almost nothing to spread Oswego's reputation, nor did he make speeches or encourage innovation. Individual staff members were excellent, but there was no real coordination or substantial support of their efforts. On the national level, general improvement of the nation's normal schools caused Oswego's status to diminish.

Poucher had been an outstanding teacher, despite his less than brilliant performance as a principal. He advised his students to "use your brains or else they will dry up and rattle when you walk."[21] There were several important mileposts in his life: in 1865 Hamilton College conferred upon him the honorary degree of Master of Arts; in 1902, Syracuse University awarded him the degree of Doctor of Pedagogy. In 1858, he married Catherine Allen, with whom he had three children. In 1881, two years after she died, he married Matilda S. Cooper, one of the stars of Sheldon's faculty. She continued teaching until 1886 and died in 1900.

The most highly esteemed teachers of Poucher's time were holdovers from the Sheldon period. Caroline L. G. Scales, a devotee of the classics and a pillar of the School until her death in 1926, was one. Another star was Richard Piez, who held a doctor of pedagogy degree from New York University and taught a variety of subjects, including art and psychology. Amanda Funnelle (1862), who ran the kindergarten training program from 1888 to 1911, was outstanding; even by current standards her practices were fundamentally sound. Sheldon's only son, Charles, taught nature study at Oswego from 1893 until his retirement in 1914. During these years there were three distinguished directors of the Normal's training school: Dr. Grant Karr (1899–1906) of Jena, Germany, followed by William Bagley (1906–8) and then by David Gibbs (1908–13), who had been superintendent of schools in the Philippines and also had written a series of textbooks.

Collectively, the Poucher faculty had few degrees; however, they had traveled much and while most were Oswego graduates, the majority had studied in other colleges as well, often abroad. Many alumni spoke highly of the faculty's teaching competence.

Other personnel were charged with nuts-and-bolts operations on campus, among them Mr. Corcoran, hired to help in garden work and in physical and chemical laboratories at an annual salary of $100 and a Mr. Plunkett, who helped with manual training and with the school orchestra at an annual salary of $200. In 1905 the school janitor was appointed to help Joseph C. Park in manual training when he was not otherwise employed; and in 1910, a Mr. James Fox, who had been a gardener in England for twenty-three years—one in the royal gardens of the late Queen Victoria at Windsor—applied for labor in the school garden.

With regard to curriculum, considerable progress was made in manual training during the early 1900s under Richard Piez and Earl Burchell. Joseph Park reorganized the special drawing and manual training course, a program that combined vocational training and Herbartianism by linking manual training aims with the study of mankind. Around 1908 a new philosophy presented manual training as a broad orientation to the world of work.

The educational philosophy at Oswego was a blend of Pestalozzi, Froebel, Herbart, and Dewey thinking, differing somewhat from one instructor to another.

Just as each era in college history dons a different mask, so do its students don different dress. In the early 1900s, dress was still cumbersome by modern standards. Dress-up attire was somewhat elaborate, although no one wore rouge or lipstick, and few bathed more than once a week. School dress was simpler, varying little over the years. Shirtwaists were common and short sleeves the vogue, with certain limitations at Oswego. The faculty held a conference to decide whether practice teachers should be allowed to wear short sleeves. The decision was yes, if the sleeves came below the elbow. But practice teachers were not allowed to sit down while teaching a class.

Dress varied with the weather and occasion. In winter girls were long wool underwear, leggings, and caps that covered their ears. Approved outer attire included hats—required on the street, ankle-length dark skirts, four-in-hand ties, bright cotton stockings, high-buttoned shoes, and long-sleeved, starched white shirtwaists with stiff collars. Hair was to be maintained following tradition, "and any suspicion of lipstick or rouge got its wearer in trouble." One girl was expelled when she came to class with bobbed hair, which was just beginning to be fashionable.[22]

Housing arrangements were varied, mostly makeshift, often in private homes or clubs; the clubs were no more than boarding houses for several students. Estelle Harrington recalled in 1912 "travelling along dirt roads to classes in back of a democratic wagon, a certain type of horse and buggy rig." She "basket-boarded" in one of the local houses, which meant she did her own cooking and cleaning.

Many girls still lived at the Welland, by now an old firetrap, where they were closely confined to a morally antiseptic environment. Doors were locked at 7:00 P.M. and students were not to entertain persons of either sex after 7:30 P.M. on Monday through Thursday, or after 10:30 P.M. on other nights. Lydia Phoenix, music teacher, ate there and did not hesitate to tell the girls how to behave.

Elsewhere in the country, including such women's colleges as Radcliffe, Smith, and Bryn Mawr, faculty members and students were demonstrating for women's suffrage; however, the world's issues did not impinge on the Oswego girls' sanctuary. Students' lives were still highly constricted and bound by rules. Drinking and smoking among them were unheard of, and even slang was carefully avoided, except on the sly. Students were also warned against eating candy or ice cream on the street. Some Fulton students lived at home, which they preferred to the stern rules at the Welland, and commuted to school on the Syracuse-Oswego Trolley Line.

While students of those days were mainly from nearby rural counties and communities, three girls from New York City were watched with fascination; they displayed open contempt for the "upstate hicks." The hicks retaliated by nicknaming them after three New York hoodlums headlined in a famous gangster murder: Whitey Lewis, Leftie Louie, and Gyp, The Blood.

Coed activity was severely limited both by rules and scarcity of males, whom females outnumbered twenty to one. The extent of coed interaction was walking together or dating at the Welland. In no case were girls to walk or talk with boys as they went to classes. Occasionally there were school dances in the gymnasium under the vigilant watch of many chaperones, to whom students had to bow upon entrance. At these dances, girls could dance only with girls and boys with boys. In some schools between 1900 and 1910, there was reputedly a two-foot rule, the gap to be maintained between partners in dancing; some girls were said to carry a ruler. Whether this practice extended to Oswego is unrecorded.

There is some controversy regarding six Filipinos who studied for a year at the Normal School in the early 1900s. At least some of the other students believed that the American government had financed their study here, and one was outspoken regarding his resentment of the situation. While the American students were struggling, despite very limited funds, to stay in school, why should their government educate these Filipinos? However, one of the Filipinos, José Batungbacal, who subsequently became a distinguished writer and educator in the Islands, deplores this "myth."[23] Upon visiting Oswego in 1962 he said that the young men actually lived on five hundred dollars a year, paid by their own government. Moreover, the "rumor" that one of the students returned home and denounced his parents was equally untrue. What was true, however, is that Oswego had influenced education in the Philippines through its Filipino alumni. Several decades later Oswego's Gordon Wilber spent three years (1957–60) in the Philippines directing a team of Stanford University industrial arts specialists. Fellow Oswegonian William Huss (1935), a specialist in electricity and metals, served the next two years with the same team.

In more prosperous colleges in the country students might have access to leisure sports and enjoy ragtime, but life at the Oswego Normal was stern and simple. There were no student lounges, no snack bars or well-equipped dormitories. Students spent most of the day in school, until about five in the afternoon, with breaks only for lunch and for Assembly, the latter required. Friends who attended Syracuse University thought the Oswego girls did nothing but study.

Student activities, such as they were, were both organized and informal. There were religious associations and two literary societies, with no possibility for students to choose between them. The only town affairs allowed the young women were church entertainments and lectures. Churches gave receptions for students which were stiff affairs but well attended. More informally, students played games and sometimes took trolley and buggy rides. "In the winter," recalled Mildred Conant (1908), "I remember coasting down the hill to the river on a big sled." The girls might also hum or sing some of the currently popular songs. In the first decade of this century "Good Night Ladies" was popular—and in the second, "Oh You Beautiful Doll," "Five Foot Two—Eyes of Blue," "Let Me Call You Sweetheart" and "Down By the Old Mill Stream."

Conant's most memorable experience was a visit to Dr. Mary E. Walker. "Several of us took the trolley to the end of the line and walked to her place," she recalled. "Dr. Mary gave the girls graham crackers and buttermilk and showed them old relics in the attic. All the time she talked about women's health and evils of their clothing." Even at that date, Mary Walker dressed in trousers and a coat like a man's. Dr. Walker told Conant it would be wise to use suspenders to hold up the heavy skirt she wore; clothing should hang from the shoulder, not the waist, she explained.

For the first time, around 1900, there were interschool sports.[24] Prior to that time, boys' sports were limited to informal basketball, baseball, lawn tennis, and a football team of sorts. Football in those days involved brute force, . . . the flying wedge, the revolving wedge—substitutions were made only when players were so beat up they could hardly stand. Yet to come were helmets, shoulder pads, and guards. The girls played basketball, and both sexes engaged in ice skating and tobogganing.

The Normal students' not-so-normal life, despite its limitations, apparently paid off, because they had no trouble getting jobs. An Oswego diploma was still a prestige symbol. Oswego was living on its past reputation but still had some outstanding teachers—for example, Sabra Hayden, class of 1901, taught Oswego methods to teachers-in-training at the American school in São Paulo, Brazil, and she also tutored the American consul's sons.

Thus ended Principal Poucher's era—a hiatus in the school's history destined to become extended in the decades ahead.

2

*The Darkest Years**

THE James Riggs period (1913–33) was one of near dormancy in higher education, except for the World War I interlude. By 1910 the classical colleges had come to accept as inevitable the scientific, technical, and professional features of new curricula, and a measure of stability was achieved. However, between 1916 and 1918, economic problems shrank enrollments by 20 percent, and a mood of uncertainty about higher education prevailed. The next period was one of rapid growth during which parents, in increasing numbers, strove to provide their children with advanced education while deploring certain aspects of college life. They disliked the student rebellions of the 1920s, with their antireligious proclamations, defiance of authority, rejection of traditional values, and interest in sex and alcohol.[1]

Higher education in these years won few laurels from the critics. Samuel Capen, the first director of the American Council on Education, declared that the whole development of American education had been haphazard and planless. Some called these pre-Depression decades years of no progress, as lesser individuals succeeded the giant leaders of earlier times; yet others viewed this slower-paced period as required time for adjustment.

Locally, the city of Oswego had lost some of its earlier distinctions. Railroads had diminished in importance for transporting lake freight; in the 1920s Kingsford Starch, the world's largest producer of cornstarch, folded; the salt trade disappeared in the late 1860s and early 1870s.

On campus, the Riggs years opened with the occupancy of the new building, now Sheldon Hall. The school's first home had been in the old United States Hotel, and its second a towering building on West Seneca, between Sixth and Seventh Streets. Edith Milo (1917) recalls that Charles Sheldon's laboratory, in the old building on West Seneca, had contained many stuffed birds, a human skeleton, a human brain preserved in alcohol, and many plants. These were not transferred to the new building, perhaps

---

*These years embraced the presidencies of James R. Riggs, 1913–33; Ralph W. Swetman, 1933–46; Thomas Miller, Sr., 1946–47; and Harvey M. Rice, 1947–51.

because they belonged to him personally; however, a mineral collection was removed to the new building.

Another building was also planned, a dormitory. A group chartered in 1928, under the name of Sheldon Hall Incorporated, sold shares of stock to raise money for it, promising 10 percent interest. However, because of mismanagement, the project fell through, and several faculty members lost a significant portion of their meager savings.

The Riggs period was marked by events of varying significance. World War I had a profound impact: the school's enrollment was diminished by 40 percent. At one point, only ten men remained in the industrial arts course. The main contribution to the war effort was the housing and training of an Army Corps detachment. From July 8, 1918, to December 15, 1918, soldiers used the Campus School wing as a dormitory, the cafeteria as a mess hall, and the shop rooms as laboratories. Housed on the dormitory's main floor, the men were forbidden to go upstairs. Since the Army provided students and left a a legacy of two wooden buildings and shop equipment, the school benefitted.

During the war years, the faculty and students who remained at home did their bit. Some of the male faculty assigned to teach Army cadets also held military drills, often with sticks instead of rifles. Women faculty and students adopted a war orphan, cultivated war gardens, and made bandages for "the boys."

The nationwide influenza epidemic of 1918 was a second catastrophic event. The Welland, Normal's erstwhile women's dormitory, was turned over to the Red Cross for use as an emergency hospital, and faculty volunteers cooked and tended the ill.

The next decade was generally uneventful, with a few exceptions. The first yearbook of the Oswego State Normal and Training School appeared in 1919; called the *Oshwakee*, it was dedicated to James Riggs. Former principal Poucher died in 1920, at the age of 93. Five years later, in 1925, the Regents were asked for money from a bond issue to add a wing to the present building for training teachers of vocational subjects. Since 1915, the industrial arts student enrollment had grown from 20 to 116; more space was badly needed. In 1930 the legislature voted $300 thousand for the building; and Governor Franklin D. Roosevelt, whose travel itinerary included Oswego, was asked to lay a synthetic cornerstone, since the real thing was not immediately available. Excavation for the building had been scheduled to begin on May 4, 1931, but it was postponed until 220 spruce trees had been transplanted. The building was completed and dedicated in June of 1932.

Roosevelt was obviously familiar with the art of cornerstone laying. "Give me a little mortar on this trowel," he told the workmen. "And I might add that I have a union card in my pocket." A copper box filled with records for the future was placed in a hollow of the masonry box set for the cornerstone.

Riggs retired in May 1933 because of the mandatory sixty-five year age limit, and an era ended. By this time, almost all faculty holdovers from the Sheldon and Poucher administrations had retired. The victorian behavior code had waned, but had not disappeared. The curriculum was a hodgepodge, and funds extremely scarce—the Depression had arrived. The relative status of the New York Normals, including Oswego, had sunk very low. Elsewhere, such schools had already been transformed into teachers' colleges.

The Riggs faculty compared favorably with those of the other New York Normals, but poorly with those in the country at large. In 1930 only one in three of Oswego's faculty held a master's degree, compared with 60 percent in all teacher-training institutions. Many were aging holdovers from the earlier Sheldon and Poucher periods. On the other hand, many had traveled widely and were wholeheartedly committed to teacher training. A few were quite strong, among them Richard Piez and Caroline Scales, both outstanding faculty since the time of Edward Sheldon, and Caroline Sinnamon (1894), who taught here thirty-seven years.

The "top four" of this era were President Riggs together with Piez, Scales, and Sinnamon. Riggs, whose elevated status derived mainly from his role as principal, was a gentleman of the old school, friendly but formal. He showed little concern for the students' academic performance (he left that to the instructors), but had much interest in their morality, especially that of the girls. He encouraged social functions, even at faculty meetings, where tea and sandwiches were served. Riggs once said to Frank Schneider, "I'm just the oil can around here trying to make things go smoothly." "He had the nickname of 'Slippery Jim,'" said Schneider, "but he wasn't that type in his dealings." Riggs was also called "Smoothie" by the students, who had little contact with him.

Riggs was paternalistic toward the women faculty and served as a self-appointed guardian of their morals, a common practice of principals in those times. For example, he opposed women faculty members' smoking and placed pressure on them not to smoke anywhere. Also, according to Isabel Kingsbury Hart (1907), in physiology class one could mention "every bone in your body and locate it, and know the muscles and process of digestion, but there was no mention of sex."

Richard Piez, who taught at Oswego from 1893 to 1936, was probably the most highly respected man on the staff. "He could teach almost anything anyone else could," affirms one alumna, "and do it better." Grace Hynch (1913) remembers his trying to make students think and always search for reasons. When a teacher complained that a child in the practice school was too stupid to learn, Piez called the child to the blackboard, drew two lines, and said, "Jimmy, this is a railroad track. Make believe the eraser is the engine and run it up the track." An examination showed the boy was almost blind.

Caroline L. G. Scales was equally prestigious. She taught history and English from 1884 to 1926, and was preceptress at the Welland from 1887 to 1906. She was often described as "brilliant—all intellect and brain." Scales invited her English class to her room on West Sixth Street on Saturday evenings and read classics to them while they sat at her feet. It was she who composed the words to "Oh, Blue Ontario's Waters," the Normal School's first alma mater. No knowing what her initials stood for, students bought the rumor that her name was Carolina Louisiana Georgia Scales; they never knew her full name.

"Miss Scales always wore dark brown dresses, and two stories circulated about them," noted Edith Milo. "One was that she bought a large bolt of cloth and had a dressmaker make it up; the other that she had been in love with a man by the name of Brown who died, so she wore brown in his memory. Imagine what a sensation it was when Miss Scales, a day after we moved to the new building—now Sheldon Hall—appeared with a navy cape around her at Assembly, sat down on the stage, and threw back the cape, which was lined with cerise."

Caroline Sinnamon was the highly respected head of the Campus School's senior department. She, like many of her contemporaries, was a strict disciplinarian. Once she caught a student chewing gum in class; although he immediately swallowed the gum, she dismissed him from class and henceforth ignored him.

Another star was Amos Farnham, for whom the local crisis center is named. He always insisted on students' pronouncing words correctly, and he truly knew his subject, (Geography) said Edith Milo. "He took us on field trips and on one showed us glacial markings on the bedrock of the lake shore. He taught us how to enlarge a map which resulted in my receiving an A in a history course in college later."

Helen Nielsen (1931) and Lois O'Grady (1931) thought highly of Lucy Norton, their history teacher. "She taught things we could use when we were teaching," says Helen. "And she gave so much extra knowledge," adds Lois. "She told us of her trips through the world."

Edith Milo (1917) recalls Charlotte Waterman, supervisor of music for twenty-two years, with regard to an incident in Assembly. On that occasion another teacher, Leslie Savage, young, attractive and dark haired, wore a bright red jacket with a white shirt. Her attire was quite noticeable as she sat on the platform with the other teachers, most of whom were dressed conservatively. Waterman, who led the singing, announced, "We will sing 'Fairest Lord Jesus,'" and when it came to the part, "robed in the blooming garb of spring," she glanced at Savage.

Joseph Park was also important. He taught industrial arts from 1903 until his retirement in 1939 and headed the department from the time it was organized in 1908. He became a leader in his field and in 1932 was named among the one-hundred outstanding industrial arts men in the country. By this time his department was recognized as one of the best in the country.

The curriculum during these years displayed important changes. A third year was added to the general elementary curriculum in 1922, differing little from the earlier version. The same classifications were offered: kindergarten, intermediate, and industrial arts; however, their content was mainly a review of high school work. It was also subject-matter centered and fragmented. The child-centered curriculum had yet to arrive, and methods were rigid and unimaginative; one method simply required children to copy a picture.

In short, progress in methods and curriculum was at a stalemate because of the lack of a consistent philosophy to support them. The two major philosophies of the period, those of Edward Thorndike of Columbia and C. H. Judd of Chicago, were sharply opposed. Thorndike, whom most of the Normal School faculty followed, popularized drill and attention to specific details, while Judd stressed basic principles and generalization.

Certain curricular innovations and special events also related to this period. In 1913 an open-air school was begun for children with a tendency toward tuberculosis; swathed in blankets and Eskimo suits, the children were taught with windows wide open. The experiment was discontinued after a few years. Another innovation was the training of retarded children, which began in 1916 and lasted about two decades. Among the reasons given for this program was that they were likely to wander about, become thieves, firebugs and murderers. At that time New Jersey was the only state with a law providing special classes for subnormal children.

In 1916 the Normal School severed its remaining ties with the Oswego city schools, which hitherto had furnished teachers for the training school. A few years later, in 1919, the first regular summer session at Oswego began; a popular feature was a tent colony on Camp Shady Shore. Later, this colony grew to embrace twenty-one cabins, six tents, and a larger trailer area.

When James Riggs arrived, industrial arts was still a formal discipline, based on the theory that certain fundamental skills in every trade should be taught through set exercises. The problem was a lack of appropriate instructors; most were tradesmen and craftsmen. A brief era of vocational education began in 1917; shop programs at Oswego and Buffalo were scrapped in favor of preparing teachers for general industrial shop work. The industrial teachers' training program graduated its first class in 1920 and, in 1921 industrial arts education revived, at least in avowed purpose, although vocational objectives persisted. Only in 1925 did major change occur, when Arthur Hauler revised the practice teaching program and arranged off-campus teaching centers.

Except for the brief vocational interlude, the first truly significant curricular changes in industrial arts since 1911 came in 1929 with the initiation of a three-year program, expanded to four years in 1932, and the emergence of the general shop. The idea was that students, in an industrial culture, should learn how to integrate a broad range of skills and processes. Nevertheless, these shops, like the industrial arts philosophy they presumably reflected, still existed mainly in name only. For the most part, the general shop was simply an aggregate of unit shops.

The industrial arts curriculum mostly ignored the humanities. Despite the addition of a third year, the so-called cultural offerings were tinged with professionalization. Students took shop math and shop English, and every effort was made to relate so-called cultural subjects specifically to industrial arts.

The industrial arts division had become the males' exclusive domain. In earlier days, a few girls had been in the program, and a few took shop courses during the war, which helped instructors to hold their jobs. However, during the vocational education interlude, 1917–20, women were excluded.

Students of the 1920s were often the first members of their families to attend college. Few were commuters; hence, most became active in extracurricular life. Chapel was still compulsory, and the gap between faculty and students was wide. Students could be dismissed, even for dubious reasons, without raising questions. Anti-college demonstrations were in general looked upon as horseplay, rather than symptoms of a need for change.

A carnival atmosphere prevailed. It was a "mad, bad, glad" period, the flaming 1920s: the Jazz Age.[2] Common campus crazes included working crossword puzzles, flagpole sitting, and marathon dances. Among technological advances were radio and, in 1927, the first feature sound film, *The Jazz Singer*. By 1920 Studebaker had stopped making horse-drawn wagons and in 1927 Lindbergh made his solo flight across the Atlantic. The music of the day was jazz, Charleston was the dance, and ukuleles became popular. Girls used rouge and powder but usually not lipstick. There were strict rules about smoking and liquor for women and sometimes for men, although they were not enforced for the men. A man at Harvard might entertain two women in his room, but not one.

The smaller isolated colleges, such as the Normal School, were far more conservative than the others. Perhaps a vestige of the sophistication and autonomy in other colleges seeped into Oswego's Normal School, but it was only a trace. Even here, bobbed hair and shorter—but not very short—skirts became popular. Social life had changed little except for the dance music. Favorite pastimes continued to be skating, tobogganing, walking, and swimming. Elsewhere in women's colleges, rules about chaperones were relaxing, but not here. Drinking and sex still were rare at Oswego and uncommon among colleges generally. Student sentiment, here as elsewhere, strongly favored prohibition.

With the advent of women's suffrage at the close of World War I, women in larger, more urban universities revolted against various social and religious traditions, but not at the Normal School. On the whole, girls at the Normal were still adolescent and unsophisticated. Nor did aspects of the communist scare flooding other institutions reach the Normal School.

Calvin B. T. Lee described the college generation of the 1920s as marked by "a charming superficiality, a semi-sophistication and a semi-innocence. In short, it was an era of fun, self indulgence and optimism."[3] At the Normal School, this judgment might be modified to describe the students as unsophisticated, innocent, not so self-indulgent, and perhaps less superficial, because it was a professional school.

The Jazz Age came to an abrupt end with the famous market crash of 1929, and in the early 1930s the Depression enforced new limitations. Students might hike instead of go to the movies, or go to the library instead of to town. For entertainment students might listen to the radio, hearing variety shows starring Jack Benny, George Burns and Gracie Allen, Edgar Bergen and Charlie McCarthy. Bing Crosby and Mae West were popular, but students rarely had fifteen to twenty-five cents for a movie.

In those days Oswego's students came mostly from nearby counties. Many of the girls continued to live at the Welland until 1918. When it was someone's birthday, the girls often entertained in their rooms, but their boyfriends were not allowed to attend. Nor were girls permitted to walk along the lakeshore except on Saturdays, when they could go for picnics.

Once when student Pearl Smith was invited to go with a young man to the Masonic Hall, she could not accept becaue it was a Tuesday night; seeing young men was permitted only on Fridays and Saturdays. The girls at the Welland were upset and said they would tie sheets together and let her down outside the window. However, she didn't want to risk expulsion, as some girls from Yonkers had. The girls couldn't even step outside at night, except to walk straight to the mailbox and return.

In the early 1930s several girls lived at Jakeway's, across the street from the school. They had five rooms on each floor and a kitchen where they did their own cooking; Mrs. Jakeway maintained the required college rules. Students had three floors: freshmen lived on the top floor and, when they reached their second or third year, descended to the second floor where seniors also lived. Jakeway and her husband occupied the first floor.

During the later Riggs years, a faculty member, Frank Schneider, and his family lived on the first floor of the Sheldon home, while male students lived on the second. Charles Young (1934) recalls that in 1931–32, "seven of us lived there, paying two-fifty a week rent. There was no bathroom on the second floor and only a toilet and lavatory under the stairway. There was an unsealed stovepipe hole in our closet over the dining room, and we sometimes amused ourselves eavesdropping on the quite frequent family arguments that went on below."

Living expenses were reasonable; however, after the crash of 1929, penny-pinching was the rule. "Textbooks and tuition were free," recalls Helen Nielson, "and all my expenses, including $3 for rent, came to $10 a week." Helen worked in a drugstore in Phoenix after school and on weekends. She received five dollars for the weekend, working from eight in the morning until eight or nine at night, with an hour off for lunch. Lois O'Grady said that she worked part time in Woolworth's, beginning at age sixteen, while she was still in high school. He job paid very well, she said: "$1.25 from 12 noon to 9 at night or 13½¢ an hour if you worked by the hour." With her wages she bought an accordion-pleated skirt, very much the in-thing then, for $1.49. She had joined a Christmas Club and paid 25¢ a week until it was paid for.

Women students in general wore skirts; around 1913 they abandoned their corsets. After the war, in 1919, skirts had risen about six inches above the ground and another three inches by 1920. This the *New York Times* called "far beyond any modest limitation."[4] At Oswego, the girls wore skirts even when they walked up the hill during snow storms, often supplemented with long woolen stockings over their regular hose and long underwear. The men wore suits, collars, and dress shirts but had no dress code.

Strict rules for girls and almost complete freedom for boys continued. Girls could not go out in the evening or over the bridge, where Navy men were stationed. Edith Milo tells of a student whose parents had a hotel, the Wheeler House, on West Second Street, less than half a block from the Welland. Required to wear hats when they went to town, girls would leave the Welland properly attired, stop at the Wheeler House, and park their hats until they returned.

When asked what would happen if a girl had a child out of wedlock, alumna Helen Nielson said she would have been put out of college. When asked if the male would also have been dismissed, she replied: "Of course not." Alumna Lois O'Grady added: "He wouldn't have even been involved. That was the way it was." Helen concluded with, "If they had known who the boy was, it wouldn't have mattered either." When asked if girls resented the restrictions, Helen replied, "No, at the time they believed them a good idea—they just expected them." When asked about women's rights, she said, "We didn't think about them." Lois added, "You felt you were as good as any of the boys. The matter of equality didn't enter in. We thought we had it."

Asked whether students paid any attention to the outside world, Lois remarked that, at least in Miss Norton's class, students were interested in nations getting together into a confederation of nations, and earlier, a class had assumed charge of an Armenian orphan girl through Near-East Relief. In 1927 the Normal's Student League of Women Voters had programs on water power, fate of the women's juror bills, the forty-hour work week for women, and child labor. However, students were most actively interested in campus matters; for example, class leaders of 1926 sought to keep the Main Building trellis extending to the sidewalk from being torn down.

They were concerned over course work and making adequate grades and spent considerable time in the library. "However," said Helen Nielson, "the librarian was jealous of letting a book out—books were supposed to be on the shelves. You would almost have to steal them to get them out to use them." "Yet," added Lois O'Grady, "the Oswego library was one of the finest I had used."

The shops remained the males' almost exclusive domain. Most of the boys took "IA," the term often used after 1924 and 1925; and the girls enrolled in the elementary education course. Only under exceptional circumstances were girls allowed to take shop; Nielson could not remember any girls taking it. However, O'Grady, when preparing for a particular class certificate, was given special permission to enroll.

Recreation was informal and cheap. In summer students had tennis, swimming, and picnics; they could buy ice cream cones for five cents and sundaes for fifteen or twenty cents. Occasionally, there were proms and costume parties, and even dances, all strictly supervised. In summer there were rides on open-ended trolley cars and an amusement area, Ontario Park, where girls could go as a group, but only as a group. In the winter there were sleighing and snowshoeing; for these activities the girls wore heavy ankle-length skirts.

Greek organizations rapidly gained status after Ransom Libby and Max Ziel organized the first Oswego fraternity in 1924–25, Psi Phi, with just four charter members. It had its own house by 1927, and other fraternities quickly followed. The second fraternity, the Kappa Kappa Kappa, changed its name to Delta Kappa Kappa so that its initials, KKK, would not be confused with the Ku Klux Klan. The first women's Greek organization, Clio, was organized in 1923, and others soon followed. Initiations among the Greeks were immature and harmless affairs, requirements being to serve as ushers in chapel, scrub steps, or wear ribbon pigtails.

Campus interest in organized activities increased in the 1920s and by the 1930s the school had many extracurricular activities, among them social clubs, special interest and avocation clubs, subject matter clubs, music organizations, public speaking or literary clubs, and athletics organizations.

Clubs used assorted means of raising money, such as candy and popcorn sales to pay the expenses of parties. They also undertook a welfare project, for which each student sold twenty-four bars of candy; however, as a class historian remarked: "It proved so much easier to eat the bars ourselves instead of asking people to buy them, that we were our own best customers."[5]

Student governance was under the aegis of the General Organization, or GO. An annual fee of $2.50 supported student affairs; half of the fee was allocated to the athletic association, composed mostly of men. The GO had responsibilities such as assisting with Faculty Assembly programs and the further allocation of student funds.

The first student annuals were called *Normalians*, retitled *Ontarians*, in 1927; their content was more varied than has been the case with recent ones. The 1927 issue contained a section of humor called "The Bunkville Bladder," with articles on "A Lotta Bunk," "Overnight Miracles," and "A Kiss as Defined by One of Our Coeds."

Oswego men had informally organized athletic teams in the 1890s, and off-campus games were arranged, but not for two more decades would there be a varsity sports team. Under the aegis of coach Max Ziel the basketball team was organized in 1918, and football in 1920. When Max called for football players in 1921, only thirteen students appeared. He ran the boys through some pine trees near Old Main, now Sheldon Hall, and designated the first four through the trees as the backfield, and those who bumped into the trees as the linemen. He had almost undefeated seasons in 1927 and 1928. In basketball, he used his "magic" figure eight: a five-man vertical weave offensive. Funds were so short one year that the baseball team was composed only of boys whose fathers had railroad passes, allowing the team to travel for nothing. Kent Northrup (1926) tells of going with a team on Dynamite Gould's bus to play in another city and, when the bus ran out of gas on the way, Ziel had his players practice impromptu on a nearby field.

Relationships between students and faculty were formal but friendly; and the faculty never hesitated to give students extra time and help. In 1929 Louis DeLaVergne (1932) and Gerald Crozier (1932) came to Oswego in DeLaVergne's Model T open touring car to find out about the industrial arts program. They were given a tour of the shops in the basement of what is now Sheldon Hall. IA instructor Harry Karcher even gave them a demonstration of his famous "spark gap" machine, which could be heard almost throughout the building.[6]

Despite its low fortunes during that era, the students were proud of the school. Pearl Smith, president of her class in 1917, said, "Nowhere else could I have gotten an education like the one I got here." Another alumna said, "As an Oswego graduate I had a better chance of competing for jobs." They were still proud of their Oswego heritage and said the students felt a genuine school spirit.

Certainly, many alumni of those years were quite superior, often highly successful people. Dr. Clifford Lee Brownell, class of 1915, later became chair of the health and physical education department at Teachers College of Columbia University. Other well-known alumni included John Enders, head of State Rehabilitation for years; John Burns (1967), superintendent of schools in Palisades, New Jersey; and Hoover Mackin, who held an important government post.

Ralph Waldo Swetman's years (1933–1946) which followed Riggs's retirement and the one year of acting president Thomas Miller (1946–1947) spanned the Great Depression and World War II and their aftermath. Everywhere, college enrollments and state budgets declined. Colleges fought back, often engaging in questionable recruiting practices. Oswego faculty members joked that "if live bodies came by, we tried to grab 'em." Because of the grim economic situation, the federal government increased its support of higher education. Its student-aid programs helped vast numbers of students and became the precedent for post-war assistance for veterans, the greatest scholarship program in history. Responsibility for helping students in higher education, a concept which became widely accepted, took root during the Depression.

Locally, the budget crunch was keenly felt. One casualty was the school publication *The Vocationist*, published by the IA faculty since 1910. The only permanent building was poorly kept; its halls were dark, and worn cork covered its floors. Temporary wooden buildings were constructed in 1946 to house classrooms and dining halls, an assemblage nicknamed "Siberia." Former Army barracks housed GIs and their families, while other students rented rooms in town. Landlords promised to change beds at least once a week and supply light bulbs of at least forty watts.

The student housing problem became so acute in the fall of 1946 that Swetman split up a local telephone directory, and each faculty member called the homes in his or her section to inquire about available rooms. Even this drastic measure produced meager results.

"When the draft had all but cleaned out the IA division," recalled George Pitluga, retired science professor, "we had only forty-one male students left and the state was seriously considering closing the college. Swetman called the faculty together and asked: 'We have a problem: what should we do about it?' Among other things, faculty members, at their own expense, traveled all over the state recruiting students, necessarily female. Swetman himself went to Washington and procured a 300-man contingent of the Air Force in a program which 'saved the homestead.' There was a pervading sense that faculty and administration must work together to save the college. It was *our* college, not *the* college."

Adding to this grim picture was a serious fire at the Normal School during the night of January 18, 1941. A sheet of flame swept through the auditorium, causing much damage. Edward Austin Sheldon's bust was partly damaged, a big chip broken from it. This bust had been made from a death mask of Sheldon by the National American Sculptor, Herbert Ames. Despite the damage, Old Main was revived again, although still in a decrepit condition.

There were brighter events to offset this scenario of gloom-and-doom, among them the inauguration of a new tradition. The Torchlight Ceremony was born in 1936 on the seventy-fifth anniversary of the founding and has been repeated annually ever since during alumni week. In this ceremony, in front of Sheldon's statue, the torchbearer hands the torch to the college president; the president then hands it to the oldest graduate, and so on around the circle.

Perhaps partly because of his Herculean efforts, on November 3, 1946, President Swetman was abruptly stricken with coronary thrombosis and, shortly thereafter, driven nonstop to Florida by physical education chairman Golden Romney to recuperate. Dean Thomas Miller became acting president. Swetman did not return to Oswego but rallied enough health to run for mayor of Boca Raton, losing by just a small margin.

In retrospect, Swetman may best be recognized for rescuing the school from its near-mortal status, through upgrading the faculty and completely reorganizing the curriculum. It was a gigantic task in which he was assisted by Hermann Cooper, appointed to the newly created office of New York State Assistant Commissioner of Education in 1933.

Even after all these years, Oswego was still remembered for its historic contributions during the Sheldon period. In 1951 George Pitluga spent a semester traveling in Britain and northern Europe to study educational systems. He recalls that, when asked where he was from, he would somewhat apologetically say, "It's a small teacher-training institution in upstate New York called Oswego." They would always respond, "Oh, Oswego, indeed. We know about Oswego." He was greatly surprised to find that Oswego was known so widely in England.

In Swetman's time, higher education faculties across the country were hardly thriving. Because of the Great Depression, cutbacks were common and casualties were mostly young professors. Appointments were short term, opportunities for moonlighting almost dried up, and pension arrangements were meager. Some instructors simply abandoned academia and found employment in newly created state and federal agencies, which now had posts requiring college degrees. Meanwhile, faculty involvement in administration had become common, although many complained that it was not enough, especially in financial decisions. Hence, the gap between faculty and administration widened, leading to faculty councils and committees.

This picture only partially reflects the situation at Oswego. The 1933 faculty of about thirty-five were mostly holdovers from the Riggs era. Pay was poor, participation in administration minuscule, and the morale of many very low. Only one instructor possessed an earned doctorate, and 55 percent of the faculty had no degree. True, the faculty compared very well with those of the sister New York Normals but poorly with those countrywide. In 1926 the American Association of Teachers Colleges raised the standards by which Normal schools were rated. As a result, many such schools had come to rival liberal arts colleges in terms of faculty preparation.

Despite having little in the way of inducements to offer, Swetman resolved to refurbish the faculty. Hence, he pronounced an ultimatum in 1934: no faculty member could remain after 1935 who had failed to get a master's degree. Some individuals managed to get bachelor's and master's degrees, in some cases by deliberately taking easy courses and piling up credits as fast as they could. Others, especially older ones, simply resigned because they lacked the funds or stamina for the task. Some observers felt that Swetman's dictum had been harsh, even cruel; after all, it was in the depth of the Depression. Others believed he simply did what had to be done.

Swetman also set out to obtain faculty members from all over the country to make the school less provincial and to add more men to a largely female faculty. On public occasions, he took special pride in naming the newcomers' home states. One such import, with a brand new Ph.D. from Duke Univesity, was this writer, who was paid the grand salary of $2,928—annually, that is—and resolved to stay just one year.

Swetman made a great show of being democratic. He kept faculty meetings in session indefinitely until he could get a unanimous vote on some matter, one that agreed with his view. He was an apostle of the normal curve in grading and, in effect, required staff members to employ this standard. He held daily assemblies that both faculty and students were required to attend. He limited smoking to designated rooms, including the faculty dining room. In short, he ran the whole show, and with a very firm hand.

The faculty, old and new, were a dedicated lot, and deserve much credit. Among them were Leo Cribben, a math instructor who, when meetings dragged on, would loudly say, "Move we adjourn"; and Marietta Odell, whose mother graduated from Oswego in 1875. Odell supervised off-campus teaching and was prominent in New York State education. Other notable faculty were Harold Alford, also a state leader, who was director of the New York State Elementary Education Division; Lida Penfield, an English teacher and another star, to whom the local Historical Society dedicated its 1943 yearbook—the first woman to be so honored. Helen Hagger, a librarian and an admirer of Penfield, saw to it that the new campus library was named for Penfield. Other standouts were Isabel (Izzy) Hart (1907), one of the state's early organizers of field trips for summer session credit and author of three series of geography tests for children; Marian Mahar, a history instructor from 1931 to 1957, who had studied in Berlin, Edinburgh, and Paris. They and their colleagues would always rise to a challenge. Two of those collegaues, physical education chair Golden Romney, and English professor

James Moreland, successfully raided high schools for students. And in 1937 many of the faculty drove the 150 entering freshmen, including 90 industrial arts education students, on a tour of the city.

There were occasional events of an amusing nature, one of which occurred in the shabby basement cafeteria, called Mongeon's Dungeon after its manager and locale. President Swetman's large dog often wandered through it and, on this occasion, sparked a misunderstanding. A tall, elegant teacher from the campus was in the cafeteria talking with a colleague when she felt a nudge in the rear. She wheeled around and slapped the hapless gentleman just behind her, mistaking him for the offender.

The college had only two main programs at this time, elementary education and industrial arts; the latter after 1933 had its own building just in time for the extension of the three-year IA program into four. However, the building was more modern than the curriculum. Having no clearly defined concept of industrial arts, the instructors modeled the curriculum somewhat after vocational education. In 1933 the IA curriculum focused on methods; the new one in fall 1935 was more balanced, consisting of professional work, technical, and liberal-cultural courses. Two years later, in 1937, the Regents authorized a four-year curriculum for both industrial arts and general elementary divisions. Another giant leap forward was made when Gordon Wilber became director in 1940. Prior to that time, under the aging Park's leadership, the industrial arts men had gone their individual philosophical ways. Industrial arts graduates of 1940 were the first to receive the degree of Bachelor of Science in Education. Such degrees were granted to all four-year graduates two years later; and, in 1947, authority was granted for offering the Master of Science in Education degree.

In the meantime, other events of significance occurred for industrial arts. In December 1941, Hermann Cooper sent a memorandum to the president of the New York State Commission on Education raising the question as to whether separate industrial arts teacher training should be continued at Buffalo and Oswego, or one combined center should be at Oswego. He noted that the new building contained space at Oswego for an automobile shop, but there was none at Buffalo, and he recommended discontinuing the elementary education division at Oswego. However, neither was done, mainly because Harold Johnson, chair of the Board of Visitors, strongly opposed such a plan.

During World War II, the largely male student body shrank drastically: just nineteen industrial arts students graduated in 1943, and fourteen in 1944. The college might have expired had it not been for Swetman. He encouraged 4-Fs and cadets' wives to enroll and had assigned to the college the 324th College Training Detachment of preflight cadets. They came in groups of three hundred, taking classes at the college and flight instruction at the airport near Fulton. Everyone in industrial arts made model airplanes for the Navy, and the IA faculty instructed the preflight Air Corps trainees. Along with the ending of the war in 1945, trainees were gone, and the enrollment trend reversed. In 1946 Swetman stressed the need for a fifth year for men in industrial arts, but the Board rejected the request because it would tax the facilities of the institution.

Meanwhile, the elementary division's overall educational philosophy was progressivism, as propounded by John Dewey. Formerly, teachers had focused on subject matter, and children themselves were incidental; now they must consider the nature of children and how they learn. A related principle was learning by doing, implemented primarily through the use of projects.

The faculty was reorganized; individual chairs of instruction became leaders of subject-matter departments. Another step toward achieving academic respectability was through increasing the ratio of liberal-cultural to professional courses. These additions were no mere accretion; they had to be packaged together, balanced, and organized. In 1939 Harold Alford integrated methods courses into four broad areas: child development, child curriculum, student teaching, and seminar in education.

An examination of the records for these years uncovered items which, in their own way, reflected the times. For example, single women, but not married ones, were required to take physical education—did that mean that homemaking in itself provided sufficient exercise? Also, in 1934 women student teachers in the Campus School but not their counterparts were assigned to launder the curtains in their classrooms. However, a woman on the cafeteria staff came to their rescue and did the job.

Swetman's two greatest accomplishments were upgrading the faculty and earning for Oswego the right to award degrees. Colleges and universities from their intellectual pinnacle had long fought this development, believing that extending degrees to the lowly Normals would tarnish the degrees' worth. However, in 1937 New York's Board of Regents authorized a four-year curriculum which became standard for all Normals in 1938. In 1942 Oswego belatedly changed from a Normal School to a teachers' College, a change begun elsewhere years before; more than 150 Normals had become teachers' colleges by 1930. When the Normal School was formally designated a teachers' college, recalls Carol McLaughlin (1945), classes were canceled, and the whole student body marched to the bridge on Bridge Street and tossed into the river the old Normal School sign that had graced the entry to the grounds.

Across the country in the 1930s student activists were concerned with demonstrations against war, abolition of ROTC, opposition to discrimination against minorities, and to any restrictions on free thought and expression. Students defended their rights to campus-based political activity, and opposed censorship of student newspapers, institutional control of visiting speakers, and disciplinary action without student participation. Students were somewhat subdued because of the economic crunch. In 1936 editors of *Fortune Magazine* concluded that most college students were fatalistic, "a generation that will not stick its neck out . . . it is a cautious, subdued, unadventurous generation, unwilling to storm heaven. . . ."[7]

As noted earlier, the advent of World War II on December 7, 1941, brought dramatic change. College life had changed drastically. Parties had become much more spare because of wartime austerity and the lopsided sex ratio. Students felt that while men were going to war they shouldn't squander money at home and minimized purchases. They enjoyed the records and radio programs of Dinah Shore, Frank Sinatra, Perry Como, and certain folk singers.

With the war's end in 1945, the GI Bill of Rights sent World War II veterans scrambling off to schools in droves. The result was a serious shortage of classroom space, teachers, and facilities. Everywhere there were housing problems for veterans and their families. Trailer camps sprang up, often with communal bath facilities and outdoor toilets. A married veteran received $90 a month in 1945, later increased to $105, and then to $120. Many babies were born to these veterans' wives; many wives had already finished college and were now helping husbands get their degrees.

Both married and unmarried veterans were very serious about their work. They were older and more mature and cared little for traditional extracurricular activities. They made the highest grades on campus and expected a high quality of teaching. A few joined fraternities but wouldn't put up with such childish things as hazing. Also, they had the effect of democratizing the campuses, having no patience with religious and racial barriers. One might call these students of the late 1940s a settled-down generation—a regimented military life doesn't produce rabble-rousers. They aspired to jobs which insured security.

The situation at Oswego was much the same; there were no activist groups. Teacher-training schools are typically conservative; the local area is conservative, and most students were from the area. However, the addition of growing numbers from New York City added a touch of cosmopolitanism and sophistication. In the meantime, post-war recession dictated very simple habits and recreation. Students' clothing was whatever they could scrounge and put together. A hundred or so of them had $15-a-month jobs with the National Youth Administration, helping in the library, in offices, or on the grounds. Otherwise, self-employment was largely limited to domestic help, nursemaid work, odd jobs, and occasionally work in stores and restaurants.

Female students continued to be treated almost as children. In the 1941–42 *Student Handbook*, comments regarding Men's Recreation Association contained references to "men." In the very next paragraph, in the women's sports section, females are referred to as girls. A sentence in one paragraph notes, "All of these varsity letter sports are open to all men"; in the next paragraph, "All girls are encouraged to participate. . . ."

In the same handbook, there is this statement: "A list of approved rooming and boarding houses is available in the office of the dean of women. Girls must live in approved rooming or boarding houses." That same year, smoking regulations included prohibition of smoking on campus by women students, while limiting men students' smoking to specially designated rooms and entrances of the industrial arts building. In 1937 "many prominent young ladies of our campus could be seen flocking to Fords and Chevys in the rear of the school for a bit of smoking." The students of 1964 argued that the student council and faculty should have taken hold of the issue and allowed "the girls" to smoke if they were so inclined.

Both sexes were encouraged to adhere to quite formal and traditional behaviors and values. Swetman often addressed students in chapel about "PA" or professional attitude. As stated in the 1941–42 *Student Handbook*, one requirement for graduation was that character, personality, and other traits must meet the standards that are deemed essential to the teaching profession. No indication was given as to how these characteristics might be validly measured.

Gradually, the overall campus atmosphere grew more relaxed. Faculty–student relationships became more friendly and less formal, especially with the arrival of younger faculty members. Students also had plenty of inexpensive fun, spending what miniscule amounts they had on food, beer, and jukeboxes at their favorite hangouts, especially Conzone's, Buck's, or the Snakepit. Boys' on-campus activities included photography and woodwork, while girls were involved in music, reading, knitting, and stamp collecting.

A popular pastime of upper classmen was the hazing of freshmen. "They would make it tough for the freshmen," recalled Charles Shoemaker (1947). "They would paddle them right on the stage. . . . Freshmen would get paddled if they couldn't sing the alma mater," added Vernon Tryon (1958). "They had to carry a little notebook in their pockets with a set of rules. For example, one day they might have to wear their suit coats on backwards or wear their ties down the back of their necks. It helped to create a sense of rapport with the institution."

The Greeks continued to maintain a high status on campus and by 1941–42 there were three sororities: Alpha Delta, Arethusa, and Clio, and three fraternities: Beta Tau Epsilon, Delta Kappa, and Psi Phi. In the 1930s Delta Kappa Kappa members sponsored Big Brother nights for children of Oswego. During World War II the Arethusa sisters sold war bonds; and in 1943 the Clio sisters worked in the field to help compensate for the shortage of men at home.

Swetman became concerned about students who were not invited to join the Greek societies and encouraged, literally mandated, the formation of non-Greek social clubs. The most successful of these was the Sons of the Wilted Wallet, organized in 1939. A parallel women's club, called itself The Daughters of the Wilted Wallet, with the permission of the SWW, began in 1946, but it 'wilted' within a few years. Also established were two honorary scholastic organizations, the Sheldon Forum for boys and Sigma Phi Rho for girls.

Dean Thomas Miller was the acting president from the time of Swetman's sudden illness in November 1946 to fall 1947, and again from Harvey Rice's resignation in December 1951 to the arrival of Foster S. Brown in fall 1952. In his brief stint as chief executive, Miller kept the wheels running smoothly and helped pave the way for expansion. In fact, he performed so well that several faculty members plotted to give him the top job for good; however, the board dug in its heels and stood by the unwritten rule that the chief executive must come from the outside.

The result of the ensuing canvass for candidates was the election of President Harvey Mitchell Rice, a tall, gray-haired, distinguished-looking man, who was formally inaugurated on October 28, 1947.

Rice, his attractive wife Dorothy, and his faithful dog Pal, installed themselves in Shady Shore. Dorothy Rice, who had taught dramatics on one occasion assumed the leading role in a campus play, *Good-Bye, My Fancy*. Harvey Rice was an accomplished administrator and good speaker (during his West Virginia high school years he had won a statewide oratorical contest). During World War II, he served as a lieutenant in the United States Navy's special services division. Rice was self-confident; some critics thought him cocky and, taking as their cue his initials, H. M., referred to him as "His Majesty."

Rice went to work with vigor, both locally and statewide. He was especially active as president of the New York State Teachers Association and of the State Parent–Teacher Association. He was at the helm when the college became a part of the newly constituted State University of New York. After a full, but relatively placid, four years, he left to become president of the State College for Teachers at Buffalo and later of Macalester College in St. Paul, Minnesota.

Rice's faculty, fewer than one hundred in number, were mostly inherited from Swetman, with a few survivors from the Riggs years. The top brass included Dean Thomas Miller and Gordon Wilber and Harold Alford, the latter two directors of industrial arts and education, respectively. During these years the faculty lost three of its stars. Marietta Odell, well-known educator was killed in an automobile accident in California while on sabbatical leave; Golden Romney, chair of physical education, left in 1950 to chair physical education at the University of Washington; and James Moreland, known to one and all as Jimmy, died suddenly in 1951.

The chief curricular development was a shift in emphasis, except in the professional studies, from liberal to general education. The main difference, as interpreted then, was the perception that liberal education was an end in itself, whereas general education used the heritage as a tool for understanding and dealing with the diverse problems of modern life. Despite many discussions, no real consensus developed about how such a concept should be implemented. Substantial changes did occur, but some were later questioned. Electives multiplied, and, as a consequence, requirements shrank. The industrial arts division added several shops. Driver education emerged in 1947 and the elementary industrial arts program was developed in 1951.

The State University of New York was created in 1948, thereafter commonly called SUNY, and not to be confused with the University of the State of New York, founded in 1784. The latter, the first of its kind, was a governing body, not a university. Thus, just as New York was the first state to centralize control of higher education, it was the last to have a state university. This fledgling creation, whose first president was Alvin C. Eurich, consisted of forty-two units, including community, technical, and teachers' colleges.

In addition to its inclusion in the state system, there were other boosts to Oswego's status. One was the introduction of a graduate program; the first graduate degrees were granted in 1950. The tangible evidence at graduation exercises was the first contingent of candidates, seven in all, to wear the green and gold graduate hoods. Another mark of progress was the acquisition of certain temporary buildings. On the shores of the lake, Army barracks, dubbed Splinter Village, were erected to house married student veterans of World War II. The wives were warned to keep their doors closed, not to keep out thieves but to bar entry to the many stray dogs and cats. Other wooden barracks were added which served, only passably well, as classrooms, a cafeteria, and a gymnasium; they were drafty, the acoustics were a horror, and the floors were squeaky. A temporary residence hall for women was also built, with board of $4.50 per week.

Among more permanent acquisitions during this period were additions to Sheldon Hall, the Industrial Arts building, Park Hall, and a combination student union and dormitory. The long overdue advent of a dormitory was marked by the cornerstone-laying in June 1950 by Governor Thomas E. Dewey, who also delivered that June's commencement address. Student occupation of the dormitory began in fall 1951 at a cost of $17.50 per week for room and board.

The first stirrings of faculty claims to a hand in the administration of the college came in the late 1940s, and in 1949 the Faculty Council was organized, with this writer as the chair.

A less significant but noteworthy event occurred when someone—no one ever knew who—removed President Swetman's portrait (an oil painting only recently commissioned and given to the college by the Alumni Association) from the wall in the library, placed it on a pile of books, and set it afire. At the same time, fire was set to the library's lounge furniture. The portrait and many books were destroyed, and the remaining 40,000 volumes had to be carefully washed.

The most distinctive change in the student body was the influx of a large number of veterans, more at Oswego than at any other New York teachers' college. This tidal wave created a housing problem, and students often lived six in a room prior to completion of the dormitory. Some students lived at the Fort, and many lived in town in approved dwellings, with "boys and girls" never in the same house.

To ease the space shortage, no new IA students were added to the spring 1950 total of four hundred ninety. The situation eased in fall 1951 with the completion of the new wings of the IA building. Further easing of the facilities problem came with the gradual reduction in the number of veterans after 1950.

Even so, other campus buildings and facilities had become rundown and out of date. To give the campus a facelift, cleanup days were held in 1947 and in 1951. Groups of students, supervised by faculty members, scrubbed down, painted and repaired buildings, built benches, and cleared the pond. At noon all workers shared in a picnic served on the athletic field. The writer, who supervised and shared chores with a contingent working in the hot sun, resented the fact that the top brass, including the all-male chairs' group, spent the time indoors at a meeting.

The lifestyle and customs of students were relatively simple, giving little hint of the turbulent times soon to come. The males wore mainly sweatshirts and dungarees; the females wore sweaters and skirts, the latter which tended to be longer in fall 1947. Rules for women were relaxed ever so slightly but continued to underscore their second-class status. Women who failed to sign in or out or get weekend permission were automatically campused. If one was no more than fourteen minutes late, a first offense produced a warning, but for a second, if not over twenty-nine minutes, the offender was campused on Saturday and Sunday night. Female students were still called girls, never women.

Both sexes lived somewhat controlled lives. Two chaperones, either faculty members or "responsible friends of the college," were to chaperone all events. Greeks were limited to entertaining females in their lounges on Saturday from 8:00 A.M. to 1:00 P.M. and on Sunday from 2:00 P.M. to 8:00 P.M. There were campus-wide attendance rules for all classes, and until the early 1950s, attendance was required at chapel.

Sports affairs were well attended but funds were inadequate and outstanding teams uncommon. Nevertheless, although head coach Max Ziel was popular, pressure for big-time sports was nonexistent. One top basketball performer, Armand "Mags" Magnarelli (1950), became a prominent civic leader in Syracuse.

On two occasions the women faculty drubbed the students in basketball. Among long-term women faculty members on the team were Marian Strickland, Helen Hagger, Louise Ostberg, Dorothy Mott, and Dorothy Rogers.

One popular recreational event was the annual daylong boat trip to Kingston, Canada. Students were advised to bring a coat and, to save money, a box lunch; the round-trip fare per student was a mere $2.78.

The Alumni Association revived somewhat in these years. New York City's Oswego Boys Club, organized in 1900 and quite active until World War II, was reorganized in 1947. In that same year, a clock purchased for $300 by the alumni was placed in the Industrial Arts library. Also, the Hammond Organ, destroyed in the 1941 auditorium fire, had been replaced by the state. The original had been given to the college by the Alumni Association.

3

Years of Transition

THE presidency of Foster S. Brown followed that of Harvey M. Rice. Brown's tenure, 1952–1963, was comparatively quiet. True, McCarthyism tainted the generally bright picture and fostered rumors of students' spying on politically "dubious" professors for (presumed) FBI (Federal Bureau of Investigation) men on campus. However, the country prospered generally and conservatism reigned. The St. Lawrence Seaway opened in 1958, and the 1960s began quietly, almost a continuation of the 1950s. By 1961 Governor Nelson Rockefeller had dropped his program for mandatory fallout shelters, though still urging they be erected on State University college campuses. Overseas, barbed wire split Berlin and divided the world.

President Brown's last year in office, 1962–63, saw the curtain rise on a different era. The spaceship Marina set out for Venus; astronaut John Glenn orbited the earth; and the Cuban missile crisis erupted. That same year a black man, James Meredith, escorted by a federal marshal, registered at the University of Mississippi.

Acting President Charles S. Turner's years, 1963–1965, were mostly peaceful locally but quite eventful nationally. The stage was being set for the dramas to come! In 1963 astronaut Leroy Gordon Cooper, Jr., voyaged into space; President John F. Kennedy was assassinated, and Lyndon B. Johnson became president of the United States. That same year Betty Friedan's *Feminine Mystique* appeared and students struck for free speech at the University of California, Berkeley. The Beatles came to America in 1964. Martin Luther King led a rally in Washington, D. C., in 1963, while Governor George Wallace of Alabama solemnly vowed, "Segregation now, segregation tomorrow, segregation forever!" Two years later, in 1965, Martin Luther King led a march from Selma to Montgomery, Alabama; and thirty-five people died in the Watts (California) riots. On the industrial scene, technology was sweeping the land including the debut of computers, and the economy prospered.

In the meantime, higher education had undergone significant change. After World War II academic scientists had been involved in harnessing atomic energy. Faculty members had served an important wartime role for business, government, and industry; and institutions of higher education won widespread approval for their responsiveness to veterans' needs. In the early 1950s post-war planning committees produced a tremendous ferment in education.[1] Major concerns included the need for articulation between high school and college education and to improve higher education, especially teacher education. As veterans left the campuses, decreasing enrollments became a problem. Growing inflation was also straining the academies' financial situation, and the higher salaries offered in industry and business made it difficult to obtain top-quality instructors and researchers. Another problem was limitations in physical plants which, since World War I, had not kept pace with enrollment growth or demands for extra services, including research. Moreover, as knowledge grew more complex, costs of research increased.

By the end of the 1950s a new concern had arrived on the scene, an anticipated tidal wave of students.[2] After World War II, millions more were predicted to seek nondegree education in private technical and occupational training schools as well as through correspondence, adult education, and other programs. The 1957 presidential Committee on Education Beyond the High School predicted a doubling or tripling of college enrollments by 1970. The GIs had helped popularize going to college, and colleges were now perceived as both a service to society and a means of eliminating discrimination. Demographic factors, including an increased birth rate and lower infant mortality, had increased the number of college-age youths. In addition, business and industry were placing a greater premium on higher education because of technological advances. Automation was predicted to create a demand for incredible numbers of people in highly skilled jobs as machinery designers, draftsmen, system engineers, mathematicians, and logicians.[3] Also, more people would be needed for new managerial jobs who had the ability to think, analyze, make decisions, and assume risks. Clearly, more space and resources were needed to prevent a massive denial of educational opportunities.

Foster Sargent Brown, Oswego's sixth president, became widely regarded as the right man in the right place at the right time. In real-estate deals he was a "wheeler dealer," said Sherwood Dunham.

"In charge of everything," added Richard Wheeler. "The college operation was far less complex than now. We had a single-purpose institution for training industrial arts and elementary school teachers—that was about it."

Brown was an administrator of extraordinary efficiency: he expected and obtained quality performance from his staff. His earlier experience as a public administrator had served him well. "When I first came into higher education," he recalled, "I was astounded at the lack of accountability. In public schools, if children do not learn to read in the first grade, something has to happen. In the twelfth grade, if graduates can't get into a respectable college, something has to give. But in colleges remote from the family home, it is assumed, partly because it is difficult to get into colleges, that they must be very good, but it doesn't hold at all."

Brown held his staff accountable. "He wanted efficiency and he knew his campus," noted Charles Shoemaker. "He would walk through the buildings with a pleasant smile, and shake hands. He knew what was going on; he had his ears to the ground. He could be a real iron man. He would frequently come into faculty members' classrooms or offices."

"He was also effective in follow-up," added Vernon Tryon. "He would assign people tasks and then check on their progress. You could be sure he would touch base with you. He wouldn't just let projects sit on the back burner." Brown was in charge; the days of genuine participatory democracy were yet to come.

Brown was a master at maintaining healthy human relationships. Writes Gordon Mangel: "I can still remember Foster Brown's greeting me by name as I strolled toward his residence. He had met me only once, or at the very most twice, yet I was a person to him."

Ed Boardway, campus electrician, added this anecdote: "One day I was working on a lamp at the top of a post, and since students often shook them and made them go out, I said under my breath, 'Those damned students.' Brown heard me and said, 'Ed, if it weren't for those damned students, you and I wouldn't have a job.'"

Brown was also successful in his community relationships and was once named Oswego's "Man of the Year." He was highly approved by the College Council, chaired by James Lanigan, retired resident manager of Niagara Mohawk Power Company, and for whom a campus building was later named. Other Council members in 1961 were John Aylward, Watertown attorney; Dorothy Barclay of Pulaski, owner of Douglaston Manor farm; Samuel Castaldo, Oswego alumnus and partner in the Castaldo Construction Company; Clarence Leighton, president and editor of the Oswego *Palladium Times;* Marian Mackin, Oswego alumna and president of the Oswego Housing Authority; George Penney, managing director of the Savings Bank Association of the State of New York; Margaret Mansfield Richardson, who obtained her master of science degree from Oswego in 1929; and Marion Steele Adams, prominent in the Parent-Teacher Association.

Brown's statewide relationships were equally amicable, both with SUNY and with the independent colleges. He always found Albany and the State University Budget Office "very cooperative." Nor did he assume an adversarial stance toward the independent colleges, despite their long-standing favored status in state priorities. He saw private and public education as supplementing each other.

In 1963 Brown left Oswego to become the president of his alma mater, St.

Lawrence University, from which he had received an honorary doctorate; his earned doctorate in education was from Columbia University. Six years later he retired and moved to Chapel Hill, North Carolina. Of Oswego he said, "My family and I loved it here. Just thirty years ago today we were driving to Oswego from Cortland, where I had been dean, and the children were singing 'Os-we-go into the wild blue yonder.'" While at Oswego, Brown always worked within the SUNY framework.

SUNY developed its first master plan in 1950 and revised it in 1952. In 1961 the SUNY Board of Trustees presented to Governor Nelson Rockefeller a ten-year, six hundred million dollar program designed to expand SUNY's student capacity from 42,000 to 145,000 by 1970. The colleges of education at the Albany and Buffalo Centers would immediately become multipurpose institutions. Buffalo Center had already become a multipurpose institution with medical, law, and engineering schools. The other nine units would incorporate liberal arts and sciences at the upper division levels. Students would then be able to transfer from the University's network of two-year colleges to the four-year colleges to complete their liberal arts degree requirements. The plan also called for full-time master's degree programs in the colleges of education (heretofore, graduate programs had been carried on solely through extension courses and summer school programs). Governor Rockefeller called higher education the biggest remaining untackled issue for the 1961 legislative session.

Locally, an upgrading of buildings and expansion of grounds were long overdue. On campus were three main buildings and several temporary wooden structures built during World War II, and the grounds encompassed fifty-five acres. When Brown left in 1963, the campus spanned eleven thousand acres; three buildings had grown to fourteen, including one nine-story high-rise residence hall (with another under way) and a large field house with a seating capacity of 3,500. Five temporary wooden structures remained, although the old Splinter Village had been torn down. The architect for the new buildings was Skidmore, Owings and Merrill, the firm that designed Lever House and the Chase Manhattan building in New York City, the entire town of Oak Ridge, Tennessee, and the Air Force Academy in Colorado. This firm was sometimes referred to as "the General Motors of the architectural world." Brown also managed to have legislation passed enabling the city to sell the City Home to the foundation he and the council had created. Dean Charles Turner noted that SUNY's slogan for its tenth birthday celebration in 1958, "A decade of growth," would apply just as well to the College at Oswego in Foster Brown's time.

The south athletic fieldhouse, completed in 1963 and named in honor of Golden Romney, chair of physical education from 1935 to 1950, had the first indoor skating rink within the SUNY system. (Today when the skating season ends, the rink becomes an indoor track.) Occupied in 1963, the fieldhouse was the site of graduation exercises for the first time in 1964.

Other additions to facilities included a refracting telescope presented by Lillian Wells in 1955, an observatory built under the direction of George Pitluga in 1956, and carillon bells given by Mr. and Mrs. Walter P. Phillips in 1956. The bells were programmed to run a sequence each day from 8:00 A.M. to 8:00 P.M. and to signal each hour. The Alma Mater was played at noon, and at 6:00 P.M. three light musical selections were heard. At first, hours were struck from 8:00 A.M. to 11:00 P.M., but neighbors complained and the time frame was restricted. After nine decades of miniscule expansion, the enormous growth seemed almost abrupt, as one huge building after another arose. Ultimately, the plan was complete, except for three dormitories designed to complete the circle around Glimmerglass Lagoon; plans for the dorms were canceled by a shrinking budget.

Off campus, Fallbrook Farm, formerly home for the aged, became a recreation area with a ski lodge, ski slopes, and an indoor riding arena. Meanwhile, the fifty-seven acre south athletic field provided facilities for various outdoor sports. The Shore Acres Park at Fair Haven Bay, an eighty-acre bird sanctuary, was used for field studies, sports activities, and picnics.

Throughout the construction period, Brown proved himself a master strategist. He recalled his attempts to buy one property that seemed to be out of reach because of its cost. He kept raising the amount of his offer until the matter seemed to be getting out of hand. Finally, Brown, with Cary Salander, the business manager, went to see its owner. "First, we talked about chickens for a while. Then we said that we were prepared to offer him that day 'x' dollars for his property. The man stood up, excited, and said, 'Mr. Salander, did you offer that?' He said, 'Yes.' 'Well,' I said, 'if we offered it, we will stick by our word until tomorrow, but tomorrow the price will go down because your offer was much too high.' The man asked, 'What time tomorrow?' and I said, 'Nine o'clock.' At eight o'clock he called and said he would take it."

On another occasion, Brown arranged a tour around the campus for Governor Averill Harriman. In one place, a plank about six feet long straddled a mud puddle and Brown made sure the Governor had to walk across it to emphasize the fact that a bit of help was needed around here. He also showed the governor the old World War II barracks and the men's gym where just two shower heads were working.

An anecdote recalled by Harry Charlton, Oswego's publicity man, points up the reputation Brown had for large-scale thinking. In the early 1960s Brown asked Charles (Bud) Coward to produce some plans for some sort of bridge or physical expediency which might give students safe access and egress when crossing Route 104 to attend events on the South Athletic Field.

Shortly thereafter, Bud Coward happened to be in Harry Charlton's office and saw on the wall a schematic photo which had come in the mail. Coward said it was "an architect's rendering of a huge interstate highway cloverleaf. Traffic moved six lanes in either direction, and there were bridges, on and off ramps, spurs leading in several directions—certainly at least a one hundred million dollar project." Coward noted that he and Charlton decided on a joint memo to Dr. Brown "enclosing the schematic photo as our solution to the Route 104 bottleneck. With some misgivings, we co-signed the memo and gave it to his secretary." Three days later Coward went to Charlton—in stitches—with a memo from "FSB." It read something like, "Impractical, far-fetched, feather-brained. But your best work to date. Keep it up."

George Pitluga calls Brown "the best building and grounds man the state ever had," a view shared in Albany. Years later SUNY's budget director introduced him to some people, saying "You people always complain about people who spend money. Here's a man who saved the state millions because he bought land before homes were built on it."

Events of special interest or significance during these years were highly varied. In 1956 James Lanigan, who had served on the College Council for fourteen years, ten as chair, retired. He had graduated from the Cortland State Normal School in 1911, attended Syracuse University from 1912 to 1913, where he returned in 1951 and graduated in 1953 with a Bachelor of Science degree, *cum laude*, at the age of 60.

The deepest snow in local history came in December of 1958. The town was cut off from the outside world, and the college had to shut down.

Dr. Takashi Kurasawa, professor of education at Tokyo Gakugei University, spent several days at the college in 1960 studying documents regarding early Japanese students at the Oswego Normal. That same year, Oswego alumnus Hideo Takamine's granddaughter was the principal of a college for young women in Tokyo. From time to time over the years Japanese educators have come to Oswego, which Japan acknowledges as the model for its schools of teacher education.

Other assorted events occurred during Brown's last years, 1960–1963, and Turner's, 1963–1965: the 1962 flu epidemic was so severe that consideration was given to using basement dormitories for housing the ill; in 1964 the largest judo tournament ever held in the area was held on campus; and the first Parents' Weekend was held. During Turner's acting presidency, the College Council considered more than 120 presidential candidates. Although very popular, Turner was not considered because of a rule, since abandoned, that presidents could not be chosen from the local staff. Several faculty, along with the overwhelming support of others, met with the Council in an attempt to have the rule overturned, but to no avail. Turner retired in the fall of 1965, James E. Perdue assumed the presidency, and Samuel Gould became the Chancellor of the State University of New York.

Commencement is an event of significance every year and, from 1913 until 1964, the site for Oswego's graduation exercises was selected dependent upon the situation and conditions of the moment. Old Main was first occupied in 1913 and from that year until 1946, with the exception of 1941, commencements were held in its auditorium. Fire destroyed the auditorium in 1940, and the 1941 commencement took place in the Oswego High School. Lacking a large enough campus facility, commencements were held in the Oswego Theatre from 1947 until 1960, followed by outdoor exercises in 1961 and 1962 on the North Athletic Field. In 1963, largely due to inclement weather and the unusually large number of graduates, commencement was held under a tent erected on the lawn of the Lakeside Dining Hall—the only year under a tent. The Romney Field House has been the commencement site since 1964; its size makes unnecessary limiting the number of guests, and neither the size of the graduating class nor the prevailing weather is a factor to consider.

Except for changes in speakers and locations, these occasions were, and continue to be generally similar. A notable event during one commencement concerned two women and several men students who had been out late one night, resulting in an unsuccessful campus-wide search for the women. The women were denied the privilege of walking across the stage during the graduation exercises. Their co-conspirators, the men students, were not punished at all. The women did, however, receive their diplomas.

The 1961 exercises included a series of events commemorating the college's Centennial Celebration, beginning in April with a major address by SUNY's executive dean of teacher education, Hermann Cooper, and culminating in a convocation on Founder's Day, October 18. The events included an address by SUNY's then president, Thomas Hale Hamilton, and the dedication and naming of several new buildings. Old Main, first occupied in 1913, was renamed Sheldon Hall; and the college residence hall, formerly known as Piez Hall, was renamed Farnham Hall. Amos W. Farnham, Normal's class of 1875, joined the college's faculty in 1894 as a teacher of geography and, in summers, taught at Cornell University. During the Civil War, Farnham served with the United States Christian Commission as a nurse in the Depot Hospital.

Eight of Sheldon's twelve living grandchildren and two great grandchildren attended the Founder's Day Convocation and were personally escorted through the new buildings.

The Centennial observances included a Festival of the Arts with the theme "A Century of Americana," a ballet adapted to portray the history of the college, and a concert by the U.S. Navy Band. WHEN-TV Syracuse presented a special one-half hour Centennial television program on April 29 featuring students and faculty.

More than five hundred alumni and friends of the college attended the

Centennial Alumni Weekend, and 586 attended the alumni banquet on June 10, the largest assemblage of alumni in the college's history. James Lanigan, chair of the College Council, and President Foster S. Brown were honored at the banquet, each receiving an honorary life membership. Centennial plates were presented to the oldest alumna, Emily Dashley, Class of 1884, and in absentia, to Dorothy Rogers, author of the just-published Centennial History (and of this book). Rogers, professor of psychology, and Louise Ostberg, then chair of the Women's Physical Education Department, were circling the globe in a Jeep truck.

The 1962 commencement speaker, Charles Garsiele, a New York attorney, offered his own prescription for teacher education. His proposal: no education courses in the first four years; in the fifth, or graduate year, courses in one's major, perhaps including a course in philosophy or history of education and one in the psychology of learning; and about six weeks of practice teaching. The graduate would receive a Master of Arts in Teaching degree. Garsiele also said there was no reason why Oswego could not, within ten years, become "one of the great liberal arts colleges in the East."

Foster Brown of necessity took very seriously the role of casting director of his staff. During the 1950s, well-prepared faculty members were in demand. In 1957 the President's Committee on Education stressed the need for recruiting talented people and recommended that faculty income be doubled within five to ten years, and fringe benefits added. Brown made his "number one priority" the acquisition of a quality faculty. "One year," he said, "when we had ninety people to hire, I traveled to California to make contacts at the University of California and Stanford. After I brought back candidates' credentials, department heads took it from there."

A comparison of the 1957 and 1963 college faculty reflects the magnitude and success of his recruiting efforts. The faculty tripled from 88 to 270 and those holding doctorates quadrupled from 22 to 90. In 1952 the eighty-eight faculty members represented thirty-four alma maters, 54 percent of which were Columbia, Syracuse, and New York Universities. By 1963 seventy-four institutions were represented, but only 30 percent were from these three universities. The same trend continued during the acting presidency of Charles Turner. By the fall of 1964, the teaching faculty numbered 310, with an additional 30 in other positions, such as administrative and library staff. Of the total, 37 percent held doctorates.

The change in mission from a teacher-training college to a multipurpose institution ushered in a new era. It altered the composition of the faculty, with mostly favorable outcomes, but at least one unfortunate result. Recalled Richard Wheeler, director of placement and later Associate Provost, "They had some contempt for the earlier faculty and what it had been doing. The latter, in turn, adopted many of the rather unflattering mannerisms that they observed in their new colleagues." In any case, the winds of change were blowing and the curriculum was destined for at least a 350-degree change in course.

Within the framework of their mission, the Brown–Turner faculties included many outstanding individuals. In the Brown administration the next in rank was Harold Alford, director of the Education Division, and then dean until he left in 1960. Sherwood (Sherry) Dunham succeeded Alford as Director of Education from 1958 to 1962 and was named to the deanship in 1962. Charles Turner, director of Education following Alford, was named acting president in 1963, a post he held until 1965.

These three men were talented administrators, masters of human relations, and widely recognized for their leadership in teacher education. They had a special knack for inspiring the entire staff to perform well while maintaining high morale. Dunham said Turner was a "champion" insofar as he was concerned. "He had the intelligence and stability to hold the institution together from a curricular standpoint. When Brown was here, administrators consulted him about financial and personnel matters, but he left the curriculum to the faculty. Charlie Turner, in contrast, supervised the development of the curriculum." Dunhan believed his chief ability lay in making conditions appropriate for the achievement of others, and for creating conditions that made his staff productive. While dean of the college, Dunham enjoyed most working on the curriculum, and he found Richard (Dick) Wheeler of particular help in that regard.

Wheeler deserves special mention, as do two other administrators of that era: Virginio Piucci, principal of the Campus School; and Robert Helsby, alumni director and later chair of Industrial Arts. Wheeler was—and is—an excellent team player and a master of detail, a nuts-and-bolts specialist. Piucci, always called Dit, was truly a progressive educator and the father of two sets of twin boys. About Helsby, whom Foster Brown leap-frogged over others to head Industrial Arts, Brown recalled, "Art Hauler said, 'That was a bold move, but I was for it.' "When there is such evidence of talent, you must have the courage to make use of it." Brown's praise was no exaggeration of Helsby's talents; he had been valedictorian of the Class of 1940 and received the college's first Bachelor of Science degree. "I came to Oswego in the middle of the Depression with $30 and a dream," said Helsby. Helsby went on to become the executive director of Oswego's Alumni Association, and in June of 1967, while serving as the State University's dean for Continuing Education, he received Oswego's Distinguished Alumnus Award.

From 1951 to 1965, Industrial Arts had four division directors. The first was Gordon Wilber, who retired in 1957; next was Robert Helsby, who left in 1959 to become Deputy Commissioner of Labor of the State of New York; he was followed by acting head Arthur Hauler, whose work across the state was so outstanding it won him the nickname of Mr. IA; and in 1960, Paul DeVore was named.

Two other well-known administrators of this era were Norman Whitten, professor of history and, for a time, dean of students; and White Warner, coordinator of Field Service. Sherwood Dunham declared that "White did as much as anyone to make Oswego what it is today. He would get in his little MG sports car, go to the high schools, and assemble students in the auditorium. After he was through, if they didn't think that Oswego was the best place in the world, they simply hadn't been listening."

Members of the teaching faculty also made notable contributions. Charles Snyder, history professor, wrote *The Little Lady Who Wore Pants*, about Dr. Mary E. Walker; the author of the present book wrote the centennial history of the college, *Oswego: Fountainhead of Teacher Education*, a book about her travels, *Jeopardy and a Jeep*, published in America and England; and *Mental Hygiene in Elementary Education*, which won the Delta Kappa Gamma International Society's award. Carlton Gerbracht and Frank Robinson brought out a book called *Understanding American Industries;* and the National Council on Geography Education presented to Melvina Svec its Distinguished Service Award. In 1964 Maurice Boyd, chair of the music department, his wife and their three children gave their sixteenth annual Christmas Vesper Concert, playing the piano, autoharp, clarinet, flute, and bells. Helen Buckley, author of children's books, received the Junior Literary Guild Award.

In addition, several faculty members were taking Oswego's name abroad. Harold Richardson, emeritus chemistry professor, and Arthur Greer, associate professor of industrial arts, directed educational programs in Vietnam; their families were evacuated along with other American families. William Reynolds and Carlton Gerbracht directed industrial projects in Brazil, and from 1963 to 1965, Emeritus Dean Harold Alford headed SUNY's and the Ford Foundation's Indonesian projects.

In the meantime, several well-known faculty members died or retired. Marian Mahar, who had taught social studies from 1931 until 1957, died in 1960. She had studied at three foreign universities, organized the Refugee Children's Council in Oswego, and worked on the Fort Ontario Refugee Project. Carol King, associate dean of students since 1954 and dog-obedience trainer, died in 1959; and in 1963 Isabel Kingsbury Hart (1907), former dean of women, died. Later three campus buildings, Mahar, Hart, and King Halls, were named for these three women. While vacationing in Barbados in 1958, former President Swetman died. For various reasons, the following departed during this period (the year each arrived at Oswego is included): Harold Alford, director of education, then dean, 1934; Marian Angel, the Campus School, 1924; Leo Cribben, mathematics professor, 1929; Melvina Svec, geography, 1947; Charles Wells, physics, 1929; and affiliated with Industrial Arts, Gene Essex, 1929, Harry Karcher, 1921, and Jay Rudolph,

1918. Among other faculty members who retired in 1957 were three old-timers: Gordon Wilber, long-time director of industrial arts, who had arrived in 1933; Max Ziel who had arrived in 1921, was a major in the Air Transport Command for thirty-one years and Oswego's physical education legend; and Frank Schneider, who had arrived in 1926 and was an industrial arts instructor and well-known designer of model speedboats.

During Brown's presidency, faculty–student relations and faculty relations were close. The college was still small; all were united in the same teacher-training process; and times were relatively good. Brown judged faculty–student relationships during this period as "above average." True, some individuals were "restless," he said, "as they were elsewhere . . . seeking issues, often artificial ones. Oswego's difficult time was just beginning when I left. Even before I left there were some incidents that made me wonder what was lying ahead."

In those days men faculty made weekend trips to Paul Shaver's "Earth Sciences" cottage in the Thousand Islands where, in addition to fishing, there was story telling and feasting, and Bob Sykes, "Earth Sciences" prepared "the most elegant gourmet meals I ever ate," recalled George Pitluga.

The faculty in the science department often indulged in horseplay, that was, in retrospect, seemingly juvenile. On one occasion, Ernie Wise stapled John Weeks's classbook to the ceiling over his desk. Another time, Charles Yager had taken raw eggs to use in chemistry class that afternoon only to discover that Orla Loper managed to boil them without his knowledge. On yet another occasion, Loper and Yager conjured up some sort of painting—a real mess—which they took to Joseph Schoenfelt in the art department for appraisal. They said they had bought it and wanted his opinion. Joe, at least temporarily, took it seriously.

Another trick faculty men sometimes played on each other involved leaving a note on someone's desk, reading, "Please call 342-0490 at your earliest convenience"; the returned call was answered by Dial-A-Prayer. Nor was it unusual for an instructor to glance at the door while lecturing and see one of his colleagues yawning exaggeratedly, just out of view of the students.

The science faculty now and then acted somewhat humorously toward students. The physics lab had acquired a very powerful magnet which Orla Loper hid behind the blackboard, and he had also placed a nail in the blackboard eraser. After finishing his lecture, Loper would let go of the eraser leaving it stuck on the blackboard. His students would look on "bug-eyed." Vernon Tryon (1958) recalled that when a student would ask Loper for permission to leave a class early, he would reply, "Yes, on one condition, and that is, when the time comes for you to leave, you must slam shut your book, stand up, and announce to the class, 'I've had all of this I can stand.' A few did it; others just couldn't bring themselves to." Tryon also recalled, "There was a work table in the back of the lab and Loper always carried a cigar. Once he left the cigar there and while he was gone, Hop Powers nailed it to the table."

Some faculty humor was not intended as such. Psychology Professor William McGarvey had large classes and many papers to read, and he found himself writing similar comments over and over. Therefore, he requisitioned rubber stamps for the twelve most commonly made statements. After a long interval, (getting special purchases approved in those days wasn't easy) the rubber stamps arrived. To his dismay, instead of receiving separate stamps for each of the twelve comments, he received twelve stamps, each containing all twelve comments. Since some of the comments were two sentences long, each rubber stamp was huge.

During those years, there were the earliest glimmerings of the faculty's insistence on greater participation in college governance. The Faculty Council, begun in 1949, was succeeded in the 1950s by the Faculty Assembly, shaped mainly by Sherwood Dunham, Robert Sloan, and Johnson Cooper. "I wanted to make it collegial rather than adversarial," recalls Sherry, "but the faculty was becoming too independent."

Curricular trends during Brown's years could be described as follows: from 1952 to 1957 the emphasis was on expanding facilities and curricular offerings because of the anticipated tidal wave of college applicants.[4] Because of this rising tide, as well as the growing emphasis on equality of opportunity after World War II, colleges everywhere, including Oswego, lowered admission standards. When Russia launched its Sputnik in 1957, however, the country almost panicked. America's superiority in technology and education had been taken for granted, but Sputnik spelled the end of such complacency. The results of Sputnik's success, plus other technological developments, set the stage for a reversal of the trend toward more electives and renewed an emphasis on fundamentals.

It is important and appropriate to compare in detail the curriculum at the time of President Brown's arrival to what it was when he left in 1963. Oswego's mission in 1952 was to train elementary and industrial arts teachers. As the teacher shortage grew, Oswego added junior high, secondary, and early childhood programs. To the junior high program, academic specializations were added in art, music, psychology, mathematics, science, social studies, and English. The industrial arts division also expanded its offerings and by 1963 had courses in industrial arts education, kindergarten through grade 12, manual arts therapy, driver education, and elementary industrial arts. Areas of instruction in industrial arts were technical, professional, and general studies. Preprofessional experiences for both divisions were provided in the Campus School and in public schools.

The graduate and extension programs also were expanded during Brown's tenure. In 1952 approximately 200 students were enrolled each semester in extension work; in 1963 the enrollment reached 893. The 1952 graduate offerings were in industrial arts and vocational and elementary education; in 1960 school guidance was added; and by 1963, offerings included junior high school English and social studies. An important aspect of summer sessions was the Intensive Training Program to prepare liberal arts college graduates to become teachers.

During Brown's last year, a basic change occurred in the college's mission—the first in 101 years. Oswego moved from a single to a multipurpose institution. In the fall of 1962, thirty liberal arts students were admitted to the curriculum, then restricted to transfers at the junior level. It was not until the fall of 1964 that freshmen were first admitted to the liberal arts program. The first liberal arts majors were in five areas only: communications, specializing in public address and modern languages; humanities with specializations in art, philosophy, and theater; science and mathematics with specializations in biology, chemistry, physics, and math; social studies with specializations in economics, history, political science and sociology; and behavioral science with specialization in psychology.

A sharp upgrading of teacher-training programs occurred during Turner's two years as acting president, along with a rapid expansion of the liberal arts. However, because of the teacher shortage, the major emphasis was still on teacher education, and Oswego rose to the challenge. Oswego was one of the seventy-five colleges cited in 1963–64 for programs of excellence in teacher education by the American Association of Colleges for Teacher Education at its annual conference in Chicago.

In his 1963–64 report, Turner reported an increasingly intellectual climate on campus. The number of academically and culturally oriented artist series, assemblies, and convocations was growing rapidly. Important days were Founder's Day in spring, the Honors Convocation in October, and the Festival of the Arts in spring. "In addition," recalled Sherwood Dunham, "some of the new liberal arts faculty members were arguing for a more liberal education, and the education people were quite concerned. They felt threatened—no question about it."

In most classrooms the lecture method still ruled supreme; however, there were variations, two of which are noteworthy: On October 3, 1964, under the direction of Peter Pratt, 190 students undertook the largest archeological expedition ever conducted in New York State, and one of the largest in the nation. Near Auburn, New York, they explored a village site occupied in the fourteenth century by ancient Cayugas, one of the five member nations of the Iroquois confederacy. Among objects the students found were stone axes, mortars and pestles used to grind corn, polished stone beads and pendants, and pottery fragments. Another innovative educator was Robert Sykes, earth science professor and associate of the State University Atmospheric Sciences Research Center. He used a broad network of instrumental stations and volunteer help, including talented high-school youths and senior citizens, to gather extensive data on weather factors related to lake-effect storms.

Certain departments were innovative, and still are. For example, under the leadership of Robert Canfield, the Reading Center compared the effectiveness of machine-oriented adult reading instruction to teacher-oriented programs. Meanwhile, the psychology department, the largest in SUNY, initiated and hosted the first annual intercampus undergraduate psychology conference. At each of these, students delivered (and still do) original research papers.

Instructors with strong personalities sometimes transcend the courses they teach. One such was the legendary Max Ziel. Vernon Tryon recalled that during his student days, gym classes were held in one of the temporary buildings and, on very cold days, Ziel would cancel classes. Before class, students would place a snowball at the thermometer's base, removing it before Ziel arrived. Upon his arrival, Ziel would check the thermometer to determine whether to hold or cancel the class. Such stories notwithstanding, Ziel was one of the most admired and beloved faculty members Oswego has ever had.

Paralleling and supplementing the regular curricular programs were various professional events and lectures. In the summer of 1961, the first-ever Coast Guard Reserve Training School held in the United States was conducted at the college. Four two-week sessions involved one hundred Coast Guard reserve officers and enlisted men from all parts of the country east of the Mississippi. Other periodic events included various distinguished lecturers; among them David Schoenbrun, news commentator; George Estabrooks, retired chairman of psychology at Hamilton College, temporary Oswego professor and authority on hypnotism; and Robert Kennedy, U.S. Attorney General. "In 1963 when a representative of the Communist Party spoke on Campus," recalled Charles Turner, then acting president, "the townspeople were very disturbed. I explained that a part of becoming educated is to hear all sides of issues."

College students across the country were still somewhat traditional, and iconoclasts were the missing persons. Students did not dissect currently conflicting philosophies or debate world issues. The male students studied hard, and expected to make it in their careers. The coeds dreamed of a husband, children, a house in the suburbs after graduation, and a stint in the classroom. These students, male and female, had missed both the Depression and World War II; theirs was an era of prosperity; There were some changes, however. College attendance was becoming more broadly based, partly because families were more prosperous. Most GIs had finished college; only a few were still enrolled.[5] By the mid-1960s a small fraction of students were activists, but most were concerned with personal goals. A full

85 percent were satisfied with their college experience and a mere 12 percent dissatisfied. American students were a "reincarnation of the nineteenth century Oxonian aristocrats, securely ensconced in their 'sweet city with her dreaming spires.' "[6]

Students seemed in no hurry to get away from campus life, perhaps because it offered security. A small majority (52 percent) intended to go to graduate school, while a considerable plurality (36 percent) indicated their first jobs would be in education or teaching, followed by a minority (21 percent) who indicated their first jobs would be in engineering and science. Most students looked benignly on their parents, and the gap between generations dwindled from that of the recent past. Despite their tumultuous new world, the majority held similar beliefs to their parents in politics (53 percent), religion (57 percent), self-image (53 percent), and sex (52 percent). Almost two-thirds believed their parents held values similar to their own. Some students felt they had let their parents down by doing poorly in their studies or for not pursuing directions their parents had wished.

The entertainments of the 1950s had been relatively tame with no great sense of excitement and no rebellion. The show "I Love Lucy" was popular at that time, and popular tunes from Broadway musicals were "South Pacific," "Pajama Game," and "My Fair Lady." Students could be heard singing "Some Enchanted Evening" or "I Could Have Danced All Night."[7] "Hi-Fis" (mon-aural, high fidelity), which appeared in 1948, were popular with the college crowd. Elvis Presley was of course the rage. Also rising to popularity was the pilgrimage to Fort Lauderdale during spring vacation, when the sun had melted down the snowmen and the undergrads' resolution to study.

The 1950s had also been the era of strange fads, one of which was panty raids—a few bold males even tried to collect them directly from the maidens themselves. The more obliging girls sometimes tossed panties and bras out of windows; others tossed buckets of water. Other fads were the wrecking of pianos and crowding into telephone booths (Missouri State College claimed a record capacity of thirty-five).

Modes of youth entertainment are fickle, and during the next decade the entire scene changed. In the early 1960s guitars were still popular, as were Grand Old Opry music and folksingers. Square dancing and folk festivals caught on, and jazz was the rage. Beginning in 1961, the twist was the most popular dance, to be succeeded by the mashed potato, the hully gully, the dirty bird, and the slop. The discotheque arrived in 1964, where couples danced the watusi and its variations.

The Beatles stole the musical scene in 1963 and held center stage for several years. Soul music gained a wide audience, folk music changed into folk rock; and gospel tunes were well liked. In reading matter, restraints disappeared, censorship diminished, and campus publications reacted accordingly. Even humor changed as "deliberate absurdities raged through the college campuses . . . there was the elephant joke: 'What do you get when you cross an elephant with a jar of peanut butter? A peanut that never forgets or an elephant that sticks to the roof of your mouth.'

Simmering in the background were more serious issues: the restlessness at Berkeley had begun to spread; emphasis on national issues grew; the status of Greeks diminished; and the day of the campus hero had passed. Lyndon B. Johnson succeeded the assassinated president, John F. Kennedy, and Johnson's wife, Lady Bird, inspired a concern for the environment through her national beautification efforts.

The Oswego student population had changed in size and in character. The total enrollment tripled from 1,076 in 1952 to 3,599 in fall 1963. The gap between numbers of men and women had narrowed—from a 3:1 male–female ratio in 1952 to a 1:1½ ratio in 1963. Students also hailed from greater distances than ever before. In 1952 Albany and Schenectady counties sent a total of four students to Oswego, compared to sixty-one in 1963. The number from Westchester rose from 63 to 151 and Nassau from 53 to 345. Oswego County still led in numbers with 502, followed by Onondaga with 355. Five downstate counties, Nassau, Westchester, Suffolk, Queens, and Kings, were among the top ten.

During Brown's tenure, freshmen Regents Scholarship Examination Scores increased on average by eleven points, and college board scores compared well with those of college students nationally. However, beginning about 1964, scores declined for a time, both here and elsewhere. "Those were the days of civil rights," observed George Pitluga. "Everyone now had a right to a college education, or at least a four-year hiatus between high school and the workaday world. As a result the quality of students deteriorated."

At least until the mid-1960s, far more males than females came from working-class backgrounds. Males from more affluent families generally went to schools providing entry into better paying occupations. Females from these same families often went into teaching because higher status occupations were largely closed to them. In poorer families, the limited monies available mostly went to sons. Finally, more easily than their female counterparts, working-class males could find part-time employment, thus enabling them to stay in the more expensive schools. As a result, many upper-middle class girls had same-sex friends of similar background, but where dating was involved, the young women were often conscious of a social-class gap.

Where student styles were concerned, more traditonal dress prevailed in the early 1960s. The 1961–62 Student Handbook suggested as everyday attire for women skirts, sweaters, blouses, and sport shoes. Recommended for schools when practice teaching were hose and flats or heels, and for evening assemblies and concerts, dress, skirt and blouse, hose, and heels. "Slacks and bermudas may be worn by women on Saturdays. Blue jeans are worn when participating in athletics," decreed the handbook. Men wore to classes "sweaters, sport shirts, slacks, bucks, saddle shoes, loafers—and to church and Sunday dinner, suits or jackets, ties, dress shoes, and top coat."

In the early 1960s students were far more clothes conscious than formerly. The males wore Ivy League styles; gone were the dungarees and sloppy slacks. Girls wore a popular bouffant hairstyle with locks arranged in puffs, making their faces appear small and round. They wore skirts to classes, although slacks and bermudas might be worn after 4:00 P.M., but dungarees were frowned upon as sloppy attire.

However, as student revolts spread, clothes at Oswego began to change, the men's earlier than the women's. The theme was toward becoming individualistic and dress was unusual, if not strictly appropriate. An *Oswegonian* article chided males for their attire: "Certainly, bleached, stained, skin-tight jeans are not appropriate dinner time dress; nor are bermudas. Perhaps a male counterpart to AWS (Associated Women Students) should be devised for establishing a dress code."[8]

The female dress code survived awhile longer. Patricia Harrington (1965) often wore cut-off jeans and a raincoat to classes so it would appear she had on a dress. Maria Kimmel Ricketson (1965) remembered that "PA, professional attire, was required because the school's primary concern was teacher training—which meant dresses, hose, and heels for Sunday dinner, concerts, or lectures. If you didn't conform, someone representing the AWS would place a mark on your record; and after you had several you would be campused, which meant that you couldn't leave your dorm on Friday or Saturday night, or some such thing."

Margaret Garno Helmke (1965) recalled that "Levis and Wranglers were worn only during recreational functions. Sweaters, plaid skirt, sneakers, and knee socks (to match the sweater, of course) were the uniform of the day. On Thursday one must wear his or her fraternity or sorority blazer. The sheath was the 'dress-up' thing to wear, and cocktail dresses for formals were 'in'. The bouffant 'flip' was the hairdo for women, and the cleancut 'Princeton' was the chosen coiffure for gentlemen."

Food and drink habits had changed little. Many students of both sexes drank alcohol, mostly beer, but few used other drugs. Fraternity parties centered around drinking. Women students, especially, were shocked when any student—usually a male—was arrested for using marijuana, and judged him "seedy." As for food, many students skipped breakfast and, as customary in colleges, found dorm fare uninspiring. Women students sometimes loaned their meal tickets to fraternity boys, "who were always hungry."

In the meantime, student expenses were steadily rising and would escalate still further later on. In 1961–62 room and board cost $680 to $750, and books and supplies another $50 to $60. Just two years later, in 1963–64, these same items cost on averge $1,352. Student–faculty association fees of $15 twenty-five years earlier had risen to $23.50. Nonacademic expenses were moderate, unless one owned a car. Car ownership was a status symbol, and half of the men students owned one compared to only one in thirteen women. "I had $25 a month allowance for spending money," recalled Maria Kimmel Ricketson, "and that was plenty. Most students had very limited allowances." Many more scholarships and loans were available than in the past. Some were underwritten locally, and others came from outside sources such as the state level, from the New York Higher Assistance Corporation. Moderate federal funds had also become available, but only to students who would sign a non-Communist affidavit.

Campus life varied by student category, each with its formula for fun and frolic, or serious endeavor. Fraternity men were social kingpins on campus and regularly partied. Protestors, a product of the dawning civil rights movement, often participated in demonstrations. The non-frat, more traditional, students had fewer parties, but sometimes shared pizzas delivered to the dorms. Students in general enjoyed going to Vona's and Canale's for food, the Country Inn for atmosphere, and Bucklands for the TGIF or Thank-God-its-Friday celebration. Social life was also modified by the lopsided sex ratio: getting a date was an achievement for the women. An *Oswegonian* editorial contended that the males "got superiority complexes. They could date any time, while some of the girls would drift into Bucklands to pick up a guy."

Freshmen were inducted into the rituals of college life by the orientation committee. As a member of it, Margaret Garno Helmke recalled "all-night stints painting huge posters for Homecoming Weekend, making thousands of tissue flowers to stuff into chickenwire shapes for a winning float in Float Parade and dreaming up disgusting concoctions for pledges to drink."

The off-campus local students, who shared only marginally in campus life, were called "'towners'," explained Helmke. "They were as distinct from people in the community who didn't go to college, who were 'townies'." Helmke, herself a 'towner', added, "Being a towner had its problems, such as explaining to parents why you were in the shape you were in after a frat party. Also, I missed something by not living in a dorm or sorority house. On the other hand, it was nice to have well-balanced home-cooked meals and drive Dad's car sometimes."

In the early 1960s college traditions began to crumble, including Greek societies, secret societies, attendance at athletic events, and formal proms. However, many schools, including Oswego, still maintained dress and behavior codes, and curfews. Oswego abolished compulsory chapel attendance in 1953 although, even in the early 1960s, students were encouraged to attend. Women were still treated like children and freshmen initiations were childish. In 1955 freshmen were required to "wear the original caps given to them every day but Sunday; attend all social functions of the school; not smoke on campus; obey all commands of upperclassmen; tip their caps to upperclassmen and say hello first; not keep their hands in their pockets at any time; learn the alma mater, football songs, and school cheers within two weeks; keep off the grass; not wear athletic or class insignia from prep schools; render services during athletic contests; meet on the front steps every Wednesday noon; and, above all, be a good sport."[9]

Sections of Oswego's 1963–64 *Student Handbook* read like relics of some bygone era. Students were warned that "liquor by those under 18 is prohibited by law in New York State and use of alcoholic beverages is prohibited in college buildings and sorority houses. Any marriage is opposed by the college which involves secrecy, lack of parental approval, or contravention of law. It is suggested that students consult with a spiritual advisor or members of the personnel staff before they get married in college. Married women students are not permitted to live in residence halls." The reason for this last restriction was never made clear. In that same year, 1963–64, a student editorial demanded that the women's dress code on campus conform to the will of the majority.[10] However, the Associated Women Students' executive council said it would enforce the code even if it was not approved by the majority. Although from present perspective it seems like comic soap opera, curfew still prevailed in modified form. In April 1965 the new closing hours in women's residence halls were midnight, Sunday through Thursday, and 1:30 A.M. on Friday and Saturday nights. Also tried was a midnight closing hour for all the women in Funnelle Hall, a change from 10:00 P.M. for freshmen and 11:00 P.M. for upperclassmen.

Maria Kimmel Ricketson, then president of the Associated Women Students, explained the situation in greater detail. "Women students were not allowed away from campus overnight. You had to be in by curfew unless you had written permission from your parents to spend the weekend somewhere. Some sort of permission slip was sent to them before the school term began and they could give different types of permission. My parents gave me permission to go away on weekends if I wanted to go home with roommates; it only had to be cleared with the dean of women. Otherwise, parents had to give written permission each time you wanted to spend a weekend away. Yet the women students were not particularly unhappy with the rules. I recall no big outcry that dorm life was too restricted or that there were too many rules for women. Some individuals didn't like the curfews and wanted freedom to stay out as late as they wished but the administration argued that rules were necessary for women's safety. The administrators were our surrogate parents—when they took us to live on campus they were responsible for our well-being—and if they didn't know where we were, how could they uphold their responsibility?

"During my four years there, I can't recall anyone's ever putting forth an argument, saying 'Hey, wait a minute. Why do these men have free run of the place while the women are locked in?' There were always women students who just didn't show up, and if they were very late, Campus Security would be summoned to find them. It was always approached from the angle that something could actually be wrong—maybe they were in an accident or something. There certainly were no coed dorms or coed visiting in the rooms, and this didn't bother anybody. The girls were comfortable with the fact that they could walk around their floor in their underwear and not have to be concerned that men students were visiting there."

Most student activities centered around going to class, but on Friday nights it was the in-thing to go to Bucklands; and those who didn't drink beer stood around and pretended they did. In warm weather the crowd went to Nunzi's on the lakeshore. Most of the social life was restricted to the campus because few students had cars. A few students watched television; others almost never watched it, unless some highly significant event occurred, such as the Kennedy assassination or the Cuban missile crisis. Then the television set remained on for anyone to see and hear.

Playing pinochle and bridge was popular in the dorms after studying, and in the Union between classes. Students were always at the tables playing games; and others might sit around drinking coffee or talking, prepared to replace players who had to leave. There were also occasional pranks, mostly harmless, but some more serious, such as the knocking of Sheldon's statue off its base. Brown had it speedily restored to its perch.

The few students who had cars rarely had the latest model. "I had a third-hand green Rambler from my grandmother," said Pat Harrington (1965), "and we used to go off to New York City on a weekend for no reason. Most of the students either hitched rides or walked. The corner across from Sheldon Hall was the hitching corner on Washington Boulevard. People who saw students standing there knew they wanted a ride downtown. There was also a corner downtown, at Third and Bridge, where people heading toward the college would stop and give students a ride. There were no buses to and from town. However, in the early 1960s, the administration encouraged students to stop hitching rides, especially at night, after several hitchhikers had been molested or attacked."

Across the country in the 1960s, one writer observed, "Joe College was dying. Freshmen hazing and beanies were out. Fraternities, intercollegiate athletics, clubs, and dances, the traditional foci for school spirit, were fading at one speed or another.[11] Campus life underwent great change in the 1960s, greater than in the previous half century—not in the classroom wherein the traditional lecture system continued, nor in the curriculum, but in the students' out-of-class life and, consequently, in the quality of their total college experience.

Enthusiasm for athletics grew during Brown's presidency, partly due to a series of winning teams. Oswego won the annual State University invitational basketball tournament in 1958, 1960, and 1962, and, upon winning in 1964 and 1965 became the first team to win a State University Conference title for two successive years. The wrestlers won their share of victories, too. Oswego's team was undefeated in 1957 and won the State University Championship in 1965, captained by Harry Furrer (1965), who set a four-year, forty-four win no-loss record. Other sports also had their good years: Robert Thole (1962) was named to the All-American soccer team in 1961; the Laker stickmen captured the Finger Lakes hockey crown in 1965; and the swimming team had its best season ever, with Norman Harvey (1966) and Douglas Endicott setting pool records.

Some sporting events were less formal. Due to the lack of ice and snow in 1965, frustrated sidewalk surfers "took to slopes and pavement skateboarding."[12] Also frustrated by the weather, but differently, was the women's canoeing class; it canoed in Lee Hall pool, due to the extreme cold outside. Other somewhat untraditional athletes were the Guys and Dolls volleyball league, each team composed of three fellows and three girls.

Greek organizations, still important at Oswego at this time, had begun with Phi Beta Kappa in America in 1776 at William and Mary College. Such organizations were founded not as "snob groups, but by idealistic founders who were not satisfied by . . . existing societies."[13] They first arrived on Oswego's campus in the early 1920s, and early on included Beta Tau Epsilon fraternity, Alpha Kappa Phi, and Alpha Delta sororities. The number remained the same until the mid-1940s, when three new fraternities appeared: Phi Sigma Epsilon (Phi Sigma Phi), Zeta Rho (Sigma Tau Chi), and Iota Clio, (Alpha Sigma Alpha).

Greek organizations across the country were attacked in the 1950s because of their discriminatory membership policies. In 1953, in accord with a Supreme Court ruling, two SUNY coeds lodged complaints that they had been discriminated against by the Greeks because of race. That same year the State University Board of Trustees decided that social organizations with external affiliations would not be allowed in SUNY. Nor could any local social organizations discriminate on the basis of "race, color, creed, religion, national origin or other artificial criteria." As a result, the nationally affiliated Greeks reorganized under local status. A somewhat silent minority would have preferred getting rid of the Greek organizations, or else opening them to every person who wished to join.

In 1960 the Greeks were again the socially elite on campus, and they tried to upgrade their image. Pledges must have an index of 2.0, and drinking in sorority houses was taboo. Hazing disappeared among the sororities in 1952 and among the fraternities in 1959. It was traditional for the interfraternity Rush Council to sponsor pledge projects for the benefit of the city; one year the pledges donated the money from their bottle drive to a local charity. The Greek games, begun in 1949, were another important tradition. In 1965 the fraternities' thirteenth annual games included a 220-yard dash, shot put, relays, sack race, high jump and discus throw. The sororities' contests included a three-legged race, a 50-yard dash, softball throw, and shuttle relay.

Fraternity parties, said Margaret Garno Helmke, were "always crazy and usually had a theme such as the Toga Party when we all dressed like people in Roman times or the Twins Party when dates wore similar outfits. One frat had an annual 'bathtub gin' party. There was actually an old bathtub, placed in the center of the party room, into which guests would pour their gin and orange juice. Everyone would 'dip to their heart's delight'!"

Special days and events were highly varied in nature. In 1951, the Class of 1940 unearthed the time capsule it had buried that year. The drum containing it had been punctured by a post from a snow fence. When disinterred, it was "filled with water that smelled like a cross between a garbage dump and a sewage disposal plant." The contents proved appropriate, and another capsule with new contents was implanted.

"Moving-up Day" was launched in 1955; class queens were crowned and student awards were presented. A Festival of Arts was introduced in 1960 to promote awareness of the new arts developed in the twentieth century, and that same year the first homecoming celebration was held. Other events of the period involved special student accomplishments. The symphonic choir appeared three times in 1960 on nationwide CBS radio broadcasts of Christmas music, and it helped celebrate the College Centennial by giving a Town Hall concert in New York City. A quite different event was Lyn Boswell's election as the best-dressed female on campus, a contest sponsored by the *Oswegonian*. Three photos were sent to *Drama* magazine, which was to choose the ten best-dressed college women in America.

On the more serious side, one heroic event occurred when an Oswego student, Edward St. Onge, jumped into the Oswego River and rescued a man foundering in the water. St. Onge had spoken earlier in an English class on the topic of artificial resuscitation. Reminiscent of the severe influenza epidemic of World War I was a lesser but still serious one in 1962, of students overflowing the health facilities; dormitory basements were used to house them.

Oswego's severe winters always account for their share of events. In 1962 students unexpectedly gained an extra day for Christmas recess to avoid dangerous nighttime driving, and "the snack bar was ablaze with good news."[14] Two months later, in February 1963, the theme of Winter Weekend was Mardi Gras on Ice. For the snow sculpture contest, the Greek organizations and residence halls were assigned respective plots of land; they were allowed to begin work on Friday and to continue on Saturday until the latest women's curfew.

The college students of the 1950s have been called "the silent generation," because they lacked any great commitment to politics. They went along with the mainstream which itself was euphoric and somewhat subdued. Nor were the leaders of the time especially stirring. President Harry S. Truman was followed by Dwight D. Eisenhower, both moderate and somewhat traditional. Students displayed no great interest in the 1950–1953 Korean War, either for or against. Consequently, these youths were judged as having no great individuality, no spirit. In short, the young man of the 1950s was an Organization Man, expecting to participate in America's economy, probably through a job in some corporation. Most women were still in the background, their chief task a nurturant one.

Events that led to the student explosions began early in the next decade. On February 1, 1960, a sit-in by four black freshmen at a white lunch counter in a Woolworth's store in North Carolina sparked sit-in demonstrations across the country. In 1964 three civil rights workers, including two Northern white college boys, were murdered in Mississippi. Students from across the country took up the challenge posed by young President Kennedy, to unite for a better America with rights for all. The petty details of traditional college life shrank to insignificance in comparison. Students began to perceive themselves as capable of making a difference—and then John F. Kennedy was assassinated. Still, their hero had given them the feeling that they could indeed overcome.

Politics thrived, both on the left and the right. On the political right, Young Americans for Freedom flourished; their heroes were Barry Goldwater and William F. Buckley, Jr. On the political left, the movement of the early 1960s was "for something: for desegregation, for equality by blacks, for individualism." It wasn't yet "a movement against impersonalization, a battle against alienation in mass society, a revolt against the IBM card or rebellion against war."[15]

John F. Kennedy was significant in setting the tone for the youths of these times as a symbol of commitment, idealism, youth, and action. He challenged them through establishing the Peace Corps, speaking against racism, and suggesting that people "ask not what your country can do for you; ask what you can do for your country." Three in five of all college students felt it was good to grow up in the Kennedy years, and many found him an ideal role model. He was an exception in "an age of anti-heroes."[16]

These same students would learn about a new kind of world, a complex one with super-sophisticated technocracy and industrialism; yet they remained mostly unaware of issues they must face as adults, such as the population explosion. Nor did the vast majority resort to extralegal measures; and only 18 percent ever picketed, although 56 percent said that they might have, for the right cause. The students were slightly more liberal than their parents, with a tendency not to affiliate with a major political party, for many had little confidence in either party. The chief issue in 1965 was the country's commitment in Vietnam, with just 24 percent of them favoring withdrawal. The 1964 presidential election was of temporary interest: 81 percent of the Oswego students favored Lyndon Johnson, 9 percent favored Goldwater, and 10 percent were undecided.

Events at Oswego reflected this mood, although few students were active protestors. On April 28, 1960, students paraded on behalf of racial desegregation, but few took an active part. Three years later, on May 27, 1963, 225 students and faculty paraded for the same cause. Students were also concerned about the dangers of nuclear war. *Oswegonian* editorials about bomb fallout shelters appeared intermittently during 1961, one titled "Fallout Shelters a Moral Issue?"[17]

Matters of more local concern included tuition costs and the overcrowding in student dormitories. On March 12, 1963, eleven Oswego students participated in a mass demonstration in Albany against higher tuition. Students' most immediate concern was the gross overcrowding in dormitories; three students were crammed in rooms designed for two, and others were temporarily housed in study areas, guest rooms, and utility rooms. An *Oswegonian* editorial advocated allowing women seniors over age twenty-one to live in college-approved housing. The men's dorms were also crowded, but men could move to outside apartments if they wished.

The Alumni Association was still a relatively simple operation. The Association's total capital in 1950 was about two hundred dollars, and membership one dollar. The *Bulletin* was published irregularly, only when funds allowed, and the mailing list numbered 3,000 (compared to 30,000 in 1984). Hilda Bohall (1927), dedicated president of the Alumni Association during the later Brown years, used her dining room table for assembling addresses of over 5,000 alumni, (the 30,000 addresses were computerized by 1984). Bohall initiated the slogan "Graduates must be located—every single one—by the centennial in 1961." She also organized a fifty-year club, and certificates were given to its members on Alumni Day.

Various important alumni events occurred across the country. One big affair was the alumni dinner dance at the Hotel Biltmore on May 15, 1954, the first meeting of the combined Long Island and Metropolitan New York City alumni groups. As noted in chapter 1, the original metropolitan alumni organization, the Boys' Club, was formed in 1901. Another active group was the Class of 1914; six members of this class held a reunion in Wisconsin in 1960. Nine of the class had kept a round-robin letter going since they had graduated, forty-six years before. In the meantime, the number of alumni chapters had grown from two in 1953 to sixty-seven in 1961, one as far west as California. The first annual presentation of the Distinguished Alumnus Award was made to Benjamin Van Oot (1905) at the graduation exercises in 1960. He was then head of industrial and vocational education for the state of Virginia.

Many Oswego alumni continued to achieve distinction, among them

Richard S. Enders (1948), who was named Industrial Arts Teacher of the Year for New York State in 1963. Constance Del Bourgo Schrader (1954), an industrial arts graduate, became the author of *Wrinkles, How To Prevent Them, How to Erase Them,* and *Makeovers,* a major book club selection. Her classmate, Frances D'Amato, traveled across country as the vice president of the American Management Association and, as of 1981, a member of the Alumni Association's Board of Directors. Joel Block (1966), psychologist and author, capitalized on his experiences at Oswego with his book, *Friendship: How to Give It, How to Get It.* He wrote that college friendships are bonded not through fun but through the common struggles students face. Students become an important support system to each other. Joseph P. Cangemi (1959), now professor of psychology at Western Kentucky University, acted as consultant to various government officials and corporations in Columbia and Venezuela in South America, as well as in Asia. Cangemi received Columbia's national award, the country's highest award to a civilian, for his work with engineers. He received his current college's award for public service in 1983, as well as Oswego's Distinguished Alumnus Award. Jack LeBouef (1964) had distinguished himself as a real estate developer in Texas and then as a lawyer in California, where he has served as judge *pro tem* in municipal courts, belongs to three bar associations, and is listed in the Californian and national lawyers' *Who's Who*.

Thus ended an era of transition, bridging segments of two centuries of college history.

4

*The Curtain Rises On a New Era**

DURING James Perdue's presidency, the college operated against a national and international background of dramatic change. Overall, the most important external forces of the 1960s and 1970s were the social consequences of Sputnik, the surge of students following the baby boom after World War II, a growing affluence, the civil rights revolution, the war in Vietnam, and the student movement. To briefly chronicle the chain of events: in November 1968 Nixon was elected; in 1969, Earl Warren retired as chief justice; in July of 1969 astronauts Armstrong and Aldrin walked on the moon; the famous Woodstock rock concert occurred in August of that year; and anti-war demonstrators marched on Washington in October.

The decade of the 1970s began with a banner news year. Anwar al-Sadat became President of Egypt; four students were killed at Kent State and two at Jackson State, thus sparking the largest student protests in the world's history. The voting age for federal elections was lowered to eighteen; Richard Nixon was popular; disco existed only in the French dictionary; digital watches didn't exist; and video tape was what networks used.

The next two years brought a mixed bag of disturbances on the broader scene and renewed calm to campuses. A civil war split Bangladesh from Pakistan; the Pentagon papers were published; and busing to expedite racial balance in the schools was upheld by the Supreme Court (in other respects, the heat of the rights movement tapered off). In 1972, an Olympic year, Palestinian terrorists kidnapped and murdered eleven members of the Israeli Olympic team. In 1972, also an election year, Nixon visited China and burglars visited the Watergate. In the fall, Nixon won over George McGovern by a landslide, despite McGovern's strong support on college campuses, and then ordered the bombing of Hanoi and Haiphong. The 1972

*James Perdue's presidency, 1965–1977.

burglary at the Watergate, a Washington hotel and office complex, escalated into the Watergate scandal.

The year 1973 was also eventful: abortion was legalized nationwide; a severe gasoline shortage occurred; and the Equal Rights Amendment was passed by Congress and sent to the states for ratification. The Yom Kippur War was fought in the Middle East; and U.S. involvement in the Vietnam War ended. Meanwhile, the Watergate affair flared up: Vice President Agnew and White House officials Robert Halderman and John Erlichman resigned; and White House counsel John Dean and special prosecutor Archibald Cox were fired. Nixon declared he was not a crook but resigned in 1974; Gerald Ford became president and shortly thereafter pardoned Nixon.

National news, in the next year, was less dramatic than international headlines. New York City almost went broke. Supreme Court Justice William O. Douglas retired; and labor union boss James (Jimmy) Hoffa disappeared. As Generalissimo Franco hovered near death, Prince Juan Carlos became Spain's first monarch since 1931, the year King Alfonso abdicated.

By comparison, the next two years were tranquil. In 1975, Sadat of Egypt visited the United States asking for arms; two unsuccessful attempts were made on Ford's life; and four main figures in the Watergate affair were sentenced to jail terms. The economy was making a faster recovery than had been anticipated.

Most observers sharply distinguish the 1960s from the 1970s in terms of mood and values. One writer, Ellen K. Coughlin, said that "the 1960s belonged to the likes of Martin Luther King, Jr., John Fitzgerald Kennedy, and SDS (Students for a Democratic Society); the 1970s were the era of Alan Bakke, Gerald Ford, and ET. Within a few years, the great society had become the 'me' decade."[2] An *Oswegonian* editor noted that the 1960s were marked by such catchwords as "civil rights, women's lib, JFK, LBJ, Vietnam, the Middle East, and the student protests at Kent State and Columbia University."[3] It was, the editorial stated, "a violent decade; but it was also a decade of liberalism, the hippies, anticensorship movements, freedom of sexual expression in the theatre, and a marked increase in the use of marijuana, hard drugs, and LSD. It was a 'do-your-own-thing' decade. Now it's time to clean up the government and clean up the media, and shine up the national image." Thus, "the furor of the 1960s was giving way to a new and . . . quieter time."

The 1970s may have come off second best to the 1960s. According to the news media, the decade of the 1960s could be described as intense and politically active, while the 1970s were shallow and self absorbed. For every student who demonstrated for peace and social justice in the 1960s there was a jogger who got in touch with his body rhythms during the 1970s. Peter Clecak, professor of social thought and comparative culture at the University of California at Irvine, believes that the 1970s have a poor reputation because critics look at this period through "a haze of nostalgia for the 1960s."[4]

Clecak perceived the 1960s and 1970s as blended together in some ways. Both fostered an attitude of dissent which managed to erode the authority of the "male, upper middle class, WASP culture which dominated the country through the '50's." The two decades were "unified by a central cultural theme: a quest for personal fulfillment, a pursuit of a free, gratified, unalienated self within one or more communities of valued others." All of the foregoing changes had an impact on the nation's colleges.[5]

James Perdue, who became Oswego's seventh president on July 1, 1965, was highly credentialed for this role. In earlier years he had won a Phi Beta Kappa key, taught and coached in high school, and served as a naval officer in World War II. "My experiences at the University of Denver as professor, assistant to the dean, assistant to the chancellor, acting treasurer, acting director of the Social Science Foundation, and general utility man," said Perdue, "constituted a great background for understanding the scope of SUNY and how it works." That conviction, plus a chat with several Oswego wrestlers at a college near Denver, brought him east to Oswego, along with his wife, Raedeen, two horses (Rip and Lady), and his pipe collection.

The Perdues, like the first families that preceded them, had their own special lifestyle at Shady Shore. Perdue liked to walk, bicycle, build model planes, and take photographs—one taken on the beach became a college logo. On occasion, he relaxed by watching boats on Lake Ontario. His Shady Shore picture window and field glasses afforded him a commanding view of the lake. He also tried skiing for the first time, and Raedeen Perdue caught him with her camera as he made one rather unceremonious landing.

Raedeen Perdue, to whom Jim had proposed on Valentine's Day, 1939, and married on Easter Sunday, was active in community affairs, part owner of a local craft shop (the Waterfront Studio), and was herself a craftswoman. She made headboards from pieces of an old church pulpit for the beds in Shady Shore's master bedroom; and she placed at the head of the stairs a merry-go-round horse from Chihuahua, Mexico, given to the Perdues by an anthropology professor. Also, she usually took a course on campus each year and attended many lectures.

On May 14, 1966, Perdue was officially inaugurated by the SUNY chancellor, Samuel B. Gould, who placed on his shoulder a medallion of silver, jade, and gold, designed by art professor Dominic DiPasquale. It featured the state emblem superimposed against pine trees and lake shore, a gift of the class of 1966. He was also presented a mace, a symbol of power. Designed by artist Joseph Schoenfelt, the mace was a gift of the class of 1969.

During his twelve-year tenure, Perdue was invited to perform many significant tasks, often on a national and international scale, which testified to his widespread prestige. He was director of the American Association of

State Colleges and Universities, received an administrative leave grant from the Danforth Foundation, was made a trustee of Parsons College and, in 1970, was one of six college presidents invited to the White House to advise President Nixon on matters of higher education. The next year, 1971, he accompanied fifty other Protestant church leaders to Paris to discuss treatment of American prisoners of war in Vietnam. A year later, in 1972, he took a six-month's leave to study developments and trends in higher education in this country and in Europe.

Between such missions, Perdue maintained high visibility on campus. An *Oswegonian* editorial called "College Friend" noted that students often had a chance to chat with the president, "not only in his office, as is usually the case with members of the college's upper echelon, but at fraternity and sorority teas, at student–faculty coffee hours, or in the halls returning from student plays."[6] At his first meeting with the faculty, Perdue's first words were "Hi, I'm Jim Perdue;" Perdue surprised students on Parents' Weekend when "he made the rounds of the dormitory open houses with other parents and friends. He even stood in the back of Sheldon auditorium with hundreds of others when he couldn't get a seat for the Cambridge debate."[6] Perdue would ask students to lunch once in a while, causing George Pitluga to remark that "even the generals eat with the troops once in a while." Pitluga called Perdue a "real charmer who often laughed and could tell stories well."

When Perdue taught a course called "Politics and Education" in fall 1972, it was observed that "we are heartened to see that our president has returned to the classroom from the top of the power tower."[7] Perdue observed in 1974 that he had attended over half of all the "music, art, theatre, and athletic events held on our campus" and that he had "yet to refuse anyone, inside or outside the university, who requested an appointment to see me for any reason."

Perdue's tenure at Oswego was brief when compared to Sheldon's thirty-six years, but a bit long when measured against the five-year average most presidents manage to endure. He left in 1977 to assume a newly created position with the SUNY Central Administration, that of Vice Chancellor for Academic Programs, Policy, and Planning. He said he "wanted to experience how the overall system operated . . . to see the academic program at a different level."

Perdue had performed a challenging task with distinction, in mostly turbulent times. He had continued the transformation of a single-purpose institution for teacher preparation, with about 2,000 students, into a multi-purpose college of arts and sciences, with 9,000 students. Perdue identified his own most significant achievement as that of "changing Oswego's mentality from one of a teachers' college to more of a liberal arts school. . . . Teacher education had become far too professionalized and limiting in scope."

His biggest disappointment was failure to make greater impact on faculty, students, and curriculum. "My problem," he said, "was that I couldn't work with the faculty from day to day." Instead, he had to work with budgetary and political aspects of the college, with the alumni, and with gaining national recognition for the institution, especially when elected president of the American Association of State Colleges and Universities, the biggest professional organization for higher education in the country. "It certainly didn't hurt me," he said, and added, "I don't think it hurt Oswego."

Many people recall the affable, tall, distinguished-looking man with respect and affection. Virginia Radley called Perdue a "very humanistic person"; and Lewis Popham said that Perdue's years will be "long remembered for growth, not only in enrollment but in quality of students and faculty." Sherwood Dunham, first dean, then vice president during those years, perceived Perdue as having a stabilizing influence on the college and as academic in his approach.

In pursuing the path of its destiny, Oswego had and has two roadmaps, SUNY's broadly defined outlines and Oswego's detailed one, both revised every four years. Speaking at Oswego in 1968, Chancellor Samuel B. Gould described the staggering growth of SUNY and outlined its future mission. He pointed out especially the expanding continuing education program and innovative approaches such as educational TV and computer technology. He also noted the changing concept of university education—no longer always four consecutive years, but sometimes three years and sometimes much longer.

In 1973 Dean Donald Mathieu, former chair of history and of the Faculty Assembly, said the main premise of SUNY's master plan was that SUNY must be responsive to public needs and could not be conducted in ways opposing the public need and will. It did not call for doing away with liberal arts and teacher education but for expanded honors programs and establishment of a classical college-within-the-college. However, public universities were called upon to cease functioning primarily in the interest of "the articulate, the influential, and the powerful in the citizenry." Instead, SUNY must "become responsive to a wider range of economic interests and to a more diverse pattern of ethnic and cultural backgrounds and aspirations." In response, SUNY committed itself to open access on the level of junior colleges and to guaranteed entry of two-year college graduates to the four-year college programs. The idea was greater diversification to meet the needs of adults "who did't graduate from high school, the educationally disadvantaged, adults who finished high school or even college . . . and the active elderly who had raised their families and retired from careers."

Oswego itself has had five successive master plans since 1962. The 1966 plan called mainly for changing the college from a small, single-purpose, locally oriented teacher-education institution to a multipurpose, high-quality liberal arts college with a statewide and national orientation. The 1972 plan reorganized the college administration, providing for vice presidents of student administration and services, and a provost for developing the academic program with more direct supervision by academic deans. In preparing master plans, suggested Perdue, "we need a consensus of values and of what constitutes an educated person. Also, we need more hard information to keep our views from being tainted with illusion."

SUNY's 1976 master plan called for a two-year degree through an international studies program and a lower division degree program. Provost Radley said that Oswego would be the only lower division college in the country serving local students who formerly had to travel to other parts of the state, such as Syracuse, for a two-year degree. She believed the college could well serve both two-year and four-year students. For the first time, students were included on task force committees, but few were interested or willing to work.

SUNY's new Office of Academic Programs, Policy and Planning called Oswego's 1976 master plan "a thoughtful and well considered document"; nevertheless, issue was taken with certain details.[8] Most of the new programs consisted primarily of minors, but a new minor might cost more than expanding a current minor into a major. SUNY also questioned whether academic counseling, to be effective, could remain outside general or personal counseling. Finally, the evaluation indicated that the college's first responsibility was to undergraduate rather than to graduate programs. Perdue felt that the state's master plan also had weaknesses, calling it poorly planned and lacking in vision. For one thing, it did not resolve the relationship between public and private institutions in the state.

One continuing dilemma has been determining in what specific ways the college should aim to achieve special distinction. Pitluga said that when he first arrived in 1941, "if students wanted music, they went to Potsdam and Fredonia; if they wanted IA [Industrial Arts], they went to Oswego or Buffalo. However, in the later 1960s, every department in all of the four-year colleges wanted a major program—for example, at this time every campus desired a physics major."

Thomas Powell, dean of liberal arts from 1968 to 1971, believed that Oswego should indeed establish its own identity and distinctiveness, but his document did not state what they should be.[9] He cited Harold Rosenberg, art critic, who summarized what was needed: a tradition of innovation which at once meets the emotional and intellectual needs of students while fitting the needs and identities of an institution.

"In the early 1960s," said Powell, "Oswego was well known for its achievements in industrial arts, but all bets were off as to what area it might center its efforts on when it became an arts and sciences college." He believed the task was to produce quality performance in all departments while elevating some to a level that would bring to the college "real character and distinguishing hallmarks. It is simply the nature of this system, if not of the world, that we can't be conspicuously successful in all academic areas. It would be foolish to attempt to compete with certain of the other units in areas in which they already had a mandate—for example, Stony Brook and Buffalo in science."

He believed Oswego had a realistic opportunity for distinction in art, limited somewhat by unwillingness on the part of the Central Office to allow BFA programs here. The college could hardly expect to build monuments in philosophy and literature because "distinction in those fields comes to graduate schools." He noted the exceptionally high quality of language instruction, but added that "languages are a support field by nature, hence must somehow relate to some concept of intercultural studies, allied with the social sciences and the arts," if they are to play any significant role in "defining the college." But, he observed, the departments concerned had "not yet reached the point of readiness to leave off bickering among themselves and to adopt a dream."

He thought that the "main, if not sole, chance of giving the college a distinctive flavor" lay in the area of social sciences. For example, environmental studies might constitute "a main thrust, centering not merely on physical science aspects of the human environment but on social science aspects—on studies of human behavior."

Perdue believed that his role as chief administrator in discharging Oswego's mission "was to help the students and faculty to understand and accept the direction of the college's growth. All administrative officers might well teach at least one course during the year in order to reduce the gap between themselves and the students." He believed that presidents could not be all things at all times. For example, in 1974 the security police began demanding arms, but he opposed it, saying he didn't think New York State taxpayers wanted college presidents to be police officials, nor did he care to be a police chief.

During the turbulent 1960s, the deans had little time for their traditional curricular duties. "Instead," said Powell, "I was a fire fighter for the president in a period of tremendous change in relations between administration and faculty, when constant crises related to personnel matters. No one knew what the future of the college was or the kind of institution it was trying to become. In addition, the division budget was now so large that the dean needed to be a Ph.D converted from a CPA who used to be a lawyer. About 95 percent of my energy was devoted to various kinds of crises."

A perennial task of college administrations is adjusting admissions policies to prevailing rules and conditions. In the seventeenth century, Harvard's admissions requirement indicated that "when any scholar is able to read Tully or such like classical Latin author *ex tempore*, and make and speak true

Latin in verse and prose *sue marte* without any assistance whatsoever, and decline perfectly the paradigms of nouns and verbs in ye Greek tongue, then may he be admitted into ye college, nor shall any claim admission without such qualification."[10] By Perdue's time, admissions requirements had evolved into standards somewhat different from the above. Since the county had no community college or regional service program in 1970, Oswego admitted county high school graduates who did not meet the normal admission requirements. Admitted also were students from disadvantaged backgrounds, who entered under the Economic Opportunity Program. Beginning in fall 1975, 70 percent of the students were admitted according to traditional criteria (high school achievement), 15 percent under provisions of the Office of Special Programs (Economic Opportunity and Regional Service Programs), and 15 percent under special abilities criteria.

Two other admissions policies were challenged and changed. The first, initiated by President Perdue in the 1960s, provided that males and females would be admitted in equal numbers. Since female applicants made higher qualifying scores than males (Perdue was dismayed to learn), the number of women students was disproportionate. However, his fifty-fifty sex ratio policy had to be voided in 1973 because it conflicted with a federal law requiring all institutions receiving federal monies to not discriminate against students or any personnel on the basis of sex. The policy was in conflict also with that of the Regents of the State of New York.

In other action in 1973, the Faculty Assembly and admissions council passed resolutions calling for an early admissions program and to allow students to take proficiency examinations for up to thirty hours of academic credit, thus qualifying them for pursuit of courses at a level consistent with their abilities. The proposal was that this policy, already used on an individual department basis, should be employed institution wide. A student editorial applauded this move, noting that "sitting through a mandatory course when the material was old hat, served only to prevent the student from using the time for more pertinent studies. . . ."[11]

The college also developed a program to correct discriminatory recruitment practices, in accord with federal guidelines. To pull this program together, Patti M. Peterson, assistant to the president and affirmative action officer, in 1973 began a complete examination of personnel practices relating to all employees in the institution. There was considerable legislation to support such efforts, including Executive Order 11-246 and several titles of the Civil Rights Act of 1964, as well as equal rights laws on the state level. Peterson received a grant to provide selected college women on-the-job experience in traditionally male-oriented or nontraditional careers; twenty-five students registered for the program in the fall of 1975. "Some people opposed the program," said Peterson. "They would have you believe that the white male was an endangered species and that affirmative action would bring about his extinction." Faculty recruitment was another problem because of the competition between higher education and corporations for highly trained blacks and females.

Other actions related to the college's rapid expansion and adoption of a multipurpose mission. Once begun, the shift from single to multipurpose curricula was rapid. In spring 1966, 98 percent of Oswego's students were preparing to teach and, by 1973, only 54 percent; others were in the arts and science program. The ratio of women to men was about two to one in 1965, reflecting the large numbers in elementary education; however, by 1973, the sexes were almost equal in number. The academic programs had increased to fifty by 1975, and Paul Goodwin, social science instructor, told Sherry Dunham we had "become so multi that we had lost all purpose." In just five years, 1962 to 1967, Oswego's payroll doubled and the faculty had grown from 238 to 459. There were even rumors, which eventually ran their course, that Oswego would become a university center.

The task of engineering this increasingly complex, dynamically changing operation was difficult. "In this period of rapid transition," noted Thomas Powell, "we changed from an authoritarian teachers' college administration in which academic decisions were made by the president and his staff, to a college of arts and sciences in which crucial academic matters were handled by the faculty. Thus, in academics, administrators simply carried out the faculty's will, in a more or less fiduciary representative capacity. What we had was a president, Jim Perdue, expecting the faculty to manage the academic business and a faculty hitherto accustomed to being directed by a president and dean. The result was a classic gap. Such gaps get quickly filled, often on the wrong basis, in this case as the president became increasingly legalistic and was more and more legalistically challenged."

Despite the inevitable problems associated with this scenario of change and growth, Perdue sensed early on "an outlook of hope and of exhilaration. During such times, when you have money and growth, you make plans, and you don't have bad plans because money and exuberance cover them up. During good times, presidents tend to look better than they are; during hard times, worse than they are. The presidency hasn't changed that much—it's the atmosphere in which presidents work that has changed."

The Carnegie Council on Higher Education concluded that next to the 1960s, the 1970s were perhaps the best decade in all of the country's history in terms of institutional progress.[12] Certainly, the realism and optimism of administrators like Perdue were major factors in producing such results.

Miscellaneous events of interest that occurred during this time were a great blizzard in 1966 that buried Oswego under one hundred inches of snow; the college had to close, and supplies were brought to town by sled and helicopter. That same year, Governor Nelson Rockefeller was a guest of honor at a luncheon in Cooper Dining Hall. He said that watching the progress of colleges like Oswego was one of the most rewarding personal experiences he had ever had. Afterward, he shook everyone's hand, including this writer's, with a very firm handshake.

At least two notable events marked 1968. President Perdue led a tribute to Martin Luther King, who had just been assassinated, at a memorial service. That fall, Hideo Murayama, director of the Japanese Society for the Study of School Administration, spent a semester on campus studying Oswego's influence on Japan's education system.

Two important birthdays were celebrated in 1973: SUNY's 25th and the city of Oswego's 125th. On SUNY's birthday, reported Perdue, "all of the buildings on campus were open. Many departments had exhibits in the buildings, and Mrs. Perdue and I hosted a cocktail party at the college for community leaders." The city celebrated by reviewing its past and assessing its present. There were still remnants of its early years on West Water Street, including a market house constructed in 1836, now without its tower. Further north remained the Cahill Fish Market, at one time the home of a newspaper office and at another, a passenger ship terminal. By 1973 Oswego had a population of about 24,000, twenty-four churches representing twelve religious denominations, and over two hundred bars. Its major industries included Alcan Aluminum, Breneman Window Shade, Cyclotherm, Hammermill Paper, Niagara Mohawk, and Oswego Candy Companies.

In 1974 the college's special collections curator, Judith Wellman, launched Operation Attic, calling for alumni to search in their attics for memorabilia from their college years to add to Oswego's collection. The Special collections project was started in the late 1960s, after the college inherited Millard Fillmore's presidential papers, discovered by Oswego historian and History professor Charles Snyder.

The earlier Perdue years were marked by dramatic growth and included a tripling in the size of the campus and the student body. At Oswego, as elsewhere, the 1960s were perhaps the last years of growth in faculty hiring, at least for some time to come. The next growth period, according to demographic projections, will be between the years 2000 and 2010. The 1960s also saw the greatest amount of college construction in the history of New York State, and the same could be said of this college.

The college grew rapidly within just a few years. When Perdue came in 1965, the campus was limited to the Lakeside and Sheldon Hall vicinity. In 1968 several major buildings were opened: Snygg Hall, the math and science center; Laker Hall, for men's physical education; Onondaga Hall, a dormitory for six hundred students; the Littlepage Dining Hall; Tyler Hall, the fine arts center; Mahar Hall, the social science center; Hewitt Student Union; Penfield Library; and Culkin Hall, the administration building, later dubbed "The Power Tower" and, by a few, "The Head Shed." Construction was begun in 1966 on the Rice Creek Biological Field Station, a rural sanctuary and water fowl refuge site in the Town of Oswego. This structure is unique among the State University of New York units; among its features are the seminar lounge, where observers have a 260-degree view of the surrounding area. It was designed as a major study center for ecology, fresh water biology, and conservation education. And then the budget axe fell, trimming funds. Since 1970, only one new building has been opened: a service garage in 1971. Nevertheless, the sixteen years from 1952 to 1968 had seen greater physical change than did the school's first ninety.

Perdue regretted that he had no influence on the structure of the new campus, which was controlled almost completely by SUNY's Central Office. The architects were city builders with an industry mentality and wanted all administration in one building. Perdue liked it better when the president's office was in the main building on the first floor. "There were classrooms and faculty offices on the same floor. All I had to do was to step out and I was among students and faculty members, and people dropped in to see me. When you're on the top floor of a building, where the president's office was moved, devoted solely to administrative offices, the only people who come to see you are those who are angry or want you to do something."

"The college president must be like the president of a bank," he continued. "There is a tradition among bankers that the president should have a desk in the open where everyone can see him with his hands on top of the desk so they don't think he's stealing money that they are putting in the bank. Our college architects didn't agree that the president of a college is the same. Even when I couldn't get them not to build this building, I asked that my office be on the first floor where windows were all the way around so people could see I was on campus. On the seventh floor, where I was placed, no one was going to come up to see whether I was there or not."

Perdue was also disturbed about the architects' desire to have high-rise buildings. "I thought it was inappropriate for the terrain and extremely inappropriate for the weather," he said. "I asked the architects (Skidmore, Owings and Merrill) if they had done any wind-tunnel experiments on the model they were planning. The prevailing wind from the lake is almost constant and, because of the buildings, the wind gets stronger because it's pushed into a smaller area. All you have to do on campus in the winter, when we have ice and a forty to fifty-mile-an-hour wind, is to watch students being blown around in a funnel of wind. The architects looked at me as though I was absolutely stupid, said they were professional architects and knew what they were doing. They wouldn't admit that they hadn't studied the wind's effect, but obviously they hadn't."

Later, a committee for assessing the needs and interests of students was formed to test a process known as the Eco-System Model. The critical thing about this model is to consider the way students' needs and the environment relate to each other and, in the event of some discrepancy, to change either the environment or the students' needs.

At least twenty-four of the buildings were named for former students, teachers, benefactors, and Sheldon, the founder; and some for people who lived almost a century ago, including Poucher, Sheldon's successor; Funnelle, named for the founder of the school's kindergarten; and Lee Hall, named for physical education professor Mary V. Lee. Hart Hall was named for "Izzie" Hart, and Mahar Hall for Marian Mahar, both of whom taught during the Riggs and Swetman periods. Waterbury Hall was named after Edwin Waterbury, a former editor of the Oswego *Palladium Times*, who was also chairman of the Board of Visitors. In the late 1940s faculty members would make bets about how long graduation exercises or other programs would progress before Waterbury, who always sat on the stage, would fall asleep. Hewitt Union was named for Jesse Merle Hewitt, the first Oswego student to be killed in World War I (when he was just twenty years old). His sister, Hazel, taught for many years, 1947–1973, in the Campus School.

More recently, the new administration building was named the Francis D. Culkin Hall after an Oswego congressman, and the physical science building was named after Donald Snygg, first chair of the psychology department. Tyler Hall's Waterman Theatre was named for Charlotte Waterman, first director of a formal music program at Oswego Normal School, 1911–1933 and, in her last year, Oswego's first dean of women.

The health center was named for Dr. Mary E. Walker, appointed by President Lincoln during the Civil War to work with the troops, and later put in charge of a hospital. She was the first woman to receive the Medal of Honor from President Andrew Johnson, later revoked, and restored in 1976.

This writer believes that at least three individuals were far more deserving of having buildings named for them than some accorded this honor. One was Hermann Krusi, the main interpreter of Pestalozzi during much of the Sheldon period; another, Gilbert Mollison, chairman of the local Normal's council, who signed every graduate's diploma for fifty years; and Hideo Takamine, who was responsible for the many Japanese normal schools patterned after his Oswego alma mater.

A nostalgic event, in a sense, was an epitaph to an era when the college had relied for space on twenty-five World War II surplus wooden buildings. The last two of these old relics of Splinter Village were leveled in 1968. These buildings, constructed around 1941, were meant to be occupied for only about five years.

Two main factors produced higher education's unprecendented growth in the 1960s: adequate financing and increasing numbers of students. The first of the post World War II "baby boomers" entered college in the mid-1960s, and as a result, colleges experienced a period of unprecedented expansion.

There were more young people than ever before, and more of them completed high school and entered college. Before World War II, about a third of high school graduates went on to college; by the 1960s, over half did so.[13]

In the meantime, a benign public attitude and good times added a midas touch. As a result, buildings rose; shortages in supporting services and facilities were largely overcome; and faculty salaries rose rapidly, on a par with other professions, for the first time in the history of higher education.

The situation began rapidly to change in the later 1960s, as public confidence in higher education eroded and an economic recession robbed public coffers. Across the country, university endowments diminished and federal research grants shrank. Student enrollments, which had doubled in the past fifteen years, continued to increase. Already 45 percent of college-age youths were undertaking higher education, and it was predicted that the percentage might climb to 70 percent by 1980.[14] The economic problem was compounded by an erosion in public confidence. People felt that college administrators had lowered standards and "bungled" their handling of the student uprisings, and they were critical about the indignities they believed had been sustained.

Moreover, most adults of that era, lacking a college education themselves, had no clear idea of what universities meant to society nor just how shrinking budgets impaired their effectiveness. They were more willling to pay for the rapidly growing community colleges at their doorsteps. Thus, the universities were faced with the prospect of receiving the leftovers after others' needs were filled.

The local picture was a mirror image of the national scene. After requesting a budget increase of $1,200,000 for 1975–76, Oswego was granted an increase of $631,000. The industrial arts department and language laboratories had to make do with worn-out equipment; the language laboratories were unable to obtain replacement parts because the company which manufactured the original equipment had folded. A housing crisis also developed, as an *Oswegonian* editor observed: "Last year the overflow figure was 350, this year 750. Will next year's overflow clear 1,000?"[15] The next year some of the upperclassmen were housed in thirty Wine Creek apartments leased by the college.

The outlook was grim, and in October 1975 Chancellor Ernest Boyer announced that admission levels on twenty campuses, including Oswego's, had been frozen. All construction by SUNY would cease for the 1976–77 year. Perdue dubbed the first section of his 1975–76 annual report "Strategies for Survival," since money problems dominated every action. "When the first shock wave hit during the middle of the new master plan," he wrote, "everything ceased because it was uncertain in what context the college would operate. The faculty heard but hardly believed—students didn't even hear."

Nor were future prospects encouraging. The declining birthrate, especially among the better educated, would produce a shortage of students. Some people even feared that the SUNY colleges would become "underutilized ghost schools."[16] In most colleges the result was a scramble for students and a catering to student consumers, instead of to professors, in the Ivy League and more selective liberal arts colleges.

Nationally, standards of performance steadily eroded. As enrollments diminished, even among white males, most institutions found they could not revive requirements discarded in the protest era. Any requirements might keep certain prospective students away and might be viewed as depriving them of their so-called rights. In institutions where applicants were in great demand, the student consumer was clearly the winner.

Various suggestions emerged for coping with the crisis. James Walters, chair of SUNY's enrollment projection group, believed SUNY should decentralize and it would then be up to each individual campus to make or break on its own. He especially deplored the sameness throughout SUNY colleges.[17] Perdue himself said, "We have pleaded with the Governor and the legislature for over two years that if cuts were to be made, they should be general cuts, with local campuses deciding where specific cuts should be made." He also deplored the erosion of SUNY's autonomy through increased financial control by the state. Nevertheless, he believed the college should at least make the best of the situation. "It's not enough to think in terms of survival," he said, "but of affirmation of goals of the institution."

The growth in numbers of adult students shed a ray of hope on this otherwise bleak landscape. Many such students were older women who had married early or who wanted to attain credentials for employment. In contrast to other countries, such as Japan, girls in the United States often had as much or more secondary school education than their brothers; hence, women who did not receive a college education were likely to feel deprived. Locally, in anticipation of reduced enrollments, Perdue recommended increased support for continuing education to identify new student populations and to build a "student reserve."

The critical instruments in upholding faculty rights have been the Faculty Assembly, the United University Professions (UUP), and the Taylor Law. Originally, the Faculty Assembly was mandated by the policies of SUNY's Board of Trustees and chaired by the dean of the college, while the vice chairman was selected from the assembly membership. It was, and still is, composed of one to three representatives from each department, depending on the size, and four students chosen under the auspices of the Student Association. At least once a month the assembly chair must submit recommendations to the president; and the president, in turn, must report to the assembly at least once a semester.

Pending approval of the assembly's new bylaws, disagreement developed in 1971 between Perdue and the assembly regarding the meaning of consultation—that is, whether the president must follow advice received through faculty consultation. The crisis was resolved by developing interim procedures until the bylaws were approved.

Opinions differed regarding the effectiveness of the Faculty Assembly. Pitluga spoke of having served in the late 1960s on the assembly when the faculty was seeking greater participation in governance. "However," he said, "despite great effort on the part of dedicated assembly members, it became at best a rear guard action. On the other hand, the new college bylaws attempted to reduce administrative control over the faculty by reducing the department chairmen to the level of caretaker, making them responsible to the faculty rather than to the dean."

"During the past half century," wrote Paul Woodring in 1970, "American professors had indeed gained in power at the expense of administrators. Now faculty members decide what should be taught and how to teach it, as well as standards of admission and graduation. Yet they are reluctant to share any such powers with students."[18]

The United University Professions is the faculty's bargaining agent or union. It includes about half the faculty, and its representatives meet with the president or her designee about once a month. The administration and the union have often disagreed—for example, President Perdue explained that the faculty workload was the responsibility of the institution. However, James Burling, president of UUP, said that the Oswego faculty should have the freedom to set its own workloads and that the administration's efforts to preempt this freedom "connotes an improper labor practice."

The Taylor Law, passed in 1967, gave New York State public employees the right to bargain; and, through a 1971 election, the SUNY faculty chose that right. This measure received mixed reviews; some segments of the faculty strongly or lukewarmly supported it, while others outright opposed it. Pitluga believed that "it dealt a final blow to collegiality. What was once a profession was now involved in a labor–management relationship. He added, "Perhaps because of SUNY's size, all this was inevitable, but arrangements that may be successful in a factory producing egg beaters may be a cancer on the body of a university."

Perdue agreed, calling "collective bargaining detrimental to the education process because, as constituted in this country, it is an adversarial relationship. People crystallize their positions instead of constructing bridges of communication." Lawrence Delucia, president of the local branch of UUP, objected to the Taylor Law because it made faculty strikes illegal. He called the state's offer of a 3½ percent increase in faculty salaries "obscene" and felt a strike was warranted.

The question arose: How much power does, or should, the administration have? An *Oswegonian* editorial in 1976 accused the administration of taking advantage of the reserve rights principle, which indicates that powers not specified under contractual agreement were reserved for the administration. The Faculty Assembly agreed with the editorial and passed a resolution that the State University Senate Governance Committee and the chancellor investigate governance at Oswego.[19]

Perdue said he welcomed such a review, adding that he didn't know of a single SUNY president who hadn't been charged with inappropriate consultation. He said that he did attempt to get as broad a range of information as possible before making decisions. Provost Virginia Radley, who had been dean at three other colleges, said there was more consultation on this campus than at any with which she had been associated. Both she and Perdue said that the governance procedure is often misunderstood and they should seek as much faculty input as feasible, but that they were not obligated to accept faculty recommendations.

The advisory committee appointed by the SUNY Faculty Senate decided that all parties concerned should 'shape up' their act. It cited poor faculty–administration communication and confusion over the consultation process. It judged the assembly basically effective, although its various councils were uneven in quality of performance.

All parties concerned—administration, UUP, and assembly—were determined to improve the governance operation. The personnel office and union tried to develop a process whereby problems might be investigated both separately and jointly before grievances were filed; and, in fall of 1976, Faculty Assembly chair Peter O'Connor recommended a study of the state of collegiality on campus to effect greater rapport between faculty and administration. Thomas Powell, dean from 1968 to 1971, suggested that the Board of Trustees precipitated the crises by imposing on administrators "an extraordinarily inflexible set of procedures." In 1969, if an instructor's term appointment was not being renewed, that individual would be brought to the dean's office by the time required to give notice, but the department chair could do nothing more than function as a witness to what occurred. "The dean's instructions," explained Powell, "were simply to read to the person whose contract was not being renewed the appropriate section of the policies of the Board of Trustees, after which no discussion, no questions. The reason was that if anything which could be construed as reasons for nonrenewal was uttered, it was then arguable and subject to litigation. The result was that we got into a mood of legalism which began creating a gulf between the administration and faculty. Just imagine how you would feel if you weren't being continued in your department and no one would say a word to you about why—not a word." The current dean, Donald Mathieu, added, "That has not changed, it has simply become institutionalized. We only have to give reasons for nonrenewal in cases of continuing appointment."

Certainly the most colorful, and difficult, aspects of Perdue's tenure related to Oswego students' response to "the movement" of the 1960s, "the umbrella term for the cluster of related, left-leaning groups such as the student movement, the women's movement, the civil rights movement, and others."[20] According to the common stereotype, the movement "was a large, loose organization of mostly young, or otherwise disenfranchised people, whose interests were directed outward and dedicated to the improvement—or the overthrow—of society to eliminate war or redistribute wealth or guarantee racial equality, or any one or another equally idealistic aims."[20]

"The movement came late to Oswego," observes Richard Wheeler; "It didn't reach its peak here until 1970, when it was pretty well spent in other parts of the country." When it did come, its repercussions heavily affected Perdue and his staff for several years. It had many aspects and produced frequent confrontations with the administration.

Some students defended Perdue's handling of student issues; others opposed anyone in authority or who represented The Establishment. Frances Lapinski (1972) said that in spring 1970, "maybe fifty to a hundred of us showed up on President Perdue's doorstep the night of the invasion of Cambodia. It was right after Kent State. We just wanted to find out what was going on—after all, he was our leader. He didn't tell us to go home and come back in the morning. Instead we arranged to meet with him and, when we did, we put together workshops on different issues. He was always very responsive to the students."

An *Oswegonian* editor also noted that Perdue did indeed listen to students and said that calling Perdue a "reasonable man is an understatement."[21] In a later editorial called "Mishandled Activism," attention was called to the "disorderly, disrespectful" confrontations "between Perdue and students" when an effective mediator should have been there. As a result of this emotionalism and lack of order, "the few intelligently posed questions were either evaded by Dr. Perdue or were lost in the shouts of dissension of fellow activists."[22]

Running like a thread through these conflicts was a growing demand by students for a larger part in controlling their campus destinies. "In the 1950s," said Perdue, "students were a silent majority dedicated to contemplation rather than action." "Until the late 1960s," noted Betsy Auleta (1969), "the administration ran the show. There were no student representatives to the departments, or the Faculty Assembly. They had no vote of any kind in faculty or administrative matters." However, already various student power groups had formed, including one around the student newspaper, *The Oswegonian,* one around the students (the SDS, Students for a Democratic Society), and one around the Black and Puerto Rican student union. Despite the lack of strong leadership and the pluralistic nature of student demands, the first real "stirring of student power in 1968 came after a student sit-in in early April."[23]

This sit-in was sponsored by SDS in conjunction with the National Protest Movement. The students gathered at a central place on campus to listen to speeches, and about two hundred of them then marched to the administration building. While followers sat outside the president's office in the hall, the student leaders presented their demands to the president. They were demanding involvement in student disciplinary procedures, student course evaluation, and communication.

Some of the student participants in the demonstration were displeased that Perdue thanked them for coming. They apparently believed this courtesy was "a calculated attempt by him to defeat the rebellious intent of the SDS-sponsored student strike." When Perdue remained "composed and courteous to the campus dissidents," some of the students found these actions distasteful.

After a long discussion, it was agreed to establish a Committee on Governance and Scholarship (COGS), composed of three students, three faculty members, and three administrators, all elected by their respective constituencies. Much of the ensuing legislation concerned increased social freedoms, including having liquor in the rooms, and twenty-four hour visitation in coed dormitories.

Perdue called the 1968–69 academic year "disappointing," since "most of our energies have been directed toward matters of governance." He found it distressful that we should continue to be "more concerned with who is in charge than with what should go on." Perdue contended that the roles of students, administration, and faculty must somehow be articulated and the key must be "rational compromise."[24]

At Oswego, as elsewhere, students were elected to serve on most major college and university committees, and even on boards of trustees. Opinions varied regarding the effects of such decisions. Perdue believed that the administration made too many concessions, "I myself as much as anyone else. Some concessions were required in order to maintain some stability because learning proceeds best in a peaceful atmosphere. However, we suffered for it throughout the country. When controversial issues would arise in State University, people would bring up the late 1960s: 'Why did you let students do this? Why didn't you kick them out of school?' Thus there developed a large reservoir of ill feeling among many individuals, which we may have to live with another decade." Nationwide, it was believed that student protests had brought refreshing changes, dramatic in effect, for even after the furor subsided, colleges were hardly the same. Gone was the old concept of *in loco parentis:* student independence was greater than ever, and at least a measure of student participation in college governance had become confirmed.

The administration remained accountable to the local council and SUNY. Since policies often come from Albany, the council has little voice in many matters; but its members may indicate their disapproval or approval to the president and then to the SUNY Board of Trustees. The council simply keeps tabs on the college operation to see that it proceeds in a way that would please the larger community. Incidentally, as of 1975, an amendment to the State Education Law provided that a nonvoting student representative be elected to participate in council meetings. Perdue himself perceived the college council as quite conscientious regarding its responsibilities but uncertain as to exactly what these were or how to implement them. Meanwhile, the SUNY Board of Trustees had become, Perdue said, "an even more distant and mystical body than the college council." Many felt that SUNY had little interest in matters of local concern.

SUNY's Central Office staff and the Board of Trustees tend to be "boogie men, distant in time and space from the local operation," wrote Perdue in 1969. "Locally, few people understand that there is much confusion about how the people at Central Office are organized and their functions. Far too much time is required to get things accomplished through the Central Office." Perdue concluded by saying, "We are still feeling our way over dangerous ground while faculty and student tensions are high and while administrative officers become less and less enchanted with their lot."[25]

Thomas Powell observed that we "just had a loose aggregation of sometimes conflicting interests; nor did the administrators feel that State University allowed much direction in this matter. Perdue used to complain about being a branch manager instead of a president, a situation that made it awkward for individual presidents and had much to do with the kind of president that one might get on an individual campus."

"Another persistent problem," said Perdue, "was that the Central Office often made tardy decisions regarding budget and programs. Late in the summer students couldn't always be notified in advance about reductions in their programs, and faculty consultation would be limited."

Still another nagging problem was, and continues to be, SUNY's competition with private education, which receives a much higher priority in New York than in any other state. "We were prevented from giving A.B. degrees until 1960," noted Perdue, "primarily because of the private school lobby with the State Education Department. It took from 1948 to 1960 to develop enough pressure to allow SUNY colleges to give Bachelor of Arts degrees." One wonders whether SUNY's chances in this competition for funds will improve as the numbers of its graduates increase, and if or when SUNY will be freed from all the political shackles that hamper the development of its tremendous potential.

5

Dramatic Changes in Faculty and Curriculum

WHEN President James Perdue arrived in 1965, he found he had inherited a faculty inadequate to cope with Oswego's new mission and with the growing number of students in the multipurpose institution. The faculty was highly dedicated, but mainly to teacher education; the industrial arts faculty was larger, better paid, and more dominant than the elementary school training instructors. This differential disappeared in 1968 as the liberal arts faculty mushroomed.

Perdue faced a difficult challenge: to recruit a much larger and highly qualified liberal arts faculty. Thomas Powell recalls that "we replaced around forty in 1968–69 alone, so I was interviewing constantly. Fortunately, plenty of money was available and we raided the private universities unmercifully. Many candidates thought that Oswego, the fourth largest unit of the SUNY system, would become a university center. Hence, they came with great expectations about being involved chiefly in research and teaching advanced esoteric topics." Perdue himself scoured the country and offered special incentives to potential candidates, because SUNY was not then well known.

The question arises: How successful was Perdue's whirlwind recruitment and how did his catch compare with other faculties? A survey of U.S. college faculty members showed that over half had never written or edited any sort of book, written either alone or with others! Over a third had never published an article; and half had never published anything. Only 4 percent had much interest in heavy research; 21 percent were interested in teaching and research but leaned toward the latter; and 75 percent were heavily committed to teaching. For every professor strongly interested in research, nine were equally devoted to teaching. Only 28 percent perceived themselves as performing a knowledge-generating role; 85 percent found that "intellectual scholar-scientist" was the poorest description of their role, and just 5 percent thought "teacher" was the poorest description. There were tremendous differences in institutions: 80 percent of the professors in the lowest tier had not ever or rarely published, compared with 22 percent at the top-rated schools. Over half of those at the highest tier, compared with 10 percent at the lowest, had achieved a high level of publication.[1]

By some standards the new faculty had certain deficiencies. Pitluga recalls that "almost anyone with a wet Ph.D. became a walk-on in American colleges, and Oswego was no exception. But there's an awful lot of difference between a chemist and a teacher of chemistry. Besides, some faculty members who gave three lectures a week to a total of 120 students couldn't be found on campus other than during lecture hours."

By other standards, the new faculty fared better. In fall 1969 the faculty numbered 373, 170 of whom had earned doctorates. The number had grown to 451 by 1974, 58 percent of whom had doctorates representing every major graduate school in America, and many in Asia and Europe. Perdue himself described the Oswego faculty as remarkable, saying he had patterned the liberal arts faculty after topnotch liberal arts divisions of private institutions. When walking in the woods with Harvard University's David Riesman, the latter said to Perdue: "I've gone over your bulletin and I am amazed at the faculty that you've been able to get together, the institutions from which they have degrees, and obviously the quality of people you've been able to get."

In the meantime, various procedures were used for the current faculty's development. Most individuals initiated measures themselves, including study abroad; for example, Sanford Sternlicht, an English professor, served as a visiting fellow in 1966 at the University of York, England. In 1967 Oswego received one of the first federal grants, a total of $27,000, to teach college faculty members about computer-assisted instruction and teaching machines.

Less formal techniques were also employed; one was an arts and science biweekly colloquium begun in the fall of 1961. Faculty members engaged in projects, reported procedures and problems to colleagues and more advanced students, then followed up with a general discussion. There also were 'Friday Conversations', unstructured afternoon get-togethers with refreshments," which floundered in 1970, but were revived by Perdue in 1971 as 'Campus Conversations'. Interested people from the faculty or the city could and did attend.

A related matter was that of "recycling" personnel because of changing needs. The number of teacher education specialists now exceeded demand, and there was the growing problem of taking care of new needs in academic programs. Therefore, Perdue suggested using administrative and sabbatical leaves for retraining the tenured faculty. He also proposed establishing a center for the study of teaching and learning, an excellent idea but one that was never launched.

Years ago, said Powell, Frank Hulme stated that "he wouldn't give a damn for a faculty member who wasn't committed to the whole institution." "By that criterion," said Pitluga, "he might not have cared for a considerable number by the late 1960s. The college had become a series of Balkan republics; people in English never talked with people in chemistry, etcetera. Each department tended to see the college through the dark glass of its own aspirations." "In other words," said Powell, "faculty members recruited in the late 1960s and early 1970s were discipline oriented, not institution oriented, and the institution was simply an agency through which they could practice their discipline."

Many of the faculty lived far from the campus and appeared only when they were contractually obligated to do so. Several factors had contributed to this outcome. "We had become so specialized," said Norman Gordon, "that it was a barrier to interdisciplinary perspective." Besides, institutional identification diminished because Oswego no longer possessed special distinction in the area that once gave it fame. "Recruitment for a multipurpose institution brought in people of highly diverse backgrounds and interests," noted Thomas Gooding, "making cohesiveness difficult." "For another thing," added Thomas Powell, "faculty governance became pretty much *pro forma*, the parameters established by legal documents, etcetera. As a result, individual faculty members, whether willfully or reluctantly—because they didn't see anything else to do—withdrew into personal and private concerns."

Furthermore, explained Pitluga, "faculty members had grown cynical." They served on committees *ad nauseum*, but their decisions amounted only to recommendations to some hypothetical character, Joe Albany. Increasingly, they felt that their participation in the community of scholars was limited to performance in the classroom." The erosion of faculty solidarity and morale was of continuing concern to Perdue. His single greatest disappointment for the years 1965–1969 was his failure to develop a more "closely knit faculty."

Several years later, in his 1973 State of the College address, Perdue named among his priorities the development of a campus identity. Although identification with SUNY should be strengthened, local loyalty should be primary. "Some people at central office thought the first loyalty should be to State University, but I think this is foolish," he explained. "State University is not an entity that you can adhere to very easily. It doesn't have a campus; it doesn't have an institution; it doesn't have a faculty. It's an abstraction. Students and alumni rally around what they know, and that's the campuses. On the other hand "we must show them that if you put all these campuses together in a system, there is more to them than if you just count them individually. Our situation in New York is unique: we can learn almost anything someplace in the system, and that's not true of many institutions. SUNY has all kinds of colleges with almost every discipline under the sun, and faculties should become better acquainted with these other institutions. Then they can talk with students about the university so students can begin to develop that kind of affiliation."

Many of the faculty also identified with various causes. In an *Oswegonian* article about "faculty birdmen" during the Vietnam War, the doves included Warren Steinkraus and Fred Allen, while a Mr. X and Anthony Crain spoke for the hawks. During the same era, Perdue wrote to Chancellor Gould that "a growing number of young faculty members involved themselves in student causes and some faculty members utilized student discontent to win support for relatively minor faculty causes."[2]

The same specialization that splinters campus unity had brought in more highly specialized professors. In contrast, George Pitluga had observed in the 1950s that "one poor soul in the education department taught, in one course, methods of teaching biology, physics, astronomy, and meteorology—and this man could not even walk on water!" The late 1960s also brought larger classes and therefore more difficulty in individualizing instruction. Perdue suggested that large group instruction be limited to those courses which intrinsically depend on audiovisual media, and the faculty reallocated to increase the number of sections provided for lower division students. He also proposed more interdisciplinary courses, and two- and four-hour courses rather than three-semester hour blocks.

In the 1960s technology began to infiltrate the campuses. "In my early administration," observed Perdue, "some teachers feared they would lose their jobs to teaching machines. The same thing had happened in the early 1950s and 1960s with regard to television but it never came about." However, many instructors used the Learning Resources Center, which provided help with large group learning, materials production, and classroom media and instructional development. In 1973 this center received the second award in a six-year period given to an educational institution by the Association for Educational Communications and Technology, shared with the Encyclopedia Britannica Education Corporation.

Perhaps most important was the advent of the computer. Robert L. Jacobson, writing in *The Chronicle of Higher Education,* called this "the single most important development affecting campuses today."[3] Locally some departments, such as business and psychology, used computers a great deal, and growing numbers of professors employed them as advanced typewriters. Yet, despite the technological revolution, the lecture method still reigned supreme in most classrooms.

However, some faculty members developed their own special projects and techniques. Black students at Alcorn A&M College in Lorman, Mississippi, whose dialect and speech patterns interfered with their academic progress, obtained assistance from a program developed at Oswego by professor of English Paul Briand, Jr. Alcorn's program director, Dr. Mary Griffin, visited

Oswego to observe the program and applied for a federal grant, citing Briand as consultant.

In general, the impact of particular professors is a highly personal one, depending on the student. Gordon Mengel was so impressed by Seward Salisbury's experimental classes (1936–1974), which developed awareness of Judaic and Christian religions, that he incorporated the approach in his own social science teaching. Margaret Lowery (1974) especially recalled Virginia Pratt, coordinator of American Studies, for her "enthusiasm and knowledge of subject matter. For the first time I had a history teacher who made me enjoy going to class so much that I never missed one of them. Besides, she took a personal interest in each student. She knew everyone, even in large classes, by their first names, and I never felt uncomfortable walking into her office and discussing my interests. She scheduled some of her exams as oral, which involved having students in her office and getting to know them." Donald Harrison (1968) remembered Allen Bremmer of the art department as always "very vocal about anything on his mind—an exciting professor who accused us if something was wrong with the world—and of course we got paranoid about this. We didn't realize what he was doing. When the 'East Side, West Side' TV series was canceled, he screamed at us for a good fifteen minutes. We sat there asking ourselves, 'What did I do?' What he did was to bring us into the real world and help us to realize that we weren't a separate entity."

Betsy Auleta (1969) spoke of Paul Goodwin in political science (1947–1972). "You would hear about him in your freshman year. He made us feel that we were always responsible for what was going on in the world and should do something about it. Our class in Afro-American Experience demonstrated in front of the union, carrying signs, asking the administration to hire black faculty. Carol George led the march with her banner reading: 'Replace me'—and later they did. I don't know whether her dismissal was totally political or not. Who knows about these things?"

When asked about English professor Francis Hulme (1949–1969), who was greatly admired as an outstanding scholar, Don Harrison said: "We used to call him Frank, the southern gentleman—the Colonel. He had that slow southern drawl." Betsy Auleta added that "Don and I were both English majors and we respected Dr. Hulme, but he was somewhat conventional. We were more attracted to some of the younger, more nontraditional faculty." Don added: "Yes, such as John Herman, Gerhard Zeller, Tom Judd, and David King, now in the dean's office." Different segments of the student body obviously were attracted to different professors.

Perhaps Frank Hulme was most appreciated by the faculty and the more intellectual students, for whom he was a role model. Once, about midnight, he received a long-distance call from a student to whom Hulme had lent his car. After the distraught student explained that he'd accidentally driven the car "off the road and into a 'crick'," Hulme paused a moment and then said in a gentle, but chiding, tone: "You shouldn't say 'crick'—it's pronounced 'creek'."

Classes that involved unusual or frequent field trips also tend to be remembered. John Weeks, who had developed the Rice Creek program, would take twenty students on a field trip and, by the time they came back, six would have decided to become biologists.

Faculty relationships had changed a great deal since Sheldon's time. In those days, students held the faculty in some awe and greatly respected them. From the 1940s to the 1960s the distance had diminished somewhat and, partly because of the college's small size, the interaction was personal and frequent. After the college so quickly tripled in size, classes enlarged and interaction diminished. The awe wasn't there anymore, at least not simply because a person was a faculty member.

Faculty members varied greatly in degree of accessibility to students, partly because their classes differed so much in size. "We all knew faculty members who were ready to help us, to take an interest in us, and those whom you wouldn't bother with," said Betsy Auleta. "For some courses you might try to find instructors who were good lecturers and held interesting classes, yet you made no attempt to be closer to them." Debbie Roe (1973) remembered faculty members "who invited me to their homes for dinner. I appreciated that because students constitute a homogeneous age group. I missed the life I had grown up with—you have grandparents; you have younger brothers and sisters. Or you know people next door with a new baby, and I missed that mix. On campus you could become so isolated in the eighteen- to twenty-two-year old age group, you'd forget what the real world was like."

The practice of faculty evaluation by students is a highly controversial matter. A large body of research discloses serious flaws in the practice; however, some educators, for example, Paul Woodring, believe that students know more than the administration about who the good teachers are.[4] Pitluga has mixed feelings about student evaluation. "You're in trouble philosophically if you argue that the consumer has nothing to say about the product he is getting; and to say that an individual who has been a student for twelve or fifteen years has no valid opinions is ridiculous. On the other hand, one recalls such questions as, 'Does the instructor have good knowledge of his field?' How does a student know, in his first course in astronomy, whether his instructor has a good knowledge of the field or not? Some questions are important, such as, 'Is the professor readily available for help?'" A student, Steven Austin (1972), argued that "students have been evaluated by professors over the years; hence, it is time that students evaluate the professors. Many of them are boring, long-winded, and irrelevantly putrid."[5]

Regardless of the merit of student evaluations, Oswego students evaluated the faculty for the first time in 1969. Seven years later, in 1976, 347 of the 1,500 classes offered the previous semester were rated, and the results were published in the fall edition of the *Students' Oracle.*

If thus evaluated, certain faculty retirees of this era would surely have deserved high ratings. Among those individuals was alumnus James Hastings (1941) a faculty member (1948–1978) who supervised the industrial arts off-campus program for fifteen years. Mildred Larson (1949–1969), faculty adviser to the *Oswegonian,* strongly defended freedom of the press on its behalf in days when administrative interference was common. Everyone remembers Helen Hagger (1945–1970), undisputed developer of, and sovereign over, the library for many years. Others were mainly responsible for laying the foundations of their respective departments: Aulus Saunders (1937–1970), art; Charles Wells (1940–1968), English; Maurice Boyd (1947–1972), music; Melvina Svec (1947–1963), geography; Seward Salisbury (1936–1974), sociology; and Theodore Moss (1958–1979), recognized statewide as an authority on the middle school. Moss and Halas Jackim arranged to reclaim and move close to the campus a one-room school house. Twenty other veterans of the teacher-college days also retired during Perdue's tenure: they represented a quarter century or more of distinguished service to the college.

Dramatic changes in the college as a whole, as in all higher education, affected the curriculum. "When I came in 1965," noted Perdue, "there were divisions in the college: arts and sciences, elementary and secondary education, industrial arts education, and vocational–technical education, each headed by a director and collectively by a dean. The three education groupings were placed in one division in 1969, under a dean of professional studies, while the liberal arts departments functioned in a service capacity to the teacher-training function. Gradually I developed a liberal arts faculty with its own separate departments." The next year, 1969–70, students might choose from among 765 courses offered by over twenty-five departments and divisions. Programs were being developed in fine arts, literature, sociology, and modern language, and graduate programs were also being developed in biology, English, and history.

Countrywide, the shape new curricula assumed was modified by conflicting interests. Students were demanding more relevant courses and a broad choice of electives. Many people believed student idealism was still there, but that students had simply decided to work within the system. But then came the great disillusion, the surge of vocationalism. Bewildered educators, many of them veteran activists of the 1960s, sat by and watched students engage in creative career design, selecting their majors for maximum marketability. This attitude aroused opposing views on many campuses, with professors calling for a "return to basics, to more rigor . . . while administrators, aware of the need to survive, looked on and saw how the dwindling pool of students was creating a buyers' market."

Locally, Dean Donald Mathieu attributed some of the confusion to the rapid change in mission: "We were a kind of instant arts and science college, and some bowed to students' demands for electives—'the salad bar approach'." Said Perdue, "The faculty also gave in to students' demands for relevance. "They forsook the integrity of their programs in the name of human rights. They did it for all of the best reasons, but I think they moved in the wrong direction." Thomas Gooding believed that "all we seemed to care about was a student's major." "The overall effect," concluded Thomas Powell, "was to devalue the B.A. degree. It became impossible to assume anything about Bachelor of Arts graduates; and we emerged into a period of confusion, related to the confusion in our entire gigantic bureaucracy as well as to social conditions at that time."

The situation began both to stabilize and change somewhat in the 1970s. In 1971–72, academic majors were added in speech and theater, physics, and Russian. The professional studies division added a school psychology program, a Master of Science degree program with a concentration in reading or vocational–technical education, and a Bachelor of Science in geo-chemistry. Many students demanded more career-oriented programs, one result of which was the separation of business from economics. Minors were also proliferating; seven were added in 1975–76: Asian studies, astronomy, athletic coaching, health sciences, history, mathematics, and museum studies. In the meantime, the assembly had voted to allow students two majors, as long as they received the same degree.

In 1973 Perdue said that he had reached certain conclusions about the academic programs. Students had received so much latitude in deciding their own requirements that common learning experience was severely diminished, a trend that should be reversed; and all programming should be reviewed in terms of money and faculty time. Liberal education "must enliven and enlighten all manner and phases of the human condition." He believed that "the heart of most university problems is weak communication," and that good communication was seldom attained through large meetings or by memoranda. Instead it depended upon "intimate exchange . . . in the course of considering issues."

Several factors complicated the process of curricular changes and development. The rapid change to a multipurpose institution required, within a very limited time, many new courses and programs. Programs already in place had to be reviewed, and some curtailed. Decisions had to be based on whether the programs were certified, as the teacher education program was; on the number of professors and students involved; on interest shown by students; and on state guidelines. Existing factors, such as student upheavals and budget problems, made it difficult to focus on the tedious task of curriculum study. Also "a minicultural revolution" called for new vocations and values, creating a need for such new programs as women's and black studies and business programs. The conflicting interests of the various parties concerned was another problem, especially of the teaching faculty.

Meanwhile, student demands for change extended to the classroom. Students protested against large classes and were "fed up" with the old lecture method and having to regurgitate material on examinations. Oswego students sought more varied classroom activity and more participation; they demanded and received the right to take pass-fail courses, one per semester, for a total of twelve semester hours. They resented arbitrary cut policies "imposed by our beloved caretakers" as "outdated, unfair and arbitrary," Such a policy might allow one cut per semester hour with an E grade for any further "naughty absences." One student contended that if students met course obligations successfully, "they should receive passing grades regardless of absences. If they could pass courses without attending classes, fine."

Here, as elsewhere, only a few students showed much interest in basic curricular reform, beyond demanding more career-oriented work and content relevant to the world about them; however, they did want more control over curricular requirements. Laurie Bennett (1977) observed in 1975 that students pursuing a B.A. degree are limited to taking forty-eight hours within any one department; hours beyond that would not be counted toward the degree.[6] She argued that it was the student's responsibility, not the administration's, to determine such matters. She believed students were mature enough and knowledgeable enough concerning their career objectives to make final decisions. Moreover, she said, "this is not an era of expansion and of renaissance man." Rather, it is "a time of highly technical vocations— hence, students should be free to concentrate in a particular area."[6]

Students' sweeping academic demands had been at least partially met by 1975. Their representatives had become voting members of the assembly and various college councils. They participated in department decision making, even voting on matters of tenure and major departmental policies; otherwise, the record was spotty. The degree to which faculty members had made their courses more relevant was unclear. Although there had been some progress in this area, it was suggested that a problem-oriented freshman course such as "The Self in the Society" should be available. While the concept that class attendance should be voluntary was only partly accepted, the view that career orientation should not undercut liberal education was reaffirmed.

In his 1973 State of the College message to the Faculty Assembly, Perdue told of Oswego's attempts to develop meaningful statements of goals while "wrestling with a shrinking budget, a slowly expanding enrollment, and a rapidly inflating economy." He called for greater relevance within the curriculum so that students might relate their knowledge to "the world at large; liberal education should be liberating to the degree that its relevance for the present is clear." This view did not suggest that liberal education was necessarily utilitarian; it might retain its own identity yet develop relationships with career programs and professional schools.[9]

"Unfortunately," observed George Pitluga, "the rigor of the humanities requirement was watered down to accommodate the less able students. For example, it could be satisfied with one course in poetry, two in Spanish (really on the high school level), and one in stagecraft—making and painting sets; this was the humanities education of my daughter, Lisa. The twelve-hour requirement in natural science and mathematics could be satisfied with a course in meteorology, a beginning course in math, and two in computer programming. While there is nothing wrong with these courses, they hardly add up to a liberal education. Curriculum development had become a numbers game. If we could just get a requirement of twelve semester hours of modern language, that department would have it made."

At least two developments within the English department are worthy of note. Beginning in 1967, students could study English literature in England; that year, forty studied the Renaissance at York University. In 1966–67 a group studied English literature as it related to local life and thought at Nottingham.

Little progress was made toward other objectives, such as reduced stress on competition reflected in grading practices. Ronald Dygert (1975) argued that grading practices should be broadened to allow alternative means of evaluation; the pass–fail grade option should be enlarged; experimental grading practices should be tried; and a general studies pass–fail degree should be attempted.[7]

The administration's curriculum priorities were vastly different, and Perdue's advocacy of the humanities gave an overdue shot in the arm. Dean Powell believed that "the talk of relevance is not mere cant" and that "students should acquire an awareness of how humanism, as reflected in the arts and sciences, can help solve the practical problems of today." He agreed that liberal education still was, and should be, concerned with "liberation from the meaninglessness and helplessness of uncommitted, unprincipled existence." However, he perceived liberal education as assuming new forms and needing to change even more, to help young people adapt to the realities of these times.[8]

President Perdue favored development of a classical college with a humanities subdivision, oriented toward programs other than current departmental lines. Included would be communication studies, English, foreign studies, history, and philosophy. Perdue believed deeply in a broad liberal education: "If you don't have a generalized background on which to build specialization, you are not only ignorant, but I think you may be dangerous." One of Perdue's favorite quotations was President John F. Kennedy's, "Liberty without learning is always in peril; learning without liberty is always in vain." Thirty-eight sections of composition for improving students' basic writing skills were offered on campus by 1974-75.

From 1963 to 1967 the language department had only three or four professors, and only two languages were taught. Since that time, the status of language teaching had risen and, by the end of 1967, twenty-two were teaching five languages. The Foreign Studies Center was departmentalized in the 1975-76 academic year. Said President Perdue, "The marriage of the languages was a beautiful idea, but the marriage didn't jell." A language laboratory came into being in the fall of 1976, thus students were able to expedite language-learning via machines.

Margaret Nation, a gifted French major and among the first participants in the college's Year of Study Program in Paris, graduated in 1972 and died the same year. A scholarship was established in her memory to advance the cause of French studies at Oswego. The 1972 publication *Vendango,* a compilation of Oswego students' original papers—in French—was dedicated to her.

In due time, Oswego's Russian department began an exchange program with Moscow. (Oswego is the only college within the SUNY system offering a Russian language major.) For the first time, the Soviets agreed to negotiate directly with a single American institution. Edward Nordby, coordinator of the Russian program and representative from SUNY, met with the Soviet's deputy minister of higher education and cultural counselor in Washington to explore the possibility of establishing a SUNY-Soviet semester exchange program for undergraduates. Three Oswego students traveled to the USSR in 1974 for four months of Russian language study in Moscow and in Leningrad. Other groups followed.

Three Russian students, who were participating in the SUNY-Moscow undergraduate exchange program at the SUNY Center in Albany in 1975, spent a week on the Oswego campus; they were English majors from the Moscow Institute of Foreign Languages. In the Soviet, they received $30 a month to cover all living expenses; books were loaned to them for the semester. These students were required to study one major language, in this case, English, and be proficient in a second.

In 1976 the college was chosen over Salsburg, Austria, to host the forty-fifth summer Linguistic Institute, sponsored by SUNY and the Linguistic Society of America. The Institute focused on the native American: the history and language of the Onondagas, the Iroquois, and the Senecas. A native American festival was held; linguists continue to learn about language from native Americans.

In the 1940s George Pitluga and Charles Yager were the entire science department, each with his own classroom. The 1960s witnessed an explosion of science staff, and science was subdivided into four departments: physics, chemistry, biological sciences, and earth sciences. Piez and Snygg Halls were built to accommodate them.

The social sciences area in 1965 added majors in economics, political science, and anthropology to its original offerings in psychology, geography, history, and sociology. Several new courses were offered, among them Watergate—"Watergate and the Presidency" and "Watergate: Discretionary Justice."

Teacher education programs still constituted most of the Professional Studies Division and contributed a goodly share of notable events. A reading education department was established in fall 1972 and an early childhood education program began in fall 1973. In 1973 the audiovisual teacher-training program, directed by Richard Pfund, was awarded a plaque for being the outstanding program of its kind in the U.S. Other projects and courses of the education department were also successful. Education students taught migrant children in the Sodus area and through Kenneth Sipser's course, students tutored in other areas, including a day care center and neighboring schools. Chancellor Boyer announced a plan in 1975 to restructure the ten campus school programs. Several, including Oswego's, were to be phased out, others reduced, and still others continued at their present level.

The industrial arts program became the largest one in the country in 1965. Few departments, past or present, equal Oswego's in the number of different technical areas represented. Courses offered for non-majors in 1973, for example, included general crafts for the home, school, business, and industry; consumer product analysis which investigated contemporary consumer products; and two courses aimed especially at elementary school teachers.

The chancellor's requirement, since 1968, that physical education be mandatory, produced loud student protest. An *Oswegonian* writer, David Leonard (1974), argued that "preventing a twenty-two-year-old from graduating because he has not spent two hours a week for two years exercising . . . is absurd, and force-feeding physical education is as fruitless as force-feeding education of the mind."[10] The student association expressed its disapproval by freezing athletic funds, called by dean of student affairs Robert Rock, "blackmail—pure and simple" and "irresponsible." SUNY's Board of Trustees abolished the requirement in spring 1973, and Oswego soon followed.

In his 1971 State of the College message, Perdue called for more interdisciplinary programs, noting that these "arbitrary boundaries between disciplines represent the taxonomic and administrative conveniences of an earlier time." Dean Thomas Powell believed that interdisciplinary efforts should have a better "life expectancy," and he called intercultural studies "a dream in 1968–69, a hope in 1969–70, and a mirage in 1970–71," complaining that departments were still mainly interested in "self-aggrandizement." One result of these views was the initiation of a Bachelor of Arts degree in public justice, which is both career oriented and interdisciplinary. Another result was the unification of the foreign language departments within a Foreign Study Center to encourage interdisciplinary work.

Other interdisciplinary programs emerged in the early 1970s: a major in philosophy/psychology; a minor in Latin American studies requiring native American studies, to prepare native Americans for teaching on reservations; energy and environment, taking advantage of the college's location near power companies; and the classical college. Latin American studies, an interdisciplinary program, required twenty-one hours of study in such subjects as anthropology, history, and political science, as well as two years of college-level Spanish or Portuguese or equivalent.[11]

There was also an influx of many special programs. One, the Community Service headquarters, coordinated an off-campus program supervised by the various academic departments. The ROTC (Reserve Officer Training Corps) program aroused much controversy. Opponents of ROTC cited three arguments against its presence: the use of college space, provision of college credit for the program, and its presence already at Syracuse University. Those favoring the program argued that it would help pay for a college education and that students should have the right to choose whether or not they wished to enroll. In addition, it would be merely a basic training course, and those students who wished to drop it after two years could do so without any obligation for military service.

Other programs started then and still in existence were directed to special categories of students. The Economic Opportunity Program allows students from disadvantaged backgrounds to enter with lower admission scores and provides tutoring. The International Education Center encourages foreign students to come to Oswego, and its programs abroad include study of broadcasting in London, the common market in Belgium, tropical biology in Jamaica, and ancient theater in Greece; there are also special programs for the study of the culture and language of Madrid, Vienna, Paris, Pisa, and the Caribbean.

The Division of Continuing Education, initiated in 1967 to replace the former extension and evening division and directed since 1973 by Dean Lewis Popham, provides courses for those wishing to complete degree requirements as well as noncredit courses in areas of special interest. Among the choices are classes on "fly-tying or weaving," gymnastics training, conversational foreign language for those planning to travel, and piano. The program also provides institutes, seminars, and short-term courses.

Oswego's primary emphasis in the early 1970s continued to be undergraduate education; its graduate programs were still somewhat spotty. Thomas Powell observed in 1971 that "the typical M.A. degree is better than a poke in the eye with a stick . . . but not by much." Perdue described graduate studies before 1975 as paste-on-programs and urged courses designed especially for graduate students.

The so-called Third Curriculum, begun in the late 1960s, consisted mainly of a program of advisement and orientation for new students and a series of events, including plays, musicals, art exhibits, and lectures. Among the lecturers were television news broadcaster Edwin Newman who, on April 8, 1967, spoke on the population explosion and its effect on politics in a lecture sponsored by Oswego's Critical Issues program. Dick Gregory, the black comedian and author of *Nigger*, came in 1970, as did Minnesota Senator Walter Mondale, whose topic was arms limitation.

A conference having as its theme "Beyond Contemporary Thought" was held on campus in 1973 to commemorate SUNY's twenty-fifth anniversary. Later that year, an instructor in transcendental meditation discussed the "fourth state of consciousness." The 1973–74 lecture series included Eleanor McGovern, wife of then Senator George McGovern of South Dakota; Ashley Montagu, who has written extensively on anthropology and race relations and authored the controversial book, *The Natural Superiority of Women;* Shirley Chisholm, the first black woman ever to campaign for the presidency of the United States, and later a congresswoman; and William F. Buckley, Jr., controversial conservative columnist and television host. The 1974–75 series brought to the campus science fiction writer Isaac Asimov, who declared he was a feminist, "but I do treat women as sexual objects and I hope they will do the same to me." The country folk singer Emmy Lou Harris, the newest sensation in folk and country music, came to the campus in the spring of 1976. Many of these seminars and lectures drew large audiences.

Add now to the ingredients in the curriculum's vitamin-deficient diet a new ingredient—Virginia Radley, appointed in 1974 to the newly created post of provost—and the makings of a radically changed creation are present. Recruited from SUNY's administrative staff in Albany and the first woman on this campus to hold so lofty a post, Dr. Radley became Oswego's second-in-command and chief engineer of the academic operations. She surveyed the hodge-podge curriculum with a critical eye, forthwith resolved to do something about it, and did. While maintaining a continuing dialogue with all parties concerned, she set about eliminating frills, reducing unnecessary overlaps, stressing basic skills, beefing up the humanities, and knitting all together into a firmer, better designed fabric, emphasizing throughout the whole process high quality curricular content, instruction, and student performance.

The word began to get around and have an impact. Instructors resting on their laurels, if ever they had any, and students majoring in campus capers instead of class work, began to clean up their acts. Rapidly, new and higher standards were set—and met—and a resurgence of pride in academic achievement began. Of this significant and overdue development, which might be called Radley's Revolution, more will be learned in a later chapter.

6

A Turbulent Era of Student Activists

THE 1965–1975 decade was one of the most dramatic in the history of America and college life. In 1966 Betty Friedan founded NOW (National Organization for Women); Masters and Johnson's *Human Sexuality* was published; and Stokely Carmichael proclaimed the doctrine of black power. Arabs and Israelis fought the Six-Day War in 1967; and Christiaan Barnard performed the first human heart transplant.

Student protests on behalf of various issues rapidly escalated in 1968–69. The whole mood of most campuses in the country was one of confrontation, escalation, and protest. Civil rights, women's liberation, JFK, LBJ, Vietnam, and Kent State were all catchwords of the time. This was the decade of liberalism, the hippies, anticensorship movements, freedom of sexual expression in the theater, do-your-own-thing, and marked increases in the use of marijuana, hard drugs, and LSD.

By the spring of 1968, student unrest was retreating from the national to the local campus scene, partly because students' general sensitivity to rights issues made them increasingly concerned about their own.[1] Major confrontations occurred at Columbia and Harvard Universities, involving sometimes peaceful, at other times violent, demonstrations. Students sometimes lay down and blocked traffic; they picketed induction centers; and at Stanford, nearly $600,000 worth of "trashing" or random property destruction occurred. Overall, campus revolutionaries had "succeeded in creating a climate of fear and intimidation that threatened the tender, academic fabric."[1]

Then came, in rapid succession, a presidential election, the Watergate affair, the energy crisis, the unwinding of the Vietnam War, the post-war recession, and the disappearance of the draft. Attitudes changed rapidly. It seems that an era came to an end in 1970, concluded an *Oswegonian* editor and "it's time for the country to begin its 'housecleaning'." The editor correctly predicted a quieter time despite what one writer called "lingering ghosts from the 60's."[2]

College students' concerns had changed radically. "The old rallying cries for student participation in curriculum planning and the appointment of faculty were almost forgotten. This year's turmoil focuses largely on national issues—primarily the war and internal repression."[3] A new generation was emerging, concerned with ecology and committed to reversing the nation's priorities away from war and from environmental destruction and exploitation. Students had become preoccupied with the challenging problems facing them, mainly economic. Tuition costs had risen, and loan funds were no longer adequate. As a result, "the system was seemingly rediscovered" as the route by which students might attain their "pragmatic desire for a higher living standard."[3]

An abrupt change in mood had also occurred and the year 1973 saw the end of an "era of American liberalism with no equal in the country's almost two hundred year history."[4] More visible symbols of change included the return of "skirts, high heels, and short hair to campuses. Skuzzy denims became designer jeans; the standard field jacket became an oddity; ROTC enrollment began to rise; and getting grades began to matter."[4]

Peg Lowery (1974) first sensed a change in mood at Oswego about 1972. "My first two years were still part of the drug age, and part of the rebellion of Vietnam; but in 1973–74, the college took on a different look." As elsewhere, students were getting hair cuts; they didn't dress as poorly; and were more serious about themselves and their studies. They were paying less attention to the international political drama and more to Nixon and the domestic scene.

Joseph Julian, Oswego political science professor, attributed diminished student activism to the Vietnam War's end and the economic recession. In seeking jobs, he said, students feared adverse repercussion from less-than-straight behavior.

The end of the war in Vietnam also reduced the incentive for activism. Students still protested poverty, racism, pollution, quality of life, and war, but with less vigor. They joined the political action in such matters as America's move into Cambodia and the killing of four students at Kent State by National Guardsmen. Nevertheless, students did not wholly revert to their disengaged mood of the 1950s. In 1973–74, adversarial relationships were again mounting on campus, and students were protesting their exclusion from the educational decision-making process.

The foregoing scan of the years 1965–1974 serves as a backdrop for a closer, more detailed look at student issues. The main issues in the 1960s were racism and Vietnam. By 1973, according to a national poll of college editors, the five issues of greatest concern on campuses, in rank order, were ending the war in Vietnam, cleaning up the environment, eliminating racism, achieving women's rights, and combating drug addition. Almost half (46 percent) of the nation's college editors reported less unrest on their campuses compared to the late 1960s and just 15 percent reported more. Four in five (81 percent) believed that students now worked for change within the system; 75 percent saw growing student apathy; and only 6 percent reported any violent demonstrations or confrontations. Just 51 percent thought students were as concerned with social issues as those of the 1960s and only 48 percent thought their college administrations were initiating the reforms sought in the late 1960s.[5]

Civil rights for blacks was an issue of concern for students. In 1965 almost all college students approved the living of blacks and whites in the same dormitory, eating in the same cafeteria; and joining the same social clubs, although just 47 percent approved mixed-race dating, and 36 percent intermarriage. Some students translated their views into action. In the 1960s, some went South during spring recess to teach in the slums or to help blacks in social projects. On March 23, 1968, fifteen Oswego students, along with other Northern students, joined mostly black Southern students in South Carolina to assist in black voter registration. While there, the students stayed in Benedict College, a black institution, each with a soul brother for a roommate. Thus, in effect, the whites were a minority within a black community.[6]

Because of their own vulnerability, students expressed even greater concern about the draft than the war. "My graduating class in 1969 was hit very badly by the draft," said Betsy Auleta (1969). "Students were drafted if they went on what is now called academic warning, and went off to Vietnam." Don Harrison (1968) said that "students would tell an instructor, 'If I don't pass your course, you're sending me to Vietnam.' Some bought into it and passed the classroom laggards; others said no."

By spring 1967, the "Hell no, we won't go" movement had already hit many campuses, and many young men fled to Canada. Others made a plea for deferment on the basis of conscientious objection and still others married to escape the draft. Counselors helped potential draftees identify legitimate causes for deferment, such as "homosexual tendencies, asthmatic conditions, chronic bedwetting, bad backs, bad eyes and trick knees."[7] A third of the counselors believed that draft dodgers should receive unconditional amnesty. Another 31 percent believed deferment should be granted in exchange for nonmilitary service in the Red Cross, Peace Corps, or VISTA. Just 7 percent felt that it shouldn't be granted under any circumstances.

Oswego students protested intermittently. In 1970 eight students and one professor, the "Oswego nine", were convicted of fourth-degree criminal trespass after staging a rally at the local draft board. The following ad appeared in the February 1973 *Oswegonian*, in bold letters: "Sisters! Show solidarity with our Vietnamese sisters by protesting the Marine recruiters on campus at Rich Hall."[8] In the next month, eight students were arrested for disorderly conduct because they blocked recruiters from entering the placement office. An *Oswegonian* editor called the marines "highly trained soldiers, taught how to kill." On the other hand, conceded the editor, "it's their right under the Constitution to speak and present literature and the right of students to listen or read such propaganda."

Earlier, in March 1968, the *Oswegonian* had included a special supplement concerning the draft.[9] In a random sampling of Oswego students, 26 percent thought students should be given special consideration for draft deferment, 18 percent disagreed, and 6 percent were undecided. When asked, "Do you believe that so-called conscientious objectors have legitimate grounds for deferment?" 49 percent said yes, 29 percent no; 22 percent had thought little about it. A 1967 *Oswegonian* editorial supported a universal draft for both sexes, unlike "the inequitable present system wherein youth would serve in numerous areas other than and including the armed forces."[10]

Student concerns about the draft were just one aspect of the larger protest against war. President Johnson would have preferred to focus on domestic affairs. He promised to support the Peace Corps, to develop the Great Society, and to achieve progress in education. However, as the Vietnam War developed and as the draft spread, students turned against him. A turning point came in 1965 when Johnson increased the troops in Vietnam and doubled the draft quota. Protest parades on campuses were common by the fall of 1965, and chants were heard, such as "Hey, hey, LBJ, how many kids did you kill today?"

In 1966, an *Oswegonian* writer had deplored students' preoccupation with rushing, the latest hit tunes, and such trivia, while showing little or no interest in America's involvement in Vietnam. A few Oswego students and faculty members formed an *ad hoc* committee to end the war, calling it "illegal, immoral and undemocratic." By 1967, students were described as strongly opposed to "this silly jungle war."[11]

When a Vietnam moratorium committee called for a national student strike on October 15, 1969, to encourage others to oppose the war, an *Oswegonian* editor deplored the Faculty Assembly's failure to support it, saying that it "wasted two and a half hours in the worst display of intellectual cowardice, apathy and lack of commitment one could imagine."[12] Instead, the editorial maintained, it should have asked the administration to close school in support of those faculty members and students who chose to cancel or boycott classes. Assembly members had the "ironic notion that they should stand for the concept of academic freedom." One professor was more interested in the fact that he would be docked a day's pay if the resolution passed. The assembly claimed "that it tabled the resolution so that faculty representatives could get instructions from their departments. President

Perdue decided to let students decide for themselves what to do but that classes would be held. Oswego's activists were also dismayed at the students' "passive attitude toward the Vietnam slaughter."

The culmination of the Vietnam protest at Oswego came on national Moratorium Day, October 19, 1969, with a mass march to the Oswego federal building late in the afternoon. Five-hundred students maintained an all-night vigil on the steps of the Oswego post office. A brief memorial service by members of the campus ministry was the prelude to a nine-hour reading of names of the war dead, with several hundred students participating, despite low temperatures and high winds. By 6:00 A.M. only half of the list of dead had been recited.

Protest at Oswego escalated, in keeping with the mass student strikes nationwide, following the 1970 involvement of the U.S. in Cambodia. Many young people insisted on greater tolerance of individual differences, individual personal choice, and more diversity and freedom. Paradoxically, they found themselves denying tolerance to those whom they blamed for intolerance. In other words, the concept of equalitarianism that produced the protest was displaced by a spirit of intolerance and conflict between the establishment and students. On campus, a few windows were broken and a professor's car was tipped over by dissidents, "a senseless act," since the professor was himself an antiwar protest sympathizer. The result was that an "ugly atmosphere" developed, and "an academic setting can't handle force . . . because the assumption is that we settle our differences by rational discourse."[13]

Finally, in May 1970, a local student strike was called in sympathy with those in other colleges, all demanding release of political dissidents, a termination of the war in Indochina, and an end to military complicity on campus. That same evening, May 5, noted Thomas Gooding, Associate Dean for Graduate Studies, a meeting was called to discuss what action the college might take on these issues "and almost all the faculty and many students were there. I was sitting with Fred Ratzeburg, and Fred turned to me and said: 'Look at those students in the rear of the lecture hall with clubs in their hands.' I turned around and there they were—some Black Panthers. I thought we'd come to discuss the issues and to arrive at rational decisions, and it shocked me to see those students with clubs. Next morning when I drove to the campus, I found that the students had declared a strike. They stopped my car and demanded: 'Where are you going? How come you are not observing the strike?' I replied, 'I am going to my office to meet with some of my students.' They inquired, 'Are you going to have classes?' I said: 'That depends on what you mean by classes.'"

Associate Provost Wheeler recalled his experiences that same day. "When I returned to campus after lunch, there was a big crowd around Culkin. The students had entered the building while most people were out for lunch, and they told anyone they found there to leave: they didn't *ask*, they *told* them and chased them out. Some students barricaded the doors and locked themselves in; others marched outside, talking about Cambodia, Vietnam, and the government's inhuman policies. I managed to get into the mailroom myself—I'm not sure what I expected to accomplish by it—but I was in there and couldn't go anywhere else, so I just sat there.

"One reason they broke into this building was that the word had gotten around that the administration had firearms here to shoot students, and they were going to get those firearms and prevent murders by these terrible people. Of course, there were no guns in here. They opened closets and broke down doors, looking for guns. Campus personnel turned off the electricity, water, and all the power in order to drive the students out, and they did. None of the students involved was ever disciplined."

In a few instances students even attempted to take over classrooms. During Professor Ratzeburg's abnormal psychology class, a student abruptly arose and declared that we should stop talking "all this b.s. We should discuss something relevant—namely, the war." "The discussion to this moment had been going especially well" remembered Ratzeburg, "with much student involvement." Others in the room turned on the one who had stood up, told him he was out of order, and demanded that he sit down.

Ratzeburg also remembered "the long series of bomb threats on campus, sometimes several a week. Each time we all had to march outdoors, sometimes in the bitter cold, and stay there until security officers had checked the building. Finally, we caught one of the callers through the assistance of the switchboard operator. The guilty party was a young man who called in the threat in order to put off an examination for which he hadn't prepared. I was on the conduct committee and the student members, as well as some of the faculty, refused to recommend any action of a disciplinary nature. One of the women students declared that, under no circumstances, would she vote for disciplinary action because the young man might be drafted."

Hostile episodes continued but with less frequency. A fire was set in a dormitory elevator on May 9 and, on May 12, while the mayor of Oswego was speaking to the student body, minor campus violence erupted. Radicals from New York City disrupted, and took over, a conference on Puerto Rico on May 16. No violence occurred, but the conference had to be canceled to ensure people's safety.

The strike lasted until the end of the semester, and examination time was close at hand. Instructors held classes for those students who wished to attend, until the decision was made to give them grades they had made to that point. Instead of regular classes, professors mostly led discussion groups, often in dormitories or the student union, with attendance voluntary. "The president of the student body was in one of my classes," said Thomas Gooding, "and arranged a room for us in the student union. Students didn't want to cross picket lines, but I wanted to provide them an educational experience." Debbie Roe (1973) said that only four students continued going to one of her classes. "I felt a bit of ostracism from certain others because I wasn't parading around. Some of them simply got caught up in the emotionalism of events. I doubt that they had any well-thought out ideas. They were simply reacting to things rather than acting from any real dedication or purpose."

In the summer of 1970, a joint committee of faculty, students, and administrators discussed the strike. The students demanded greater relevance both in and outside the classroom; they branded communication throughout the college community inadequate; and they demanded participation in college governance. The resulting report, "Freedom and Responsibility on Campus," recommended establishment of an information center, development of campus TV, a better communication network, and student evaluation of the faculty. Following approval of a code of student conduct and bill of rights, a student conduct committee was created.

"When the spring semester ended," said Thomas Powell, "everyone heaved a sigh of relief because the college population was dispersing. People were asking each other, 'After this, what's it going to be like in the fall when everyone comes back?' But when they came back, it was as though nothing had happened. Everything was business as usual."

Nevertheless, lesser incidents continued to occur. At least three times during 1970–71 Perdue and the vice presidents assumed around-the-clock vigils to ensure that a high-level administrator was on hand at all times in case violence broke out. On May 10, 1972, a civil-service strike was called; only minor picketing occurred, however. Also in 1972, students marched on the naval base to protest the escalation of bombing in Vietnam.

Another issue of national scope that roused students was environmentalism, including nuclear power. Political activist Tom Hayden and activist/actress Jane Fonda spoke against nuclear power at Kingsford Park, despite having been refused a permit. In September 1976 Oswego's Students Against Nuclear Power showed films depicting dangers of nuclear war. In November another group, "Students Against Nuclear Energy (SANE)," held a rally for nuclear awareness at Niagara Mohawk's Nine Mile Point. About forty people, mostly students, chanted, "The people united will never be defeated" and "We don't want a meltdown."

Pollution was another concern, especially in Lake Ontario. An *Oswegonian* editorial suggested that students prepare themselves for the fare of the 1980s by mixing detergents with everything they ate and drank.[14] They should learn how to digest grass and other common plants, practice starving, and every night "drink a glass of industrial and organic waste-on-the-rocks or mix it if you prefer." Another editorial supported a local citizens' group called "Save Our Shores" in its fight against a proposed cement plant in the area. A third editorial concerned a national environmental teach-in, and a "Protect Your Environment" steering committee for the Oswego area. The editorial advised "clearing the garbage out of Lake Ontario . . . to swim without having to stake out fish nets to fight back the ecological casualties floating to the surface and rotting all spring."

A significant development paralleled these events: female students were belatedly granted a more mature status. Male students, even freshmen, had always been treated like adults; females, even seniors, had been dealt with like children. Most females simply had accepted such treatment as inevitable; however, by the early 1970s, the impact of the women's movement had become evident. *Oswegonian* articles for this period indicated the breadth of women's concerns. One issue carried the articles "Women and Health" and "The Unfinished Revolution: Lucy Stone." Another issue had articles about rape, lesbians, women hitchhikers, and women Civil War activists. On February 28, 1974, an *Oswegonian* column, "The Feminist Voice," carried the articles "Common Law Guides Name Choice," "Lesbian Mother Fights for Child Custody," "Women's Free University Plan," and "Phony Gynecologist Molested Woman." On March 21, the same column concerned a rape bill and women's right to abortion.

When representatives from SUNY institutions met at Oswego in April of 1973, the Alliance of Women Against Repressive Education (AWARE) of SUNY demanded action on the following matters: education programs for older women; discriminatory admission standards; free access for women to all jobs filed in the placement office; employment of feminist counselors in proportion to the female population on campus; full-time day care centers; an end to unfair curfew policies; a full-time female gynecologist; a birth control clinic with abortion referral; a venereal disease clinic; sex education programs at the health center; adequate funding for women's physical education programs; protection from rape, including better lighting on campuses and an after-hours escort service; courses in self-defense with credit optional; increased dorm patrols and on-foot campus patrols; establishment of a rape crisis center; a twenty-four hour hotline; a feminist therapist and legal–medical assistance; an interdisciplinary minor as well as an interdisciplinary major; and a graduate program in Women's Studies, the coordinators of which should be reputable feminists.

Locally, women felt they were treated like second-class citizens. Gloria Greenfield (1974) declared that the Student Association budget reflected the college's attitude toward women's bodies. Its appropriation for men's intercollegiate athletics was $72,537.11, for women's, $12,396.00; for intramurals the Men's Recreation Association was given $10,288.98, and the Women's Athletic Association, $3,381.00.[15] In a letter to the *Oswegonian*, Sandra Wallace (1976) and Kathryn Kemp (1976) protested the unequal facilities for the sexes on campus, observing that "males can lose their lard passing around a basketball court while females are practically compelled simply to run in place in their rooms."[16]

On one occasion, ten women clad in bathing suits held a sit-in at the Laker Hall sauna bath, protesting its policy of discrimination. When campus security officers said they must leave or be arrested, they neither left nor were they arrested. More protest was planned after negotiations with the heads of men's and women's physical education brought some, but still inadequate, benefits. Women were allowed to use the sauna only early in the day, hardly the most convenient time for a sauna bath.

Most students favored the ERA (Equal Rights Amendment), but a minority did not. An article by a student opposing the ERA appeared in a 1975 *Oswegonian*.[17] It cited the possibility of common toilets, common Army barracks for the sexes, and recognition of homosexuals and homosexual marriages. In a letter to the editor, Theresa H. Rourke (1976) wrote that she "couldn't believe that you devoted so much page space to print such an absurd article as that."[18] She wondered whether it was simply a satire or someone's genuine opinion.

Despite the large Catholic contingent on campus, student sentiment was mainly pro-abortion, especially among the feminists. An *Oswegonian* editorial applauded the Supreme Court's overruling state laws which prohibited abortion during the first three months of pregnancy and it condemned the local assemblyman, Edward Crawford, for introducing a bill to repeal New York's liberalized abortion law.[19] Abortion advocate Bill Baird spoke in December 1972 to a Hewitt Union audience of mostly women; he berated churches that opposed abortion and he displayed birth control devices (after showing these at Boston University, Baird was sent to prison). The district attorney said it would "make whores and prostitutes of women" but, when he asked for a show of hands of those who might be turned on sexually by seeing these devices, the audience just laughed.

Another issue was the women students' dress code. "Until about 1965," recalled Don Harrison, "women couldn't wear jeans in the library." "Or in the dining hall for Sunday noon dinner," added Betsy Auleta. Continued Auleta, "What we did to protest the Sunday skirt rule on Sunday was to try to look really ugly. We would wear ankle socks, sneakers, and a plaid skirt with a striped shirt. Even those who went to church were angry that they couldn't come home and put on a pair of comfortable jeans and go to the dining hall."

In 1966, groups of students protested the library hours and the rule that forbade women students from wearing slacks in the library; there was no dress code for men. When one hundred people confronted a college official on the matter, he told them they were interfering with the normal function of the college and were making themselves liable for disciplinary action. They were told they should go through the Associated Women Students. Later, after the librarian, Helen Hagger, met with officers of student groups, signs indicating proper dress for women were removed. For a time, the dress code was supervised by the Associated Women Students but was dropped by 1968.

Curfew rules for women, another major issue, simmered for several years. In 1966 most women had to sign out after 7:30 P.M. to go anywhere outside the dorm, even to the front steps. According to the Cinderella-hour policy, a girl or her date might purchase time, from 1:30 to 2:30 A.M., at the rate of a penny a minute. However, girls had to sign out individually for the one-hour extension.

A 1967 editorial asked, "If it's necessary to regulate a coed's night hours, why aren't daylight hours regulated?"[20] The Associated Women Students proposed a cylinder key system whereby girls planning to return after closing hours could sign out a cylinder resembling a roller skate key; the cylinder would open a deposit box containing a key to the dormitory. A second proposal, submitted by Dean Robert Rock, suggested that curfews be eradicated and a night watch system be implemented instead. The next year a Student Association resolution, approved by fourteen members, with four abstaining, recommended that the no-curfew privilege be given to freshmen. An *Oswegonian* article was titled "Is Our Parentis Loco?"[21]

Betsy Auleta recalls that "one night we told the administration that men and women were going to sit in each other's rooms (there were male and female dorms then) beyond the curfew, to challenge the whole thing. An administrator quoted in the *Oswegonian* had said that students who did this would be suspended. However, President Perdue asked the administrator, 'Are you crazy? Five-hundred students will be involved. We can't expel five hundred kids tomorrow morning.' There may not have been 500, but between 250 and 500 did break curfew. Each student was assigned a room to sit in. I didn't even know they guy whose room I was sitting in with a couple of other girls. We were simply trying to make a point, that we were no longer going to be kept."

"There was a three-tiered system when I came," said Debbie Roe (1973), "and parents might sign for what level of privileges they wanted their daughters to have. On one tier you couldn't leave campus for a weekend without written permission to your residence hall director two days before leaving campus. Even if you were just going to your parents' house, you couldn't be out past the time that the front doors were locked. On the second tier, you had to be in every night by the time the doors were locked, but if you wanted to go home for the weekend you could just leave. The third curfew type was carte blanche—'I'll leave it to my daughter to set her own hours.' Few of my friends were on the most restricted tier; but one who was two years older than I, and an RA in Hart Hall, had the restricted curfew.

She came in just seconds late one night and had to go before the judicial board, and was very upset. By my sophomore year, 1970–71, we had our first coed dorm on campus, Seneca Hall, and everybody was carte blanche."

Another issue that simmered throughout the 1970s concerned arming the campus security officers. Most students strongly opposed this move but the security officers argued that not carrying handguns could be hazardous. During one two-year period in the early 1970s, one student "was shot at; a couple of students were stabbed; several students were assaulted."[22] There were also many rapes, at least one involving display of a firearm. Many searches of trespassers resulted in firearms being found. One security policeman deplored the administration's desire to maintain the college's image as a "quiet little college by the lake" to appease parents who wouldn't want their "children" to go to a "crime-infested" campus. Reputedly, eleven men had left the security department in the past two years, mainly because they believed they had one hand tied behind their backs.[22]

The ROTC was also controversial, at Oswego and elsewhere. Some students supported having the program, others did not, and disturbances were common during ROTC graduations and award ceremonies. In one instance, eight students, including two women, were arrested by campus security police at Rich Hall because they sat in a hallway blocking the path of two U.S. Marine recruiters to the placement office. Originally, about twenty-five students had gathered at an entrance of Rich Hall to block the Marines from entering. After the students were told that demonstrators blocking the men would be arrested, all but eight left. These eight continued handclapping and chanting, "Life, life, we love life!" until they were arrested, handcuffed, and placed in a shuttle bus. Taken to the police station, the students were charged with disorderly conduct and released on $100 bail each. Security officers denied that weapons or clubs had been used, while admitting that "a little pushing and shoving" simply could not be avoided. Security officer Ronald Guile was puzzled, saying, "Now that the war is over it's hard to understand just what this was all about." The students countered with, "This is an educational institution, not a factory for killers."[23]

The ROTC forces rallied, pro and con. The Marine officers noted that Oswego had more candidates, seven for the officer training program, than any other school in this area. Dean Rock said he placed Marines in the category of employers and didn't object to having them on campus; and he argued the students' right to have access to them. Such remarks produced a volley of letters to the editor and editorials in the *Oswegonian*. One student, James Bethany (1980), observed that "America was once a land willing to commit millions of men to fight tyranny."

Implicit in many of these upheavals was students' challenge to authority, catching many speakers for the "establishment" by surprise. In the early 1960s psychologist Nevitt Sanford said society appeared so stable that the college generation had little hope of changing because students were concerned about finding their own place within it. Moreover, observed Columbia's Frankel, youth's elders speak in so liberal a fashion that the young have little to rebel against. But students did find a cause celebre: university administrators! Certain early protests were against faculty members' intrusion into students' personal affairs. In a letter to the editor, a student protested against several faculty members, who had suggested that students should look more professional and cut their hair. The student observed that John F. Kennedy, Leonard Bernstein, Albert Einstein, and even some professors on campus, wore their hair long. To some extent, even after 1970, many students' college careers still consisted mainly of "co-curriculum—in other words, activist activities involving attending rallies, committee meetings, etc."[24]

Until 1967–68, observed Perdue, confrontations with administration and faculty were minimal because of student "apathy, disinterest, and fragmentation among them." However, by this time, added Perdue, confrontation had become "exciting, albeit frustrating, as students began to 'rally around issues' that they believed significant—and these were many." In 1967, student B. C. Smith proposed that students aid in course selection and evaluation of professors, which he termed student power and, he argued, would increase the college's effectiveness.[25] Burt Naznitsky (1971) called on students to demand a voice in various matters, including student housing, curfews, alcohol, and student discipline.[26] He deplored the administration's having taken unto itself the power to act on student affairs without student consent.

However, in 1966 students were protesting faculty control of their funds. Even though students were involved, they were recruited and apparently controlled by faculty members. In that same spring, the student body voted to allow the Student Association to collect a mandatory student activity fee. In fall of 1967 the SUNY Board of Trustees declared that such a fee was a tax on the Student Association's constituents and, hence, illegal—a policy later reversed.

Students made considerable gains between 1968 and 1970. The results of mass demonstrations were meetings Perdue called "punch-the-president" affairs. Before 1965 there were no student department representatives and none in the faculty assembly; students had no vote of any kind on faculty or administrative matters. However, by 1970, *Oswegonian* writer Steven Austin (1972) could point to considerable student progress: "alcohol has finally legally arrived . . . open dorms and coed dorms are close to coming. A faculty evaluation system is being established."[27] An *Oswegonian* editorial, "Student Rights," called the no-curfew and reformed alcohol policies "great leaps forward," but concluded that we have "barely scratched the surface."[28] President Perdue observed in 1972 that students had begun to recognize they could exercise power through student activity fees and the ballot box.

He predicted that in a few years faculty and students might be jointly involved in the bargaining process.

Students even came to insist on a role in hiring and firing the faculty. A 1975 *Oswegonian* editorial took the administration to task for neglecting students' rights as consumers with regard to academic cutbacks.[29] The next month, Robert Tompkins (1976) and Paul Dupont (1977) called on students to become as involved as their predecessors of the 1960s in demanding input.[30] They deplored the loss of sixteen professors, a speech pathology program, a third of the social work program, and the undercutting of other programs. They noted that just "eight to ten people are forced to do all the work and all the fighting on this nonviolent issue."

Student protests extended past the local campus to SUNY at Albany. In fall 1972, SUNY Chancellor Ernest Boyer had asked student body presidents to help develop a structure which would make their involvement operationally effective. However, the students were impatient. In March 1975, SASU, the Student Association of State University (SASU), demanded that student housing rents be kept down. Demonstrators arrived in New York City by the busload while police stood by. One student carried a sign reading: "Free Rent—Avoid Lament."[31] Another placard read: "Boyer Sleeps Free, Why Can't We?" One female student on crutches carried a sign. Finally, the chancellor appeared and told the students that a rent increase would not take effect without student input. Locally, students held a rally to protest SUNY cutbacks for the Hewitt Union ballroom. The United Student Social Workers organization sponsored the protest; its purpose was to "fight for quality education." Students were also protesting faculty cutbacks, declaring that "SUNY schools would soon be 'floating in a cesspool of mediocrity.'"

The student housing situation was a major source of contention. In 1975 350 students demonstrated peacefully to show their concern over anticipated housing conditions, specifically the decision to limit to 2,200 the number of upperclassmen housed on campus. Students urged that funds be allocated for temporary housing to be built on the Oswego campus by September 1, 1975. President Perdue replied by noting legislative budget cuts, the statewide moratorium on housing construction, and other factors outside his control. One student fired back this question: "Can I rent a room in your house?"[32] Later that year, seventy-six students planned to go to Washington to talk to their congressmen about New York State's financial crisis. Because of an oversight, the Greyhound bus did not arrive, but SASU did send 1,300 students.

Students were oblivious to Albany's excuses on such matters. The following year, 7,000 SUNY/CUNY students, including thirty-four from Oswego, were transported to Albany (in 160 buses) to protest state cutbacks affecting the quality of education. They were proported to have converged on the

State Capitol building, fighting capital police at every stairway, pushing them aside, chanting: "The people united will never be defeated." The police responded by flourishing nightsticks, trying to push the students away from the chambers.

Down the years, even centuries, food has been a major source of college students' concerns. In the 1970s the *Oswegonian* carried a column called "What's Cooking with Food Service?" The most popular items offered by Food Service in 1973 were roast beef, fried chicken, grilled cheese sandwiches, and tuna fish.[33] The least popular were hamburgers, beef burgundy, fried clams, pizza, scrambled eggs, and cordon bleu. In a letter to the *Oswegonian*, "Welcome Back to SUCK-O," one student protested the fact that those students who returned to campus shortly after the dining hall's 6:30 P.M. closing hour could not be served. In April 1973, when students boycotted meat because of its rising cost, the Food Service supported the boycott, but served meat to those who asked for it. An *Oswegonian* writer observed that, by turning down the Student Association's request to open a food and record co-op on campus, Dean Rock had "overextended the bounds of his authority with unfair decisions, but he got away with it." In short, student "beefs" about food service are perennial.

Lesser issues were highly varied. An *Oswegonian* editorial called "Going to the Dogs" protested the invasion of the campus by canines.[34] Never before had there been "so many, so dirty or so large." They interfered with driving on campus, crawled under tables in the dining hall for scraps, and went food-begging in the dormitories. One perennial issue was the use of alcohol on campus. *Oswegonian* editors called such use unnecessary except for selected events, such as formals and receptions but they opposed registering them. A related issue concerned the smoking policy. In response to student suggestions in fall 1973, Oneida and Cayuga dormitories provided nonsmoking sections. The no-smoking policy had been erratically enforced in classrooms, depending on the instructor. However, because of fire laws and student complaints, the administration imposed a more stringent campaign against such violations. As a result, a spate of letters appeared in the *Oswegonian;* a few students supported the right to smoke in classrooms, but a majority opposed it.[35]

The 1960s activists, who had made a name for their generation, were a small minority. By the late 1960s, it is certain that all students had been influenced by some kind of protest; however, only about 20 percent of all students—and not all sit-ins—were favored by the student body.[36] However, students in general supported protests whenever administrations used repressive measures. Locally, President Perdue estimated that only 2 or 3 percent of the students had caused disturbances on campus, but he agreed that "a small fraction manages to give its stamp to a generation."

Some observers sensed a diminution of student activism as early as 1969.

A *Life* Magazine survey suggested that "campus radicals are suffering from the blahs; the liberals are frustrated; and the movement is turned back toward oneself. Yet the main issues—Vietnam, and draft and drugs—are deeply felt, and there is no chance of returning to the passive detachment of the 1950s. While students are pausing to reexamine their commitments, the first is still dangerously close to the surface."

The question arises: Had students become truly apathetic or was protest simply dormant? "In the early 1970s," observed Debbie Roe, "I found my peers pretty open-minded and tolerant of people's differences. There was an interest in social justice, in world affairs. Compared with students today, they were more aware of what was going on in the world and what the issues were." Peg Lowery agreed, noting that students of the early 1970s "read the papers, and watched Walter Cronkite—and the women were as involved as the men. Today's students don't."

Student sit-ins and strikes were widely publicized, but there were other forms of protest. "In those times," commented Betsy Auleta, "the yippies, led by [national activists] Jerry Rubin and Abby Hoffman, popularized media events through guerilla theatre. At Oswego you'd go someplace and make theater happen right there, as in the dining hall or cafeteria." Don Harrison added that in the union, students would "sometimes just take over the cafeteria, get a table, and begin some kind of play." Another device was the so-called "bitch-in." In 1968 Oswego students were invited to get together to unload their feelings. Topics of "bitch-ins" which drew the largest crowds were curriculum revision, birth control, abortion, housing, Greek row, threat of Communism, riots, and the legalization of pot. However, most of the "bitch-ins" were poorly attended.

The activists' close network also contributed to their effectiveness. They had a long-distance telephone network linking almost all the colleges. Locally, via their telephone desk in the student union, Oswego activists could contact the network and get information about what was going on, such as what the president and university trustees were doing. In addition, an extant National Underground Student Press paid $20 for each accepted article. In contrast to the earlier, more strident tactics, by the mid-1970s student writers of poetry, criticism, and other works displayed a milder, quieter activism.

In retrospect, the activists of the 1960s might be called rebels, but not true revolutionaries. Many, if not most, lacked any clear ideology or well-thought out programs. Their rallies were over issues, not philosophies, and they had no real theory regarding their society and its future. Nor were they as dedicated as often portrayed. Demonstrations, though they had the aura of excitement, were only occasional.

Activists themselves viewed lesser involved students as hedonistic and lacking in social responsibility. Perhaps these critics were right, or at least the moderate majority had different priorities, such as making high enough grades to get into graduate school. Still, many quietly supported the activists, despite remaining aloof themselves; only a minority viewed with scorn the more radical activists. Several students writing in the *Oswegonian* observed that "as hair grows longer and skirts shorter at Oswego, the same fadism which has brought change in dress has failed to bring maturity and tolerance which the new appearance has been acclaimed to carry."[37]

What, if anything, did the activist minority accomplish? At Oswego, concluded President Perdue, "the overall effect of the student upheavals could be healthy if the results proved corrective." At any rate, after the dust has settled, some decades hence, historians will write their versions of the best epitaph for this era.

7

Campus Life—Some New Directions

FROM a broader perspective, what were they like—the college students of the years 1965 to 1976? For one, they were becoming a common breed. Just a million and a half were enrolled nationwide in 1940. By the 1960s, over five million crowded the campuses. When the economy plunged in the early 1970s, however, a bit of shrinkage occurred. Hence, 65 percent of those applying to Oswego in fall 1972 were accepted, compared to 51 percent in 1971, and just 2,290 new students arrived. The very next year, the tide turned again: SUNY-wide, student enrollment increased by 5.8 percent and by 7.2 percent at Oswego.[1]

It is easier to count students than to define them. Appraisals of the college students of 1965 amounted to "educated bafflement . . . what in the world can youth be, this wondrous creature with so few defenses and so many changes. What can the student be up to, this preposterous unicorn with a graceful gait and eager eye?"[2] These students have been described as "explosive," "cool," and "committed." And while the future is usually conceded to the young, these young people had "staked out . . . a claim on America's present"; and their "tastemakers stamped a vigorous imprint" on fashions, entertainment, and speech.[2] "They sought to establish their identities, yet they copied their crowd"; and they disdained the material world, yet relished its fruits. Never had any generation in history been "such complete strangers to famine, plague, want, or war."[2] Times were prosperous and The Great Depression was history.

A new morality, more flexible and tolerant than before, had emerged. Students acknowledged an individual's right to do her or his own thing. Armored with the pill, premarital sex won the day—and the undergraduates' approval. Students loudly proclaimed the need for honesty and openness, but cheating in classrooms was still common.

Dress changed along with morality, a truism throughout history. As the tempo of the 1960s quickened, clothing grew more extreme. The somewhat traditional garb of the early 1950s, decreed for women by the campus dress code, was transformed. Blue jeans were "in," and also miniskirts, which

Oswego's often frigid climate fixed at about two inches above the knee, about five inches short of true "mini-status." Culottes were popular and, until the dress code gave up the ghost, were often sneaked into class by virtue of looking like skirts. Some of the men, at least, opposed this retreat from ladylike femininity. Calling themselves the LEGS, or League for Emancipation of Girls' Skirts, they declared that 97 percent of men on campus favored women's wearing skirts during class hours and to social functions.[3]

Men's fashions did not undergo a revolution in the 1960s. Men continued to wear sweatshirts, dungarees, and shirts for everyday, and more formal attire on special occasions. Some students went barefoot around campus, even to class, and many wore no socks. However, crew cuts had become obsolete, displaced by long hair, often falling to the shoulders, as popularized by the Beatles. Many students grew mustaches and some wore beards.

Most of the more extreme styles were abandoned in the early 1970s. In 1973 The Stall, a clothes store, advertised clothes that would achieve "that coordinated well-dressed look." In 1972, minis became midis, often worn with maxi coats. The maxis soon disappeared, but the midis remained. Said Debbie Roe, "Some attire looked like what we call preppy today—penny loafers, crew-neck sweaters—a well-dressed, casual style. Or maybe docksider shoes and bright-colored blazers."

In the meantime, men's long hair had retreated a bit, but not all the way to crew-cut length. By 1975 hair was supposed to "tickle the collar instead of completely cover it. The early Beatle bangs across the forehead are still all right and tend to be practical also. Even the slick-back look may be an alternative in the near future."[4]

Other significant developments related to student housing. The 1968-69 academic year "promised a giant step in the direction of the sexes' total integration through coed residence complexes," Marilyn Witney said in *The Oswegonian*.[5] Housing placement would be made through campus-wide drawing by classes, with preference based on seniority, she predicted.

Nevertheless, the first coed dormitory, Seneca Hall, was not approved by the College Council until the fall of 1970. President Perdue balked when students proposed also making Cayuga and Oneida Halls coed, partly because upperclassmen preferred not to live in mostly freshmen dormitories.[6] Perdue wanted to balance the lifestyles on campus, arguing that coed housing had reached the saturation level. In addition, some people in the community disapproved of such housing. However, after a rally, in which students indicated that just 38 percent of them lived in coed dorms although 78 percent wished to, Perdue surrendered; Oneida and Cayuga would go coed by May 1, 1976.

The results bore out the apparent wisdom of the students' wishes. In 1967, James Wassenaar, director of housing, had reported that Moreland and

Lonis "would be evacuated . . . someday to allow workmen to scrape dried shaving cream and other delights from the walls of rooms and halls."[7] In contrast, students in the coed dorms behaved better and took better care of the property. Overcrowded facilities were a major problem of this period. In fall 1976, 4,463 of the 9,000 students were housed on campus, and 1,800, mostly freshmen, lived in triples. Some people put dressers inside closets so they could do without bunk beds. Many used one of their two desk tops to hold a stereo or TV set; others constructed lofts attached to the ceiling.

The lofts soon produced a storm of controversy. State fire inspectors declared them a fire hazard.[8] Charles Weeks, assistant housing director, pointed out that lofts standing four to five feet above the floor and covering a major portion of the room would "fool the heat detector should a fire start underneath that expanse." As an alternative, the Save-Our-Lofts Organization investigated two fire-proofing methods, one called Pressure Impregnating, a fire-proofing material, and the other a fire-retardant paint. The housing office subsequently acknowledged that specific prohibitions against lofts did not exist and those already constructed could remain.

Crowded or not, many students were in favor of dormitory living, at least for the first two years.[9] Randi Chernov (1977) said that dorm life was socially advantageous, where you "get thrown together with all types of life styles and ideals. You share, live, and work together until you all have a lot in common." Terry Lydon said he "could not imagine a better transition to coming to college than living in the dorm. I valued friendships and socialization there highly; however, as my academic priorities heightened, my toleration for lack of privacy lowered."

The approximately 135 RAs (resident assistants) had mixed feelings about their dorm experience.[10] They worked about forty hours a week, were on call once a week, and were on desk duty a total of about sixteen hours; all this was in addition to their personal interaction with students. John Robbins (1977), third floor RA in Scales, said that when "people at a party find out you are an RA, they tell you to go hide in a corner." Paul Mongiello (1977), an RA in Funnelle for three years, at first felt intimidated in his job and tried hard for acceptance as an RA and a friend. Nevertheless, in general, the RAs found their role rewarding. Barbara Wolfe, RA in Hart, said that "financially, it's the pits. The pay would probably work out to about a nickel an hour, but it's worth it. Let's just say I like my work." Qualities taken into consideration in choosing RAs are level of integrity, leadership, and maturity.

Some students stated a strong preference for living off campus. Wanda Little (1977) said that off campus she became more "attuned to the world, things like preserving gas, shutting off taps—these things became relevant." She commented on the lack of privacy in the dorms, and said that once she moved off campus "my grades zoomed up." Terry Lydon said he felt a need for more space. "In the dorms it was as though you could never feel alone.

The whole sense of mass impedes a certain type of contemplation." Jean Goslin (1978) was a "top bunk lady" for one term, and "it wasn't claustrophobic, but it cramped my style." Others said they got fed up with dormitory food, in more than one sense. Liz Loonan (1978) claimed that the food was "so unnutritious that you might as well be eating paper." (For better perspective, let it be noted that almost everywhere institutional fare earns low ratings.)

Over the years, expenses for everything, including on- and off-campus housing, had continued to mount. Room rent increased to $365 for the 1965–66 academic year, and it was projected that a $10-a-year rent increase would occur in each of the next three years. In the later 1960s, living expenses, including room, board, supplies, and spending money, were about $1,500, and tuition was $400. The price of snacks around town would seem cheap today. The Parkside Drive-In advertised itself as being "the only place on or near campus where the 20¢ hamburg still thrives." Other items on the menu were French fries—15¢, milk—13¢, coffee—10¢, pizza slice—18¢, and fish sandwich—30¢.

Students spent much of their money at Hewitt Union, which was rated both a plus and a minus development. In 1972–73, students planned and designed a tavern in the basement where they could enjoy various assortments of jazz, folk, pop, piano, and ragtime music, plus seeing movies and even magicians. Despite some raised eyebrows in town that such a place should exist on the campus, the Tavern thrived and beer imbibing became incidental to conversation and entertainment. The next year, the students sustained a blow when the budget crunch lopped off the erstwhile hot-meal service on the floor just above. They lamented what some people referred to as the "destruction of the college's town square" in favor of vending machines.

Meanwhile, traditional hangouts continued to thrive, such as Buckland's and Nunzi's where students came for kill-the-keg specials. Sam Tesoriero, operator since 1957 of Nunzi's on the shore of Lake Ontario, said that many students returned for visits after they had graduated, especially married couples who first met there. He guessed that about a hundred couples met first at his tavern, and he believed that the students' college education had helped them. "I've seen some kids come in here and have a ball . . . and some of them have awful good jobs today. . . . College is almost a must today to get anywhere at all."[11] Nunzi's opens the first of April, and on that night the place is mobbed. Tesoriero, age sixty in 1977, expected to pass the business along to his grandson.

Hangouts were far more popular than sports at Oswego, in contrast to the nationwide trend. Elsewhere, since the 1960s sports were in an era of expansion: major-league baseball mushroomed from two eighteen-team leagues into four sixteen-team divisions; pro-basketball tripped across the continent; and pro-hockey was catching on. Pro-bowling became a big sport. The National Football League expanded into Dallas, Atlanta, Minnesota, and New Orleans. The larger colleges continued big-time football; however, smaller ones, including Oswego, had trouble maintaining it because of little interest and less money. Nevertheless, in October 1973 the National Clubs Sports Association ranked the Oswego's Great Laker Football Team fourteenth in the nation, in its category.

In other sports, too, Oswego's teams continued to shine. In 1967 Oswego Laker intercollegiate squads won the all-sports trophy, awarded by the State University conference to the college whose teams had the highest overall standing in eight designated sports. Oswego's golf team won the SUNY championship in 1970; the baseball and tennis teams came in second; and Richard Ames (1972) was chosen for the all-SUNY soccer team. In the next year, 1971, the lacrosse team—at that time a club sport—competed in its first and undefeated season. A year later, in 1972, Glendon Widrick (1974) pitched a no-hitter baseball game against Plattsburgh: the score, 14 to 0. The year 1976 was a mixed bag for men's varsity; the hockey team won the SUNY championship, but football folded, after a checkered history. In the meantime, after eight straight victories, seven Laker skaters fell victim to the flu, and the team lost to Buffalo, 7 to 6.

Half of the members of the 1974 hockey team were Canadian, an *Oswegonian* editorial posed the question: "Why is it, in spite of the fact that exactly half of our hockey team is Canadian, only the Star Spangled Banner is played at the beginning of hockey games?"[12]

Ever and anon, sports seasons are marked by special situations or unusual events. In fall 1973, during the energy crisis, the finals of the Max Ziel Classic were shifted from night to afternoon to allow players to return to campus before gas stations closed. On April 1, 1974, after the college's lacrosse players had completed a contest with St. Lawrence University, they spotted a building on fire and then, to their horror, saw a third-floor window open and an elderly woman appear. As the room filled with smoke, she climbed on the ledge. After her strength gave out, she fell and struck guidewires of a display sign which tossed her into a horizontal position. The whole lacrosse team moved, with tremendous agility, to where she was, and with all their hands and arms reaching up, caught her, and prevented her from experiencing major injury and probably death.[13]

Women's teams also had some notable successes. In the 1971 season their hockey team was undefeated; and in 1973 Marcia Girolamo (1973) won the women's intercollegiate pocket billiards championship held at Idaho State College, Boise. She had been playing the game for only the past three years and attributed much of her success to suggestions given her by pocket billiard legend Arthur (Babe) Cranfield. Two years later, in 1975–76, Oswego's women's swim team completed its best record ever, defeating, among others, Syracuse University, 9 to 2.

Sixteen sports were offered at Oswego in 1962–63. By 1968, just five years later, additional sports were ice hockey, skiing, speed skating, hole-in-one, punt-pass contest, three-man toboggan run, billiards, and coed activities in volleyball, bowling, and tennis. Of these, tennis became the hottest sport on campus and court time was scarce. This was one craze that wasn't just a craze, for it's still going on. Hockey classes for women were instituted in fall 1973, taught by the men's varsity coach, Herb Hammond.

Earlier, long-distance walking had been popular and in 1966 five Hillcrest Hall students walked to Syracuse and back. The Syracuse *Herald-Journal* covered the walk with articles and pictures. Two walkers had to drop out due to blisters, and a third walker gave up after walking to Syracuse and ten miles back. The other two walkers, however, walked all of the approximately eighty miles.

In budgetary terms, sports are a big-ticket item, subject to perennial controversy. The coaches, especially, have lamented their inability to lure potential stars with big enough carrots; and in 1969, when student fees were voluntary, Coach John Glinski perceived varsity sports to be in real jeopardy. Perdue attacked this policy in 1973, saying that, according to national intercollegiate athletic association rules, the faculty had the ultimate responsibility for athletic policy, and it was illegal for students to make all such decisions. That fall the students responded by voting to freeze athletic funds until the Student Association received a written guarantee that students would decide all policies affecting athletics; however, in January, the Student Association Senate lifted its freeze, "provided that student opinion receive due consideration in the future."[14]

Perhaps Oswego's most distinctive sports, planned or otherwise, relate to its sometimes "sub-Arctic" weather and include building snow structures, ice skating, and expecially on snow days, when classes are cancelled, simply going out to challenge a blizzard. Debbie Roe (1973) recalled how friendly people were "during those bad snow storms when the wind was incredible, with a chill factor that froze your eyebrows. You might be walking across campus and wondering why they didn't put tunnels underground. People would band together, making human chains to fight the wind; and someone might take your arm whom you never knew, someone you'd never met in the classroom, so you could team up against the wind. We would joke around and laugh at some people, the way they'd get blown down, but the weather helped bring us together."

The interest they shared in drugs also brought some students together. At Oswego, as elsewhere, most students tried marijuana, and many tried hard drugs. The hippies had popularized the so-called psychedelic drugs, which presumably produced pleasurable, creative sensations. Along with drugs came psychedelic art and culture. As the serious side effects of LSD became apparent, the use of "acid" proceeded rapidly to decline. Marijuana became the drug of the day, the symbol of alienation, and undergraduates' challenge to their parents and authorities.

Oswego was no exception—experimentation with drugs was common—and students sometimes had brushes with the law. Seven Oswego students and a student's wife were arrested for various drug offenses in 1967, including possession of narcotics and purchase of cough syrup. One also was arraigned for fireworks violation because he had seven cherry bombs and thirty-four large firecrackers; troopers also uncovered evidence of glue sniffing and a marijuana party. One student wrote to the *Oswegonian* complaining of its coverage of the students' arrest before they were tried.[15]

The No. 1 drug at Oswego remained alcohol, and in 1967 President Perdue established a Committee on Alcohol Use, made up of faculty, administration, and student representatives. Its purpose was to look into all matters relating to the use of alcohol on campus. An alcohol policy was adopted in 1968, and its first authorized use was in a dorm-sponsored Halloween party in Mackin Hall on October 31, 1968.

Debbie Roe said that when she came to Oswego in 1969, "it was illegal to have alcohol in your residence hall room. There was a lot of sneaking going on but you did have to sneak it. However, by the end of 1970, the alcohol policy allowed you to buy a six-pack of beer and bring it in with a pizza. That same year there were quite a number of changes in residence life, resulting in people assuming greater responsibility for themselves. Finally, alcohol was legalized in Seneca Hall after a vote by the residents, with 371 for and 12 against. In the next month, December, the on-campus Alcohol Beverage Committee accepted policies from eight more dormitories. Also in 1969, the Student Association Council endorsed a policy that would allow students "to have alcohol beverages in their rooms."

Hard drugs were mostly gone by the early 1970s; marijuana and alcohol remained. In 1973 most college editors indicated that students on campuses were using wine, marijuana, liquor, and beer more than during the previous year. A large majority (71 percent) felt that marijuana should be legalized and 69 percent reported that most other students also believed it should be legalized.

There was much evidence of Oswego students' widely acclaimed drinking habits. For example, in a 1973 *Oswegonian* there was a large ad for the Ferris Wheel: ALL THE BEER, WHISKEY AND WINE YOU CAN DRINK AT POPULAR PRICES. An advertisement called Buckland's "your home away from home and invites you on December 11th (1972) for free beer." In his 1973–74 annual report President Perdue observed that the "beer bash is once again fashionable. Liquor provides the high without the hassle." He noted that 10 percent of the 95 million Americans who drank were full-fledged alcoholics or at least problem drinkers and that the high-density population on college campuses aggravated the drinking problem.

Marijuana use seemed to have become a permanent part of American life. A national marijuana survey showed that among secondary-school students, ages twelve to seventeen, 14 percent had tried marijuana and 5 percent were current users. Among adults, 39 percent favored getting rid of the criminal penalties for sale or possession of small amounts of marijuana and its private use; 40 percent believed there should be tougher laws for possessing even small amounts; and 13 percent favored laws as they were.[16]

Most Oswego students used marijuana temperately; only a few tested the boundaries. A student who signed herself "Busted," noted that the Oswego City Police had searched her house and arrested her and her apartment mates for growing five very handsome marijuana plants. She advised other students that if they grew any to be sure to put it where it would not be noticed.[17] An *Oswegonian* editorial warned students to be aware of Governor Rockefeller's hard drug law.[18] The editor branded it "a reactionist, short-sighted political move."

Marijuana was mostly a weekend luxury. Class days were pretty routine, as evidenced by this description of a typical day by students Ellen Tracey and Sandy Shear.

> The girl, whom they call Candy Coed, runs through the tunnel from Cayuga to Pathfinder and finds Pathfinder as well as her breakfast cold. The only creature enjoying the breakfast is a fly which lights on the eggs and dies a watery death in Candy's coffee. She goes hungry to Sheldon Hall for an eight o'clock class which runs a bit overtime. She sprints out of class for the social science building and is late, but so is the professor, so there is no problem. After class she returns to Cayuga, changes her clothes, unkinks her hair, eats a cold unhearty lunch, and prepares a mandatory library assignment.[19]

More creative individuals introduced their own variations on the usual theme. Melissa Hall (1975) said that Hart Hall, an all-women's dorm at the time, 1974, had an organization of tall women. She had put up a sign asking any women 5'8" or over to come, but doubted that anyone would. "However, about forty of them came," she said, "and it was great. We all just stood there, looking at each other eye-to-eye, and discussed such things as short men and short women." She felt that "in some ways, short men want tall women. It's almost as though they feel they can borrow your height. We exchanged experiences and met once a week."

Enterprising students found many things to do. Thomas Berson (1967) said "some people complained that there was nothing to do in Oswego, but Oswego is at Crossroads U.S.A., a hub of transportation, and before the ice cometh there is usually a ship or two tied up somewhere in the harbor." He also suggested reading the local newspaper, *The Palladium-Times*. Some students did indeed capitalize on Oswego's lakeside location. In April 1967, five of them hiked to the Oswego Port Authority, "just under the shadow of the guns at Fort Ontario" and went through a freighter from Ghana, Africa, called "The Bean Boat."[20]

Students generally, including the more innovative, were avid consumers of films and music. Many films were created by the young for the young and so-called underground films found their way to campuses. Music was very popular and most college students had a guitar, hi-fi set, or tape recorder. The music idiom of the times included country and western music, folk rock, soul, and hard rock; the music represented the soul of the the counterculture movement. Young America, via television, in effect shared the Woodstock rock festival attended by 300,000 young people. Rock music was the expression of "revolt against the sham of Western culture; it was direct and gutsy and spoke to the senses; and it attacked the war, middle-class values, even the PTA."[21] Rock music symbolized the search by young people for authenticity, rejection of authority, and distrust of tradition.

Much of the same could be said of Oswego students' lifestyle and mood. Older students remained somewhat traditional in tastes, but a majority dressed in jeans, had tape recorders, and swayed to rock music. A very few— vastly fewer than at Berkeley and other places—wore love beads, unisex garments, and high boots or no shoes.

The student culture had become increasingly pluralistic by the late 1960s, with different groupings having their own diverse causes and ways of life to espouse. Campuses differed among themselves and from one part of the country to another but there was an underlying theme of anti-tradition and anti-establishment.

Even fads reflected that theme; streaking, or dashing *au naturel*, in a public arena was among the stranger fads. Don Harrison said it was reported incorrectly that he had cruised about the campus on his motorcycle minus clothing. An earlier fad, in 1969–70, was tie-dying. "You took a shirt," explained Debbie Roe, "tied it together, and dunked it into dye. When you took it out, part of it was dyed, and part had white lines where the dye didn't get to it, and it came out in crazy patterns. You did it to jeans and you did it to shirts. We took all of my roommate's underwear one night and dyed it purple for her. Another ridiculous fad in 1969 was calling everybody 'baby cakes'."

Some pranks are perennial, varying only in detail; others are mostly one-time occurrences. Doing something to Sheldon's statue is one of the Oswego perennial pranks. Someone placed this inscription on it in 1976: "My son, the day Albany straightens out our budget is the day I drop this apple." Making crank calls is another perennial prank. An *Oswegonian* editorial called "Spring Fever" pointed out that "phony bomb threats . . . have replaced the traditional panty raids as the spring thing to do at Oswego."[22] The editor pointed out that nothing can be done to stop the cranks, but one can only hope they [students] will grow up.

Other episodes are of the one-time variety, some unusual enough to record. In 1966, the actress Jayne Mansfield was performing at Three Rivers, and the men at Hillcrest Hall invited her to come to Oswego to be named their honorary housemother, never expecting a reply.[23] However, she did come to Hillcrest, heralded by shrill sirens and cuddling her two small dogs, Momsicle and Popsicle. Hillcrest president Joseph Alff (1966) presented her with a scroll, declaring her to be the men's honorary housemother. She, in turn, said she would try to be a good housemother, declaring "that we will now have a 5:30 A.M. curfew and champagne parties until 5:00 in the morning."

Crime was a much more serious aspect of campus life; events involving outside perpetrators were sometimes grim. In 1972–73, auto accidents, theft, and vandalism declined, but serious crimes rose slightly. Vandalism arose again in 1975, reaching an all-time high. By November 1975, seven large plate glass windows on academic buildings had been broken, each costing from $500 to $800.

The biggest concern regarding off-campus intruders was rape. In fall 1972, a Syracuse University coed had accepted a ride from a businessman, and disappeared. At the time, women students in Rogers's phychology class said they would more readily trust an offer of a ride from someone who had long rather than short hair, but the same question, posed in the late 1970s, brought the reverse reply. Two Oswego coeds who had been hitchhiking were raped at gun and knife point by two youths, ages seventeen and nineteen.

Various measures were suggested to prevent such crime. An *Oswegonian* editorial called for flood lights around such areas as the Campus School, the Learning Resources building, and the library, and others called for arming the campus police.

One relic of the macho era (early 1960s) was the panty raid, resurrected in spring 1968—in this case called "the lace riot," when clothing was taken as well as money and valuables. In a panty raid that fall, about 250 male students attempted to storm the women's dorm, while the women poured pails of water on the railing below. Men on the ground attempted to boost others up so that they could get in through the windows. However, this time their efforts proved futile.

Male reactions to the panty raids were mixed. John Berninger declared in a letter to the *Oswegonian* that American males had proved their masculinity in their panty raid at Cayuga and Funnelle Halls on May 13, 1968.[24] Females on campus now had no excuse for complaining about the decline and fall of the men students' masculinity. Other male students, in an open letter to President Perdue and the student body, called the raiders "perverts who rob the girls of clothing and other articles."

Two alumnae differ regarding the severity of male sexism in the early 1970s. Debbie Roe said that "a lot of the guys were beginning to question the idea of the male as head-of-household and the traditional marriage relationship. They were beginning to see marriage as a partnership, not with the male dominant. It was in keeping with this whole attitude of accepting people with different points of view and value systems." However, Peg Lowery said she hadn't found men "any less macho than formerly, in spite of all the protests in these hot years." She had seen no changes in the way men viewed women.

Greek life was an area in which change was indisputably real. Greeks were still big on campus in 1965, but their status was declining. The Beta House was gutted by fire in October 1966, and its shell "remained dark and lonely in the late evening sky." That same evening the Beta brothers gathered in the barn behind the Phi Sigma Phi house to eat a free meal donated by the owner of Buckland's Grill.

Nationally, several factors contributed to the Greeks' decline. Certain advantages of belonging to a fraternity, such as having opportunities to drink and entertain the other sex, disappeared as campus rules diminished. Also, the Greek lifestyle had its detractors. The film *Animal House* portrayed it as anti-intellectual, rowdy, and sometimes sadistic. An *Oswegonian* writer, Sam Waggoner, questioned the value of certain pledging activities which included "paddling, ingesting putrid concoctions, and other physical abuse."[25]

Interest in joining Greek Societies was rapidly eroding by 1970. A former president of the inter-fraternity council, William Stata (1969), said that students lacked interest in joining the Greeks because they were trying to find themselves. They were irked to see "groups of silly girls singing some idiotic song or around a bar to proclaim their togetherness." To survive, he suggested, Greeks must come to accommodate people who want to think and who have intelligence.

Another factor in Greek decline was the nationwide movement toward the leveling of society; cutting down the snobs. In 1966, student Joseph Alff deplored the Greek minority's seeming rule over the majority, noting they monopolized large portions of the school newspaper, special weekends, athletic events, and other school affairs. He declared in a letter to the editor of the *Oswegonian*, "The Greeks are dead."[26] In a reply a week later, William Tevendale (1968) argued that any group might try to gain a dominant position, and that if 93 percent of the students are ruled by 7 percent of the students and there is no general reaction, the majority must be satisfied.

On most campuses, Greeks numbered only about one in ten in the student body by 1973. The same picture prevailed at Oswego. However, here as elsewhere, a few more organizations began to appear. The first coed fraternity, previously Lambda Chi Delta, incorporated in 1973 on a trial basis and, by 1976, Oswego had eight fraternities and seven sororities.

Although the Board of Trustees had yet to lift its 1953 ban on national fraternities in SUNY institutions, by 1974 local Greeks were thinking of going national. The Greek organizations were exempt from the sex discrimination prohibitions that some feared would force groups to open membership to persons of the opposite sex, since these groups were neither professional nor the recipients of federal monies.

As for Greek life in the early 1970s, apparently the Greeks did some studying. In 1973 their average index was 2.78, with one house having a high cum of 3.2; the lowest was 2.3. Some houses had students who had earned 4.0 cums for the preceding semester. The Greeks also took part in money-making and community projects, including calendar sales, vaudeville night, Greek games, and charity projects such as the cancer drive. Social affairs were also a very important part of Greek life. They had two semiformal or formal parties a year, as well as frequent mixers with other Greek organizations or dormitory floors.

One important factor in the success of a Greek organization was whether or not it had a house; all those at Oswego either owned a house, or were renting or buying one. Having a house reduced room and board costs, which averaged $951.28 annually for sorority members and $782.44 for fraternity members, compared with dormitory costs of $1,270. The houses also provided a familylike atmosphere, open kitchens for eating whenever one wanted, soda machines, laundry rooms, telephones, and a party room. Some of the frat houses had pool tables; most had cable TV; the majority had cooks; and some had cleaning help. Ordinarily, enough people in the house had cars to provide everyone transportation to and from campus. The one disadvantage was not feeling quite in the campus mainstream and therefore feeling somewhat isolated.

Neither Greeks nor non-Greeks could be said to conform to the image of "the college student," for students had become increasingly diverse. One rapidly multiplying variety was the older student, and undergraduates older than age twenty-five numbered almost 500 by 1976–77.

Older students have always said that returning to school was well worth the effort, but there are problems.[27] On one hand, they lack the opportunity for interaction supplied by traditional dorm situations. On the other, David Emerson (1977), a 25-year-old philosophy junior, found that dormitory life required major adjustments. "It brought me back to a mentality that I'd been away from for a long time. However, everyone in education should be forced to live in a dorm just to see where the students are coming from." Kathy Johnson (1977), taking a regular course load at age thirty-five, agreed with Emerson. "One of the main things about being an older student is being completely outside the mainstream of college life." Johnson, who had been a secretary, knew that if she was ever going to advance, she should have a degree.

Helen Hicks entered college as a business major for the first time at the age of forty. "I was a little afraid," she said, "that when I went into the group of young people I would be a little intimidated. It was completely the opposite. They were the ones intimidated by the class situation. When you've been bumped around a few times and you know that people won't bite, you're not afraid to ask questions. Indeed, older students are more likely to speak up in class discussions; and they find themselves motivated more by a need to accomplish than to compete." A twenty-six year old, David Hickey (1977), said, "I used to get upset about tests, but not anymore. I know I'm going to pass and I don't pull all-nighters."

Special strains are involved for married women with children. Ann Robson (1977), age thirty-seven, portrayed her life as "rushing through dinner, arranging for a babysitter, trying to study in between a child's chickenpox and bronchitis, trying to maintain some semblance of family and social life similar to pre-college days, and putting up with put-downs on the holiday cocktail circuit."

Robson suggested an orientation program for the part-time returning students, including a review of registration procedures and techniques for library use. Another common request among these older students was for adjustments in course offerings and scheduling, many of them would have liked weekend and evening courses. Another need was a particular place where they could meet to discuss their situations among themselves. On the other hand, none of them wanted to give up their contacts with younger students. Ann Robson said, "I want to shout at griping younger students who can't see that their chance to get an education the first time around is something to be grabbed and lived to the full." But she added, "They've kept me from becoming an entrenched thirty-seven year old."

Blacks, who, like older students are a distinct minority on campus, gained special attention after the black movement of the 1960s. The Black Student Union (BSU) was initiated in fall 1970, funded by the Student Association, to educate people regarding black culture and to establish a black community at Oswego. Perhaps as a result of the women's movement, in 1973 all officers of the BSU were women. Two years later three minority groups on campus formed a coalition: the Black Student Union, the Latin Student Union, and the Native American Brotherhood. Its purpose was to increase the minorities' power and spirit of community; however, the minorities' response was not enthusiastic.

The blacks' column in *The Oswegonian*, "Uhuru Sasu," pinpointed a variety of issues. One was a protest against blacks going to Vietnam, partly because nonwhites typically had been exploited by "white imperialists."

Other issues concerned the performance of lobotomies on black prisoners, voting rights, unjustified arrests, and equal-education opportunities. A national profile of black youths in 1971 indicated that almost 90 percent would work full time if necessary to stay in college, and 80 percent wanted to help blacks. However, at this time they feared President Nixon would cut back programs that helped them attend college. An *Oswegonian* editorial expressed concern for black faculty and student recruitment and retainment. It noted that Dr. Patti M. Peterson, who became affirmative action officer in 1972, was supposed to deal with such matters but that it was important "to find out whether or not this office is serious or just an office that sounds appealing but does not produce."[28]

The blacks also wanted to spruce up their image and show that indeed "black is beautiful." In April 1970, the Black Student Union sponsored a Black Week to give people more understanding of problems facing them and to promote black cultural and intellectual achievement. In a Uhuru Sasu article called "Black Messiah . . . Jesus Is a Black Christ," Elijah Beamon (1973) observed that "Christ has been personified as a blue-eyed honky. Black people need to dehonkify him and thus make him relevant to the black condition. He becomes the essence of blackness."[29]

Individual blacks disagreed about their treatment at Oswego. Two in five, mostly female, experienced no unusual pressures; the males had mixed feelings.[30] One might be "branded an Uncle Tom in that he had abandoned the blacks and joined the whites." Most of the males "felt more indifference than anything else." However, a small majority (60 percent) "felt the social pressure which stems from the fact that blacks aren't considered in the mainstream in programming social activities." About 25 percent had "losers' attitudes" in social life and were hermits.

Certain individuals questioned the effectiveness of the blacks' efforts. In a 1973 issue of the *Oswegonian*, there was controversy over whether the "Uhuru Sasu" columns said something or nothing. Another article noted that "the dominant white culture manipulates and restricts social events to the white perspective." At the time, with just three minority representatives in the Student Association Senate, "it is next to impossible to institute liberal and broad-minded policies." The college tavern had two minority student employees, but "their status is one of mere tokenism."[31] The Black Student Union is the only organization where minority groups are capable adequately of expressing their views. Overall, it was concluded that black participation had increased at Oswego, but the effect was slight; yet, despite this note of pessimism, some progress was being made.

Winsome Tulloch (1975), the first "sister" to head the BSU, believed that blacks should be more political on campus. In particular, the campus should have more black students, more black faculty, and recognize that whites are unlikely to take the initiative for blacks because they are white-oriented.[32]

Another campus group, the gays, was also a product of the 1960s rights movements. The Gay Brothers and Sisters of Oswego was organized in 1971 by Thomas Phillips, former history instructor and campus minister. These students reported considerable harassment both on the campus and in the city. Because three gay friends lived on a particular floor it was called "the gay queer floor," and they received obscene phone calls. In town, a bartender avoided serving a certain gay and later barred him from coming to that establishment. However, the gays did receive "quiet support" from administrators and the Student Association, although they were allowed the smallest budget of any student group funded.[33] One student declared in the *Oswegonian* that "gay brotherhood and sisterhood is not only powerful, but inevitable."

Another special category, the so-called hippies of the 1960s, represented rebellion against such values as materialism, overconformity, and oversophistication. Some Oswego individuals were, at the very least, borderline hippies, and most of the students reflected some of their influence. Writing in the *Oswegonian*, Richard Galloway concluded that "people will someday consider the hippies more than just unwashed, unshaven, shoddily dressed trouble makers. They are concerned individuals 'not content to sit back' and simply put up with the foibles of society."[34]

The nation's students may also be categorized according to their religious views; however, a large majority, three in four, were alike in asserting a belief in God. Almost 40 percent of the total said the college experience had caused them to question some aspect of their faith, seniors twice as often as freshmen. There were far more atheists and agnostics in the private nondenominational schools than these figures indicate and far fewer unbelievers in the church-related schools. The chief observable change in religion at Oswego was the appearance of fundamentalist groups. These students were and still are very devout, often carrying much-used Bibles around with them. They remain close to each other, and limit romantic attachments to others of their "one true" faith. Although committed in principle to spreading the word, only a few actively proselytize other students.

Vietnam veterans represented still another special group on campus. Most had unpleasant recollections of the war, but all said the overall impact had its positive side. A Veterans' Affairs Office functioned on campus from 1974 until 1976, when federal funding for it ceased. Like their predecessors of World War II, veterans took their classwork very seriously, ignoring the so-called "campus life."

The control center, or focal point, of campus activities was the Student Association (SA). It handled the activities fees ($64 for each student annually) which paid for such diverse organizations as collegiate athletics, the Women's Crisis Center, the Karate Club, and the Folk Dance Association.

The Student Association also funded the Student Association Volunteer Ambulance Corps (SAVAC), the only one of its kind in the nation. It began operations on January 8, 1972, and provides both on- and off-campus students with first aid and transport in case of medical emergencies. In one case, SAVAC responded to a call from Niagara Mohawk Power Corporation when a crane at one of its construction sites dropped a steel beam, injuring two workmen and fatally wounding a third. In another accident, in 1974, a Pathfinder dining hall employee climbed inside a commercial dishwasher; not knowing he was there, another worker turned on the machine. SAVAC saved his life.[35]

The college was heavily dependent on student funding for services, a fact fully appreciated by the students. An *Oswegonian* editor, Paul Murphy (1972), declared that "it is high time that the officials of this institution woke up to the fact that without the Student Association this college would be a mess. Without it and student fees there would be a lack of entertainment for an entertainment-hungry student body."[36]

Robert Rock, dean of students, was well aware of the students' access to funds. He explained that physical examinations for birth control and distribution of contraceptives were halted on campus in 1975 because other areas of health care, mandated by the state, had to receive priority. Dr. Rock said that the only alternative was for the Student Association to apply its own funds for such a program.

Students differed regarding how well they thought the Student Association handled their funds and affairs. In the *Oswegonian*, Bill Zystynaik (1973) called on students to "criticize, bitch, compliment . . . let us choose the path of activism."[37] Some students did just that. David Leonard (1974) noted student government's progress toward "phenomenal maturity" and observed that "the short-sighted luxury of violent protest and misguided allocation of funds has all but disappeared." However, two months later, Leonard compared the Student Association Senate's performance to that of a circus, with its "vicious fighting, parliamentary acrobatics and proverbial masturbation of egos."[38]

In 1970, the Student Association Senate voted to join the Student Association of State University (SASU), paying a membership fee of $3,000 appropriated from the legal aid fund. The services SASU provided (and continues to provide) included a lobby in Albany to present student opinion on matters coming before the State Legislature, SUNY and the Board of Trustees, a forum for student government leaders to discuss common problems, and a research organization for assembling information for use by student governments on particular issues.

In the meantime, the campus news media, also funded by student fees, were making news. In November 1968, the *Oswegonian*'s first full-color photograph pictured the founder's statue in front of Sheldon Hall. In January 1976, Oswego's literary magazine, the *Great Lakes Review*, received a $100 third-place award from the Coordinating Council of Literary Magazines.

Another student publication, *The Pendulum*, was controversial. An *Oswegonian* editorial supported its funding because "it would be a grand show of narrow mindedness . . . if, just as the creative writing program at SUNYCO was finally blossoming into what it should be, *The Pendulum* were killed." However, not all students supported *The Pendulum*. Peter Bernhardt (1974) declared that the *Pendulum's* office "looks like an extremely large and messy Andean condor had made its nest inside and hadn't bothered to clean up after the mating season."[39]

Reflected in student publications, at Oswego as elsewhere, were the traditional anxieties associated with college life: grades, money, peer approval, and sex. The pill became common in the 1960s, although it is uncertain how much it was used by students in those days.

Campus attitudes toward unwanted pregnancies changed dramatically over the years. In the college's earlier days pregnancies went unnoticed because unlucky girls simply left campus before their condition showed. If they remained until it did show, unmarried mothers-to-be were summarily dismissed. In the late 1960s, however, students often attended classes until their pregnancies were far advanced. Debbie Roe said that in her first two years, 1969–71, the topic of pregnancy was still hush-hush and abortion not yet legal. "Students were not rejected for getting pregnant or for having an abortion or having a baby out of wedlock, but arranging abortions was still an underground type of thing done mostly through the help of the clergy. It wasn't talked about as openly when I was a freshman as it was by the time I graduated. By then abortion was legalized and contraception was spoken of more openly and was far more available." Peg Lowery added that in her senior year, 1973–74, the infirmary quit offering the Planned Parenthood program so everyone went to one in Syracuse.

The college provided only three professional staff members in 1965 to help students with their personal affairs, including pregnancy. After this time, mental and physical health services grew rapidly and included the Mary Walker Health Center, the Farnham Youth Development Center for drug crisis intervention, a day care center, a Women's Crisis Center, and a totally confidential Psychological Counseling and Consultation Center. A series of seminars regarding sex and related problems was another resource. In his 1973–74 annual report, Perdue noted that 53 percent of the letters from student readers of a Michigan State University psychiatrist's column asked questions about sex; similar statistics were found at Oswego.

The health services were comprehensive and provided special help in emergencies. In December 1976 the Health Center arranged an on-campus mass vaccination of over 4,000 people because of the swine-flu scare. Reactions were mixed—some people feared the shots more than the flu. The Health Center had suspended most gynecological services by 1975, including examinations for birth control devices because of the budget situation, a cut protested by feminists on campus and by the Oswego Women's Center.

An *Oswegonian* editorial, "Students' Needs Ignored," noted that "pregnancy testing is permitted on campus, though funding is denied for birth control. It's a cheap political move to sidestep the real issue of family planning. . . . SUNY Central is dictating morality to its students just as oppressively as it did during the early 1960's."

Another service, initiated by Patti M. Peterson, was a mentoring program whereby women students could become acquainted with faculty women and administrators. Special events included cross-country skiing for students and faculty, a mothers-and-daughters program and a "Five Lives" panel discussion, in which five quite different women discussed their personal and professional lives. The aim was to demonstrate to young women various alternatives open to them, in contrast to those available several decades ago. The program focused on the all-female Johnson Hall residents.

The establishment of the Women's Crisis Center was one outcome of the women's movement. The center provides such services as a 24-hour hotline referral, birth control courses, abortion referral, and help with special problems. The Women's Center also maintains the Matilda J. Gage Library, the largest public collection of material by, for, and about women in New York State. The Rape Crisis Center was a corollary service, established chiefly to give rape victims and their families immediate help, as well as follow-up counseling. In its first year of operation the center had six calls from rape victims, whereas the Oswego Police had received only one.

Students were not only recipients of, but also dispensers, of services, often in the larger community. In the college's Adopt-a-Grandparent Program, begun in 1974, grandparents were adopted by teams of two students each. Members of a sorority would meet with their grandmother each week and, on special occasions, entertain her for dinner at their house. Prior to her adoption, one grandmother had called a local agency often, expressing her needs, but, since adoption, had not called once.

Students also helped in drives to conquer various diseases. In 1966, using as their theme "Stop: Help Pave a Road Against Cancer," and wearing their Greek letter society blazers, hundreds of students marched from the top of the hill down West Bridge Street to a bandstand beneath the American Cancer Society Office in town. When they set out, they began unrolling a mile of paper symbolizing paving a road against cancer and they continued laying the paper all along the march. The college received widespread attention through Hank Bonn's mile-of-money jingle. At the request of state and national units of the American Cancer Society, the jingle was recorded for use in their campaigns.

Several years later, in 1973, the local environmental group, Ecology Action, asked Oswego students for help in a trash-a-thon, a combination cleanup day and fund-raising drive. Sponsors promised to donate to Ecology Action anywhere from 10¢ to 50¢ for each bag of trash collected by an individual on Trash-a-thon Day.

Other community services for which students volunteered were highly varied. These included helping handicapped children in swimming and gym work; being involved with the Big Brother, Big Sister program and the Oswego Teen Center; and providing entertainment for residents of extended care facilities. Students also became involved in county social services, the probation department, and even the family court, sometimes working as interns in certain agencies.

Town–gown relations could not always be painted in such rosy hues. Students and townspeople became embroiled in zoning disagreements in 1973. Students reported occasional and unnecessary harassment. Five male Oneida Hall students, arrested by an off-duty policeman when hitchhiking toward campus, had to put up bail and one was jailed. The community housing controversy flared again in 1975. At a public hearing, charges were made of maintaining dormitory-type residences in the city of Oswego, virtually an attack on the college's off-campus students.[40] The charges were based on a city ordinance which indicated that a dormitory situation existed when six or more unrelated people shared common kitchen and hygienic facilities. One man argued that "young people and old people lived in different worlds. We are in danger of being overcome by this type of dormitory housing on First Avenue." Another specifically argued against "those kids playing football in the street and blocking traffic, and 'revving up' motorcycles." Even when it was pointed out that on-campus housing was very tight, one individual argued that the college should provide on-campus housing and if it weren't possible, "let them live in Oswego's landfill."

Just as town–gown problems vary with the times, so do reasons that students go to college, or to any particular college. Nationally, in the 1970s, men no longer entered college to escape the draft, and the proportion of women entering continued to rise. Yet, unlike earlier women, they were no more academically diligent than men. Locally, both sexes gave highly varied reasons for coming to Oswego.[41] Shep Narkier (1976) said the various materials the college had sent gave him the feeling it really wanted him to come. Jeffrey Greenberg (1977) and Wayne Gould, both in business administration, said they were accepted by other colleges but came to Oswego because they believed it was the best of the SUNY colleges. Karen Steiger (1975), secondary education major, believed Oswego would help her get a job because of its name in the field of education.

Fifteen thousand students applied for entrance in fall 1975. Robert Schell, associate dean of students, asked thirty-two of those accepted why they had chosen Oswego. Their top priority was academics: the high academic standards, the courses of study offered, and Oswego's reputation. The next most important factors were the scenic location and social life.

Having chosen Oswego, students soon learned the local traditions.[42] One bit of local folklore is that students should wait a specific number of minutes for teachers who are late for class—longer for a professor with a Ph.D. than for an instructor without. Most campuses also have a traditional way of recognizing a virgin: "Statues stand up or speak as she walks by; fixed gates close; stone animals twitter and roar; paintings and statues or angels blow horns and flap wings." At Oswego, "the apple will fall from Sheldon's hand (on the Sheldon statue) when a virgin graduates." (Of course, the object Sheldon holds is not an apple.) A large boulder on the SUNY-Potsdam campus presumably will split when the first virgin graduates; at Russell Sage College in Troy, New York the statue of a minuteman, under the same circumstances, will fire his musket.

The Greek houses with their close-knit groups and rituals often contribute to campus folklore. All Oswego alumni can recall the colorful fraternity tradition of painting the elk statue in front of the Elk's Lodge on West Bridge Street. At the Phi Omicron Xi fraternity house on West Cayuga, Eugene, the resident ghost, is the reason for the disappearance of objects and the various maladies that befall the century-old house.

There are also other folktales. These range from LSD (Lakeside dysentery) to the troll on the Seneca bridge. There are nuns in Cayuga Hall, pigs in Riggs, and prudes in Johnson. A colorful Seneca foyer mural depicts the friendly flying man who was created by an eccentric ledge walker, who delighted in startling late night pedestrians by yelling down at them from his precarious and highly illegal perch, seven stories above the ground. It is, of course, common knowledge that a male toothbrush in a female dormitory constitutes cohabitation.

Graffiti, typically created by anonymous persons, are among the various types of written folklore. Very often the graffiti writer is venting certain repressed feelings without revealing his or her identity. Common social slogans have been found on Oswego's walls, such as, "God is dead," "Black Power" and a Watergate favorite, "Nixon had a staff infection." In 1966 one might have found the following in Wilbur Hall: "IA is the spice of life" and "In the beginning God created IA." The oldest graffiti joke on campus is a wall sign with this instruction: "Do not write on walls, signed J. Perdue." There are also references to local weather conditions: "Where are the snows of yesteryear?"; and to academics: "Who knows where psychology grows?" One ambitious graffiti writer stamped out a message in one-hundred-foot-high words, about a quarter of a mile in length, using the frozen surface of Glimmerglass Lagoon as a tablet. The comment was too crude to be quoted but might be remembered for the scope of its creator's energy.

When asked what students prefer most about Oswego, they most often named friendliness and its location by the lake. Debbie Roe remembered one of Oswego's famous sunsets. "I will never forget it until the day I die. We were all on the west campus on the bluff watching this particularly beautiful sunset. Hundreds of people were out there. The bank was packed—the whole grassy bluff. People talked for a while, but when it came close to being sunset they were quiet; and when the last bit of sun had sunk below the horizon, one person—God knows who—began to clap, and the whole group, a couple of hundred people, stood up and applauded the sunset. It said so much about the world, and the humanness in it, and really appreciating what was around. Whether you believed in God in terms of going to a formal organized church or not, it was something we all shared in common—and that was one of my moving spiritual moments while I was here."

Unfortunately, the lake has also accounted for occasional tragedies. In the spring of 1968, an Oswego student, Wilbur Dean Yockey, and two friends drowned while attempting to navigate a homemade raft made chiefly of barrels. The raft disintegrated. All three men died.

President Perdue spoke of Oswego's widely recognized characteristic of friendliness. "Except for perhaps six years during the Vietnam War, the campus was very friendly. The students would speak to you and smile; and when you'd meet them in the student union or someplace they'd come up and talk." When asked whether the severe winters made students feel closer to one another, Perdue said, "It's [friendliness] partly because they're mostly from smaller communities where people tend to be more friendly and open. As for the hard winters, any time you get in a situation which places people close together, they either develop friendships or hostilities, and our students tend to develop good friendships."

In the country generally, loyalty to particular institutions had diminished by the 1970s, partly because many individuals changed colleges or dropped out before graduation. Both circumstances reflected an increasingly mobile society. Transfers from one college to another had also become far more common. In contrast, many Oswego students reported a strong school spirit. Despite the size of the student body, said Debbie Roe, "I felt like an individual, and that individuality came from every direction—from faculty, student personnel, administrators. It came from people who waited on you at the book store, everywhere I went. That's something that's really different about Oswego. Whenever I meet people who graduated from Oswego, we always speak positively of it; that always comes through. At Oswego, you were treated as a person. You didn't get form letters with Xeroxed signatures: they would be personally signed. That was not the case among friends I had in other institutions. After I graduated, I taught at a small college that prided itself on individual attention, but its faculty was less caring; students received less personal attention than at Oswego. And I'd hold my academic credentials and college experience up to theirs any day."

Because of such institutional loyalties, graduation exercises are normally sober, nostalgic occasions. However, at several institutions in the spring of 1970, including the University of California at Berkeley and Boston University, formal graduation ceremonies were canceled; and at many institutions these exercises became "less an academic celebration than a vehicle of social protest."[43] At small Wilson College in Pennsylvania, the seniors flourished placards of black shrouded skulls in protest against the Vietnam War before the guest of honor, Mamie Eisenhower.

Oswego's exercises proceeded normally, except for a few disruptions. In 1968, said Don Harrison, "we had a flasher. He was wearing his God-given suit under that robe and let everybody know about it." It was a funny time. A 1974 *Oswegonian* editorial protested graduation exercises as a requirement for receiving a degree, claiming that commencement itself could not seriously be claimed to improve one's mind.

Even before graduation, students begin to worry about job prospects. One observer noted that "the legendary tower of learning is not a stable structure: it is buffeted by the high winds of exam periods, by the gales of preprofessional competition; it shakes with the constant underground rumblings of adolescent cries of: "What shall I be? What shall I do? Will I succeed?"[44] Sometimes the tower sways so the student on top "sees his future in a heap of broken bones and ivory rubble."[44] Every student has his or her own means for coping with particular panics.

The employment situation was grim across the country in the 1970s. An article in *U.S. News and World Report* in 1970 declared that "jobs no longer are hunting graduates—graduates are chasing jobs," and students must be prepared for "a rude awakening. . . . Employers, after a five-year scramble for college-trained youths, are in a position to pick and choose this year." Job demand was strong for graduates in accounting, chemical engineering, computer science, marketing and finance, and secretarial work.[45]

Since it was difficult to find jobs, many Oswego students decided to go on to graduate school, or change career objectives. Growing numbers were going on to law and medical schools, or shifting to social work, or journalism, and other walks of life. Many took whatever jobs they could find, often unrelated to their area of specialization.

These former students had now become full-fledged alumni, with their own increasingly effective Alumni Association. For years its president was Hilda Guy Bohall; in the mid-1950s Robert Helsby served as president. It was not until 1973 that a full-time director of alumni relations, Robert Sweeney, was hired. Steve Sucher, Richard Collins and Patricia Ruppert followed. Margaret Lowery became the Executive Director in 1983. This more formalized operation allowed a better follow-up of graduates. In a 1976 random sampling survey of alumni, 46 percent of whom were elementary education majors, 86 percent were very satisfied or somewhat satisfied with their present employment, and the average salary was $14,000 a year. While students, 85 percent had not changed majors; 72 percent were satisfied with their current salary level.

The *Alumni Bulletin*, edited by Denise Harrigan from 1979 to the present time, helps keep in touch with graduates, some of whom have gone to other countries. One alumnus it reported on, Navy pilot Lieutenant John Crawford, a 1960 alumnus and president of the Oswego student assocation, was killed in Vietnam when on a harbor patrol assignment. Another alumnus, Thomas Oertel (1973), a biology major, worked first in Alaska and then in eastern Turkey. Dr. Victor Ripp and his wife Joan were among a group of educators admitted to the People's Republic of China in 1976 to study the culture and educational system. Gloria Greenfield (1974), an ardent feminist, had been co-founder of Women for a New World, the campus's first radical feminist organization. She also was co-founder of the Oswego Women's Center, editor of women's news for the *Oswegonian*, and creator of "Unchained," a feminist radio program aired on WRVO. Later, Greenfield became one of the founders of the Persephone Press, a radical feminist publishing house. She was named by *Ms.* magazine as one of the women to watch in the 1980s.

At least two of the 1970s alumni worked for a time with animals. Oswego alumnus Richard Rombach (1974) spent the summer of 1974 in Africa under the direction of Dian Fossey, colleague of the famed Jane Goodall, who had spent several years of her life studying gorilla life. Rombach helped Fossey in her studies of the mountain gorilla, especially with regard to mother–infant behavior. Debra Goldman (1975) became a groom for the famous racehorse, Seattle Slew, working for his trainer, Billy Turner.

Other alumni of this period have distinguished themselves in writing and the arts. Jean Miller became one-half of the Boston Symphony Orchestra's publication department. She has named Arthur Fiedler one of the most remarkable men she has ever met, who regaled her with stories on one occasion when they were caught in traffic for three hours. Alice McDermott (1975), author of *A Bigamist's Daughter*, published by Random House, credited her success as a writer to Dr. Paul Briand. "I couldn't be happier about her book if I'd written it myself," observed Briand.

Often alumni return to campus to look up former professors. In 1973, alumnus Kenneth Auleta (1963), then executive director of the New York City Off-track Betting Corporation, spoke to Luciano Iorizzo's class on "The History of Organized Crime." Auleta had served as a Peace Corps instructor, was one of the founders of the *Manhattan Tribune*, and the campaign manager in Howard Samuel's 1970 bid for the New York governorship.

How can anyone say who, among Oswego's alumni, is most worthy of mention? Who is to say what makes a life most worthwhile? In a thought-provoking commentary, Francine Israelton Roth (1966) said she found the *Alumni Bulletin* depressing. She asked "if there isn't any Oswego graduate out there who has not earned a doctorate or become principal of his elementary school? Where are the people like me, divorced and disillusioned with teaching?"[46] She'd like to hear from classmates "who botched," and wonders whether people written up in the *Bulletin* "ever have toothaches or get traffic tickets." The present writer would like to add that among Oswego's numerous alumni there are thousands just as remarkable in terms of the kinds of people they are, and for accomplishments of equally genuine worth, as those who have been cited for various achievements. Certainly, Israelton Roth's comments are food for considerable thought.

8

A New Mission:
The Pursuit of Excellence

THE period of Virginia L. Radley's acting presidency and presidency, spanning the years 1976 until now, has been eventful worldwide. In 1976, Britain's Princess Margaret divorced Lord Snowden; Viking 1 failed to discover Mars; America celebrated its two hundredth birthday; and Jimmy Carter was elected president of the United Sates. It was also the year women were admitted to the service academies of the armed forces for the first time.

The years 1977–79 saw a mix of news, some tragic and much politically significant. In 1977 the United States agreed to give up the Panama Canal by 1999; 1978 was the year of President Carter's summit meeting with Egypt's Anwar Sadat and Israel's Menachem Begin; and, in 1979, Carter reestablished diplomatic ties with China. In 1978, religious fanatic Jim Jones led the mass suicide of 900 of his cult followers in Guyana; and the Love Canal in Buffalo was declared a contaminated area. Overseas, Pope Paul VI died after a fourteen-year reign and his successor John Paul I also died after just thirty-four days. The Shah of Iran was forced to abdicate in the year 1979; Margaret Thatcher became Great Britain's first woman prime minister; and Iranian students seized the American Embassy and fifty hostages. At home, the accident at Three-Mile Island nuclear power plant provided ammunition for the anti-nuclear forces; and gasoline was rationed on an odd–even date basis in some states, including New York.

Thus ended two decades of dramatic change: social upheavals in the 1960s and quieter struggles in the 1970s. In a very brief time, a somewhat homogenized mass society had splintered into many groups with widely differing values and tastes, thus becoming a decentralized society. One may recall "when bathtubs were white, telephones were black, and checks green," but "in today's Baskin-Robbins society everything comes in at least 31 flavors."[1] In short, America's melting pot had become a myth and cultural diversity a reality.

How might these years be evaluated? Of the 1960s, it may not be easy to view favorably a period during which the leading consumer item was the pet rock and one of the most common social experiences was waiting in line to buy gas. As for the 1970s, Zonker Harris, the flower child of the Doonesbury comic strip, lifted his beer mug in a toast to their passing—"to a kidney stone of a decade!"[2] On the other hand, these years had seen women and minorities gain a stronger sense of self and more power; technology had produced new wonders; and people sought core values which would help them cope with ever-increasing changes and cultural ambiguities. Religion revived, as did a mild countertrend toward traditionalism.

The 1980s emerged on a somewhat less newsworthy tone. The United States boycotted the summer Olympics in Moscow to protest Russia's ocupation of Afghanistan, a move American students protested. Mount St. Helen's erupted; Ronald Reagan defeated incumbent Jimmy Carter for the presidency; and a United States helicopter crashed while attempting to rescue American hostages held by Iran. The next year, 1981, saw a continuation of dismal economic news, strife between warring factions in the Mideast and Central America, and growing concern over the mushrooming federal deficit. The same concerns persisted in 1982, including heated debates over such issues as the environment, abortion, and the funding of social programs—especially Medicaid, Medicare, and Social Security.

The year 1983 focused on international affairs as the United States successfully invaded Grenada to prevent a Communist takeover; American Marines stationed in Beirut dismally failed in their peace-keeping efforts; and the United States failed to quell the civil wars in Nicaragua and El Salvador that few, if any, Americans really understood or cared about. Americans were more concerned about the horrendous United States debt, acid rain, and the breakup of AT&T (American Telephone & Telegraph Company). The overall trend was somewhat conservative, a backlash (depending on one's point of view) against the excesses of the late 1960s.[3]

In the meantime, fundamental social changes left their mark on higher education, such as the increasing numbers and types of students attending college. In 1939, just before World War II, only 6 percent of Americans had attended college compared with about 60 percent in 1986. Today, students come from all social, racial, and ethnic backgrounds.[4] "Pluralism," observed SUNY's Chancellor Wharton, "has become the single most significant feature of higher education over the last three decades; and this trend dictates diverse approaches in all areas of higher education including student life, admissions, and curriculum." Education has become a popular commodity, partly because it is perceived by many as the key to social and economic mobility. More idealistic people perceive its most important byproduct to be a "more active, better informed, more humanely oriented citizenry."[5] When intelligent decision making is badly needed, college graduates make better decisions about most areas of life than do the less well educated.[5]

These contrasting views of education are reflected in opposing approaches to its implementation. The masses demand higher education for all to ensure economic opportunities. They are abetted by those colleges having trouble attracting students because of the lower birth rate in recent years. In consequence, the 1970s saw artificially inflated grades in many schools, increasing vocational and professional emphasis, and the introduction of courses especially popular with students. Meanwhile, others were insisting upon a greater emphasis on quality education. Other countries, notably Japan, were challenging America's erstwhile role as the world's chief industrial power. The quality of education was being widely challenged, causing colleges to pause and take stock of themselves.

Assessments of the current situation vary at Oswego. Distinguished Teaching Professor Rosemary Nesbitt believes that critics have gone too far, that much of what they want is "trendy nonsense. People have simply jumped on the bandwagon." Nesbitt, a sometime historian, believes that "education has been part of the warp and woof of this country. We go through this from time to time: 'Let's get on the backs of teachers'." Provost Ralph Spencer is more tentative in his evaluation of higher education's current status. "It's a time of transition in this country, and it's a little uncertain about transition to what. We've come through some very difficult times."

What course, and with what effectiveness, higher education will take will depend to a significant degree on college presidents. A national study concluded that the easiest way to change a college was to change the leader. Change occurs with each new president, for better or for worse. According to "the great man" or "the great person" theory of academic reform, faculties may try to make changes, but they almost always fail without help from above.[6]

However, all too few presidents today are the caliber of leaders prepared to lead us from the wilderness. "It's hard to remember the names of even the major institutions' presidents," observed Oswego's President Radley. "You have a hard time matching most present-day college presidents with such former greats as Nicholas Murray Butler [Columbia] or Sarah Gibson Blanding [Vassar College] or William Harper [University of Chicago]. These presidents were paternalistic, including the women. The women weren't maternalistic; they were paternalistic. They ran everything. M. Carey Thomas was one of the outstanding college presidents in the history of higher education. She supervised; she was interested in buildings; she went to Europe to select statuary for the library; and she handled the curriculum. That approach is not too popular today."

Perhaps the dearth of such giants can be charged to the changing role of presidents. During the 1920s, 1930s, and 1940s, there was little administrative teamwork; as noted above, one man or woman simply ran the show. Then, as colleges expanded and their operations grew more complex, team management became the rule and presidents less visible.

Despite this new approach, presidents are still held responsible and subject to many pressures. They face problems of budgets and funding, of faculties that protest administrative decisions, and of coping with statewide controls that limit the autonomy of units within the university system. In addition, the job is very hard work. Notes Oswego's David Glick, "The president is literally on call twenty-four hours a day. It is very lonely. Who wants to call parents and say that their son or daughter is missing? Moreover, people don't see the benefit of a leader's decisions because the results may not appear until long after they are made. Decisions are made for the long-term well-being of the institution."

Small wonder that their average tenure is just five years and that some presidents use their joint meetings mainly as a "wailing wall." "Some presidents can't hack it." said President Radley, "they can't stand the pressure. It's not the old Mr. Chips any more. Since I became president, I have seen twenty-three presidents in SUNY either resign or be replaced or go away or retire."

The mode of selecting presidents has also undergone change. A quarter of a century ago college trustees might "hand-pick a president with barely a nod toward faculty members or anyone else. However, since then, the concepts of "affirmative action" and "shared governance" have made the task of choosing presidents considerably more difficult. Searches now rely on faculty members, students, trustees, and others. Choosing a president is further complicated by the problem of deciding what kind is needed for a particular place and time. A college that has become "self-satisfied may need a mover and a shaker . . . while one that has experienced a period of turmoil may need a healer." It helps to develop "a presidential profile," but search committees are often "too idealistic and full of rhetoric."[7]

Oswego's current president, Virginia L. Radley, arrived in fall 1974, as provost and executive vice president, following several years in administration in private colleges and one year in Albany as SUNY's provost for undergraduate education. She became acting president in September 1976 when President Perdue began a study leave. Perdue returned on November 15, 1976, for two months and, upon his leave-taking of the presidency in February 1977, Dr. Radley was again named acting president. Following a nationwide search, she was named president and duly inaugurated on October 7, 1978.

SUNY's appointment of a woman president in 1978 was significant for at least two reasons. One, Radley was the first woman to head a unit of SUNY. Second, although over two-thirds of the presidents of women's colleges are women, fewer than a tenth in other colleges and universities are. Certainly, the event is rare enough to attract widespread attention, not always positive. Lewis Popham, dean of continuing education at Oswego, and a Radley admirer, said it was amazing the number of people he met on trips around that time who asked: "Will you be able to stand working for a woman?"

Women have faced a variety of barriers to achieving top posts in higher education, mainly the male networking process. Despite affirmative action, which has resulted in appointment of more female administrators, these women have had to "battle for acceptance in the male dominated academic structure."[8] Other barriers women face are lack of role models, male domination of boards of trustees, and discrimination or prejudice. In many ways, discrimination is even more damaging than before, because it has become more subtle. As a result, many women administrators are turning to other women for networking support.

The woman president's battle for acceptance is not over once she wins the job. She still faces deeply held doubts about women's new roles and the loneliness of being the token woman. In a survey of women presidents, 86 percent of the 168 replying said they often had to work twice as hard as men to obtain recognition and almost 89 percent said they had "less access to power" than men. Over half occasionally, or often, were ignored during important discussions—"they're treated as mother figures or sex objects, have difficulty establishing their credibility, and have less influence over decisions than men."[9]

"It is difficult for men to relate to women in positions of power unless they are very secure," noted President Radley. "Because of their own lack of confidence when dealing with a woman on an equal footing, they try to put you into the position of mother or wife or sister. A man relates first to his mommy, then to his sister, and then to his wife. How many female friends is a little boy encouraged to have? When he meets a professional woman, it is often a culture shock."

Certainly, Radley has experienced more than her share of controversies. One reason for controversy is her unwillingness to countenance slipshod performance or unprofessional behavior. In addition, she assumed command in a time of budgetary stress which required cuts in facilities and personnel. And perhaps some individuals could not easily tolerate a woman's calling the shots. Above all, certain critics simply had their own special axes to grind.

One persistent thorn-in-the-flesh individual stirred up a veritable hornet's nest of controversies over a five-year period, determined, for an unknown reason, to rout Radley from office. One such skirmish persisted for many months, intermittently refueled by flaming letters to the editor of the *Oswegonian* and passionate editorials, related to the use of the beach at Shady Shore, the president's home. Never mind that over the years the city had disposed of longer, more desirable stretches of beach, or that this area contained treacherous rocks and perhaps permanent pollution due to its next-door neighbor, the steam plant, or that the college had graciously offered the local citizenry the use of the shore a brief distance west. This short stretch of shore—pollution and all—said the critics, should become the townspeople's. None of these critics seemed to care a nickel about what effect such an invasion would have on the president's sanctuary where

Edward A. Sheldon
1861–1897

I. B. Poucher
1897–1913

James R. Riggs
1913–1933

Ralph W. Swetman
1933–1947

Harvey M. Rice
1947–1951

Foster S. Brown
1952–1963

James E. Perdue
1965–1977

Virginia L. Radley
1978–

Presidential portraits

Dr. Edward Austin Sheldon, founder and principal, 1861–1897.

Edward Austin Sheldon, who founded the College at Oswego as a teacher training school in 1861, is surrounded by the graduating class of 1897 together with the school's faculty.

Professor Caroline Scales teaches "The Merchant of Venice" in her English class at the Oswego State Normal and Training School, circa 1893. Note photographs of classical sculpture and architectural monuments, and examples of pottery.

The college's class of 1889, displays some examples of teaching aids used in Sheldon's "object teaching method." Among those identifiable teaching aids are geometric solids, a turtle shell, a globe, a clock, and dough or clay.

Shady Shore cottage was completed in 1858 by Edward Austin Sheldon, when he was superintendent of Oswego City Schools.

Camp Shady Shore, the most popular feature of early summer schools at Oswego. It was begun in 1919 as a tent colony. By the 1930s there were 21 cabins, six tents and a large trailer area.

Shady Share as remodeled from 1934 to 1941. Dr. Ralph Swetman, president from 1933 to 1947, restored the historical landmark with support from the Federal Works Projects Administration and the State of New York. Since its restoration, Shady Shore has been the official home of five presidents of the college.

Sheldon Hall, known until 1961 as the Main Administration Building, was built in 1911 at a cost of $340,000 and occupied two years later. It has been on the National Register of Historic Places since 1981. Taken out of service in 1983, the building is being converted to a hotel and conference center.

Construction of "new campus," with Lanigan Hall shown being built in 1966.

Hewitt Union was a mass of girders in 1966 as the "new campus" construction was under way. When it opened, it inherited the name of its predecessor, Hewitt Union, named for Jesse Merle Hewitt, the first Oswego student to die in World War I. The original Hewitt Union became Mackin Hall.

An aerial view of "new campus" as it appeared in 1974. The administration building and academic plaza are to the right of the photo, with residence halls and dining facilities at the left.

The late Dr. Paul Briand lectures in an English class of the early 1970s in Lanigan Hall.

A member of the Class of 1970 is welcomed to campus and given the traditional "freshman beanie."

Moving-in day for the class of 1970, in the fall of 1966.

Students wait to use the electric ski tow at Fallbrook Recreation Area in 1965. Operated by Auxiliary Services on approximately 150 acres of land three miles from campus, Fallbrook now features picnic facilities, a ski lodge, nature walks and cross-country ski trails.

Horseback riding, as in this 1962 photo, was available at Fallbrook Recreation Area until the 1970s, when it was discontinued due to economic constraints. Before it was acquired by Auxiliary Services, Fallbrook served as the Oswego City Poor House. The main building was constructed in 1898.

Dr. James E. Perdue, president of the college from 1965 to 1977.

Dr. Perdue visits with students on the shore of Glimmerglass Lagoon.

Dr. Virginia L. Radley, president of the college since 1978.

Dr. Radley shares her views with Dr. I. David Glick's communication studies class.

The International Relations Club in 1970. Front row, left to right, B. William, W. Bennett, and S. Strong. Back row, F. Arram, N. Francis, A. Horn, A Nader, D. Stork, R. Mageed, R. Galloway, and Mab Huang, adviser.

Black Student Union in 1970. A positive and strong presence on the Oswego campus in the 1980s, the Black Student Union was organized in 1970 to represent the opinions and interests of black students.

Students gather in the Hewitt Union snack bar in 1970.

Tyler Art Gallery, shown in 1978, houses about 18 art exhibits each year. The art exhibition program was begun in a gallery in Sheldon Hall in the late 1930s by Dr. Aulus Saunders, chairman of the art department from 1937 to 1970.

A member of the Class of 1970 unpacks in her dorm room on moving-in day, in the fall of 1966.

The statue of Edward Austin Sheldon, founder, completed and paid for through donations made by the school children of New York state in 1899. The bronze sculpture by John Francis Brines was placed in the state capitol building until 1922, when it was moved to Sheldon Hall on campus, first placed in the front hall and later in front of the building. Since the closing of Sheldon Hall in 1983, the statue has been cleaned, repaired and readied for relocation.

Students make the trek to their next classes in the fall of 1986.

"Sweet Charity," presented in 1984 at the Waterman Theatre in Tyler Hall. The musical was produced by the theatre department and directed by assistant professor of theatre Ron Medici.

Sorority members file past in a traditional homecoming parade of the 1960s.

At the "Phonie" awards celebration following the Alumni Association's Phonathon in 1986, Edith Maloney Knight of the Class of 1950 (left) and Margaret "Peg" Lowery, (1974) Director of Alumni Relations, express their gratitude for a successful phonathon which raised nearly $200,000 in pledges.

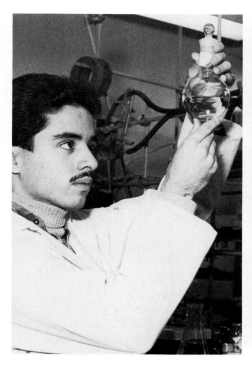

"Faces from the '80s"

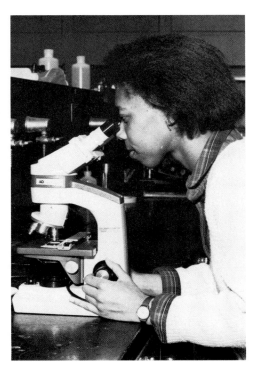

Student Louis Borrelli, a 1977 graduate of the college, works as an announcer at WRVO, the National Public Radio affiliate housed in Lanigan Hall.

Students in a typical class at the college in the 1980s.

A lake effect snowstorm blankets the campus.

The centennial class of 1961 graduates. To honor the college's 100th anniversary, several buildings were named and dedicated, an anniversary plate of Wedgwood china was produced, and the first volume of the college's history, "Oswego: Fountainhead of Teacher Education," was published.

The graduation procession begins opening the 1975 commencement at the college.

Ceremonial trumpeters, students in the music department, signal the opening of ceremonies at the 125th commencement, May 1986. Festivities in the college's 125th anniversary included fireworks, an anniversary ball, and a birthday party with cake and balloons.

Dr. Patti McGill Peterson, former vice president for academic services at Oswego, then president of Wells College, and now president of St. Lawrence University, delivers the address at the 1986 Honors Convocation. Organized by VEGA, the Women's Honorary Society, the annual Honors Convocation provides an opportunity for the public recognition of outstanding student achievements.

The poster that marked the 125th anniversary of the college depicts the statue of founder Edward Austin Sheldon which formerly stood before Sheldon Hall. The anniversary theme was taken from Ralph Waldo Emerson's essay, "The American Scholar."

visitors, many important ones from out of town or state, were officially entertained.

An even more absurd issue arose over the president's "low rental payments" for living at Shady Shore. Only one critic raised the issue, the gentleman referred to above, but he pursued it with all the vigor due a *cause célebrè*. He couldn't have picked a weaker one, since college presidents in general pay no rent and are accorded vastly more and larger 'perks' than those accorded SUNY's presidents. Nor did local presidents pay any rent until just recently. Besides, presidents are both unofficial and official hosts of the college, and their residence is a perennial "do-drop-inn" for both local and out-of-town dignitaries. Probably most presidents, weary of being on call around the clock, when off duty would much prefer staying in some less accessible retreat.

Another more legitimate controversy developed over the evacuation of Sheldon Hall. Many loyal alumni insisted the hall should, and could, be restored for sentimental reasons. After all, this building is the only one on campus, besides the president's residence, with deep historic roots. As noted earlier, it was dedicated in 1914, first called Lakeside, later Rushwood Hall, and finally Sheldon Hall. Alumni added an addition to the building in 1919, and students constructed sidewalks around it. A specialist was called in to arrange landscape around the building, including sunken Italian gardens in the rear. Other students built a pergola in 1926 to protect from the weather those students who had to walk from the trolley to the building. A contractor failed in the 1970s to properly repair the front steps, and two-thirds of the steps had to be closed in 1977.

To prevent the building's total demolition, Radley had it placed on the register of historic landmarks. However, despite her best efforts, the building had to be closed in 1983. Currently, the most likely and desirable scenario is acquisition of the property by a hotel chain; thus Sheldon Hall would become a handy place for campus visitors to stay.

In the meantime, the city decreed in 1983 that the old Welland Hotel, the long-time dormitory of early Normalites, should be torn down. Bricks and mortar have been falling on the public sidewalk, and the building is a fire trap. The owner protested and to date, 1984, the decrepit old structure still stands—barely.

Throughout these unpleasant fracases, Radley has steadfastly held firm to the course she believes right. Thus, she has maintained her professional integrity despite the unfriendly, often rude onslaughts of critics who had unfurled their banners and marched to the attack without a thorough investigation into the sometimes complex factors involved.

In no area is Radley one to be intimidated. Upon becoming president, she embarked at once on a program of developing new academic programs, improving student advisement, and developing better relationships between staff and students through a highly effective team-management operation. "A team approach is essential," she said, "for no one individual can do everything in such complex, complicated times. When I must be away from the college, someone else must be in charge. I can't be hovering over this college every minute with my personal eye on Edward Austin Sheldon's statue."

Provost Ralph Spencer has found working on Radley's team a highly rewarding experience. "Simply put, what it means is that we are less concerned with our individual roles as the dean of this or the VP of that, and more with being members of the administration, working together."

Radley's administrative style might be described as carefully thought out, vigorous, intelligent, and dedicated. She has been called controversial, mainly because she will not trade off a principle in which she believes for a critic's approval. All too often, she said, "administrators are laid back; they are more inclined not to rock the boat and to take a kind of non-stand on things. That is one reason public education hasn't progressed as far as it should, because the leadership hasn't been positive enough or vigorous enough."

When invited to be immodest and to identify her own most effective administrative talents, she said, "Every president has his or her forte, and mine is academics—I like to build monuments to the spirit and intellect. I am a combination of academician and doer; I am both a contemplative person and a person of action. You don't often find that combination in the same person. My greatest strength is that I think a lot, but I also make decisions. I am not indecisive—right, wrong, or indifferent. I make a decision, not always the perfect one."

Many people in a position to know applaud Radley's administrative style. Leyden Brown, prominent lawyer and long-time chair of the College Council, calls making her president "a master stroke. . . . She has a nice way of showing integrity at all times. She has a way of compounding what she has to say in good old horse sense—and she has that to a great degree." Professor Rosemary Nesbitt calls Radley "a fearless administrator who always pursues excellence. Nothing escapes her; she has her eye on the sparrow; she never misses a trick. She knows what is going on on our campus; and she is personally very thoughtful."

Since 1948, when the State University of New York became a reality, the local college operation has had to mesh with overall university planning and ground rules. This university is the world's largest, as well as the most geographically and academically diversified system of higher education. Its sixty-four units range from specialized colleges, such as the Fashion Institute of Technology, to four comprehensive research centers at Albany, Binghamton, Buffalo, and Stony Brook. Collectively, its campus properties equal one and one-half times the area of Manhattan Island. It has 374,000 students and offers degrees in 3,700 programs, ranging from agricultural technology to zoology. It awarded 65,000 degrees in 1981.

In its early years, Governor Rockefeller poured almost unlimited state funds into this newest of state universities and viewed it as the wave of the future—the Harvard-on-the-Hudson or the Berkeley-of-the-East. Although that vision was not realized, with its coordinated but decentralized institutions SUNY is a wave of the future in terms of its diversity. On individual campuses, said Chancellor Wharton, we are striving for "selective excellence."

Being a member of the SUNY family has its drawbacks. Oswego's Radley deplores the university's caste system with its hierarchies of university centers, arts and science colleges, and community colleges. She also regrets the "pie in the sky" approach to enrollments, the union approach to budget cuts (no budget cuts, period), and the "desperate wish to spend at any cost monetary savings from a single unit or agency."

"SUNY presidents have certain empowerments from the Chancellor," explained Radley, "but they control only 8 percent of their total budget; the rest is all allocated in advance." President Perdue said, "It makes you feel like a branch manager. I have paid more attention to the educational program because there's not much I can do about the budget. The current system constitutes a disincentive for good management. Our budget formula should have some reward system for those campuses which demonstrate high productivity, sound educational results, and substantial savings in areas such as utilities."

This desire for greater local autonomy is widespread. Hence, Senator Douglas Barclay introduced a bill in Albany, called Downstate "the Radley Bill," which would require giving individual colleges within SUNY lump-sum appropriations to spend as they see fit. He pointed out that, although college presidents are paid sixty to seventy thousand dollars a year, they control only about 8.5 percent of the college budget.

Among SUNY's chronic problems is the state's apparent discrimination in favor of the private colleges, in terms of defining mission and slicing of the state budget pie. Oswego's Associate Provost Richard Wheeler predicted that "there will never be anything remotely comparable in this state to Ohio State University or the University of Georgia, because of the private colleges and the mindless belief in New York that private is good and public is indiscriminately bad."

James Perdue, former Oswego president agreed: "There's an attitude that permeates the Board of Regents—you can document it by the actions they take—and which permeates the State Education Department, that the function of a public institution is to educate the poor and the less well-endowed mentally, while private institutions take care of everyone else. The privates would have the graduate programs and we would have few, if any. They would get the top 10 percent of high school classes and leave the rest for us. They tend to want us to be primarily vocational. All you have to do is look back and see how they prevented us for a long time from awarding A.B. degrees."

Even now, questions regarding SUNY's mission remain unresolved. The legislature, citizens, and politicians have not made up their minds about what the State University should be. Chancellor Wharton has asked repeatedly of various constituency and external groups, "What kind of state university do you want?"

William Scheuerman, political science professor and vice president of the local chapter of the Union (UUP), believes confrontation with the private sector should be avoided, because "all would suffer; yet money going to the private sector has been increasing at a faster rate than that to SUNY. The public doesn't know about it, yet has a right to know; but if we told them, the private sector would see that as an attack. This tactic would backfire politically—and the private sector is well organized. They have many alumni in the legislature and in key government positions. However, the Central Administration underestimates SUNY's potential. We have to wait until we produce more alumni."

Perdue estimated that "about seven years from now, SUNY and CUNY will have as many alumni out there as do the private colleges. Of course, one question is how much the alumni will identify with SUNY. If it doesn't mean anything to them they won't stand up for SUNY. For political reasons, we had better identify with SUNY. The chancellor suggested that we get into big-time athletics. It might be a risk, but it might be worth it in the long run."

There are problems involved in developing such an identification. "We haven't defined ourselves as a University," said Dean Barbara Gerber. "Some schools, for example, the University of California, have an overall identity, but SUNY lacks this common identity. The question is whether State University will merely remain a collection of regional institutions or develop a few truly outstanding ones that produce future Nobel Prize winners and secretaries of state."

SUNY's currently most pressing problem, inadequate budgets, can be charged in large part to its ill-defined status. "Our faculty–student ratios are too high and getting higher all the time," observed Radley. "There comes a point at which you cannot deliver quality education. We are not there yet, but it could come to pass unless the State of New York and its citizens make up their minds what kind of a state university they want. If they want a fifth-rate university, that is one thing; but if they want a decent one, which Rockefeller wanted and which the chancellors have certainly wanted, they have to realize the cost."

There are bright spots, especially from the longer term perspective.

Chancellor Wharton pointed out that, since the nineteenth century, large state universities, especially the land-grant colleges, have typically provided not only education but also technical services for small businessmen, farmers, and others. Because higher education began under private auspices, New York has not had a strong tradition in this area; however, SUNY can become a resource for solving transportation, economic, and other problems. Already, in some ways, notes the chancellor, "the University is ahead of its time. While some colleges—for example, the University of Chicago and the University of California—are decentralizing to meet the needs of students, particularly in urban areas, SUNY is already decentralized."[10]

The criticism that SUNY has overbuilt may also prove erroneous. The media, observed Wharton, persist in calling demography the determinant of university attendance "with the relentlessness of a masochist probing an aching tooth." However, the growth in enrollment of older adults will significantly offset such a decline. Moreover, shortfalls "will not affect different institutions . . . uniformly, though many policymakers are acting as if the projected decline, like St. Matthew's rain, falleth on the just and unjust alike."[11] Rather, "some campuses and types of campus may wilt or even wither; just a hardy few may flourish in a climate too severe for others. In any case, the crisis of shortfall will end; and before the next century, there will be a strong renewal of demands."[11]

To preserve diversity and recognize excellence, a multiphase rolling plan is projected, which would allow the university to evaluate resources, requirements, and program needs statewide. This plan embraces three levels of administrative action: deletions within each campus of programs of lower priority or declining enrollment; affiliations among units which allow "campuses to exchange programs for which there are insufficient student interest and institutional resources to maintain separate curricula; and reexamining, adjusting, and altering the primary purposes of entire campuses, based on state needs."

This plan is viewed mostly positively, but with some dissent. For instance, Radley believes some colleges should be closed, but that they will not be because of "political dimensions. With fewer colleges and the same money, we could do a first-rate job." Professor William Scheuerman admits that the plan is "bureaucratically rational, but irrational in the sense that diversity within individual colleges is lost; and it's crucial for young people to meet people of many different backgrounds who are studying different things."

Upon being questioned, all of a dozen or so faculty members believed that Oswego students' main identification should be with the local college rather than SUNY. "Unfortunately," said Radley, "there is something about the State University imprimatur that makes younger people identify with the university system more so than with an actual college. One of the reasons private colleges are able to raise more money from their alumni is that their alumni identify solely with the institution and not with some nebulous behemoth of a university." Associate Provost Richard Wheeler agreed, saying "a college education is a very personal thing. The important thing in the college experience is the development of relationships, especially with significant adults. Bigness is important in certain ways but that's not what you are going to identify with." Dean Barbara Gerber believes "it's hard to identify with anything as amorphous as SUNY. Most of us identify with a place, the geography as well as the psychology of the circumstance. Alumni's main loyalty is to the institution where they physically went to school and, in larger universities, perhaps to a particular college within them, or even to their departments." Industrial Arts professors Vernon Tryon and Charles Shoemaker believe that Oswego's current students, in contrast to earlier ones, identify more closely with the department than with the institution.

Regardless of how much or how little Oswego staff and students identify with SUNY, their fortunes are legislatively, if not emotionally, welded to it. After all, it is SUNY Central, guided by the chancellor, that formulates the overall framework, guidelines, and budgetary constraints within which local units must function. SUNY's fortunes, in turn, inevitably rise and fall in unison with changes in governors and legislatures—their diverse perceptions of higher education in general, and SUNY in particular.

At least currently, especially in these budget-stringent times, SUNY is fortunate to have as governor Mario Cuomo, who firmly supports education, and as chancellor Clifton R. Wharton, Jr. Wharton, a brilliant, sophisticated Harvard alumnus, who is also highly personable and empathic, has had a meteoric career. His prestigious appointments over the years, too numerous to name here, have included service on various presidential panels and missions in this country and around the world, and service as a trustee or director of the Rockefeller Fund, the Overseas Development Council, and the Carnegie Foundation. He is also a prolific writer and has authored some of the most perceptive analyses available of the current status and future directions of higher education. Before achieving SUNY's top spot, he was president of Michigan State University, which recognized his and his wife's notable contributions by naming a building for them. His wife, Dolores, is a distinguished individual of many accomplishments, including membership on boards of several corporations. SUNY could not have picked a more dedicated, talented first family to pilot it through these recent years of crisis and growth in higher education.

Locally, the college's president is advised by the College Council on many topics: review of the annual budget proposal, appraisal of student activities, housing, naming of buildings, and regulations for student conduct and safety. Members of the council represent the college to the community and the community to the college. Each member serves nine years, and terms are staggered so that as one new member arrives, another retires. The current members are Joan Fitzgibbons, chair and worker at St. Luke's Nursing Home, Oswego; Katherine Benedict, worker in Assemblyman Fink's office, Syracuse; James F. Grant, physician, Oswego; William H. Green, banker, Oswego; J. Sheridan Hillick, lawyer, Fulton; Michael Schell, lawyer, Watertown; John T. Sullivan, lawyer, Oswego; and Constance H. Timberlake, chair of the Department of Child, Family, and Community Studies, Syracuse University.

Former council chair and Oswego attorney Leyden Brown said that "the council's role should not be changed, and it would be dangerous to give it more power. Council members' task is laid out in the law, but they should add something of their own intelligence to the task, and of their own personality." Brown said it is important to have council members who have many friends in the area, who can also be made friends of the college, "for every college relies pretty much on its friends." He called Margaret Mansfield Richardson (1929) one of the finest council members the college ever had. His own greatest satisfaction in working with the college has been a "feeling that I have done my part publicly."

Richardson, council member from 1958 to 1980, was the 1978 recipient of the Distinguished Service Award of the SUNY Association of Council Members and College Trustees. This extremely popular and accomplished educator was nominated for the award, for which 250 council members statewide were eligible to compete, by former Oswego Council Chair Leyden Brown.

Another council member, Katherine Benedict (1965), was hand picked in December 1984 by Governor Mario Cuomo to become regional coordinator of New York's ombudsman program, a program he developed when secretary of state. "Ombudsman" is a Swedish term meaning "people's agent," in this context one who helps citizens understand and cope with any of their problems involving the government, such as taxes, welfare, zoning, or state agencies.

Since the college's centennial in 1961, with the support of SUNY Central, the local council, and Oswego's administration, the college physical plant has expanded greatly in size and is designed to care for at least 10,000 students. In 1937, a committee of the American Association of University Professors had advised that institutions should plan for periods of contraction, and that expansion not exceed what could be supported in periods of depression. However, there was no evidence in the 1960s, at Oswego or elsewhere, that such advice was heard by anyone. As a result, when enrollments stabilized, the perennial problem of maintaining an oversized academic plant developed.

Nevertheless, in this situation as in others, President Radley and her team have managed to do more with less. Former President Brown, among others, commented on how well kept the campus is. "Most campuses," noted Lynn Hemink, Vice President for Administration "have the attitude that all budgetary reductions should be made in nonacademic areas but here we try to provide a total life experience. This concept means that you maintain the entire environment, including the buildings. It doesn't make sense to focus all reductions on aspects of the campus outside the classroom. After all, the students live there twenty-four hours a day. As a result, the students themselves can take pride in their campus."

Hemink was asked why, as a way to save money, the college didn't have annual cleanup days such as were held before the 1950s, when all students and faculty spent one day annually repairing buildings and cleaning the campus. Each faculty member was in charge of a contingent of students, and at midday all had a big picnic. "We didn't have formalized types of unions on campus then," explained Hemink. "There are many legal ramifications to this sort of thing today. Now we deal with six different unions on campus; in the early 1950s there were none. Unions have their own prescribed work roles and they won't do anything that falls outside their role, and if a job is not in their own specification they won't do it."

"We could have a campus beautification day," suggested Dean James Wassenaar. "We could call off classes, say at noon, but it would have to be an all-volunteer kind of thing. Projects would have to be identified, and the unions would have to agree that it wasn't taking work away from someone else. But the questions is: How many of the faculty would actually get involved?"

When asked why the college hadn't explored the use of cheaper, alternative forms of energy, Hemink said, "We have, one idea being to use a federal grant to take water from the bottom of the lake at 40 degree temperatures, and pump it into the cooling towers of buildings that must be air conditioned. A plan to bring in waste heat from the Niagara Mohawk stacks was abandoned because of technological problems, and a wind machine would have to be so large as not to be financially feasible."

In the meantime, various actions have been taken to enhance the appearance and function of various buildings. Sculptor William King was invited to the campus in 1977 to create the fifteen-foot high sculpture, "Intermission," which stands in front of Waterman Theatre in Tyler Hall. In the Special Collections room of Penfield Library there are several pieces of furniture which originally belonged to Sheldon; these include a still-working grandfather clock. The most valuable of the historic collection are the many letters, documents, and pictures of the thirteenth president of the United States, Millard Fillmore, discovered several years ago by Charles Snyder, Oswego's retired history professor.

Under the direction of Nicholas D'Innocenzo, Professor of Art, art students employed in the summer of 1984 created colorful murals on campus buildings and began developing malls between them. The project for 1985 is a clock-tower sculpture.

Among other achievements was the establishment of the College Development Office by Joseph Grant, director of admissions and college relations. The development office oversees admissions, public affairs, publication and alumni affairs. Another success was Project Intervene. This program was launched by Frances Koenigsberg in fall 1978 to help reduce unemployment in Oswego County through teaching mathematics, reading, and employment strategies to unemployed adults on a one-to-one basis in their homes. In addition, the Cooperative Education Program was instituted to help undergraduates combine off-campus work experiences with full time studies. To this end, students are placed in jobs related to their academic majors. Other projects are the Oswego branch of the National Youth Sports Program and a program for tutoring the children of migrant workers. The Office of Research and Sponsored Programs has very successfully processed large numbers of research and grant proposals relating to such public service matters as acid rain, water quality, and toxic waste.

Another successful undertaking has been the Retired Senior Volunteer Program of Oswego, directed by Ellen Wahl, and co-funded by ACTION, a federal agency, and the college. This program includes literally hundreds of volunteers serving in many capacities, such as helping senior citizens prepare tax returns, organizing a pet therapy program in nursing homes, and helping in the telephone reassurance program. Older people are called every day to make sure they are not ill or in any kind of difficulty.

Providing equal opportunity for minorities and women, at Oswego and nationwide, is another area of recent concern. In higher education during the 1970s, this movement included special provisions for handicapped students, equal educational opportunities, and implementation of the 1975 federal law, Title IX. When federal regulations took effect to ensure sex equality in matters of hiring, firing, promotion, and job benefits, due process for students was also established. A 1969 court case established that students are protected by the due process clause of the fourteenth amendment.

Locally, President Radley has pursued a firm polity of antidiscrimination. Through memoranda and meetings, she has warned against sexual and racial harassment and various inequities. The personnel office and union were mandated with evolving a process whereby problems might be investigated separately and jointly before grievances were filed. Audrey Hurley, affirmative action officer and assistant to the president, said: "I investigate allegations of discrimination in the work force. These are reported to my office but the president has the final responsibility. My job is difficult but not nearly so much as that of the president because, when things get difficult for me, I have the president to talk to. Our function is to see that discriminatory practices cease, not to punish; however, a file is set up on individuals who persist in such practices, and a complaint can be refiled."

With regard to specific groups, Hurley said that "blacks and Hispanics feel discriminated against because there are not more of them in the work force; Asians and Pacific Islanders have never alleged discrimination. Most complaints have related to sexual harassment, partly because women outnumber the other so-called protected groups on campus. The area of sexual harassment is so new that even the courts are not specific regarding it. We are talking about such things as abuse of power, as when someone feels she's not been promoted because she has not granted sexual favors. Also involved are certain behaviors of males toward female students, such as sexual coercion, especially in dormitory settings, although such behaviors are far less common than in the larger society. Males are confused by the mixed signals they get from women today, from what their parents have taught them, what they hear in college courses, and what they have heard on the media. They don't know what their role is." Overall, Hurley rates the status of affirmative action at Oswego as relatively good, largely because of strong support from President Radley, Dean Donald Mathieu, Dean Barbara Gerber, and Chancellor Wharton. There has also been much progress with the faculty.

In broader terms, the women's liberation movement has significantly affected the total society, including higher education. David Riesman at Harvard believes this movement has had the most "profound effect on American society of any protest movement since the second World War." Although more traditional women may have rejected it, its effects have extended from the higher social strata down to the working class.

The book, *Everywoman's Guide to Colleges and Universities* rates 582 undergraduate schools in terms of healthy environment for women with regard to athletics, curriculum, student leadership, faculty status, and positions in top administration.[12] In general, women's colleges are rated as the best places for women who desire to become student leaders or to find role models among faculty members and administrators. Among the SUNY institutions, Oswego received the highest, or six-star, rating, which was conferred mainly on the outstanding women's colleges.

"After all," explained Dr. Radley, with justifiable pride in such recognition, "women in significant roles at Oswego include the president, an assistant vice president, a dean, an associate dean, as well as the president, vice president, and treasurer of the Student Association. When I came here, there weren't any women in the English department except Helen Simkewicz. Then, by applying pressure, we got more women, and now not all faculty openings are being filled with young white males."

Other local byproducts of the women's movement have been the Women's Studies minor, the Johnson Hall Mentoring Program for women students, and the Women's Caucus, which promotes matters of concern to women both on and off campus.

Radley constitutes a significant role model for young women on campus and is an inspiration to them. In one of many speeches before the Association of Professional Managerial and Executive Women in Syracuse, she advised career women to find a network, participate in professional organizations, never take criticism personally, have a sense of humor, be well-groomed, and have the courage to be different, without making "a fetish of it." Women, she concluded, must also be able to resist peer pressure and stand on their own feet.

Historically, college administrators have been responsible for the overall quality and performance of the faculty, with varying degrees of success. From 1720 to 1844 the chair of anatomy at Edinburgh was in effect a dynasty—as have been others at other schools—in the Monroe family. In recent years some faculty members at one American college, instead of giving classes, simply let students educate themselves.

If an administration does its monitoring job well, conflicts inevitably arise. "No matter what style of administration you have, detractors will always be with you." said Oswego's Dean Mathieu. During a psychology department meeting in 1982, as some members were attacking the administration, a large bug made its way across the open space on the floor around which department members were sitting. One professor exclaimed, "I knew the administration had us bugged!"

In these times of budget crises, one source of contention has been layoffs of faculty, even tenured ones. This drastic measure was deemed "unthinkable" until a decade ago; since the early 1970s it has been invoked with increasing frequency. Those thus retrenched ask, "Why me?" and may search for devious motives. "Some rush to the press crying 'unfair,' or use students as 'wailing walls' and 'light brigades'," noted Radley, "to fight for their reinstatement." One can only conjecture how great the outcry might have become had not the state legislature, just before the April 1983 deadline, voided the need for over 3,000 projected layoffs SUNY-wide.

President Radley has made heroic and effective efforts to minimize hardships resulting from unavoidable cutbacks in faculty and departments. Retrenched individuals have been given notice as long in advance as possible so they could seek other employment. Where feasible, they have been redeployed or retrained; for example, when Campus School closed, every one of its tenured faculty was given long advance notice. "It may not be the best way to do things," reflected Radley, "but it is the most humane way. The Campus School people were brought here for a specific purpose, and when that purpose was no longer there, we found ways of retraining and redeploying them. We did pretty well, but it was not a perfect solution."

The administration also relies on peer review within departments regarding nonrenewal of faculty members. "I have never overturned a recommendation when reviews by peers, the chair, the dean, and the provost were all negative," noted Radley. "I have overturned the peer review at times when the chair, the dean, and the provost have differed from the peer review."

Radley explained the basic principles involved in all these decisions and others regarding faculty matters made in periodic Presidential Forums. During forums, which were started by Radley, she invites questions regarding any matter of faculty concern. It is rare in the annals of higher education for a college president to go to such great lengths to protect the mental health and rights of the faculty. Despite such Herculean efforts to be fair, the administration is sometimes attacked, usually by people with an axe to grind or by those who fail to understand all aspects of the situation.[13]

SUNY faculties have less power than those in colleges where both decision making and responsibility are delegated to them, and they rely mainly on their union and assembly for input. The SUNY union, United University Professions (Oswego is one of its units), like many in higher education, was created in the 1970s primarily for the purpose of collective bargaining when inflationary pressures and poor economic conditions had reduced support to higher education. Thus, the concept of a university composed of independent individuals was displaced by that of faculty and administration as adversarial, in the manner of labor and management. Meanwhile, opposition to unionism had almost disappeared, and the collective bargaining contract had become the chief tool for teachers' power. By the end of the 1970s, most American educators were covered with contracts negotiated under state laws; their leader was Albert Shanker, head of the 520,000-member American Federation of Teachers.

Contrary to general expectations, unionization did not continue to increase rapidly; "creeping unionism" is a more valid portrayal. Approximately one in six institutions of higher education in the country was organized by 1980, over four in five in the public sector. About 22 percent have chosen not to unionize because of the lack of supporting legislation and resistance from faculties themselves, especially in research universities and private liberal arts colleges. In states with enabling legislation, most institutions have been organized, but in those without it, unionization is slow.

Advocates of unions in higher education believe they fulfill several functions, aside from collective bargaining in salary matters. Many faculty members want to share in their institution's government and planning, and a national study indicates this is more important than income in shaping faculty morale. Unions also provide at least some security in the form of normalized grievance procedures and sometimes raises in salary. Since students now sit on various college committees, the faculty union meeting may be one of the few forums wherein faculty members can legitimately speak solely among themselves.

Nevertheless, even on unionized campuses, many faculty members continue to oppose unions. One of the oddities of unionism on the college scene is that faculty members often take issue with their own local union activists, who often possess lower status on campus. One reason, claim some critics, is that unions have sometimes bargained away privileges or advantages formerly held by faculty members. Another is that unionization apparently does not result in higher salaries over the long term. Others object to the adversarial relationship which has driven top leadership to become less visible, more cautious, and defensive. Administrators tend to consult more, preserve the status quo, and try fewer new things. Still others believe labor unions are not for true professionals and prefer to dissociate from them.

Various alternatives to unions have been employed. In most colleges, faculty members rely heavily on networking groups, working together and supporting each other in pursuit of common goals. Networks in society have shifted from vertical to horizontal. Vertical hierarchies may cause people to compete to get ahead, but they produce tension, anxiety, and stress. In contrast, horizontal networking affords individuals greater power in that people come to one another's assistance. Today's world involves overlapping networks, not just a constellation of networks but a galaxy of networking constellations. Stories are heard in many colleges about the manipulation of students by faculty members to retain their jobs, as ammunition against other faculty members, or against the administration in staff skirmishes.

The SUNY union was formed in 1973 as a result of the merger of two organizations that had been fighting each other: the Senate Professional Association, an affiliate of the National Education Association, and the State University Federation of Teachers, an affiliate of the American Federation of Teachers; membership in the union had grown to 13,000 by 1983. "The union's overall mission," said William Scheuerman, vice president of the local unit, "is to protect the craft. To do that, you may ask, why do we need a union? As academics we are individualists; we have Ph.Ds; and we are research people. But the bottom line is that we are employees; we are not self-employed like doctors and lawyers. Therefore, we can be effective only if we work collectively, rather than as individuals, in matters of mutual concern."

"The present issues," he explained, "are job security, the distinction between retrenchment and reallocation of staff, and what constitutes a valid cutback of a tenured faculty member. We have to work on principle and forget faces. It's not for us to say punish or don't punish a particular faculty member, who has presumably failed in some manner. It's for us to say whether the rules were followed in implementing the punishment. Sometimes we agree with the administration that particular faculty members have done some very stupid things—all we try to do is see that all concerned follow the rules.

"A basic accomplishment of the union has been adding to job security, thus helping to maintain faculty morale. There is a real sense of terror every spring with regard to impending cutbacks, and our phone rings off the hook. Last fall, central administration was reluctant to fight, for various complex political reasons, to prevent budget cuts that would have produced large-scale faculty layoffs, but UUP was right out in the forefront. You have to put the boxing gloves on sometimes."

In the meantime, the administration has learned to live with the union, statewide and locally. "I am bound to comply with the contract which is negotiated between the faculty, various unions, and the Office of Employee Relations," said President Radley. "I have little to say about what goes into that contract, but I am bound by law to comply with it."

"We and the Union simply have different perspectives," added Provost Ralph Spencer, "on how best to achieve the goals we have agreed on to serve the students. We don't approach our task as adversaries vying for a pile of resources."

Nevertheless, many union members and their critics maintain sharply opposing views. Most of the two-thirds of the faculty who are union members defend it but with widely varying degrees of enthusiasm. Others, who are members only because of contractual benefits involved, are sharply critical, including one who said, "They just try to find something to carp about. There's no radical movement on campus, but a few would be against Jesus Christ if He walked around here—that's true on any campus." Another said, "The union reduces professionalism; and some individuals with a union mentality just teach their classes and refuse to do much else."

The present administration inherited a few controversies with students, but these have decreased dramatically in number and intensity. One student, Robert O'Connor, wrote a tongue-in-cheek letter to "President Virginia Strangelove" in 1977, making ridiculous proposals for solving the overcrowding problem on campus.[14] More recently, student criticism has greatly diminished and involves relatively few students. One reason may be that students have gained many goals they sought. Another may be that the administration has worked with great dedication to ensure a healthy environment for students on campus. Student officers confer regularly with the administration on a friendly basis.

Particular events during the present administration have been less dramatic than those of Perdue's tenure, but no less significant academically. Of prime importance was the inauguration on October 8, 1978, of Virginia L. Radley, SUNY's first woman president. "It was a gala occasion," recalled Radley, "a day when the weather gave us everything—sleet and sunshine and a rainbow." It also gave us a new era, with a new and firm hand at the helm.

Also important, especially to the students and their parents, have been the graduation exercises. Over time, such occasions have always varied a bit from one institution to another. In the year 1827, Oxford dictated that all candidates for the Master of Arts degree swear under oath their enmity against a certain gentleman who had led a mob against the school in the year 1240.[15] Oswego's version of these exercises is orchestrated by James

Howard's Public Ceremonies Committee, which manages a miraculous transformation of a hockey rink penalty box in Romney Field House into an alterlike platform. It clocks the ceremony to the minute, and this schedule includes timing the national anthem at 1:05 minutes and the alma mater at 48 seconds. The committee instructs seniors to wear dark shoes, and forbids corsages. Few colleges of Oswego's size still call the name of every graduate; however, Oswego thus far has adhered to this tradition.

Over the years, many illustrious persons have been the main speaker on commencement day, among then, in 1979, Robert Helsby, Class of 1940. He was the first graduate to receive Oswego's baccalaureate degree. His gift to the college during the 1979 ceremony was his 1940 diploma. The 1980 speaker was Stanley J. Drazek, Class of 1941. He had assisted in the establishment of the nation's Head Start Program and, until his retirement in 1978, had been chancellor of the University of Maryland's University College.

Although students at many colleges made a charade of such occasions in the 1970s, and Oswego has had a few such incidents, Radley insists that "commencement be a dignified and ceremonial occasion. At one graduation ceremony a fellow wore a funny hat, and at another, one wore a mask, but not when I was president. That is a time when my sense of humor fails me."

Categories of graduates have become increasingly diverse over time: the oldest in 1979 was fifty-one, the youngest was nineteen; the age range in 1983 was twenty to sixty-three. The class included several sets of twins, and second-, third-, and even fourth-generation Oswego graduates. Sue Clemons (1983), one of the graduates, dropped out of school at age sixteen, received a high school equivalency diploma sixteen years later and, after seven years of part-time attendance, achieved her degree.

The 1981 toastmistress suggested tongue-in-cheek improvements for the commencement ceremony, including the following: "Bright crepe paper gowns for aging faculty members susceptible to heat strokes; hot dog venders to silence the growling stomachs in Romney Field House; and lollipops for babies whose cries inevitably punctuate the ceremony. And faculty members who have had to participate a specified number of years should be allowed to hire stand-ins—or sit-ins—funded by the Alumni Association."[16]

The traditional Torchlight Ceremony originated in 1936 to mark the seventy-fifth anniversary of the college's founding. Held on the evening preceding graduation, it continues to be a solemn and memorable occasion. The circle of light, formed by everyone holding a candle, symbolizes the light imparted to graduates by their alma mater. As the torch is passed around, each person lights a candle from it, thus creating a lighted circle.

Other annual events of significance, initiated by Radley, are the Academic Fair, Honors Convocation, Parents' Weekend, and Professor Recognition Day. The Academic Fair is an open-house occasion for each department to display examples of its work. At the Honors Convocation, awards are given to students who have distinguished themselves in various college-sponsored activities. Professor Recognition Day honors new professors in a ceremony written by Rosemary Nesbitt. On Parents' Weekend, fathers and mothers tour the campus and meet their sons and daughters' instructors. These occasions, collectively, are doing much to promote the college's ideal of excellence and strengthen its traditions.

The college was visited by two nationally recognized evaluation teams in spring 1982, representing the Commission on Higher Education of the Middle States Association of Colleges and Schools (CHE/MSA), and the National Commission on the Accreditation of Teacher Education (NCATE). CHE/MSA is charged with the review and accrediting of institutions in their totality; NCATE reviews and accredits education programs only. CHE/MSA reaffirmed the college's accredited status without conditions. NCATE deferred reaffirmation action pending a report on four of twenty-eight standards, all of which must be met for continued recognition. The latter action in no way detracts from the overall strengths of the college, including its education courses, nor from its accredited status, reaffirmed by the CHE/MSA in 1982.

Among other events of note are visits by people interested in Oswego's famous history. Every few years, at least, Japanese educators visit. Two professors, Keiji Shimada and Yoshizo Yamaki, visited in 1979 to study Oswego's audiovisual and communications departments and to explore educational teaching methods. "This university," Shimada said, "is very famous in the history of education, not only in the United States but also in Japan, because of the Oswego movement." When asked what impressed them most, one replied, "The beauty of the campus and woman power."

One unusual occurrence was former President Perdue's return to campus in spring 1982, to serve as acting provost while Ralph Spencer was on leave. Thus, his and Radley's roles were exactly the reverse of those each had once held as chief pilot of the college. "I haven't heard of such a case before," said Perdue, "but I was president long enough to know what a president is supposed to do and what a provost is supposed to do. In consequence, we've had a wonderful working relationship, and it's been fun."

Especially since the 1960s, the financial strain has been felt throughout American higher education. Families' ability to pay for their children's college education lessened and, until 1983, federal and state governments assisted students in ever-increasing amounts. The Reagan administration's budget of 1983 cut student aid by a third and, at the same time, slashed support for the humanities and arts by almost a third. In effect, these reductions would limit or deny access to higher education to many students and segregate others along economic lines. The reductions would create a "two-tiered system, with elite private education for the well-to-do, and municipal and state colleges for all others. In a survey of twenty university vice presidents, seventeen expressed great concern that students, even the best ones, were simply being priced out of attending. Nor was much help to be had from the private sector because businessmen, even when sympathetic, were experiencing hard times, too. Nineteen of the twenty favored more federal help for better students who had greater financial need; and the twentieth suggested increasing support from industry as the "long-term answer".[17]

It is unclear what effects these budget cuts have had. Research results regarding their effect on the quality of instruction are ambiguous. However, faculty members clearly have experienced a decline in real purchasing power. Those institutions more selective of their students have fared best.

In the meantime, Oswego was feeling the shock waves of SUNY's budget crunch. Because of anticipated cuts, students held a "Save SUNY" rally on February 20, 1980, and attracted only about thirty people. Governor Cuomo proposed even more cuts in 1983, which would have cost 2,500 to 3,000 jobs in the SUNY system, increased tuition by $150 a year, and raised room and board by $250. The college was called on to devise a plan to eliminate 111 jobs, 48 of them teaching positions.

When asked whether Oswego should be exempt from Governor Cuomo's budget-cutting proposals, Radley replied, "I don't think anybody should be exempt when we have a 1.8 billion deficit . . . [however] we should get our priorities straight. . . . Education . . . is an investment in human capital which the State very much needs." An interviewer asked whether maintaining roads was not also an essential service. Radley replied, "Absolutely. Pioneers managed all right with a goat track. But you do not manage without an enlightened citizenry."

At a faculty meeting called to discuss the budget crisis before a large crowd, including reporters, Radley discussed plans for fighting the cuts and called upon everyone for unity. "If I were president of a private college during a budget crisis," she declared, "I would say, 'We are all going to teach fifteen hours. We are all going to take a cut in pay—and I mean all of us. We are going to do windows and toilets and clean our own offices.'" A cartoon in the next *Oswegonian* showed Radley industriously cleaning a toilet.[18] Nevertheless, Radley's remarks at this meeting were widely applauded as morale building yet realistic.

Faculty members present at the meeting responded in conflicting ways. Librarian Mignon Adams said she was willing to donate 9 percent of her salary to keep her colleagues here and called on others to do the same. Two others made the same suggestion, and these gestures received some applause. Still others suggested that the recent 9 percent increase should be given up by the faculty to retain those who would be laid off. However, Professor Donald Vanouse, president of the local UUP, said that this raise was long overdue, and giving it up would prove only a short-term solution. Professor Paul Wilbur said that voluntarily giving it up would send "bureaucrats" in Albany the message that the faculty "is a soft touch," and this statement also brought applause. At the conclusion of the discussion, Professor Herbert Van Schaack distributed paper and stamped envelopes to all faculty members present and asked them to write letters to the legislature before they left the room—and they did.[19]

Although the governor later modified his position, the college was clearly required to make do with less. Radley firmly resolved to keep the flag of excellence flying. "Until we are told to stop trying to improve the quality of life for our various constituencies, and until we are told to settle for mediocrity, the average, or half a loaf, we shall continue to exert ourselves in positive and caring ways at Oswego." The next year she wrote again to Wharton: "Despite cutbacks and retrenchment we are attempting [at Oswego] to be more available to our students. . . . We have said 'no' to frivolous and often esoteric requests by special interest groups or specified giraffes and ostriches. We have cracked down and tightened up. We have done more with less. . . . I do not have the answers. Perhaps as Alice B. Toklas is reputed to have said, 'I do not even have the questions.'"[20]

Radley continued to express confidence that even in these times of dwindling funds we could "foster excellence . . . out of our own blood and tears."[21] In defining excellence, she said: "Instead of a collection of smorgasbord, lunch counter junk food, we will be able to insure that our graduates will have been exposed to certain kinds of learning experiences and expectations. . . . We have tried to get our calendar away from a country club calendar and back to a more serious academic dimension."[21]

Dean Donald Mathieu observed that he is still often confronted by people who haven't "quite gotten over the mind-set they may have had in 1969, who refuse to understand that the pie, or whatever metaphor you want to use, is only so big. It isn't simply a matter of managing resources, but helping the staff come to appreciate limitations and to take the broader institutional view of what we can do with what we have."

"We can't afford to continue to have firemen on the diesels," said Radley, as she proceeded with the cutbacks required. Faculty office phones were removed in fall 1980, which raised a pained outcry. "The situation has gotten out of hand," explained Vice President Lynn Hemink to these protestors. "Last year's phone bill was $60,000, and 440 calls were made between 6:00 P.M. and 6:00 A.M." The administration believed these telephones were less essential than laboratory equipment and items used directly by students.

Victims of the budget crisis in 1980–81 were the Fallbrook Riding stables, the Fallbrook ski hill, two department majors (geography and audiovisual technology) and even the Campus School. "A sad affair," observed Radley, "because it was the best of SUNY's campus schools according to all reports. However, the Campus School was really a parallel public school system."

Inevitably, the retrenchment of departments and personnel produced a hue and cry, including accusations of inadequate consultation. "Ultimately, such decisions must be made by the administration," explained Dean Mathieu, "which consults with the departments, although such consultation isn't very meaningful. I have yet to encounter an academic department, faced with prospects of losing resources, that would simply nod and say, 'If you have to take staff from us, that's fine. Go ahead.'"

Throughout good times and bad, colleges must continue to redefine their mission to reflect changing times and needs. Over the past decade, in particular, the public has been concerned about America's failing leadership in science and technology and about access to higher education, primarily for career preparation. Of twenty vice presidents of midwestern universities, twelve said that the people in their states looked upon higher education primarily as a means of obtaining high paying jobs instead of a way to develop better informed citizens'; the other eight were uncertain.[22]

Educators perceive their mission more broadly and in less pragmatic terms. Chancellor Wharton believes that institutions should provide diversity to reflect a pluralistic society with diverse ethnic groups, religions, races, occupations, and life styles. These varying categories of students prefer attending institutions having a similar diversity.

Radley pointed out that Oswego's mission is stated in its master plan: "to provide first-rate, relatively low-cost undergraduate education within the public context. Within this framework, we aim for pursuit of excellence of life style. It doesn't have to be a poem to qualify for excellence." She noted a small wooden truck made by an industrial arts student. "It took 150 hours to make; that's excellence." Others, among them Provost Ralph Spencer and Associate Provost Richard Wheeler, believe that "a significant part of our mission is to build on our teacher training tradition. . . . Any institution without a tradition is incomplete. You sometimes hear the phrase 'instant tradition' but that can't be. A tradition has to be built." Oswego's mission is implemented according to its master plans, which are periodically revised. The core of the most recent of these plans is general education, to provide for each student an integrated treatment of basic areas of knowledge.

Many observers warn that any college's mission and master plan must be of a quality that preserves the integrity of the degree. The Carnegie Council expressed concern for deterioration of the "integrity of institutions." Threats to integrity include "grade inflation, reduced academic requirements, low quality off-campus programs, false promises by institutions, cheating, vandalism, and students' defaults on loans."[23] Such factors undermine the public's confidence in higher education; hence, every college should monitor its own conduct. In particular, the council expressed a need for dynamism or spirit of growth. Such a spirit is threatened by aging faculties and the growth of collective bargaining, with its focus on retaining advantages. Dynamism may be encouraged by a continuous policy of substituting some new programs for existing ones and funding new efforts.

Oswego's Provost Spencer agrees with the Carnegie Council, noting some erosion of public confidence, especially about what a degree means. "People who earned a degree in my generation simply by virtue of having a degree could go out and say, 'Here I am, world. I can work almost any place I want.' That situation has changed for various reasons, one being that so many people now have degrees. In addition, the public wonders, what actually does a degree mean? Does it mean a graduate knows anything or can do anything? We think it does, but we people in higher education must work to restore the degree's integrity."

Thomas Powell, former Oswego dean, believes that the looser academic requirements in the 1970s undermined the value of a B.A. degree. What had appeared to be democratic idealistic patterns of change in the late 1960s proved to be "pretty expensive to the young people of the 1970s." He saw a need to return to a more well-defined academic program requiring math, sciences, and foreign languages.

Spencer and Wheeler believe the college has made substantial progress. "In the past five years we have restored much integrity through our general education component and our course-control system," said Spencer. "There's been a crisis of confidence in post-secondary education," added Wheeler, "partly because some people with degrees have not performed as well as the public might have expected they would. I trust that none of these people are Oswego graduates. We have taken our own degree integrity very seriously."

In general, New York's colleges compare well with those across the country, and Oswego is among the cream in the state. New York State was one of the eleven in 1982 wherein one half or more high school students took the SATs. The average verbal score in New York was 429 compared with the national average of 426, and 467 for math compared with a national average of 466. However, this overall picture fails to show the somewhat varied admissions picture within SUNY. Oswego itself has been more selective than its sister colleges. In fall 1982, Oswego accepted only 54 percent of applicants while its sister colleges, with very few exceptions, accepted 85 percent or more.[24]

Radley refers to Oswego's competitors not as the SUNY Arts and Science Colleges, but as Albany and Binghamton—SUNY university centers—and such institutions as Rutgers and Purdue. Perhaps Oswego's selectivity contributed to its attractiveness; 11,523 applied for admission in spring 1982, surpassing Oneonta, the nearest SUNY arts and science college, by over

2,000 applications. The freshmen who enrolled scored above 1,010 on SATs, over one hundred points above the national average.[25]

Finally we arrive at the questions: What is Oswego's status now? What are its main accomplishments, the jewels in its crown, in addition to those already mentioned? "The college is in excellent shape," said President Radley, "especially considering all of the traumatic things that have happened since 1973, when the first real budget cuts came. We are now the second largest of the four-year colleges of arts and sciences, of which there are thirteen." She also mentioned Oswego's ranking in the spring 1983 edition of Barron's *Guide to the Best, Most Popular and Most Exciting Colleges*, a profile of 350 institutions representing the cream of the nation's almost 1,500 four-year colleges and universities. About 230 of these 350, including Oswego, were ranked best on the basis of admission standards; others in Oswego's rank were Tulane, Rutgers, Skidmore, and Fordham. "We are in very good company," noted Radley. In other particulars, the college also deserves high marks. For example, its campus police are the second best qualified of any in the SUNY system (after Albany's), according to the Division of Budget and Civil Service examiners. Almost all are graduates of public justice or criminal justice programs.

Radley also has a talent for economical management, a prized ability in these budget-tight times. During her first two years as president, with the aid of Robert Bieling, Director of the Physical Plant, and Frank Mazzoli, Assistant Director of the Physical Plant, she arrived at the lowest utility bills and lowest cost per student within the whole SUNY system. Vandalism, a major problem in many colleges, is lower than in any other SUNY four-year college, largely because of Radley's insistence on an orderly, beautifully maintained campus. If the president isn't interested, there can be much carnage and widespread vandalism. "If the staff recommends to me that so-and-so has gone through due process and has been found to be incorrigible, and recommends that that student be suspended or expelled, I back them," noted Radley.

Oswego's top-notch performance also embraces its more scholarly endeavors. From 1978 to 1982 library use rose 42 percent. In 1981–82, the college received a record-breaking number of grants and awards totaling over a million dollars. The Office of Research and Sponsored Programs initiated Quest '80, the first conference for scholarly activities of students and staff, and faculty: ninety-three papers were read.

Radley's main trademark as president has been the quest for excellence. When she came as provost in 1974, she decided to do something about the integrity of the college, including giving faculty members merit raises, establishing the first Honors College at a four-year SUNY unit, initiating award systems for student achievement, and supporting an advisement system for undecided undergraduates. She also resolved to improve the quality of student life. Radley believes that "higher education is, by definition, elitist, and we should base rewards on performance. We don't spread what we have all over the place because then it loses its cutting edge of excellence. There is no excuse for having junky education in this country at any level. If you don't deliver a quality education you just become a holding tank for FTEs (full-time equivalent students)."

As a result of this quest and the efforts of a superior, dedicated faculty, Oswego is winning recognition for excellence, both locally and elsewhere. Professor Rosemary Nesbitt credits Radley with achieving for the college a steadily rising reputation in academics. Alumna Kathleen Koehne (1983) said Oswego came a long way academically during the four years she was here. Professor John Mincher tells of complimentary things he heard about Oswego when working in the theater in metropolitan New York; and Dean Lewis "Pete" Popham said "the word is getting out, as students carry the message across the country, of Oswego's quality." Provost Spencer observed that "it's quite thrilling as I travel around the country, and even the world, to find that Oswego's name is known because of what its graduates have done. The most compelling example was when I was in Paris at the Sorbonne about three years ago. I met people there who welcomed me enthusiastically, not because of me but because of the long relationship they have had with the University of Oswego, as they call it. In our Paris program, over the years, our students have built a reputation for us, by becoming highly qualified and able to hold their own with the best students the university there has to offer."

Radley deplores that "we have let our traditions go so far, they are almost buried. Nobody could even find a copy of the old alma mater; we had to turn the whole library upside down to find it. The Torchlight is a nice occasion; and we ought to reinstitute Founder's Day." True, Oswego should revive and honor its tradition while, in the process, adding significantly to that heritage. And to judge from the phenomenal progress of the past few years, new and highly worthy traditions are firmly taking root.

9

A Faculty of Distinction: Its Mission and President

FROM the time of Sheldon, the college's major source of strength has been its faculty. Much has been said in earlier chapters about faculty members, but there is more to relate about them past, and present. In the academic year 1983–84, the full-time faculty numbered 357, 157 of whom were under the age of forty-five; fifty-eight were over the age of fifty-five; and the majority, 78 percent, were male. Representing minorities were five blacks, two Hispanics, seventeen Asiatic and Pacific Islanders, and two native Americans. Of the full-time faculty, 31 percent were professors, 38 percent associate professors, 22 percent assistant professors, 7 percent instructors, and 2 percent lecturers. Four held the rank of Distinguished Teaching Professor: Rosemary Nesbitt, Augustine Silveira, Marilynn Smiley, and Joseph Wiecha; and one, Dorothy Rogers, held the title of Distinguished Service Professor.

In addition to the Distinguished Teaching Professors, sixteen members of Oswego's faculty have received the Chancellor's Award for Excellence in Teaching.[1] Other recipients of the chancellor's awards are Ralph Spencer, excellence in administrative services; Bernie Henderson and Linda Syrell, excellence in professional services; and Mignon Adams, excellence in librarianship.

Another feature of the college's faculty is its quota of alumni. In 1983–84, the administrative staff and full- and part-time teaching faculty numbered 488; of these, 56 (about one in nine) hold Oswego degrees. Nine have both undergraduate and master's degrees from Oswego; 9 others hold master's degrees from the college; 38 earned undergraduate degrees here.

Of these 56 alumni, 36 are involved in instruction, the largest contingent (13) in industrial arts and technology, and 5 in theater. Among the 21 in nonteaching positions, 5 are in the library, 4 in the Office of Special Programs, and the others are scattered throughout the college. Seven of the faculty alumni, 5 in industrial arts, have attained the rank of full professor; 2, Sanford Sternlicht and Vernon Tryon, are department chairs; and 9 have the rank of associate professor. The college's alumni include three other star performers: Celia Sgroi, the college's lawyer; Margaret Lowery, the alumni director; and Dorothy Brown Clark, recent president of the alumni association.

Some critics might argue that employment of alumni encourages provincialism and inbreeding of ideas. However, perhaps some are needed because, as Robert Carter of the history department pointed out, faculty members who are products of the system have a special feeling for it. Carter, who himself possesses two State University degrees, said, "I can identify with the students and understand them because I went to SUNY colleges, too."

A feature of the faculty in general is its high quality. "If you look at the faculty's background, you'll see that all of the major universities in this country, and some abroad, are represented," observed President Radley. "These people came at a time when quality faculty were scarce and the State University paid better than most."

A second feature, the growing number of tenured faculty, had some negative results. This factor, here and elsewhere, has made it more difficult to meet changing instructional needs in areas of specialty. In consequence, concluded the Carnegie Council, faculties had to be retrained to teach in related fields and the older faculty encouraged to retire.[2] Nevertheless, the persistence of inflation and consequent shrinkage in the buying power of pensions causes many professors to cling to their jobs as long as they can.

In New York State, and nationally, another result has been a surplus of young Ph.Ds, but fewer than often estimated because their numbers are decreasing.[3] Because of increased emphasis on college graduates' access to jobs, holders of the doctorate are declining in the fields of engineering, mathematics, physics, the social sciences, and the arts. On the other hand, in these same fields, the percentage of older faculty is low, suggesting that few positions will open because of death or retirement. Hence, in faculties generally there is a bulge in numbers in the central age range. It might be added that this country is not alone in this problem, for most industrial countries lack opportunities for promising young scholars.[4]

At Oswego, as elsewhere, the effect of this situation on younger faculty members has been demoralizing. They are very dedicated, but have no security; hence, they cannot have a sense of the future. Understandably, they perceive older colleagues as blocking their professional careers. "When they have a chance to leave," said Thomas Gooding, Professor of Psychology, "they may say 'I've had enough'. We lost two outstanding young people in psychology this year, Frank Dane and Josh Stoller, who were already building national reputations."

"The failure to replace them, [older faculty]" observed industrial arts chair, Vernon Tryon, "leaves us inadequately staffed with an aging faculty who haven't the energy to do extra things—for example, curriculum development lags. We have enough faculty to get by, but not enough to function with distinction."

"When we were worrying about retrenchment," recalled Charles Shoemaker, "I heard a young faculty member say he didn't know what to do. 'I'm last in, first out. I don't know whether to stay here or not.'"

This situation—last in, first out—as stipulated by the union contract, has been especially hard on women, few of whom have had the chance to join the ranks of entrenched professors. Those who remain have difficulty rising through the ranks, for most of the slots are filled. Nevertheless, President Radley has done what she could to improve the situation. In 1979 she wrote to Chancellor Wharton:

> I take some pride in our progress here regarding women. Dr. Patti Peterson has one of the four vice presidencies; Dr. Diana Balmori is the new director of the Honors Program; and Dr. Barbara Gerber is Dean of Professional Studies. We have just hired a woman as Director of Institutional Research; and we have recently put a lawyer, Ms. Gail Erwin, on our payroll. Nonetheless, when I consider the number of presidencies that were open in the State University of New York system, and then see almost invariably that a white male has been selected, I cannot help but be disheartened and somewhat dismayed.

Women suffer in less detectable ways. "Many truly self-confident teachers turn in an outstanding performance," wrote Harvard's David Riesman in 1980; "however, women, who are still in a minority on the higher levels, are less confident than men, and often too perfectionistic to be completely natural and relaxed."[5] Women also lack the networks possessed by the overwhelming male majority, although the situation has improved at Oswego under Radley. Dr. Marilynn Smiley said that when she came to Oswego's music department in 1961, "it was a male club with serious discrimination." Added Dr. Patti M. Peterson, "The sort of informal network by which jobs are obtained and promotions received, which has always existed for men, has not existed for women."

Another countrywide concern has been that of racial and ethnic minority representation on college faculties. In the United States in 1975, only about 7 percent of professors were minority group members, except for Japanese and Chinese-Americans. This may be due in part to the fact that well-educated minority members are able to obtain higher paying employment outside academia.

In general, the strategy for achieving equality of opportunity for minorities has involved legal remedies for preventing discrimination, reducing inequality in financial resources, and somehow reducing, or at least compensating for, inequalities in preparation of those seeking admission. As a result, institutions of higher education, including the elite, have made progress in affording such opportunities to minorities as well.

Locally, the administration has strongly enforced a policy of fairness for all segments of the faculty, and claims of discrimination have been rare. Oswego's 1979 faculty included 300 white males and 80 white females, 6 male and 1 female blacks, 3 male and 2 female Hispanics, 15 male Orientals, and 1 American Indian male, for a total of 408: 300 white males, 108 females and minorities.

The Carnegie Foundation reports a somewhat low morale among American faculty members in general. They may be disheartened through decreased real income, losing to students control of certain aspects of academic life, and to having difficulty in achieving tenure. There is also the interference of government and the courts, thus reducing their feelings of independence and autonomy. Campuses and their faculties are no longer as independent as they once were, the result being "less of a community and more of a professional life or economic pressure group."[6] In addition, observed Dean Barbara Gerber, "everything in the country, including higher education, which used to be mystical, has become demystified. The critical nature of reporting about higher education has lowered its image. It has had a leveling effect, and we are no longer seen as high-flying intellectuals, but as ordinary folk. The oracular nature of the faculty has diminished in the eyes of the student body and perhaps of each other."

Despite this situation, many faculty members at Oswego and elsewhere have delayed retirement for two main reasons: current economic conditions; and elevation of the mandatory retirement age to seventy, with the possibility of a one- or two-year extension by request of the college's president and with special permission of SUNY's chancellor. As of 1984, twenty-five (4 percent) of the faculty had been on the staff at least a quarter century, two— Frank Robinson and Dorothy Rogers—over thirty years. Eighty-seven (18 percent) had been at Oswego twenty years or more.[6]

These individuals include many people employed during higher education's rapid expansion in the 1950s and 1960s who might not retire prior to the end of the century. This factor, along with reductions in enrollments, meant that few faculty openings would occur except through death and retirement. Hence, few new faculty members could be hired, and recent appointees had trouble attaining permanent appointments. For this reason, in addition to the high salaries paid the older faculty, the state allowed an additional three years' service credit to all staff members fifty-five or older who would elect to retire in 1985. As a result, an unprecedented number seized the bait, leaving the staff stripped of key people.[7] In Dr. Radley's administration, faculty and staff members representing a quarter century of service had retired.[8]

Several people have suggested that greater advantage of the retired faculty's talents should be taken. Rosemary Nesbitt suggested "they might be invited to give guest lectures, or we might have an emeritus forum. There is nothing wrong with their bodies and minds, yet they have been put out to pasture." George Pitluga suggested that "retired faculty members might be used to fill in for faculty members who have been absent a few days for some reason. Of course, this is no time to be picking up free labor if it means displacement of jobs. But there is a tremendous amount of accumulated wisdom, and also folly, in retired faculty members."

Oswego's senior faculty members, with rare exception, oppose mandatory retirement at any specific age. Associate Dean Thomas Gooding called it "an invasion of human rights," and doubts that it can be legislated in any way that doesn't violate an individual's freedom of choice. "However," he added, "apart from competency tests for people of all ages, there must be some way to deal with people going through the aging process. I presume all of us would begin to lose competence if we continued to teach into our nineties. I would prefer that people make the retirement decision themselves, but it's a complex issue."

Others admit that some aging instructors actually retire before they leave the classroom, serving up last decade's lectures slightly warmed over, but argue that many continue to perform with distinction until late years. "At age sixty-five, many people are just reaching the apex of their achievement," said Professor Rosemary Nesbitt. Associate Provost Richard Wheeler agreed, saying, "Some of our most effective teachers are older ones. The most significant factors in obtaining students at an institution are current and former students' satisfaction with their experience and developing a relationship with some significant adult there. Most students develop such a relationship with some faculty member and often it is an older individual. I hate to see gifted, dedicated, hard-working young people hired for just a year—and that's what is happening all over the country—but to cut off that other quality, the seasoned richness that the experienced veteran faculty member can provide, is also wrong."

Provost Ralph Spencer believes people should be allowed to stay "as long as their services continue to be valuable, although some faculty groups are concerned about what they perceive as deadwood. I'm concerned about that, too, and matters of contract and tenure make it difficult to handle." Former Vice President Sherwood Dunham concurred, saying he opposed mandatory retirement but favored "some sort of control to insure that the quality of the institution will be maintained because, after all, people do get older. Besides, room must be made for younger people coming along, for there are those who would hang on forever even though they are not capable."

Because current faculties are aging, and the rate of retirement increasing, a different scenario for younger faculty looms ahead. "Over the next twenty-five years, a half million faculty members will be hired by American institutions, replacing practically the entire professoriate. The big 'surge' is a decade away, and will be equivalent to "founding our institutions anew."[9]

Student evaluation of instruction is often used to keep tabs on young recruits, as well as on all professors. A survey of over two hundred institutions indicates that student evaluation of teaching occurs in 86 percent and, in two-thirds of these institutions, results are available to university administrators. However, since research does not indicate that instruction improves as a result, administrators are "flying blind" if they use the results in decision making. Perhaps instructors should select items pertinent to their objectives, suggested Richard Renner in the *Phi Delta Kappan,* else content designed to identify good teachers will reflect the personal judgments of its originators, and might even crystallize into "official orthodoxy."[10]

Mass-based student ratings also encourage catering to the average student concerned about presentation of subject matter, course organization, and grading procedures, while the top 10 percent prefer more independent thinking. In short, argues Renner, these evaluations "inhibit academic free expression and encourage the faculty to target instruction at the lowest denominator." Instructors who wish to win the statistical ratings game cater to the average and "emphasize at their own peril qualities that the rating form omits." It should be assumed that college instructors know their subject better than the students do, but the imposition of student ratings constitutes an "implicit demand" that professors suppress their own judgment in favor of student opinion.

The practice prevails in some of Oswego's departments but not in others, and it is favored by some people, but not by others. Professor William Scheuerman noted that the same instrument is used to evaluate small and large class sections, majors and nonmajors. "It's like comparing apples and oranges." This writer believes it discriminates heavily against instructors of large classes and those who employ unconventional though effective methods of instruction.

President Radley pointed out that "faculty evaluation is only as valid as the instrument used. Such evaluation is an attempt to stay away from the personality of the professor and to get into such questions as quality of class preparation and time taken to return papers after they have been handed in, and so on. I have found student evaluations helpful to me. You always get one or two who wouldn't like anything you did, no matter what. If, on balance, the majority of the evaluations are positive, you are probably doing a pretty good job. However, such evaluations should be only one measure. I believe in the chairs' visiting classes, and in senior professors sitting in on junior professors classes."

For whatever reason, including inefficiency, some faculty members must inevitably be dismissed; and, just as inevitably, squabbles will result. Radley has carefully followed prescribed procedures and, in almost every case, accepted recommendations of department committees, chairs, and deans. Nevertheless, pained cries of foul play have been heard. In one case, abetted by faculty members, political science students struck, demanding reinstatement of a faculty member. In another instance, positions had to be cut. A German professor, the last in the department to receive tenure, was retrenched. Rejecting an offer to take a two-year leave and thus become eligible for tenure in the English department, he took the matter to court, claiming he had been retrenched because he had once remarked that "the administration used gestapo-like and undemocratic tactics." Brought before a federal district court in November of 1977, the case was dismissed.

To reduce the incidence of dismissals caused by changing curriculum priorities, instructors may need to be retrained to move into related fields and programs. Moreover, as retirement age is raised, some may need to be retrained for greater teaching effectiveness. The same technological advances which will revolutionize colleges will require retraining faculties to use new technologies.

Whenever departments or positions are cut, Oswego's administration makes every effort to save tenured faculty members' jobs through redeployment or retraining. A philosopher and a historian were retrained in computer science, and two industrial arts instructors began working with computers. Instructors sometimes are reassigned to another department, on at least one occasion over the objections of the recipient department. In 1979, members of the Spanish department pledged unanimously to support the students' protest against the hiring of a Russian professor to teach Spanish 100. Credentials for this new assignment included fluency in Spanish, twelve hours of undergraduate work in Spanish, employment in jobs in which it was required to speak that language, and a record of effectiveness in language instruction. However, student and faculty protestors planned to deliver a formal letter of complaint to SUNY Chancellor Wharton and to stage a rally at the Syracuse hotel where the chancellor was scheduled to speak.

Dramatic changes in the college over the years, including those just discussed, have altered faculty relationships. Before the 1950s, when the college was small, all faculty knew each other. As the campus and faculty greatly expanded, and as the college changed from a single to a multipurpose institution, relationships became more impersonal. "Walls exist not simply between faculty and students or faculty and administration," said Vice President Lynn Hemink, "but within the faculty and within the administration. We haven't had a get-together of the administrative staff, crossing division lines, in ten years."

Departments are sometimes like small fiefdoms, in effect walled off from much social intercourse with others. "I'm now finishing my sixth year here," said psychology chair Norman Gordon. "When I arrived I felt I had come into a tight-knit community, and I still feel like a relative newcomer." In any case, observed Dean Barbara Gerber, "because of the economy, we people on the staff seem to be stuck with each other, so we might as well learn how to live and love."

Others paint faculty relationships in rosier hues. Oswego's retired meteorologist, Robert Sykes, said he was especially affected by certain great teachers on the faculty: Frank Hulme, Harold (Hop) Powers, George Pitluga, and Charles Yager. Provost Spencer perceives a real change in the faculty's social climate, but still much that deserves merit: "One thing that hit me full force, at the banquet for retiring professors, about today's faculty in comparison to that of ten, fifteen, or twenty years ago, is that many of the older faculty regret that personal relationships are not the way they used to be. Some of this change is a function of the growth of the college, some of departmental walls. But, even so, there's a tremendous reservoir of good will among a great many faculty. Most of them have great dedication and loyalty and, as we go into the future, I hope that we will be able to retain that sense of loyalty to the institution—it's a great thing, believe me."

While faculty relationships are sometimes neglected, those between faculty members and students have always been judged significant. In medieval times in Italy the majority of students were mature men studying advanced medicine and law, and their guilds held great power. The students themselves paid the teachers, decided courses to be given, and fined the teachers for various things, including not letting them exit promptly at the time of the bell.[11]

Nor has college teaching always been a safe occupation. A disgruntled student fired upon Aulard, a famous historian of the French Revolution, during a lecture for praising Danton at the expense of Robespierre. Sainte-Beuve, who lectured brilliantly on literary criticism in the days of Napoleon III, addressed students under the protection of several gendarmes. The great Viennese philosopher Moritz Schlick was shot on the steps of the university by a student whose thesis he had turned down.[12]

Some centuries later, in the 1960s, students began assuming a critical, sometimes hostile, though rarely so lethal, attitude toward the faculty. A 1975 *Oswegonian* editorial, "Students Screwed Again," declared that the "scheduling of the three-day final exam week by the Faculty Assembly was made for the convenience of the Assembly and not for the benefit of students. This decision seems to support the theory that the institution revolves around the desires of faculty and administrators, not the welfare of students."[13]

James Wassenaar, dean of students, believes that "students' uprisings of the late 1960s drove a wedge between them and the faculty. As a result, faculty members became less willing or less comfortable about doing things for them. Students insisted on defining their own rights and taking autonomous control of their own destiny. The relationship of advisers to organizations became almost nonexistent. not just in the Greek societies, but even academic clubs associated with particular departments. Students and faculty no longer related to each other in extracurricular activites to the degree that they did in the early and mid-1960s."

Faculty members have their own special ideas about how they should relate to students. Harvard Professor David Riesman views as counterproductive those campuses where students do their own thing and the faculty do not asert themselves with regard to curricular requirements.[14] President Radley encourages faculty members to be mentors to several students. She encourages students to get to know their professors better and professors to spend time with students, "not hovering, not mothering, but helping their minds catch fire." Dean Gerber believes it is important "for us, the faculty, to keep our ear to the ground and communicate with students. Sometimes, in doing so, they can tip you off on how attitudes are changing around campus."

An important but often ignored factor is student influence on teachers. Students may demonstrate their rejection of professors, or indifference to their ideas, through acting bored in the classroom, or by avoiding those instructors' classes. Students rarely look internally for the causes of their boredom and indifference, but instead place the blame on instructors. Often the student's attitude is one of "come entertain *me*, or I won't listen." For their part, professors' morale and effectiveness hinge importantly upon their own perceptions of student feedback.

Every Oswego professor questioned on this matter agreed that student impact is important. Rosemary Nesbitt said she learns from her students every day, and if she didn't, she believes she should leave the college. Her own main interest is in classical theater, so she depends on her students to keep up with what is going on. Modern theater "doesn't mean much to me, but it says a lot to these kids, and in theater there just can't be a gap between faculty and students."

As an example of students' impact on him, Associate Dean Thomas Gooding recalls an experience when teaching a senior seminar in existential psychology. He and the class were discussing family relationships, and Gooding noted he had not been as close to his sister as he would have liked. "The class responded, saying, 'If that's bothering you, why not go home tonight and do something about it?' So I did. I wrote my sister a letter, laid all these things before her, and in a few days a letter came firing back, saying how much she appreciated my letter. She said she had never felt estranged at all but was glad to know that I wanted a stronger relationship." Gooding also noted how inspiring he had found working with graduate students on research relating to a grant he and Education Professor Nathan Swift received from the National Science Foundation. "These students," he said, "have given us new ideas that spark us off. They have been instrumental in helping us define some of the parameters we wished to look at next."

Coordinating the foregoing faculty functions, and the nuts-and-bolts academic operations, are the department chairs; however, over the past two decades their power and status have sharply declined. Former Dean Thomas Powell observed that "years ago they were called department heads, but I haven't seen that term in years. The department head concept is that of director of the department; the chairman is essentially a housekeeper. In past years the norm was closer to the head concept, and there was not much consultation. The chairman's role was held in high esteem and carried considerable prestige. Now this position carries no prestige and is a thoroughly unenviable assignment."

Dean Donald Mathieu, also a former chair, agreed, noting that "in the 1960s when all those young faculty members were hired, there was no longer a real policy governing faculty roles. Untenured faculty members began showing up on personnel committees, and these things became institutionalized. In contrast, in our social sciences department, including thirty-three or thirty-four members, the chair consulted with a few of the senior faculty, but that was the extent of it. Even today, we have as many styles of chairing departments as we have chair people—covering the whole spectrum. Some are like officers presiding over meetings of the board when everything is voted on, and so on. The majority are probably in the middle, taking the only viable stance that one can take long term, and that is to exercise whatever influence they can with their colleagues yet give everyone an opportunity to make their views known when decisions are made."

Norman Gordon, who became chair of the psychology department in 1977, inherited the revised role. "When I first came, I had the feeling that they wanted a chairman who was not so strong as to override all their wishes but strong enough to represent their views to the administration. Instead of trying so much to initiate ideas, I tried to encourage them, which some persons might have perceived as a sign of weakness. Also, the department was so organized by committees that they took care of most curriculum matters. Therefore, I was reticent about assuming roles that I might otherwise have taken, and I respected that sort of elan."

"A major problem in this college," said President Radley, "is that, by and large, our chairs are not strong enough. The chair has to be a kind of benevolent despot, and I speak from eleven years' past experience as a chair. You have to be in control, and you have to see to it that all people are treated fairly whether they belong to the prevailing department clique or not. However, in SUNY the chairs have little power because they are not in management, but in the bargaining unit. The chairs control money, and have much to say about hiring and firing—hence, have no business being in that unit."

The various departments and their chairs differ widely in their mode of operation. The chairs of some departments exercise the deciding influence in choosing new faculty members; in others, committee members prevail. Some departments are run mostly by senior faculty members, others by juniors who may outnumber older colleagues. Cliques exercise much power in some departments, through planning strategies and voting as blocs. "Our so-called democracy backfires," said Professor Thomas Powell, "when cliques meet before the main group convenes and control the direction that the main group moves."

Departments may also have problems with each other, stemming mainly from the isolation of different disciplines. The result has been a combination of duplication of effort and neglect of topics that spill over the boundaries of single disciplines. Interdisciplinary cooperation is badly needed between departments, between schools within a university, and within universities themselves.

Nevertheless, Policial Science Professor William Scheuerman believes that "departments give faculty members a sense of identity, although those from different disciplines should talk more with each other." Former President Perdue would go further and encourage professors "sometimes to teach out of their main field despite some views to the contrary. It's the mark of a scholar to get out of your own field at times."

It is not always easy to distinguish between the powers of administrators, including chairs, and the faculty. Hence, the assembly was created to discharge SUNY's mandate that the faculty "shall have the obligation to participate significantly in the initiation, development and implementation of the educational program" and to represent the faculty in matters regarding its welfare. In contrast, the union (United University Professions) has the right to be responsible for the terms and conditions of faculty employment. Either or both of these bodies (assembly and union) may become involved when the faculty and administration disagree on certain issues. For example, Charles Eaker, Faculty Assembly chair in 1979, complained that the faculty was not consulted by standard means before President Radley granted the public safety officers the right to bear firearms. Actually, Radley was required only to consult with the College Council, which she had done. Eaker later acknowledged that the faculty had no real opinion on the issue, believing it did not affect them.

Radley pointed out that conflicts regarding college governance have arisen because the assembly misunderstands what constitutes consultation. She explained that "the SUNY Policies of the Board of Trustees place the responsibility and authority squarely upon the chancellor of the university, and he delegates that empowerment to his designee. The bylaws speak of the president as being in charge of all hiring, firing, budget preparation, the whole sphere; and the president is responsible for all those things. The president is also obligated to consult with the faculty and various other constituents, but 'consult' is defined in the *Policies* and in the contract as 'to seek advice from.' There is nothing about participatory governance in the *Policies* or in the contract. Some of the faculty have claimed that I never accepted their recommendations and never consulted with them. However, in 98 percent of all cases, I had accepted the Faculty Assembly's recommendations without emendation. In the other 2 percent, I sent them to the deans and the provost for review."

The union and the assembly sometimes disagree with each other, such as defining their respective functions. "Recently," said Assembly Chair Herbert Van Schaack, "the assembly and the union have come into conflict over a very basic issue, and that is whether or not the faculty, via the assembly and its priorities committee, should participate with the administration in deciding upon academic programs to be cut. The union argues that voiding programs means cutting employees; hence, this falls within its area of jurisdiction: terms and conditions of employment. If the faculty has participated in the decision to make such cuts, the individuals concerned in effect forfeit their prerogative to initiate grievances against the administration. The assembly, on the other hand, supports the interaction of faculty and administration on such matters, for to do otherwise would mean abdication of responsibility as mandated by the Board of Trustees. How this impasse will be settled is still unclear."

Opinions vary regarding the assembly's effectiveness. Noted one longtime professor, "it spends too much time on chit-chat and not on what really could be accomplished. The assembly really doesn't represent the faculty—it just talks about representation. It wastes time doing what is the business of the administration. The assembly has not clearly defined itself as the representation of the faculty. People on the assembly don't want to deal with real problems: they would rather invent them."

In contrast, Chairman Van Schaack believes that "the assembly has proved its effectiveness. A comparison with other SUNY colleges shows that Oswego is well ahead in its reaffirmation of the traditional role of faculty governance through its active participation in the decision-making process. Although possible onslaughts of drastic cuts in budget, coupled with sharp protests by the union, may test this participation to the fullest, I believe that the vitality of faculty governance at Oswego will survive and flourish, as it has done in the past."

Leadership of the college is ably provided by Dr. Virginia L. Radley. The first woman president in the State University, she is one of the most influential women—or persons of either sex—in higher education today. College presidents within SUNY are held wholly and solely responsible for their Colleges' destinies—hence, are granted much power. During their tenure, their policies strongly impact upon their college's destiny; and strong presidents tend to shape their institutions in the image of their own philosophies. Such personal stamping of institutional destiny is especially significant in critical times, as they were when Dr. Radley arrived at Oswego in the wake of the turbulent 1960's and early 1970's.

Inevitably, presidents' styles and philosophies reflect their own origins. President Virginia Radley grew up in Marion, New York, the youngest in a family of four brothers. "My father was a businessman," reminisced Radley, "and my mother was a teacher, but she didn't work after marriage because she had her hands full. I had a solid background with good ethical values—the whole Protestant ethic. My parents set standards and lovingly expected us to live up to them. We were always treated fairly and justly. If we deserved a reprimand, we got it whether it was withholding allowances or a spanking. I also had two high school teachers who made a great difference, one who taught English and physical education, and the other English, Latin, and French."

Now, some decades later, Radley's demeanor and character reflect this healthy upbringing. She is a poised, distinguished-looking woman whose image conveys a blend of dignity, strength, self-confidence, and warmth. She speaks very correctly in decisive, low-pitched tones; she dresses impeccably and professionally. Journalist Antoine Clark wrote to her: "I haven't seen a hair out of place, even the slightest hint of not standing up straight; and the answers she gives are always honest, factual and formal." Once, he said, "we all got a laugh when she said if she came in looking like a throw rug we'd hear about it all the way down to Fulton."

"Our president has style and flair," noted Professor Fred Ratzeburg. "The Kennedys will have to move over; we have our own Camelot right here in Oswego." Her personal behaviors are likewise presidential in quality. She displays good manners and dislikes bad ones. "When I find someone annoying," she said, "I recite Keats to myself. It's wonderfully soothing, and it works 99 percent of the time."

Radley will go to great lengths to defend and support people in whom she believes. Dominic Gangi, who said he has known Radley for "the past 100 years," since they were students at Syracuse University, remarks upon her "intense respect for human dignity. Her respect is so intense that she won't let individuals tear down their own dignity."

Dr. Bruce Dearing, then University Professor of Humanities at the SUNY Upstate Medical Center, described her as "an embattled champion of the underdog: people, institutions, and values threatened by unconcerned power, complacent laxity, or short-sighted expediency. In such contests she can be a formidable, and often victorious, adversary. She has courage and determination but does not confuse resoluteness with intransigence. She can be persuaded, but not bullied."

Virginia Radley is also warm and thoughtful, despite her hectic schedule. As any number of people can testify, a stream of notes from the president's office offers condolences to individuals who have experienced some misfortune, or congratulations to those who have achieved something special.

On the lighter side, Radley is thoroughly wholesome and human. "She's not going to let herself be shoved around," writes University of Rochester Professor Kathrine Koller, "but she has a well developed sense of humor and the ability to laugh at herself, as well as at the rest of the world."

Radley is also complex. One may identify specific traits, but it isn't easy to define the total configuration. Antoine Clark noted that "it's easy to think she's either properly British or a graduate of Harvard at times. At other times she seems to be a self-made woman who has become one of the area's most important figures."

Radley's life style is as distinctive as her personality. Every hour of every day is packed chock-full of highly varied duties. On a typical day, wrote Denise Harrigan, editor of the *Alumni Bulletin*, "she's up at five with her cats, preparing classes, reading and writing by the window that overlooks the lake. 'It's my most productive period,' she said; 'nobody calls me then.' After bacon and eggs, she heads for her office in Culkin Hall, driving an antique black Lincoln in fair weather and a CB-equipped Wagoneer in the fall and winter. She is at her office at 8:00 A.M., and evenings are devoted to dinners, meetings, and speaking engagements, which she considers important for public relations." Often she pauses to pat her cat, Sheena. Kathrine Koller, Radley's college mentor, observes that T. S. Eliot would have found her a kindred soul because of her delight in cats.

Over the years, Radley's main roles have been as teacher and administrator. She has always been a superb teacher, as the record clearly shows. She was evaluated the most effective teacher at Russell Sage College, and she received superlative ratings at Nazareth College and at Oswego. Cynthia Lovelace Sears, who was in her class at Chatham Hall, recalls, "Those of us lucky enough to have her as our English teacher quickly spread the word to the others. Miss Radley possessed the wisdom of the ages, the mystery of the sphinx, the prescience of Nostradamus. We were convinced that she must have been on close personal terms with Socrates, Shakespeare, Pope, Emerson, Hardy, Hawthorne, and every poet of the Romantic era. Clearly she made an impression. She had just turned twenty-five. In public we were always appropriately formal and polite. In private, among ourselves, we referred to her as "Rads," feigning casualness—but with a surreptitious glance cast skyward, waiting for the thunderbolt. As we worked our way through the reading list, we acquired new epithets to apply: Pallas Athena, the Dark Lady; Stern Daughter of the Voice of God; Tiger, tiger, burning bright.

"The process of learning in her classroom was fun; it was also exciting, challenging, exhilarating, demanding, and scary. She was not an easy teacher. She expected a great deal from her students, not in terms of knowledge already acquired, but in willingness to learn, to think, to grow. To be ignorant was all right—who isn't at fifteen?—but to be complacent about that ignorance, to be indifferent to cultural and aesthetic values, was to be a Philistine, a troglodyte—and we soon learned that those were the worst things one could be. Just as 'sloppy scholarship' (which, in her lexicon, covered everything from inaccurate quotations to outright plagiarism) was the gravest error one could commit."

As a successful woman, Radley has been especially helpful to younger individuals of her sex, although she's helped numerous young men, too. She says that being a feminist "is a quality of mind that believes wholeheartedly in the concept that human beings have the potential for good, regardless of what sex one happens to be. People aren't used to seeing women in the power spectrum. That's been a male domain, and it's threatening to some people, but it needn't be."

At speeches before various groups she has offered practical advice on how women can succeed. "You're not one of the boys, so you need neither drink nor smoke your business associates under the table. Have the courage to be different, but don't make a fetish of it."

Over the years, many of her students have chosen her as their role model. Diana Lauria, one-time president of student government at Russell Sage, wrote, "Although I was not an English major, and did not have the opportunity to take one of her courses, she was the role model for me of the educated, independent woman. She encourages women to be brave, not to be afraid to stand out, and to think clearly. The Russell Sage alumnae who used her as their role model didn't need the Women's Liberation Movement. They were always, and still are, way ahead of it, thanks to her!"

Virginia Radley's career as an administrator elevated her to evermore responsible roles. She was assistant dean of students at Goucher, dean of freshmen, associate dean, and chair of the English department at Russell Sage, dean of the college at Nazareth, provost for undergraduate education at SUNY Central, executive vice president and provost, then acting president and president at Oswego. In the process she established several firsts for women: she was the first laywoman to be dean of Nazareth College, first woman provost for undergraduate education in SUNY's Central Administration, and first woman president in the SUNY system.

In her Oswego inaugural speech, Radley predicted that America's further expansion into unknown areas would be not so much a physical one as in the "mind and heart of man;" and "our expansion will be one of mental rigor, of mental exploration." She promised that "we will turn ourselves to that which is quintessential, to a consideration of the quality of life."

College presidents come to be identified with particular emphases, and Radley's is academic excellence. Ruth Healey, art gallery director at Russell Sage College, recalled Radley's "struggle against her alma mater's shift away from the liberal arts towards professionalism. Only after she relocated at Nazareth College did the requirements of four semesters of English for all students cease."

Bruce Dearing, then SUNY's vice chancellor for academic affairs, recalled that "we were fortunate in being able to attract her into the Central Administration of the State University at a time when our mission was to attain and maintain rigorous standards in undergraduate education throughout SUNY, and at the same time continue the adaptation of the four-year colleges to a broader and still evolving mission in liberal education. Well in advance of the current vogue for reemphasizing the role of modern foreign languages, revitalizing the study of history, and seeking balance among the essential components of the arts and sciences, Virginia Radley was fighting valiantly in support of these values."

Locally, Radley has persisted in holding high the academic torch. She insists that baccalaureate holders should be able to "read and write, to cipher, to speak, to present themselves well, to have some historical perspective (hence, to avoid lumping World War II with the Peloponnesian wars, Socrates with Elvis Presley and the like), to have the knowledge of a culture and a language other than their own, and to have some appreciation of the arts."

President Radley is also widely recognized as a no-nonsense, effective, and talented administrator. Her own mentor, Kathrine Koller of the University of Rochester, notes that "she is able to identify a problem quickly, and her experience as a teacher, scholar, and administrator has taught her how to deal with people and to analyze the full significance of a situation. The wide range of her interests enables her to make wise decisions." Another of Radley's special strengths is the systematic review of all sides of issues, both in total configuration and detail.

Radley carefully reflects upon the validity of criticism—the inevitable result of action-oriented decision making—but doesn't buckle under to the whims and irrational attacks of others. In this regard she is reminiscent of Edward Austin Sheldon, who sustained his own share of hostile attacks throughout much of his illustrious career. "She's a real bulldog when it comes to quality," noted former President Perdue. "Some critics do not pause to realize that administrators, by the nature of their role—if they discharge it properly—will incur criticism. People forget that when you make a decision for one person it often means a decision *against* someone else. Presidents themselves must realize that criticism is not of them personally but of the way the function is discharged—else it can devastate you."

President Radley is intolerant of staff members' mediocre efforts or carping criticism but is unusually supportive of those who put their shoulders to the wheel. "She's not a watchdog, but she does like to be kept informed," said former Vice President Patti M. Peterson. She described Radley's administrative style as "very comfortable. She is very comfortable with, in fact she encourages, diversity of opinion. She is compassionate with her staff and also extremely action oriented. When a problem arises, particularly a problem that is plaguing students, she likes to move quickly. She is not a back-burner administrator."

Inevitably, because of the miniscule fraction of women chief administrators, Radley is perceived not merely as a college president but as a woman president. When she was acting president and asked whether she was criticized unduly simply because she was a woman, Radley replied: "Right or wrong or indifferent, I have too big a job to do to pay any attention to those sorts of hangups. This is 1976, not 1820."

The following episode vividly points up the still widely held image that significant people are necessarily male. Radley was invited to be the main speaker at a men's club in a nearby city. Arriving early, she stood by the cloakroom waiting for her hosts to arrive. Men began to arrive and, assuming her to be the cloakroom attendant, handed her their wraps, which she graciously placed on hangers.

Many college presidents become so preoccupied with their executive roles that they lose sight of students. With Radley, students are a priority consideration. Sherman Spector, professor of history at Russell Sage College, spoke of "her intrepid defense of student rights," while she was at Russell Sage. Diana Lauria, now with the Lincoln First Bank of Rochester, recalled Radley's "support of [Russell Sage College] students' efforts to reorganize their bylaws and to make student government a meaningful entity on campus." During those same tension-filled times, Mary Ann Oppenheimer, former editor of the Russell Sage newspaper and now Citibank branch manager in Fairport, recalled Radley as "most supportive and encouraging. Although I was a history major, I spent more time in her office than anywhere else on campus, except the newspaper offices. There are several of us who might not have made it through in one piece without her. I am proud to be part of her history, and proud that she is part of mine. I don't know if I have always been able to live up to her example of truth and beauty, but I do know that having that example, that role model, has been a never-ending source of strength. Even though I don't see her as much as I would like, I think of her often. In difficult times I remember the words she often quoted to help us through: 'to strive, to seek, to find and not to yield.'"

Cynthia Lovelace Sears, former Chatham Hall student and Bryn Mawr alumna, aptly describes Radley's capacity for helping individual students. "As she guided, prodded, and encouraged us intellectually, so she was also the one we turned to when things were troubling or confusing in our lives outside the classroom. To one another we agreed how formidable, how unapproachable, she was. Yet secretly, singly, we crept downstairs to her office during evening study hall and, one after another, would pour out our anxieties and preoccupations, our problems with roommates, French class, boyfriends, overweight, parents, whatever. She was and remains the most *complete* listener I've ever known. Without belittling our concerns, she would put things into perspective and send us off with lighter hearts and firmer resolves to 'develop inner resources'—her antidote for almost all ills."

As is true of all nationally known college presidents whose widespread activities elevate the prestige of their campuses, Radley is not always available in her office, a fact some students have criticized. When asked about a president's visibility, Radley said, "That's not the president's job. Wheeling around a dressed mannequin might do just as well." However, she contends she is among "the most visible presidents in the entire Northeast." She has set aside hours especially for seeing students, and she often sees them informally.

Sue Castrigno (1984), Oswego's Student Association president in 1983–84, found Radley "very gracious and approachable." She spoke of talking with Radley about her plans for the future. "She's accessible," said Castrigno, "and now that I'm president of the student body, she said she couldn't emphasize strongly enough that I should call on her when I need to."

Within the span of a decade, Radley's efforts as provost and vice president, then president, have yielded outstanding results. Despite the state's widespread economic problems, Oswego's enrollment has remained stable, with over two thousand more applicants than any other arts and science college in the System. In full-time enrollment, Oswego is SUNY's second largest four-year college unit. Faculty members, encouraged by the administration to upgrade the quality of their research, received over a million dollars in grants in 1983. In the meantime, anecdotal documentation indicates that students think highly of the college and of their life on campus. Residence halls, collectively, have sponsored over seven hundred organized activities during the past year; over half of these have had cultural and intellectual emphases. Students have also participated enthusiastically in campus-wide intellectual programs such as the Honors Convocation, academic receptions, and student orientation.

Many current academic events and practices are Radley innovations. One, the very effective Student Advisement Center, staffed by sixty-four faculty and student advisors, has helped to decrease attrition. Another is the highly respected Honors College, awarded a $74,000 grant for the establishment of interdisciplinary seminars. A Writing Institute, which focuses on all aspects of students' written communication, is in place. Other innovations include two summer institutes: the Methodology Institute for Foreign Language Teachers and the Gifted and Talented Institute (Sheldon Institute).

President Radley has done more than any of her predecessors, since Sheldon, to foster good relationships among all those concerned about the college, and to make its achievements known. In just one year, 1981–82, she held forty-nine receptions at Shady Shore, the official presidential residence, for students, faculty, townspeople, and visitors to the campus. Across the country, that same year, she gave forty-eight speeches to many prestigious groups. And twice, in 1982, she was voted the most effective of the guest speakers at national conventions.

Radley also does much to forge links between academia and the larger society. She has served as consultant to at least eight colleges in New York and Pennsylvania, as well as to the University of Europe in Brugge, Belgium, and to the University of Pisa in Italy. She holds memberships in, or is affiliated with, several professional associations and is listed in numerous editions of *Who's Who*. She has also served on, and sometimes chaired, many important committees and boards, among them the Marine Midland Bank Advisory board, the Sentry Life Board, the College Board Planning Committee, the Governor's Advisory Task Force on Women in State Government, the Advisory Committee on Women of the American Council on Education, the Board of Directors of the Chamber of Commerce of Greater Oswego, and the Advisory Committee of the New York State Senate Education Committee.

President Radley has been especially diligent as a commissioner on the prestigious Middle States Association of Colleges and Schools' Commission on Higher Education. Dr. Bruce Dearing, chair of the commission, testified that "her shrewd and informed judgments and wise counsel, often laced with sardonic humor, are always given respectful attention by her associates on the commission. She is often sought out by authorities in government and the educational community for advice and assistance, and she responds generously. She is appropriately recognized as a major figure in American higher education, and a person to be reckoned with as well as depended upon."

Within her own special field of academic expertise, nineteenth-century romantic poetry, Radley has contributed scholarly and widely acclaimed writing and research. She is considered an authority on both Elizabeth Barrett Browning and Samual Taylor Coleridge; and her books about them are classics in their field, widely consulted by students and specialists.

The foregoing is far from being a complete list of Radley's accomplishments—one marvels that this remarkable individual could have accomplished so much. Certainly, her daily habit of rising before dawn yields a substantial bonus of time. Also, she is favored with unusually good health and stamina. She admits the pace of a presidency is wearing: "At this point I can't even keep house plants." Only someone highly skilled in lifestyle engineering could be so productive.

Not surprisingly, in the course of her distinguished career, Radley has been accorded numerous honors. In 1969 she received Syracuse University's Distinguished Alumnus Award and the Association of Professional and Managerial Executive Women's Distinguished Administrator Award. In that same year, the New York State Legislature, the assembly and senate, passed a resolution honoring Radley for her "considerable academic and administrative talents" and for "the advancement of ideals and aspirations of academic women everywhere." She received a Distinguished Administrator citation in 1976 from the New York State Association of Foreign Language Teachers, and, from the president and faculty of the University of Pisa, a citation and its Galileo Medal. The Greater Oswego Chamber of Commerce honored her at a luncheon in 1982, and the Central New York Chapter of NOW presented her with its Trailblazer in Education award. Her alma mater, Russell Sage College, awarded her an honorary L.H.D. degree in 1981, and she was named to the Board of Trustees of Goucher College in 1983. Radley received two very significant honors in 1984: Governor Mario Cuomo appointed her to the Regional Economics Development Committee, and Russell Sage College gave her its Crockett Award, the highest a graduate can receive. These many honors accorded its chief administrator have helped to raise Oswego's prestige and to make its name widely known.

Although presidents undoubtedly are the key figures in institutional destinies, they cannot function effectively without the support of their faculties. In this respect, Radley is fortunate. Oswego's faculty is and ever has been, studded with a galaxy of high performers. Their functions, and examples of individuals who perform each, will be examined in the next chapter.

10

The Roles Faculty Members Play

THE objective of this chapter is to pay tribute to the Oswego faculty and administrative staff for their performance, and to convey at least an idea of the many complex tasks a university operation entails. A university operation is a complex enterprise involving varied tasks and many individuals with their own unique personalities and special abilities. Regardless of who is at the helm, inevitably and within all college faculties, staff members assume particular functions and roles. First, therefore, a review of several of the administrative staff who perform the key roles in any enterprise. Because of space limitations, many equally competent individuals have been omitted.

"Ours are the crème de la crème," declared Dr. Radley of her lieutenants. "We have Provost Ralph Spencer, a steady-in-the-boat person with experience in public school education and a very fine educational background. Spencer's right-hand, Associate Provost Richard Wheeler, is a doer—he accomplishes much with little fanfare and is skilled at working with committees and deftly discharging multiple duties. Equally effective is Lynn Hemink, vice president of administrative services, James Wassenaar, dean of students, who knows how to hold the line and work in the trenches. Donald Mathieu, dean of arts and sciences, is a hands-on person; he believes in face-to-face contact with his faculty. He has a fine educational background and helped to initiate the Honors College, the general education program, and many, many other programs. Dean of Professional Studies Barbara Gerber is a different kind of dean. Many students have found her to be both supportive and appealing. Finally, Dean of Continuing Education Lewis Popham, a Harvard graduate, is a man for all seasons. Probably he has the best outreach to our many publics of any of the administrators. A former dean of students, David Glick, made a truly noteworthy contribution; he managed to change the then-prevailing laid-back climate in student services dramatically and to introduce the important element of accountability. He also ably implemented the president's plan for a coordinated, college-wide advisement center and service."

The associate deans, Elizabeth Moody of professional studies and David

King of liberal arts, also deserve superlative ratings. Moody is a widely recognized authority on teacher education, a top-flight teacher, and talented organizer. Her counterpart in liberal arts, David King, is an all-round performer—competent, popular, and skilled at oiling the springs in difficult operations. Another standout is Bernie Henderson, director of business affairs, who is a master of human relations as well as budgets.

Also highly effective is Linda Syrell, dean of student advisement services, and currently vice president of the Oswego Chamber of Commerce. "She's a high-energy person," said Dean Gerber. "One of the most selfless people I know," added Elizabeth Moody.

Another administrator well known for her expertise is Patti McGill Peterson, who made an indelible mark before she was lured away to become president of Wells College. She served in the administrations of both President Perdue and President Radley. As Oswego's first affirmative action officer, Dr. Peterson was the college's pioneer in enforcing rules protecting the rights of minorities and women on campus.

Department chairs are important administrators, too, despite the recent erosion in their status and power. Although plagued by shifts in policy and budget, among those who have led their departments well are Marcia Moore, communications studies; Philip Downum, mathematics; Bruce Lester, counseling and psychological services; Richard Smernoff, foreign language and literature; Vernon Tryon, industrial arts and technology; and John O'Dwyer, physics. Augustine Silveira has made the chemistry department a model in its field; and Norman Gordon, psychology, has adroitly directed a department of highly productive, articulate individuals who differ considerably in their philosophies.

Turning to the teaching faculty, some on-campus individuals—for example, Rosemary Nesbitt, Herbert Van Schaack, and Judith Wellman—have such diverse skills as to defy classification. When asked what accomplishments she was proudest of, Nesbitt said, "being named distinguished teaching professor, being a founder of the Heritage Foundation, and bringing up exceptional children, who've 'done me proud.'" Largely as a result of her initiative, the oldest port city on Lake Ontario acquired a maritime museum. She was named a Woman of Achievement by the *Syracuse Post-Standard* in 1972 and Woman of the Year by the Oswego Jaycees in 1974. The Freedom Foundation at Valley Forge gave her its gold medal in 1975, in recognition of her original dramas for children. Another faculty member of varied skills is psychology professor Herbert Van Schaack. This alumnus and former student body president (1950–51) received the Chancellor's Award for Excellence in Teaching in 1983. A third all-rounder is Judith Wellman, historian, writer, speaker, book reviewer, and researcher, *par excellence*. She is the nation's leading specialist on the 1848 Seneca Falls Women's Rights Convention, and many of her history students intern at Seneca Falls.

Every campus has its colorful personalities, eccentric and unique in the best sense of the words. A more intrepid writer than this one must identify the eccentric; of the unique, I shall venture to name a few. Historically, there was Mary V. Lee in Sheldon's time—and Sheldon himself; later came Richard Piez and Max Ziel, both of whom survived several administrations. Currently, there is President Radley, who makes news because she is news. Rosemary Nesbitt, theater department, can make elegant drama of the least event; and Lewis "Pete" Popham has a certain class, flair, and expertise that have made him well known in his field from coast to coast. Nor can anyone forget foreign language expert Joseph Wiecha, after watching him gesture his way through an eloquent speech—which means any segment of his conversation. Or anthropologist M. Estellie Smith, whose sparkling repartee and showmanship are her students' delight.

Another very special category includes an impressive number of people who are authorities in their respective fields. These include Augustine Silveira, chemistry chair, distinguished teaching professor, and winner of over thirty awards and research grants; Kenneth Hyde, also a master teacher and research chemist; and Geraldine Forbes, historian. Sanford Sternlicht is an Elizabethan scholar; and Albert Leighton is one of the world's foremost cryptologists. Recently retired Robert Sykes was the world's leading authority on lake-effect weather.

In addition to these experts, Oswego has a bumper crop of writers and editors in wide-ranging areas of scholarship. Among its well-known poets are Lewis Turco and Sanford Sternlicht. Other poets favor a particular theme: Joan Loveridge-Sanbonmatsu's poems are political, and Nancy Osborne's feminist. Poet Paul Briand wrote Amelia Earhart's biography, *A Daughter of the Sky*. Writers of children's books are John Knapp, whose *Pillar of Pepper* contains children's nursery rhymes, and Helen Buckley Simkewicz, recently retired, who won a Literary Guild award for children's stories.

Others, especially in the social sciences, have been editors of and contributors to prestigious journals. These include Charles Bishop, M. Estellie Smith, DeWight Middleton, Ivan Brady, and Thomas Judd. David Hill is an editor of the important Emerson papers. Faculty member James Smith, who died in 1977, authored several series of textbooks for publishing house Allyn & Bacon. Ruth Everett, a now retired faculty member, edited a volume on William Blake.

Certain departments are especially prolific. Historians who have produced important books include Robert Armeson, Thomas Powell, Geraldine Forbes, Luciano Iorizzo, Albert Leighton, and Tsuyoshi Hasegawa, whose *The February Revolution: Petrograd, 1917* was reviewed as the best book on the subject in any language. The psychologists, among them Thomas Gooding, Paul Roodin, and Richard Izzett, have written a profusion of journal articles, as have the social scientists. Prolific journal contributors from other departments include David Hill and Donald Masterson (English), William Doll (elementary education), Ernest Luongo (physical education), and Harry Hawkins (technology).

Researchers, many of whom are especially adept at obtaining grants, are scattered throughout the college. Unlike the common stereotype of researchers as remote and cloistered, almost all of those at Oswego are also excellent classroom teachers. Certainly, this dual competency applies to such individuals as Thomas Gooding (psychology), Helen Daly and Richard Izzett (psychology), Terrence Hammill (biology), Karen Elias-Button and Donald Masterson (English), and Nathan Swift (education).

Oswego also has its especially creative persons, including the ones named above and many in the areas of theater and the arts. Among these are the poets already mentioned, as well as Thomas Seawall, nationally known authority on printmaking, and George O'Connell, whose work was selected for a tour of the Soviet Union in an exhibition of contemporary American graphics sponsored by the Institute of Soviet-American relations. Other creative artists include Dominic DiPasquale who, with Joseph Schoenfelt, designed the college mace; and George Stark and Socrates Sampson, accomplished cartoonists. Others, whose trademark is fresh ideas, are viewed as especially creative thinkers. Candidates for this designation are John Belt, industrial arts; Ivan Brady, anthropology; Nicholas D'Innocenzo, art; and Ronald Brown, physics.

A special sort of on-campus creativity is initiating something new—a department, a special service, or whatever. Mainly responsible for launching the Women's Studies program were Barbara Gerber, Judith Wellman, Blanche Judd, and Chris Pierce; the Department of Counseling and Psychological Services, Lucy Wing; and Experienced-Based Education, Frances Koenigsberg. Other program directors who perform in distinctive and productive ways are Donald Harrison, coordinator of services for off-campus students and veterans; June Vescio Johnston, whose office produces over three hundred publications; Robert Schell, coordinator of Information Systems; and James Howard, wrestling coach, who instituted an invitational tournament in 1957, the first of its kind in New York State.

Some individuals, so creative in the conduct of their specific functions, elevate their performance almost to an art. Among these is Coy Ludwig, director of the college's Tyler Art Gallery, always a visual feast. He was one of the ten New York museum professionals to take part in the 1973 International Museum Studies Program. And alumna Constance Bond (1951), elementary education, whose name is quite apropos, for she has constantly bonded school folk in the field to the college program by means of countless contacts and a warm personal touch. Others are James Howard and his public ceremonies committee, including two long-time members, Grace Mowatt and Shirley Hodge. This team engineers a myriad of formal programs, including graduation exercises, with a time-clock precision that would make any corporation's management envious. Among the many librarians who make an art of serving their clientele are Anne Commerton, Blanche Judd, Mignon Adams, and Nancy Osborne.

Others, known more for special skills than functions, go that extra mile in helping their colleagues: Robert Moore and Donald Masterson in writing workshops for faculty, Paul Wilbur and Thomas Mustico in matters involving computers, and Mark Morey and Robert Schell in lecture evaluation.

Such individuals often make their contributions campus wide, while others are mainstays of their departments and dedicated to helping define and implement their objectives. Among such stalwarts are Helen Daly, Owen Pittenger, Paul Wilbur and Thomas Gooding (psychology), Paul Liebenauer (physics), David Richmond (anthropology/sociology), Paul Mormon (history), Sara Varhus (English), Vincent D'Ambrosio (industrial arts), Eleanor Filburn (secondary education), Manuel Mena (business administration), and John Cooper (elementary education).

Conflicts may arise within departments and in the college generally, as personalities and ideologies clash and tempers flare. Fortunately, all colleges acquire a quota of level-headed mediators, individuals who help somehow to identify elements of agreement, allowing solutions to emerge. Examples of this essential breed are David King, Donald Mathieu, Paul Liebenauer, Thomas Gooding, and Jay Button.

Another role, that of representing the faculty, also requires unusual skill in human relations. Ever since college faculties, here or anywhere, began to gain enough power to make such a role viable, certain individuals have played roles in representing them. Over the years, Lee Marsh, John Fisher, Herbert Van Schaack, and Paul Wilbur have persisted in this task at Oswego, despite the inevitable sacrifices of such work.

Faculty members often exert leadership roles in the community or serve in other capacities. Stars in this area are, or have been, Sherwood Dunham in many capacities; Herbert Van Schaack, county legislator; and Luciano Iorizzo, chair of the county's Democratic party.

Other faculty members share their expertise with institutions abroad. While on leave, Herbert Van Schaack taught in Germany and Sanford Sternlicht in England; Geraldine Forbes, who chaired the committee that developed an international studies program, is an authority on the history of women in India. José Perez has developed an outstanding foreign studies program, and many of the faculty, including George Markow-Totevy, Frank Messere, and Lewis O'Donnell, have served as directors or instructors in Oswego's study centers abroad. Cheng Liu initiated a unique exchange program in China, and Saisuke Ieno organized the Japan program.

Another mainly "off-campus" role is that of supporting various causes: Edward Lonky, Jacqueline Reihman, President Radley—and this writer—

are all vehement supporters of animal rights. Wilma Beaman ardently defends civil rights, and Mab Huang is a champion of international human rights. Sue Weber and Helen Daly are especially concerned about the environment and are sworn enemies of nuclear power.

Perhaps the most vocal contingent, waving the banner for a cause on campus, are the feminists, beginning with President Radley herself. She defends everyone's rights and is fully alert to the obstacles confronting women. Dean Barbara Gerber is especially active in this area. She has chaired the local Women's Caucus and helped in the development of women's studies programs at Oswego, and nationally, in her work with the National Women's Studies Association. Gerber is on the Central New York Girl Scout Council Board and was a member of the founding board of the National Women's Center and Educational Institute at Seneca Falls. Nancy Osborne, librarian, is a board member or officer on national, state, and local levels in many women's organizations, among them Women Against Rape, the Seneca Falls Women's Center and Educational Institute, the National Women's Studies Association, and the Oswego's Women's Caucus. She also helped develop the library collection for Women's Studies at the college. Judith Wellman, history professor, writer, speaker, and book reviewer was a recipient of a National Park Service award for her work as historian for the Women's Rights National Park at Seneca Falls. Betty Bartkowiak, physical education, has won over sixty athletic trophies in country-wide competitions and, in the 123-year history of SUNY Oswego, is its champion of champions. She was a pioneer in promoting interscholastic athletics for women.

Joan Loveridge-Sanbonmatsu has proved both versatile and innovative regarding feminist issues. She was a founding member and first president of the Women's Career Center in Rochester, New York; co-ordinator of Women's Studies at Oswego; and chair of the Model Curriculum Committee of the Women's Summer Institute on Multicultural Curriculum Development in Chicago. During this past year she has given significant papers relevant to feminism at conferences in Washington, D.C., Rhode Island, Texas, Chicago, and Japan, and she writes political poetry, some concerned with women's issues.

Other staunch feminists abound on campus. In 1984, Marilynn Smiley gave an excellent presentation on the status of women to the local American Association of University Women. Dorothy Rogers, after many years on the National Council of the National Women's Party, was elected its first vice president. Karen Elias-Button (English) and Bat-Ami Bar On (philosophy) currently co-chair the Women's Studies program.

Perhaps the most significant of all faculty roles is that of serving students—that is what colleges are all about. President Radley advises that students are not merely to "be looked upon as English majors, psychology majors, or history majors. Students may or may not be marketable items.

There is no question, however, but that each is a man or woman studying, playing, thinking, sometimes goofing off and, most assuredly, breathing. We can and should use management systems to facilitate the student's work and life, but we must never forget that students are organic, dynamic."

Throughout its century-plus history, Oswego has been well known for its personalized faculty-student approach, and among the best at this are psychologist Mark Morey, with his always-open office-door policy, and Lewis Popham. Often such people adopt a very personal role, acting as mentor and adviser to individual students. "Celia Sgroi was very supportive of me in the public justice program," said Howard Hooper (1983). And Karen Donnellon (1984) said that "Dr. Barbara Shineman always made time for me in her busy schedule to discuss my academic work, or just listen to me." "My own personal mentor," reported Leslie Radin (1983), "is Dean Barbara Gerber. She has guided me through four years of college joy, accomplishment, tears, and problems."

Other students named faculty members who proved especially supportive when they needed it. Mike Chewins (1984) said that "Bill Lundy of the accounting department motivated me to pull myself together and get on the ball." Linda Comploier (1983) appreciated James Molinari and William George "for listening to me. They care—and are warm and friendly."

Students often credit faculty members with having helped to plan their futures. David Canfield (1985) testified that "Dr. Sorensen helped me decide what to do with my life." Andy Wray noted that "Professor Freedsen was a major factor in my deciding to become an economics major." William Scheuerman is adept at getting students excited about political science. Timothy Cochrane (1983) took an accounting course from William Lundy, "in a kind of exploratory way, and after the first week I had become an accounting major."

In many cases, a student develops a continuing relationship with a professor who serves as counselor and mentor. Sometimes a more experienced professor may become mentor to a younger professor. For instance, President Radley's guidance of her young assistant, Patti M. Peterson, groomed her for her later role as president of Wells College. Rosemary Nesbitt's mentor was Helen Buckley Simkewicz: "She talked me into writing my first book, and she took my manuscript to a publisher. She's a generous woman without a tinge of jealousy."

Some faculty members, often including mentors, keep tabs on their students after graduation, a service of much worth. Such follow-ups help to evaluate the long-term effectiveness of the college's programs, and to build a constituency of supportive alumni. Preserving faculty-student relations, and not severing them when the sheepskin arrives, is also a matter of personal satisfaction. In addition to formal follow-ups by departments, some faculty members have been especially avid pursuers of their ex-proteges' fates and futures. Charles Shoemaker in industrial arts, Elizabeth Moody, formerly in education, and Grace Mowatt in women's physical education, all have a coterie of faithful alumni on whom they keep tabs. "I keep track of my swimmers," said Mowatt. "Two are now attending, or have recently completed, law school: Dawn Slater (1977) and Laurie Irving (1983)."

Among the most significant roles of all, and one not always discharged effectively, is that of instructor of academic disciplines. Sponsored by the Carnegie Corporation, a committee of fifty-one outstanding leaders of higher education, science, government, industry, labor, and philanthropy has called for "dramatic improvement in America's whole educational system, and for an effort comparable to the ones sparked by Russia's launching of its first space satellite in 1957. It stresses the country's needs for "highly trained and talented scientists, engineers, technical personnel and persons skilled in foreign languages essential for economic growth as well as diplomacy and world understanding." For their part, students have become accustomed to doing passively what is required of them; nor has true intellectual engagement ever been common among American students, whose aims have been primarily "pragmatic."[1]

Various qualities are named as characteristic of effective teachers. David Riesman believes that the best instructors are those who remain very concerned about their teaching and view it as "an ever-renewed experiment with an uncertain outcome."[2] Oswego's Ivan Brady said we change every time we teach a course and we must, at all times, relate our approach to the students' cognitive structure. Associate Dean Elizabeth Moody advised that students should be helped to resist their need for closure and for labeling answers right or wrong. Nicholas D'Innocenzo stressed the student's personal growth as the focus of teaching; and Ivan Brady added that "you shouldn't prostitute your discipline to the language of the grocery store, yet you should make course content comprehensible to students."

Joseph Epstein, editor of the *American Scholar*, who reported students' memories in *Masters: Portraits of Great Teachers,* said that what all these great teachers appeared to have in common was love of their subject, satisfaction in helping to create this love in their students, and an ability to convince students that what they were being taught was "deadly serious."[3] Their classroom initiatives constitute a frontal assault on obsolete methods.

Joseph Wiecha, a one-of-a-kind language professor, came to Oswego from Harvard. For four straight years he was evaluated by students in their *Confidential Guide* as "probably the best language teacher in the Harvard College." One of his students, Ursula Walker, called his dedication, commitment, and personality "truly electrifying." He founded Oswego's Department of Foreign Languages and Literature, which became the Foreign Studies Center in fall 1972. In addition to the rave reviews by his students, he is recognized nationally and internationally for his foreign language teaching methods. Wiecha has given many talks and workshops on his progressive reflex method of teaching in America and abroad, including in Puerto Rico, Italy, Austria, the Soviet Union, and Poland.

Despite her crowded schedule, President Radley teaches an English course from time to time. She's adept in raising classics to prime-time status, even in students with a media-over-mind mentality who cut their teeth on TV cartoons and melodrama.

Other instructors are known for innovative teaching approaches, among them Leland Marsh. "Student roles should be active, involving discovery. Just lecturing doesn't do anything more than establish the ego of the lecturer."

Raymond Bridgers (education), like Marsh, practices the philosophy of inspiring students to be self-activators. "He would help you structure your goals," recalled Fran Lapinski (1972), "and your progress was measured in terms of the goals you had set. He helped you put a twist on something to make it your own. He helped you build a puzzle and, to the extent that you solved that puzzle, you were satisfied with the outcome. He would also put comments on your paper. Individual effort and self-expression were required."

An industrial arts professor, William Hanks, teaches his classes the morality of design, that certain things—such as beer mugs with cigarette lighters—should not be designed. He tries to teach in an interesting and human way: he had one of his classes support a one-pound brick using a minimum number of toothpicks.

Virginia Pratt's distinctiveness lies in a rare combination of knowledge of her field (American studies), enthusiasm, and personal concern for students. "Even in large classes she knew everyone," recalled Peg Lowery (1974), "and I never felt uncomfortable going to her office and telling her what my interests were. Sometimes she had individual oral exams and would sit down with you and get to know you."

Herbert Van Schaack (psychology) is another state-of-the-art instructor. "It's his ability to stay in touch with the students that helps make him so effective," said Thomas Gooding. "When we team-taught a course he suggested that every week, or every day in the beginning, we do a course evaluation. He'd say to the students: 'We would like each of you to take a sheet of paper and mark down two numbers, one on the content and one on the way the professor instructed the class. Give us a 1 to 5 rating on each.' We would discuss any respects in which we didn't get a high evaluation and talk to the students immediately. We asked, 'What do you think is wrong?' If we got a high evaluation, we'd conclude we were doing something right and must continue doing those kinds of things."

Some instructors, such as Vincent Barone, secondary education, are exacting without destroying students' self-confidence. "I worked my tail off," recalled Debbie Roe (1973), "and he expected so much of you, you just had to live up to it."

Particular courses are made popular by the instructors; three of these are James LeFlore's "Women and Culture," Terry Hammill's "Biology of Sex," and Fred Ratzeburg's "Abnormal Psychology." Individual students report highly varied courses as having had a special impact, often because of their own special needs. Randall Barnes (1985) found a communications course beneficial because he'd had "a terrible fear of speaking and of being the center of a discussion." Linda Comploier always "looked forward to going to James Molinari's class in marketing research and advertising. I'm a business major and such courses gave me direction for the future." A "high-level wellness" course, taught by Charles Davis and Thomas Chapman, impressed James Branigan because it "helped students deal with social and school pressures." Howard Hooper (1983), a public justice major, said that a criminal law course taught by then district attorney Robert Hurlbutt, "gave me tremendous knowledge of the workings of criminal courts." Thus, courses with potential impact on classroom consumers vary as much as do students themselves.

Apart from courses that have gained special reputation, Michael Wager pointed out that "students take teachers, not courses." The criteria used in judging professors include whether they are stimulating, amiable, and "incorporate into their classes a sense of kinship." Thus, faculty members come to be identified differentially according to their respective strengths or weaknesses. Sherri Marty (1984) enjoyed Professor Tullio Garzone's classes "because he's like an actor on a stage." Alice Turcotte (1984) credited Professor Helen Daly with having made psychology "understandable, and helping me pull it all together." Ronnie Vaillencourt appreciated "Professor Robert Salisbury's opening the biology lab for me whenever I wanted to use it." Halas Jackim, education, who died in 1980, has been called "intellectually rigorous," and both Thomas Judd, history and Tsuyoshi Hasegawa "very dynamic: they don't spoon-feed students." Debbie Roe called Elizabeth Moody a master teacher, whose helpfulness and criticism "never put you down but built you up. You may really have bombed, but after talking with her, you'd find another approach." Similarly, Ed Awad (1983) said he liked teachers who related to him "eye to eye, who made you feel as though you were worth something."

The following comments afford additional testimony that professors are admired for highly varied reasons:

> I only earned a C in Dr. Estellie Smith's anthro class, but she was very interesting and thought-provoking (Steven Baker, 1978).
>
> Dr. Terrence Hammill showed enthusiasm for what he taught [biology]. He's funny—and humor is important (Diane Cutler, 1986).

When Dr. James Lackey [zoology] talked about mammals, I was amazed and respectful of his knowledge. He also made you feel important and that you could do a good job (Nancy Neary, 1984).

Dr. John Belt [industrial arts], who believes in students' learning instead of being taught, develops students' creativity and self-expression; and he showed us how to relate to the unrelated (Tom Simmonds, 1984).

Dr. Norman Weiner [sociology] is extremely professional, well-spoken, interesting: he's great (Allison Morgan).

I asked Dr. Celia Sgroi (1970) [public justice] a question after class, then we got into personal philosophy. She took the time to talk with me and shared herself with me as I did myself with her (Gary Dievendorf, 1984).

Dr. David Richmond [sociology] is the most worldly, intelligent, and fair professor I ever encountered (Joseph Dodd, 1984).

Dr. Jerry Exline [music] is extremely talented, gifted, and positive in his approach (Darcy Brown, 1986).

Dr. Joseph Alessia [Italian] developed in me an interest in my past, and a desire to return to Italy to find out more about my roots (John DeFrancisco, 1983).

Students find especially appealing those professors who go out of their way to be friendly and concerned. One student noted that Gerhard Zeller (English) "was not only a good teacher but a sort of father figure and friend." William McGarvey (psychology) always struck students that way, too. "He put his subject across," recalled Debbie Roe. "He was concerned about the student as a whole person and would spend hours in the snack bar talking with us about all sorts of things."

The physical educators who are involved in both academic and extracurricular programs are in a special category. Down the decades, beginning with Mary V. Lee in Sheldon's time, Oswego has had a perennial parade of outstanding people in this area. Louise Ostberg, once a guide in the forests of northern Minnesota, almost single-handedly laid the foundations of the current women's physical education department. Hildegarde (Babette) Guttendorfer spoke several languages fluently, played several musical instruments, and made teaching dance—or anything—an art. Elizabeth Bartkowiak pitched two no-hitters in semi-professional softball games, one against the Phoenix, Arizona, four-time national champions. She won a Most Valuable Player award in softball, a Best Skier award, many championships in bowling and tennis, and one in badminton. In addition, she is one of the most popular instructors who ever tossed out a ball at Oswego.

Certainly, other women physical education proctors should not be ignored: Chair Patricia Peterson, Joan Huff, Grace Mowatt, Alice Struzinsky, JoAnn Meadows, Hilda Sorensen, Shirley Hodge, and Nancy Sigman have collectively conducted an A-1 operation.

The men have also been outstanding. Coach Walter Nitardy, whom the players call Doc, has turned out top-notch baseball teams since 1956, winning six SUNY conference titles. Thomas Brennan, golf coach since 1962, had produced by 1982 fourteen all-American national champions and compiled a fantastic 250-to-31 winning record in dual meets. He at one time was ranked among the top fifteen golfers in the state. The wrestling coach, James Howard, is another top-notcher. Between 1962 and 1980 he produced thirteen all-Americans, and he has been elected to three coaches' halls of fame.

Finally, every college has its rising stars, individuals who make their presence known within a brief time. Among these are Edward Lonky, psychology, an excellent all-rounder; William Whipple, co-director of the Honors Program; Jacqueline Reihman, Psychological Services and Counseling, a brilliant young scholar with a flair for research; Celia Sgroi (1970), Oswego alumna (valedictorian) and college lawyer; and Bat-Ami Bar On, co-director of Women's Studies, a colorful individual of many competencies.

The foregoing is a mere sampling of an unusually large fraction of talented instructors, reflecting the current administration's primary concern for academic excellence and student growth. Students, Beth Carroll (1982) among them are generally appreciative of their instructors' excellence. She observed that "in comparison with my experience at other colleges, my classes here have been far superior. They are more relaxed; there's more interaction between students, and between students and professors. Professors are more genuinely concerned about whether or not students are making progress and understanding content. It's easier to speak up in class, and even to disagree with professors than I've found true elsewhere."

In surveying students on the above matters, the writer was struck by several observations. Students have a deep need to be perceived as individuals and to feel that faculty members know their names and are interested in them. Many and diverse types of faculty members were named, not just a few stand-outs, suggesting that colleges need many kinds of faculty members to accommodate highly varied types of students. It is true, however, that certain faculty members have strong appeal to students generally. Note, too, that students often look at faculty members with eyes different from those with which the faculty view each other. Finally, Oswego's faculty as a whole is unusually strong in many areas, including student relations. Throughout its ranks, its quality deserves a four-star rating.

11

Crafting a Curriculum: Basic Issues and Liberal Arts

STUDENTS everywhere tend to show no great concern for becoming truly well educated. A report prepared for an international conference in Rome, based on 1,500 student interviews throughout the world, indicated that only one-fifth expressed any interest in studying subjects to clarify moral and ethical issues. One business major said that "morality has nothing to do with the study of business."[1] One-half of the interviewees indicated they often discussed cultural, moral, and social concerns in private conversations; however, an equal number wanted college work confined to technical competence and career training, arguing that values are formed outside the classroom.

Locally, students overwhelmingly agree that the most meaningful aspect of their Oswego experience is campus life outside the classroom, more than either the arts and sciences, or professional studies. "That's very unfortunate," said Professor Rosemary Nesbitt. "Part of that attitude is a reflection of the times. Students have been brought up on a diet of 'If it feels good, do it.'"

Concerning academic matters, a struggle developed nationally and locally during the 1970s between the student clientele and faculties, with students demanding career-oriented programs and faculties preferring a broad-based liberal arts curriculum. Great gains had been made by the professions, while the humanities experienced losses. Increased time had been allotted to electives, less to general education. Meanwhile, alumni often said they wished they had taken more of the humanities.[2]

Prominent critics and educators have united in deploring this preoccupation with vocation and have suggested other emphases. Peter Drucker notes that knowledge production has become the primary industry of our country, yet information, if not organized and rendered usable, does not constitute a viable resource.[3] The informational technology which "brings order to the chaos of information pollution" gives value to data; otherwise, the data are of no consequence.[4]

The Carnegie Council emphasizes that scientific research must become more sophisticated, since all advancements are based on knowledge. "Knowledge . . . along with land, labor, and capital is a basic factor of production."[5] Production itself depends on new technologies and expert skills which depend on the quality and level of education. This productivity, in turn, is required to advance standards of living, eliminate poverty, and employ raw materials more efficiently.

In the meantime, the more technological our society becomes, warns the Carnegie Council, "the greater is the need to offset it with more humanizing 'high-touch environments.'" For one thing, we must use our physical selves more in our leisure activities to compensate for continuous mental output in the workplace. This outcome has become apparent in the popularity of home renovation, cooking, and gardening.

Faculty attitudes toward curriculum have also been in a state of flux. In response to student demands in the late 1960s and early 1970s, more career-oriented programs were developed and more electives allowed. When he came in 1965, then-President Perdue recalled, matters of curriculum were "overshadowed by the fact that the college was moving so rapidly. When you have to hire sixty new faculty members in a year, everyone thinks about things other than curriculum." When he returned in 1982 as acting provost, a different climate prevailed. "Then," he said, "the Oswego faculty were far more concerned about curriculum than I had seen since I first came to New York."

The faculty often speak out in favor of an in-depth liberal arts education. "One thing that disturbs me," noted Professor William Scheuerman, "is how the colleges today have a tendency to put out technicians. The economy requires doing that, but it is nice to have things going besides business and computer science majors. It is helpful for these majors to be able to talk to other kinds of people."

Associate Provost Richard Wheeler calls the present situation a challenge. "We have a constant selling job, because it is not a widely held perception that one can major in history and still sell securities successfully. We do have to reckon with students' expectations, but we are convincing some students, at least, that certain of our more traditional programs can prepare them for the world of work rather effectively."

Others comment on special emphases they would like to see in Oswego's curriculum. Physics professor Ronald Brown wants a truly challenging intellectual offering for "the growing number of very bright, sometimes brilliant students we are getting here, because they can't afford to go to the private colleges. We must touch up courses and take a sharper look at the upper-level students." Dean Barbara Gerber is particularly interested in ending sexism in all aspects of the curriculum; in her "Women in Management" course she developed in students an awareness of women who have succeeded.

There is some difference of opinion about just how, or to what degree, Oswego should try to be distinctive. Sherwood Dunham, retired vice president, said, "I think we should have identifying characteristics so that we are not just like every other institution." Former President Perdue believes the college already has a certain distinctiveness, the Sheldon tradition, that should be built upon. "Perhaps it's a wishful thing on my part," he said, "but Sheldon's whole theory concerned activity—searching, feeling, demonstrating—more than being theoretical. A look at the college shows that we have art, music, theater, industrial arts, all areas where you learn and do quite directly. I can't help but think there is some sort of relationship there that we should exploit."

The question arises: should the college try to do something different to call attention to Oswego, as Sheldon did over a century ago? Richard Wheeler believes that "to the extent that we can do something better than other places, even if it's something that other places do, if we do it better, to me that is uniqueness. Everybody has chemistry programs, but I think ours is as good as any you'll find anywhere. And there are our language programs—all colleges have them, but ours are tops. And there are other examples, too."

Theater Professor Rosemary Nesbitt would oppose deliberately singling out particular departments to focus upon and make distinctive. Instead, "we should do as well as we can all the way around, and then let distinction emerge where it will. After all, uniqueness grows like Topsy. If it is there, it will surface. The worst thing that SUNY colleges can do, including Oswego, is to single out certain departments and push them for excellence. That would create poor morale. The theater is very visible and gets much attention, but people in some other departments may toil away and never get any publicity. We aren't out there seeking special attention; it is all in the nature of our work. Departments should seek out these special ways of attaining distinction, but it shouldn't be the other way around."

The local college may not have the full or final say in deciding which areas it will emphasize. According to SUNY's multiphase rolling plan developed in 1980–81, no single campus within SUNY would attempt to be all things to all students. Differences in college mission would reflect variations within service areas and type of institution and facilities. Each institution would have standards of excellence reflecting its particular mission.

Provost Ralph Spencer is well known throughout the State University as an advocate of this plan. In 1983 Vice Chancellor Sherry Penney distributed to all units Spencer's description of this plan, asking campuses to make some assessment of their own programs with this idea in mind. "In the long run," explained Spencer, "the best hope for SUNY is to coordinate and consolidate its curricular offerings. Rather than every institution trying to do more or less the same things, pick out certain areas of focus—I won't call them specialities because I'm a bit leery of specialities—and have an overall plan for SUNY. At Oswego I advocate maintaining our traditional role in teacher education, though not exactly in the old style. In contrast, many SUNY colleges are diminishing their commitment in this area."

In contrast, the faculty gives priority to general education, which has five main goals, according to Dean Donald Mathieu, a master tactition of curricular engineering. "It should provide for basic skills, including the ability to write and speak clearly, and mastery of mathematical and computational skills. A second goal is scientific literacy, which means understanding the mathematical and experimental models and the methods scientists employ. Third is knowledge of one's heritage, 'the history of Western thought', a requirement which can be met in various sequences—historical, artistic, philosophical, and literary. A fourth aim is that students become well acquainted with at least one other major cultural tradition than our own, for our very survival has become dependent on our capacity to understand our neighbors. A final objective is to understand the significance of the aesthetic dimension, and to develop an appreciation of the arts. An overall goal must be to acquire an understanding of the interrelatedness of knowledge and one's own relationship to the total environment."

Chancellor Wharton cautions that general education and basic literacy are not the same thing. The basics constitute the "fundamental building blocks," while general education involves, in addition, "analysis, criticism, and synthesis," all "very sophisticated mental processes." Students should come to college with basic skills and, when they do not, remedial programs should be provided. In all pluralistic societies, such programs are necessary to help students who come from deprived backgrounds. Wharton also disputes the notion that the content of general education has a never-changing core, rooted in past centuries. Such a nostalgic view of general education as "eternally relevant knowledge is passé, and these persistent continuities deserve examination."[7]

General education is often contrasted with two recent trends in higher education, career education and educational "consumerism," added Wharton, who described the foundation for this view. "Perhaps the single most dramatic development in American higher education during the 1970s was the demand for career programs, and the trend persists." Career-related courses, Wharton said, are the "shopping basket or consumer approach to choosing courses." Students choose among various offerings, often defending them as being more personalized or suited to the individual. The result has been a fragmentation of the traditionally integrated course of study with its orderly sequences, patterns, and general education core. This trend has borne the banner of relevance, education designed for achieving certain individual and social goals. However, what one generation may find relevant another does not. Also, those courses may appear most relevant which are least so. Courses designed specifically to relate to today's world may be quickly out of date, while presumably irrelevant courses that focus on basic concepts have a more enduring value.

Wharton suggests that career education and general education merge under the broader umbrella of educational competence, which includes symbolic competence (basic literary skills and foreign languages, including non-Western and emerging ones) and epistemological competence (dealing with structures of knowledge required for modern society, including the latest skills in "research, information organization and knowledge management . . . and computer literacy as well").[8] Cultural competence more closely resembles what has generally been termed general education, having to do with the individual's relationship to the cultural milieu, past and present, including the cultural and artistic heritage of present-day society. However, successive generations "reinterpret" tradition in their own manner.

General education for cultural adequacy in the next century will have to do much more than did the old Western civilization courses. Students must learn to live in a whole series of overlapping communities: family and home, workplace, state, nation and world. The trend toward globalism is proceeding fast, yet most students have little interest in other cultures. Globalism suggests not only more and better courses in foreign languages, but also much stronger offerings in world history, area studies, and non-Western approaches to science and the humanities. In short, the overall goal of higher education is to produce educated people in the broader sense of the term. In a knowledge-centered society, this kind of education isn't simply a symbol of distinction but is necessary for participation in the modern world.

Nationwide, the colleges quickly fell into line behind the general education concept. Harvard's Rosovky Plan became a sort of Magna Charta for such education in the early 1980s. About that time the Alfred P. Sloan Foundation reported on "the new liberal arts," insisting that general education be adjusted to a culture in which "quantum theory and Shakespearean drama are equally important—and equally humanistic."[9]

Since fall 1980, Stanford University has required all entering students to take a year's course in Western culture, jointly taught by faculty members from varied departments. In addition, students are required to take at least one course in each of seven broad areas: literature and fine arts; philosophical, social, and religious thoughts; human development, behavior and language; social processes in institutions; mathematical science; natural sciences; and technology and applied sciences. Thus, notice was being served that the academic permissiveness of the 1960s had "been found wanting."[10] In the meantime, throughout the SUNY system, there had been a move toward general education, or core courses, that students took during the first two years; and English composition courses, in particular, were being upgraded. As Chancellor Wharton points out, learning basic skills is only the foundation for general education, but an important one, and this learning was dismally neglected in the 1960s and the early 1970s. He added that many young high school, even college, graduates, "cannot write acceptable English, or even do simple arithmetic. For the first time in American history the generation moving into adulthood is less skilled than its parents."

More specifically, Oswego's revised general education program was designed to provide students "a broad, yet deep, perspective, which would relate their subject matter to general and fundamental intellectual issues and would stress the development of skills of thought and expression. Basic requirements would be at least three to six hours of English composition, with an emphasis on expository writing, and the same number of hours of basic mathematics. The revised humanities requirements would include nine semester hours each of natural and of social and behavioral sciences, and a six semester-hour sequence in Western heritage, as well as nine hours from two areas, which would include fine and performing arts, literature, historical studies, and ethical philosophical analysis."[11]

Locally, this development has been favorably acclaimed, at least by the faculty. "When I came here as provost in 1974," recalled President Radley, "there was no structure or rationale in the curriculum. Oswego had gone the way of many colleges and had a lunch-counter sampler with a junk-food curriculum. A collection of 122 hours of almost anything would suffice to get a baccalaureate degree. This new program is a great improvement, with one basic flaw, that there is, as yet, no foreign language requirement. Certainly, the humanities majors should have a language other than their own, and all majors should have some acquaintance with a foreign language. To date, however, we have not found the means to accomplish this desired goal."

Radley disagrees with faculty members who argue that "our general education curriculum is 'Europeanist'. I say, 'Now listen. First of all, we don't have the faculty who know all of these countries, and all these cultures in the Middle East, the Orient, and Africa. Secondly, our students desperately need to know something about their own Western culture, including America. Our students don't know American history, let alone English, French, German, Italian, and Spanish. Students need this 'History of Western Civilization' course that all must take at one time or another. We should offer courses in Eastern civilization and Eastern art, and certainly we should emphasize Russia. We have faculty members here who know something about Africa, but those courses cannot be in the mainstream at present, because Western World priorities are greater now."

Reprogramming curricula around a general education core has not been all smooth sailing. Each department, of course, insists on its slice of the pie. Those students (and their parents) who want career-oriented programs, especially in business and computer science, must be coped with. "It's the whole program that counts," observed Provost Spencer, "not just the major, but it's a difficult message to get across."

Among the most highly respected areas of on-campus general education are the fine and performing arts, wherein students of all varieties and gradations of talent develop their creative skills. "The staff members involved," noted Dean Mathieu, "develop excellent rapport with their students, and spend much time with them out of class at special events and ceremonies." Adding to this healthy ambience is Tyler Hall, the fine and creative arts building, a "second home to some three-hundred majors in the areas of art, theater and music," Mathieu said. It was built in the 1960s and named for a local artist with a national reputation. In Tyler, said Mathieu, "students may be seen toting portfolios and canvases, carrying musical instruments, or be heard singing choral scales, or be observed reciting lines and gesturing." There are studios for print-making, jewelry, sculpture, painting, drawing, and design, and a ceramics studio where students create forms in clay. Student voice and instrumental recitals and programs by the Tyler Chamber Readers are held in the Tyler Galleries, in which there are musical studios and practice rooms. The main foyer is a visual treat, reflecting Tyler's "cosmopolitan world of creativity and talent."[12]

The art department grew from six staff members in 1960 to eighteen in 1984, and its courses from thirty-four to about eighty, including minors in art history and museum studies. The first art chair was Aulus Saunders (1942–1967), followed by George Stark (1967–1977) and, since then, Thomas Eckersley. The art department offers courses in painting, drawing, two- and three- dimensional design, photography, graphic design, print making, ceramics, sculpture and metalsmithing/jewelry. Both lecture and studio courses are supplemented by instruction in the campus art galleries where colorful, mind-stretching exhibits are regularly held, including national shows. "In art we have a number of very productive people and very good teachers," noted Dean Mathieu. "I'd put them up against any in the system. Some of them are quite unusual—for example, Coy Ludwig, who is in charge of the galleries. He does a magnificent job with the kind of budget he has, and the galleries attract a lot of attention."

The art staffers make their subject more meaningful by placing it in historical, cultural, and sometimes local perspective. Nicholas D'Innocenzo and some of his students developed a riverfront park on the edge of town in the early 1970s; they built the park benches and fencing themselves. Several years later, during a park "face lift", members of the Student Industrial Arts Association "bent over backwards to help us out," Mathieu said. They repaired the fence, dredged the waterfront, and repainted the park benches.

The highly versatile art staff involves its students in other projects as well, such as erecting murals, creating sculptures, and compiling a slide library (now containing about 32,000 images). Each year the department takes students on trips to New York City and to Washington; they visit major galleries and museums, chat with well-known artists and critics, and visit artists' studios. Not surprisingly, a campus evaluation rated the art department as one of those on the verge of national recognition.

Music is another of the college's top-rated departments. Chaired by Marilynn Smiley from 1975–1980 and since then by George Cuppernull, the department has three areas: history, literature, and performance or applied music. SUNY's main music schools are at Potsdam and Fredonia, but Oswego's distinctiveness derives from its emphasis on the liberal arts. Its program has been rated among the best of its type in the country.

The music department has a long history of exciting tours; on a 1967 tour the symphonic choir performed in the International Band festivities at Montreal's World Expo. The band shell was located amidst small shops "selling everything from a run-of-the-mill cold hot dog to a . . . Belgian waffle, which tasted like soggy shredded wheat."[13]

The department's musicians, both staff and students, provide a smorgasbord of delightful entertainment. The State Singers, a vocal group directed by James Soluri, tours a great deal, sometimes for the Alumni Association, and often visits high schools. The Chamber Singing Group, a select group of twenty-four singers with a classical repertoire and directed by Paul Mueller, goes on many tours. About five years ago it was chosen to perform in several European festivals, one of about four groups from the entire United States. On one occasion, in 1978, the college choir toured Washington and Baltimore; it sang in several churches, including the first Roman Catholic Church in the United States (Baltimore).

In some years as many as sixty concerts have been given, ranging from rock to the classics. Some concerts are given in high schools during student recruitment programs, often by Professor Hugh Buritt's Solid State jazz-rock group. And a string trio, composed of Professor Jonathan Shallit, violinist Daniel Barach, and cellist Walter Freimanis, has gone to high schools for the past four or five years to conduct recruiting workshops.

Other concerts are conducted each year to raise money for scholarships, both for present and prospective students. One concert, given by the local musicians' union, paid for a scholarship commemorating the late Paul Rogers, a long-time member of the music department; and an alumni scholarship is named for Maurice Boyd, former music chair. Another group, the SOS Rock Band, gave a benefit for the Delta Kappa Kappa fraternity when its house was destroyed by fire. This band, formed by James Soluri in fall 1982 for Parents' Weekend, first called themselves the Sons of Sam, later the Sons of Soluri, and then just SOS. The band's bass player, Luciano

Iorizzo, says, "We are just a bunch of nutty guys." Members of the music faculty also perform frequently, sometimes individually and sometimes as ensembles. One piano duo, Anthony Crain and Jerry Exline, make their own personal musical arrangements.

Music activities have proved a healthy tonic for community relations. The College Community Orchestra, directed by Walter Freimanis, puts on children's concerts, using child musicians from the community. The Festival Chorus has toured the United States and gives two or three concerts a year. Directed by Leon Carapetyan, the chorus specializes in large ensembles as in "The Messiah" and, on one occasion, was chosen to perform in a concert by the National Piano Teachers Association. The Oswego Opera Theatre, a college-affiliated organization managed by James Soluri, has made Oswego something of a regional opera center. The Oswego and Bronx Opera Companies work jointly, a relationship that grew out of the directors' friendship.

Another fine-arts area, speech and theater, became two departments in 1973, theater and communication studies. Sanford Sternlicht became chair of theater, with Rosemary Nesbitt as supervisor of acting and directing, and John Mincher in charge of scene design. All three are master coordinators of talent and widely recognized for their expertise, as indeed are their six fellow staffers. Both Sternlicht and Mincher have worked with off-Broadway plays. Sternlicht designed a course called "Introduction to Theatre," in which students are introduced to theater history and to the role of the critic, a course now widely copied by other colleges and universities. In addition, said Nesbitt, "Anderson McCullough, our resident playwright, teaches the art of play writing. Demonstration classes are provided in such areas as scene building, costuming, makeup, acting, and directing. Theater majors see four plays, review them, and each designs a box set or produces a play." Nesbitt herself is a director and prolific writer of plays, many for children; and Kathleen Macey has done important work in costume design. Every year the department's repertoire includes about twenty one-act plays, a summer theater program, a tour by the Chamber Raiders, productions directed by students in experimental theater, and four major plays in the Waterman Theatre. The plays include musicals, classics, modern drama, black theater, and children's theater.

Nesbitt captured the flavor of the current department in a few cogent remarks. "Because of changes in staff personnel we have shifted from dilettantism—'theaters are nice places to go to all dressed up in the evening'—to professionalism. The theater is a place of hard work and absolute dedication, a place of ultimate truth. It is one of the great original fine arts, and we must pull the scales from in front of students' eyes. Theater people have to know liberal arts upside down and back and forth. If you do a Shakespearean play you must know all about the Elizabethan period, politically, philosophically, and socially."

"Our students are more mature now than formerly," continued Nesbitt. "There is much scene selection in the theater, and their maturity in that area is many times better than it used to be. There was a time when a boy, on his own, would never select Hamlet, but he does now."

Many of Oswego's theater alumni have achieved positions of distinction, some as scene designers in the Metropolitan Opera House. Those who double-majored in theater and music or communications include Thomas Morse (1974), Broadway sound designer, whose credits include "Playing Our Song" and "Joseph and the Technicolor Dream Coat"; and George Dummit (1969), a Broadway stage hand and master electrician for "Children of a Lesser God" and head rigger for "Best Little Whorehouse in Texas." Others are Jeffrey A. Billings (1971), costume designer and assistant to Bob MacKee who costumes Peggy Fleming and Cher, and Alice Maguire (1976), who was prop master for the Juilliard School, the Santa Fe Opera, and the movie, "Friday the 13th." Jon Vermilye keeps a complete file of the theater alumni and maintains a very personal contact with them.

Theater's former academic partner, Communication Studies, offers three areas of concentration: general communications, communications studies, and broadcasting. The number of majors has burgeoned from ninety in 1973 to six hundred in 1981. Initially this program was part of the English department; in 1973 the Department of Speech and Theatre split, with theater becoming one department, and speech and broadcasting another. The latter, renamed Communication Studies, was chaired by Vernon Rank until 1975 and since then by Marcia Moore. This department initiated an internship program in which students work in industry at such locations as Broadway, Wall Street, and Madison Avenue in New York and in Washington, D.C. Also, through participation in a national telecommunications hook-up, the department provides an upper-level broadcasting course. One of its most unusual courses in fall 1982 was Joan Loveridge-Sanbonmatsu's intercultural communications class, which concerned controversial issues such as racism, prejudice, sexism, and homophobia. Students were admitted to the class by interview only, to ensure representation of a wide variety of ethnic, racial, and religious backgrounds.

In a more traditional area, English, chaired by David Hill, a revival of interest in the classics is evident. The development represents a reaction against the largely social relevancy of the 1960s, writes David Riesman. "An education clearly beyond utility is essential, not just for life but for the good life," observes University of Chicago's Eva Braun.[14] The study of the great classical works provides a fulfilling means for appreciating the Western tradition.[14]

When Radley came to Oswego as its provost, she deplored the status of students' knowledge of English literature and communication. "I saw that students couldn't write very well," she said, "and they hadn't read literature in terms of any cohesive pattern. They didn't know anything about Shakespeare, Chaucer, Milton, or major writers of the eighteenth or nineteenth century. I don't even know whether they knew the twentieth-century writers. They had had a dab of this and a dab of that. They didn't know how to use the library, how to handle secondary sources, or to read primary sources. They didn't know how to read poetry. They were no worse than students in many similar colleges, but this situation couldn't be allowed to continue because many of them were going out to teach. I convinced the English department, through some rather strenuous methods, not always happily from their point of view, to revise their major curriculum."

Typically, Radley took firm hold, increasing freshman composition sections from three to forty, and tossing out the window courses in "folklore, witchcraft, sex, and literature." She confesses she "might not have won any popularity contest" but would rather be disliked than not do what she believed was correct. Henceforth, English majors would be extensively trained in writing, critical reading, and research, as well as in literature. She insisted on resurrecting the classics and restoring them to prime-time status.

Radley also restored respect for composition and properly written sentences. She believes a college degree should connote, among other things, an awareness of displaced commas and respect for diagrammed sentences. "Because of Dr. Radley," said Dean Mathieu, "Oswego was well ahead of the pack in its emphasis on composition and expository writing, not only in SUNY but nationwide. Of course, they [other colleges] are all trying to catch up now."

Lewis Turco, founder of Oswego's writing arts program, calls the program "second to none in the United States" and the quality of students in the program "fantastic." What distinguishes this program from that of other schools, he said, is that "here we prepare people for careers in writing. A high percentage of our graduates enter careers related to this field."

Also remarkably effective is the college's Foreign Language and Literature program, a fortunate emphasis in these times. Rapidly progressing globalization makes it essential that a language and cultural renaissance occur. Earlier predictions that English would become the one world language overlooked the world's cultural diversity; hence, Americans must learn other languages and learn them well. Indeed, for individuals to be successful it has been suggested that individuals be trilingual: fluent in English, some foreign tongue, and the computer.

Oswego's foreign language programs embrace three departments: French, Italian, and Classics (chair, Richard Smernoff), German and Slavic (chair, Edward Nordby), and Spanish (chair, John Demidowicz). Not only do language majors acquire proficiency in their respective languages but also an appreciation of the cultures involved. Majors often take courses outside their department in international trade, economics, law, health services, and communication studies. Foreign languages are important also, in such fields as writing, the airline industry, and export divisions of international corporations.

The language staff is widely recognized for its unusually effective methods. For example, in spring 1973, Susan Smernoff of the Russian faculty used a Soviet daily newspaper as the class textbook in her course "The Soviet Press" to introduce advanced students to everyday Russian vocabulary. Through reading the newspapers, the students also gained first-hand knowledge of daily Soviet life to the extent the government press was willing to disclose it. Another master of the language teaching art, Joseph Wiecha, demonstrated before the college council several students' facility for switching easily from one language to another; it was an incredible performance.

Of special significance in these programs are opportunities to study abroad. Spanish majors study in Spain or Puerto Rico; French majors participate in a summer program in St. Malo or a year-long study program in Paris. German students may choose exchange programs with either the University of Wurzburg or the University of Gottingen, or a summer program in Bregenz, Austria. In 1980, four Oswego students, Diane Travis, James Osborne (1980), David Madore (1979), and Edward Marron (1980), were cited by the Goethe Institute of Munich for their performance on a worldwide test, administered twice yearly by the institute.

The Russian exchange program is especially noteworthy, partly because Oswego has the only Russian major in SUNY. Then SUNY students spend a semester studying at the world's most prestigious language institute in Moscow, while ten Soviet students attend a SUNY college. Of the ten SUNY undergraduates chosen for the only exchange program between the Soviet Union and the United States, five in 1982 and six in 1983 were from Oswego. More often than not, the on-site coordinator of the program has been from Oswego, for example, Drs. Sue Fines and Edward Nordby.

In the meantime, foreign exchange students have had memorable experiences at Oswego. On Halloween weekend in 1982, Oswego's Russian club entertained eight Soviet students who were then enrolled at SUNY's Center in Albany. They toured the campus, played frisbee, and stopped at a downtown store to see "punk clothes." One bought a pair of shoelaces with red and blue stars. Later they went trick-or-treating with members of the Russian Club and saw a cult film, "The Rocky Horror Show."

A group of West Germans, ranging in age from eleven to seventy, came to Oswego in 1977 to study U.S. culture. While here they attended classes and worked in the language lab at Sheldon Hall. They said they would always remember the sunsets and their afternoons on the tennis courts. Many played frisbee, a game new to most of them. Among their favorite places in town were Buckland's, the Great Laker Inn, and the Ferris Wheel. One of the Germans left proudly sporting a green-and-white Oswego sweatshirt.

An exchange program with Japan was added in the late 1970s. Fourteen Oswego students spent a semester in Japan in 1977, studying film making, slide photography, AV (audiovisual) media and technology, and taking a Japanese language course. This program is unique, since it is the only government-funded program between two universities within the AV media and technology field of study.

Such diverse experiences might simply produce confusion and conflicting values if students did not understand basic human philosophies; hence, the significance of the philosophy department (chaired by Charles Echelbarger). However, it is somewhat uncertain these days just what the role of philosophers should be. Writer Ronald Labuz believes that students avoid philosophy courses because "the image of the philosopher in America is that of an inessential, somewhat mystical academician."[15] Princeton University Professor Richard Rorty contends that contemporary philosophers' debates have become fruitless and often boring, having little to do with other areas of current cultural and intellectual life. Philosophers are rethinking traditional methods and theories, as well as their basic assumptions regarding the relationship of philosophy to the rest of Western culture. No longer can philosophers look upon themselves as overseers of other disciplines; they may not even have a distinctive discipline of their own. Rorty suggests that the philosopher's real role may be "to become the socratic intermediary between various Discourses."[16]

Certainly, philosophy has a role in a pluralistic world with competing, often confused, ideologies. Especially when ethics and values are shaken loose from their bearings, students need to develop a philosophy onto which to anchor their own beliefs. Locally, said Oswego's philosopher Chris Pierce, a current emphasis is on applied ethics and on a combination of the applied and the traditional. Students often intern in Washington, D.C., agencies and, later, many go on to law school.

The gap between the foregoing areas and the traditionally more "practical" subjects, among them mathematics (chair, Philip Downum), has narrowed as the latter now stresses theory as well as practice. Its members have shed their orthodoxy and called a truce with pragmatism. The mathematics department prepares students for careers in applied mathematics and for advanced degrees in mathematics and related fields. Its graduates become employed as statisticians, mathematicians, systems analysts, mathematical economists, and teachers; they also gain expertise in modern computing techniques. "After all," noted Professor Ronald Brown, "students preparing for many areas need a basis in mathematics because it is the language of science."

Most of the current staff were theoretical mathematicians when they came but retrained to embrace also the new applied emphasis, particularly after the arrival of computer science. Therefore, with the advent of sophisticated mathematical models, students can look at the economy and the stock market more scientifically than previously.

The department has employed various techniques to make its instruction more palatable, effective, and useful. Students with deficiencies receive tutoring at the math center in the Office of Special Programs. Noncredit courses in basic math are also provided, including a lab follow-up. Frederic Fischer's course, "Math for the Math-anxious," has been especially helpful: students no longer get mangled in scrimmages with logarithms and lost in jungles of statistics. Several instructors do intensive work with individual students. In the meantime, Fischer and psychology's Mark Morey keep tabs on students' progress through careful evaluation.

Neither mathematics nor a related area, computer science, need be dehumanizing. After all, concludes John Naisbitt, an authority on current trends, computers represent the only way to keep track of numerous groupings in our society and to allow for individually structured adaptations.[17] In confirmation of such views, the 1983 annual conference ("The Entry of Colleges and Universities into an Information Society") of the American Association for Higher Education predicted that there would be over twenty times as many microcomputers in use on college campuses in 1985 as there were in 1980; within two decades computers would replace the book as the chief delivery service in educating students; and personal microcomputers would increase "scholars' freedom from centralized bureaucracy, by allowing individual control of the technology and direct access to widely dispersed sources of information."[18]

Students and most faculty members, except for the more theoretically, less practically inclined, believe computer literacy to be essential. Oswego student Ed Awad (1973) notes that we live in an age of computers and will continue to do so. Many Oswego professors use microcomputers for such tasks as word processing, computation, record keeping, recreation, creation of teaching programs, graphics, and accounting.

Oswego's eight-member computer science department (chair, Elizabeth Brindle) combines a sound theoretical approach with high standards of practical expertise; its graduates obtain positions as programmers, research assistants, and systems analysts. Theirs is the wave of the future and, for now at least, they are riding its crest. Nonmajors, too, find computer skills helpful in getting jobs. As an illustration, Associate Provost Wheeler tells of an experience communication major Steven Shapiro (1978) had while on spring break in Fort Lauderdale. While lying on the beach "baking the Oswego frost out of his bones, he began wondering what he would do that fall after he graduated. So he decided, just for fun, to apply for a job there. In a Fort Lauderdale newspaper he found a help-wanted ad placed by the Motorola Corporation and said to himself: 'Well, since I'm in communications studies and that's Motorola's business, I'll reply,' so he made an appointment. He was talking with the interviewer and coming to the conclusion that the man would simply tell him, 'Thank you very much for your interest in Motorola. If something comes along that you may be interested in, we will call you.' However, at that point the man asked: 'What courses other than communication and broadcasting have you had?' Steve replied, 'Let's see. I took four courses in computer science and some in psychology.' The guy sort of jumped out of his chair and asked: 'Do you know FORTRAN? Can you program it?' Steven's answers to the questions that followed were mostly yes, and he was hired right on the spot, not because he was a communication major but because he had taken electives in computer science. They were also interested that he had taken electives in psychology. Now he is part of an internal executive training program which some people in Motorola require years to enter. At least at Motorola in Fort Lauderdale they think Oswego is Harvard, Yale, Princeton, and MIT all rolled together, because of this young man's success."

Change in science instruction is as exciting as the development of computers. After all, it is essential to understand scientific principles in a world dominated by science and to appreciate that scientific knowledge persists in a forever state-of-flux, wrote Harold Shane in the *Phi Delta Kappan*.[19] Science fiction has turned out to be for real. In addition, all knowledge is to some extent subjective, and choices of action are open to debate. Despite this need, noted James Rutherford of the American Association for the Advancement of Science, science education in the United States has declined rapidly in recent years, thus "dangerously undermining our economic health, productivity and national security."[20] At the same time, other countries, including Japan, China, Russia, and West Germany, have been stressing it ever more heavily.

Given this grim scenario, how well are Oswego science programs faring? In the chemistry department, chaired by Distinguished Teaching Professor Augustine Silveira, Jr.—the college's longest continuously serving chair and among Oswego's most talented at putting the intellect back in vogue—students pursuing B.A. degrees prepare to enter professional schools, such as medical or dental; those pursuing B.S. degrees anticipate chemistry careers in industry and government or attendance at graduate schools. The department has developed a cooperative program with chemical engineering departments at other colleges; students study for three years at Oswego prior to spending two years at the cooperating engineering college. Upon graduating, these students receive Oswego's baccalaureate degree in chemistry and a Bachelor of Science degree in chemical engineering from the cooperating college.

Associate Provost Richard Wheeler declared that "Oswego's chemistry department is as good as you'll find anywhere," and the evidence confirms it. In 1967–68, it became the first within any SUNY college to receive accreditation for its programs by the nationally recognized American Chemical Society. It was also the first SUNY college to offer an ACS-accredited Bachelor of Science degree, and the first to offer a Master of Science degree in chemistry. In addition, Oswego's chemistry department has often led all SUNY colleges in graduating the largest number of students with ACS-accredited degrees. Moreover, not one of the approximately one hundred Oswego chemistry graduates who has gone on to earn a Ph.D., or to an M.D. or a D.D.S., or other advanced professional degrees, has ever failed.

Indeed, Oswego's chemistry students and staff bear strong and continuing testimony to the department's excellence. For many years, Oswego's American Chemical Society student affiliate has been one of the 34, out of 767, designated as outstanding by the society, a well-deserved honor. On one notable occasion, a paper presented at the thirty-fifth annual Eastern College Science Conference by Gregory Kon, one of Silveira's students, was chosen the best of the more than one hundred papers presented. Silveira and Professor Kenneth Hyde are among the leading chemistry researchers and writers in the country.

Another Oswego science department, physics (chair, John O'Dwyer), focused on theoretical and experimental emphases until a decade ago. There was almost nothing of an interdisciplinary nature or offering that might appeal to liberal arts majors or one that attracted physics majors with special interests in that area. However, over recent years, the picture has dramatically changed, as physicists seek answers to phenomena which could result in cosmic upheaval. The physics department provides programs in theoretical and experimental physics as preparation for careers in technologically oriented businesses and industries. Some of the course work is derived from engineering texts, such as electronics, thermodynamics, and electromagnetism. In undergraduate experimental work, the department's nuclear laboratory has been heavily involved in trace metal analyses using x-ray flourescence techniques, which are of special interest to the environmental sciences. Many students go on to graduate programs in various branches of applied science, and some to engineering colleges. To pursue interdisciplinary studies in graduate schools, many students couple a physics major with another major in chemistry, mathematics, meterology, biology, or zoology.

Perhaps the greatest change in recent years, noted O'Dwyer, has been in developing attractive general education options for liberal arts students and increasing the applied content of the physics programs. A comparison of the four-year SUNY colleges showed Oswego's general education offerings in physics to be about twice the average. Especially popular general education options have been the courses "Realm of Physics" and "History of Ideas and Concepts of Physics." The "Light and Color" course has attracted students in art, photography, theater, and communications. "Sound of Music" has appealed to students in music and theater, whereas the course on energy has proved of great appeal to students in general.

Also popular are the biological sciences, focused in two departments: biology (chair, James Seago) and zoology (chair, Sigurd Nelson), the only four-year program of this type in SUNY. "The single most notable development in the biology department since the 1960s," said Seago, "has been involving students in science research, which has inspired many former students to achieve advanced degrees or enter the world of science. In one of the most unusual programs in New York State, if not the country, our students are required to undertake solution of problems relating to their own special interests."

Many biology graduates have pursued careers of distinction. Two Oswego graduates, Steve Wolniak (1972) and Suzanne Schwab (1975), while graduate students in California, won awards for the most outstanding presentation of a Ph.D. thesis in plant physiology at annual meetings of the Botanical Society of America.

About one-half of the students enrolled in the biological sciences program major in zoology. After attaining a degree, they work with animals in some way, usually in laboratories, fisheries, or in the wild, as well as in zoo technology. Oswego has an articulatory agreement with a community college in Gainsboro, Florida, which operates a teaching zoo. Zoology students also use the Rice Creek Biological Field Station in Oswego, directed by Donald Cox; here they gain a background for future careers in such areas as dentistry, medicine, veterinary science, physical theory, medical technology, optometry, and podiatry. Graduates prepare for advanced studies and for employment in laboratory, environmental, or ecological work. Also important for biological instruction is an electron microscope, which magnifies to 70,000 times. Valued at $80,000, the electron was donated to the college in 1983 by the JEOL Company of Oak Ridge, Tennessee. "The field station has also done marvelous things for public service," said Dean Mathieu, "in terms of mini-courses, Saturday and evening courses. Some of these courses are quite unusual—for example, studies in taxidermy, and the effects of winter on habitat." Another zoology program, which has involved many students, is the study of myrex (a pesticide) in fish, supported by Kathryn Martin's significant research grant. "The biological sciences," observed Professor Sigurd Nelson, "are no longer merely descriptive. They have changed greatly through their emphasis on molecular biology and genetics."

Like biology, the earth sciences department (chair, David Thomas), offers two majors, geology and meteorology, as well as minors in astronomy, marine sciences, and geology. Currently, geology has a more or less unified theory that explains many geological phenomena, such as the production of mountains along the sea.

Oswego's meteorology program is the only one of its kind in this area and is outstanding. Its recently retired professor, Robert Sykes, has been rated by experts, including the head of the U.S. Weather Service, as the world's leading expert concerning lake effects on weather. Graduates of the program are much in demand and obtain positions with the national meteorological and weather services, some as forecasters and some as radio and TV weather personnel. Oswego's location is especially favorable for meteorological studies because of the lake and accompanying weather events.

Turning to the social sciences, Bachelor of Arts students in psychology (chair, Norman Gordon) study behavior within the framework of a broad liberal education; they prepare for graduate work in psychology and related fields. The Bachelor of Science degree is designed mainly for students preparing for careers in psychological research. Psychologist Mark Morey believes that a main emphasis in psychology today is the return of interest in the mind and how thinking occurs. Upgrading the quality of life is another theme. This department, the largest in SUNY arts and science colleges, offers a wide variety of courses.

Gordon's first impression of the department, and "one that still remains with me, was one of fierce pride which seems to unite people of quite diverse views. This pride is well deserved." The department is well known throughout the East, and especially in New York, as a place to study psychology. Students who transfer here from other schools say they heard that if you want to major in psychology, you come to Oswego. We know, too, of institutions that welcome our graduates because they have had real success with them." The department has other distinctions. Its staff members are prolific writers, among the best grants winners on campus, and dedicated researchers who involve students in their research. Richard Izzett explored the views of 131 psychology students regarding the Vietnam war; 65 of the subjects interviewed had demonstrated against U.S. involvement in the war by boycotting classes on October 16, 1969, the day of the moratorium.

In anthropology, a related science, students learn that people's behaviors are a result of their unique cultural backgrounds.[21] They also learn to look on the peoples of the world as "we," not "we and others." Moreover, coping with modern-day changes necessitates an appreciation of cultural relativism and of cultural compromise to reduce inter- and intra-cultural tensions. It is also important to learn at least one language other than one's own for better cross-cultural understanding and to learn to identify with people from other cultures.

"The major thrust in Oswego's anthropology studies (chair, Richard Loder)," said Professor Charles Bishop, "has been into the applied areas." "In other words," added M. Estellie Smith, "Students will apply the concepts of anthropology to the world around them. Students will become conscious of their whole world system, of the world-village concept. They will look at all aspects of the culture. For instance, in the course 'Death and Dying' they learn how customs relating to death vary within different racial and ethnic groupings."

Anthropology staff members, noted Dean Mathieu, "are strong in research," and, along with their graduate majors, are highly productive. Several of the faculty hold editorships of major journals; and Oswego alumna Julia Luyster was the first to receive the University of South Florida's doctorate in anthropology.

Sociology, anthropology's fellow discipline, noted Harold Shane, demonstrates that "a global society requires new concepts of mutual understanding and an appreciation of the impact on life of mobility and urban sprawl." Also emphasized is the problem of growing numbers of subgroups with their own special interests, a fragmentation derived partly from the high mobility and disruption of families. Another current trend is the movement toward voluntary frugality, the opposite of a throwaway society, of developing voluntary simplicity, or "decluttering future life styles."[22]

In sociology the emphasis is on social relations and on social problems. Traditional areas—the family, religion, and urban affairs—are covered as well as areas of special contemporary concern such as sex roles, sexual behaviors, and minorities in present-day society. The Native American Studies program is an interesting adjunct to this department. Directed by Richard Loder, a Native American, it is one of the few such programs in the country.

This department also has several well-known researchers, among them M. Estellie Smith, who studies the Pueblo Indians. Several staff members, recent or present, have been associated in some capacity with churches, which helped to shape their interests. Claire Humphreys, for instance, a former nun from Ireland, has researched the role of women in religion.

An interdisciplinary minor in African and Afro-American studies (coordinator, Alfred Young) introduces students to African people, to their descendants and cultures. The courses include such diverse topics as slavery, African archeology, black drama, black movements and messiahs, jazz and rock, and colonialism in Africa. One course, "Modern Jamaica," is taught in Jamaica, West Indies. "This area of study has finally become recognized as part of academia and not simply peripheral to it," observed Young. "However, we still don't have an adequate appreciation of our pluralistic society." Course offerings are interdisciplinary, often involving specialists in several fields.

Political science, a related discipline (chair, Richard Funk), concerns describing and analyzing governmental and political institutions and processes. An internship program, guided largely by Frances Koenigsberg and Fred Bartle, provides practical experience for its students in such organizations as law firms, the state legislature, and election campaign committees. Students also go to Albany and Washington to serve as interns to state senators. Graduate majors may go on to law school, earn a doctorate, or take positions in government.

"It's incredible what's happening in the field of political science," observed William Scheuerman. "Over the past thirty years, we've come to realize that attempts to extract phenomena that are uniquely political from the larger social context obscure the view of what's happening around us, so that we miss the connection between social structure and political institutions. Rather, we must develop a sense of the social totality. Fortunately, our department is pretty eclectic."

New emphases have also emerged in history (chair, Thomas Judd), including the need to know the whole world's history and to gain insight into the different degrees and interpretations of democracy. Also, some historians think that recent historical scholars "have not produced a coherent overview of the past." Harvard's history professor, Bernard Bailyn, says, "It is now time to incorporate the great mass of social data that has so occupied recent historians into a more general narrative." The goal now should be to develop a consecutive history that "takes account of the massive body of specialized scholarship and synthesizes it."[23]

Donald Mathieu, dean and historian, notes the current preoccupation with social history. "Historians are confused as to whether they are humanists or social scientists. These days, instead of looking at the impact of particular personalities, of presidents or kings, on history, we may look at the impact of minorities on the historical process—of women, the masses, the French Revolution, Russian Revolution, or whatever." It appears that footnotes to history are now perceived as having greater significance than its main stream of content.

When Oswego's social science department split into separate disciplines in the mid-1960s, Charles Snyder became the first chair of history. Later, upon his discovery of the Millard Fillmore papers, he resigned to establish a special collection archives. He was followed by Cecil Cody as chair in 1968 and by Thomas Judd in 1981. The current history program acquaints students with their own historic heritage, with that of another culture (Africa, Asian, Latin American, or European), and an in-depth knowledge of one historical area. Majors in history may find career opportunities in law (presupposing an understanding of the past), and in governmental positions. Graduates with a history major and effective writing skills may work with the media in preparing research articles about current events or education programs with a historic perspective.

A quite unusual course is Albert Leighton's "Code Breaking and History." Leighton is the founder and coordinator of the Center of International Research in Historical Cryptanalysis, which seeks to unlock information hidden away in archives, for hundreds of years in some cases. Several years ago Leighton decoded a Papal Cipher, the contents of which had been secret since it was written in 1573.

Various Oswego historians have distinguished themselves as classroom instructors. In the years 1976–78, four history professors won teaching awards: Thomas Powell, Irwin Flack, and Thomas Judd received the Chancellor's Award for Excellence in Teaching, and Alfred Young received Oswego's Black Student Union's Excellence in Teaching award.

The department has also yielded a bumper crop of administrators. Historian Thomas Powell, who became dean of liberal arts, was followed in the deanship by fellow historian Donald Mathieu. Others who have been or are administrators include David King, associate dean of arts and sciences; Geraldine Forbes, half-time assistant dean; Diana Balmori, first director of the honors program; and David Danahar, director of general education. Historians coordinating programs are Virginia Pratt for American Studies, Judith Wellman for Women's Studies, Albert Leighton for Medieval Studies, and Alfred Young for Afro-American Studies. (Why, one might ask, do historians become such outstanding administrators?)

Economics (chair, U-Jin Jhun), another of the social sciences, offers studies of economic systems and their relations to social phenomena. Its majors often pursue graduate study in economics, industrial relations, business administration, law, and related fields. These students are preparing for careers in teaching, research, government, the unions, and business, as well as in government research and advisory positions. U-Jin Jhun said that the department excels in econometrics, research techniques that are used in economics, and perhaps is SUNY's best in this field. The internship program is another strong feature; students work with the Federal Reserve Board, the Departments of Treasury and Commerce, and with private consulting firms in Albany.

The above data afford ample proof that Oswego's liberal arts programs are first-rate, with many claims to distinction. In the next chapter, the reader will become acquainted with the professional studies and special programs.

12

Professional Studies and Special Programs

THE liberal arts were late in coming to Oswego's curriculum. For almost a century, the teacher-training program was career oriented. This educational area has caused great concern nationwide in recent years and, in 1981, the U.S. Secretary of Education appointed an 18-member National Commission on Education to evaluate the American education system. The commission's 1983 report refers to America as "a nation at risk," a condition that mandates massive change.

Issues of concern cited by the commission include the following: about twenty-three million adults are functionally illiterate on simple tests of everyday reading, writing, and comprehension; functional illiteracy among minority youths may be as high as 40 percent; and the average achievement of high school students on most standardized tests is lower than it was a quarter century ago. From 1963 to 1980, scholastic-aptitude test scores steadily declined; average math scores dropped almost forty points, and verbal scores over fifty points. These marks of decline were coming at a time when highly skilled workers were needed more than ever before: computers were rapidly becoming more widely used and, by the end of the century, millions of jobs would involve laser technology and robotics. Technology is dramatically transforming many of the more traditional occupations, such as medical science, health care, and food processing. Moreover, international comparisons have shown that American students often lag behind.[1]

The commission recommended that schools and universities adopt more measurable and rigorous standards, as well as require all students to have a foundation in English, mathematics, science, social studies, and computer science; teachers be more accurately evaluated and more highly paid; and a career ladder be devised to include the beginning, the experienced, and the master teacher.

Contributing to this dismal picture is a dearth of properly trained teachers. Over the past decade, the preparation of mathematics teachers has declined by 79 percent and of science teachers by 64 percent, and further deterioration is expected. Nationwide, a quarter of all high-school mathematics positions are occupied by temporary or uncertified teachers, and 65 percent of physics teachers did not study it either as a minor or major in college.[2]

Oswego's Dr. Elizabeth Moody, who is also president of the American Association of Colleges for Teacher Education of New York State and a Regents' appointee to the Teacher Education and Certification Board, pinpoints certain obstacles to producing superior classroom teachers. One problem is that "many people think training in pedagogy is unnecessary and that teachers simply need expertise in their content area. Such knowledge is important; however, students also need to understand the teaching–learning process." Another problem, said Moody, is: "Where are the future teacher educators? We have successfully wiped out a generation of them. In colleges of education over the past decade, student enrollments have declined; therefore, college faculties have been retrenched, and, as [faculty members] have retired, they have not been replaced."

The closing of the Campus School created another problem at Oswego: all student teaching and experimentation must now be done in the public schools. "Perhaps it could have been saved," said former Vice President Sherwood Dunham, "if it had performed its true function as a demonstration center where truly innovative ideas could be tried, or as a research center. We lacked the staff for such a function; they were employed because they were good teachers, not for being researchers."

Nevertheless, where teacher education is concerned, Oswego isn't about to toss in the towel. Provost Spencer believes Oswego should maintain its long-standing leadership in this area, and Moody recommends "development of a professional school. It would not admit students until they had completed three years in the arts and sciences, wherein they would gain a solid foundation. They would complete their bachelor-degree requirements in the fifth year, that time being necessary to become today's true professionals. In the meantime, we must take into account the diversity of our student population and the complexity of the teaching operation."

The Division of Elementary and Secondary Education was established in the early 1960s, with Theodore Moss as elementary education chair, Robert McManus as secondary chair, and Sherwood Dunham as director. John Cooper, elementary-education chair from 1966 to 1972, developed a triple-track program for early childhood, middle school, and elementary school teachers. In the early childhood track, the emphasis is on nursery school through grade 3; in the middle-school track, the focus is on a particular content area; and the third, the generalist track, includes levels from nursery school through grade 6, the emphasis is on breadth of studies.

The elementary-education department undertook certain important changes in fall 1982, "for the first time in almost twenty years," said Professor William Doll. "Schools are requiring more reading today," added Dr. Tullio

Garzone, "and teachers are asked to do more with mathematics, computers, and exceptional children." The new program, initiated by Dr. Elizabeth Moody (chair from 1976 to 1980), involved three levels: theoretical, methodological, and field placement designed to integrate theory with practice.

Students, for their part, are well satisfied with the program. Sue McNally (1984) said, "It fits me and I love it." Sherri Marty (1984) likes it because it "lets students get involved, with experience on each grade level." Mary Beth Butler (1983) enjoys the diversity of student teaching.

Oswego's secondary-education department, like most in the country, is trying to help schools cope with the current shortage of English, mathematics, and science teachers. Unfortunately, this challenge coincides with a time of diminished college resources. Nevertheless, in the manner of the Oswego tradition, the department is busily upgrading its program. It is collaborating with both the English department and the schools in which students do their practicum and student teaching. "We welcome input from the schools about what they'd like student teachers to know," said coordinator Charles Linn. "It's important that students stay on the edge of their disciplines and keep up with the journals because of the fast-changing contents of all the majors."

Industrial arts, like elementary education, has been a major feature of the Sheldon tradition. This program, renamed the Department of Technology in 1985 and chaired by alumnus Vernon Tryon, has involved experiences with the tools, materials, and processes associated with modern industry; and it has prepared students to teach industrial arts in New York State in grades kindergarten through twelve. The current program had eleven technical areas in 1984, including microelectronics, a tribute to the present computer age.

In addition, the department has designed certain electives for nonmajors. These include such courses as "Today's Technology," a study of the effects of technology on society; "General Shop," which involves individual and group instruction on the safe use of tools and machines; and "Photography," which allows students to develop a familiarity with conventional photographic equipment, films, and darkroom procedures. "Automobiles," taught by Willard Allen, author of *Know your Car,* is available to both majors and nonmajors.

A development of recent years, within the Department of Technology, is the gradual demise of shop courses and their replacement with technical/industrial courses. Across the nation, courses in metal work, drafting, and woodworking are on the way out; taking their place are courses in computers and robots. New York State is in the forefront of this movement, as evidenced by the recommendation by the Board of Regents that industrial arts be changed to technical education. The Regents plan would require every student by 1986, male and female, to have had a year in technology by the end of the eighth grade.

Locally, the department has submitted a letter of intent to the chancellor regarding the establishment of a program that would lead to a Bachelor of Science in technology/education. The program would be dual, the present one parallelled by substituting industry-related courses for those in education, with an internship in industry for student teaching.

The participation of women in the department has been minor, and at times over the years, they have been excluded altogether. In Radley's administration, the number of women industrial arts majors has grown from four to over fifty, but it remains primarily a male domain.

In fall 1979, the Oswego Industrial Arts Curriculum Library was renamed the Arthur Hauler Memorial Resource Center. Hauler, who died in 1976, taught industrial arts for twenty-three years (1925–1948) and, until he retired in 1964, chaired industrial arts education. He twice served as director of the Division of Industrial Arts Technology, and, in 1938, initiated the first industrial arts conference, which brought together teachers in the Eastern United States and their best students.

A continuing feature of the department has been its closeness, among all concerned. "Much of it is because of our hands-on activities," explained Tryon, "and Charles Shoemaker is a good example. You don't see him standing around with his hands in his pockets. He will be hunched over looking at something a student is doing. You constantly get close to students physically, talking about some project or other. Another reason is that we have small classes."

Special programs and conferences also help to bond faculty and students. Industrial arts students held their first annual self-propelled transportation competition in October 1977, in which students contrived prototypes of vehicles operated by the student designer without the use of commercial wheels or tires. One design, the Ritzen rocker, used a bicycle frame and two iron rocker assemblies that moved symmetrically when simultaneously rocked and steered. Another used a bike frame along with beer kegs wrapped in rubber material as the main propulsion device. Some worked quite well; others simply fell apart.

The department does have its problems, one of which is the difficulty of attracting enough students to maintain the program. In addition, certain critics view the program as too traditional, saying it should be abandoned or dragged into the advanced technological age. Others believe it is too expensive in terms of staff and equipment required.

Nevertheless, the department has ample reason for pride. It is one of the biggest and best-known such departments in the world, and 99 percent of its graduates are placed. Dean Lewis Popham said, "Wherever I go across the country it's not unusual for someone to come up to me and say, 'I'm an Oswego alumnus and head of industrial arts in such-and-such school.'" Shoemaker noted that very often feedback is received from students some years after graduation. Shoemaker told about former student Charles Hadley, who went into dentistry: he said his industrial arts education had been a natural for drilling teeth. Tryon told of an IA alumnus, John Fox, who was chosen as New Mexico's Industrial Arts Teacher of the Year, after having taught just seven years there. Fox said that Oswego provides much greater technical diversity than do that state's IA programs.

The school psychology and counseling department, so designated in 1978, is a newcomer compared to the Department of Technology. It provides two sixty-hour programs, one in school psychology, the other in counseling; both are devoted to teaching skills required for the helping professions. It began in the late 1960s when Lucy Wing initiated and developed a graduate counseling program. It later became the Department of School Psychology, with Wing as chair. When Wing died, after sixteen years at the helm, first Eugene Perticone, and then Bruce Lester chaired the department. "It was Wing who established the department's foundation," said Dean Barbara Gerber, "although Frederick Ratzeburg, Frances Koenigsberg, Owen Pittenger, and Bruce Lester all made contributions. The current chair, Lester, truly puts his shoulder to the wheel when he believes in something. He never asks 'What's in it for me?'"

To date, the department has been a stellar performer, including that it has never failed to place a graduate. In 1981, Provost Spencer referred to it as one of two departments of special excellence on campus, the other—industrial arts.

Another outstanding team, the vocational-technical education department (chair, John Glenn) offers programs leading to a Bachelor of Science degree and prepares vocational-technical education personnel to teach occupational subjects in secondary and post-secondary education, as well as in industry. The curriculum is designed to accommodate trade specialists from industry with such occupational specializations as air conditioning, food preparation, graphics, and metal trades, as well as transfer students holding associate and applied science (AAS) or associate of occupational studies (AOS) degrees in occupational specializations. The program offers courses in marketing, distribution, secretarial science, agriculture, and the trades, such as carpentry. The vocational-technical faculty is composed of about seven members and serves New York State, mostly the eastern half. There now are two such programs within SUNY, at Oswego and at Buffalo.

This department was reestablished at Oswego in fall 1982, after a decade's interlude. The program was transferred here from SUNY's Utica-Rome college; a similar transfer from SUNY's only other program at Buffalo may be made in the future. "Oswego has the most comprehensive vocational-technical program in the state," said Glenn. "We encourage our students to combine their vocational-technical work with general education. A new trend is studying clusters of skills spanning several occupations instead of particular ones. In these times of high technology, the content of these areas has changed dramatically."

The business administration department (chair, Charles Spector) also is vocationally oriented. No one knows just who contributed most significantly to establishing it, although several people were involved: Richard Hyse, James Stamm, and John Parr. This interdisciplinary program provides students with a broad range of experience in computer operation, modern media technology, and an internship program with business and industry. It prepares students for graduate schools or for entry-level positions in management, business, industry, or public organizations; its faculty have both experience in various fields of management and expertise in academic fields.

This program has proved very popular and successful. "If we admitted all who wished to enter our business and computer science programs," observed President Radley, "we could easily increase our total enrollment by 2,000. Of course, there would be no beds for them unless they brought their own—Oswego has an academic capability for 12,000 students but beds for only 3,770. Three dormitories remain on the planning boards."

Business majors have won important honors. Brenda Debandi and Amy Schattle (both Class of 1984) won first prizes in the 1983 student research competition of the American Society for Personnel Administration, and two other students received national scholarships.

Business majors are staunch defenders of their program. Michael Chewins cited three main reasons why his experience had been so favorable. "The classes were not so large that you lost the personal touch between student and teacher," he recalled. "Also, the professors had had real life experiences, as in accounting, and students thus gained in-depth knowledge of how it is going to be out there. Finally, and something very special, the professors are very personable and relate to students like friends."

More deeply rooted in Oswego's history than business are the health and physical education departments (women's chair, Patricia Peterson; men's chair, Charles Davis). Currently, they provide courses in dance, physical education, and health science, most of them coeducational, as well as programs of intramural sports and intercollegiate competition. Across the country, including Oswego, colleges have flagrantly discriminated against women in the areas of physical education and athletics. Illustrative of this, the proportion of women's teams coached by women decreased from 58.2 to 52.4 percent nationwide during the 1977–1982 period. Meanwhile, more than 80 percent of women's athletic programs were supervised by a male director. No women are involved in administering over 30 percent of women's athletic programs, and that percentage is growing.[3]

Until Radley's presidency, women at Oswego also fared badly. True, the department, chaired by a man until 1950, was split and Louise Ostberg named chair of women's physical education. In that role this talented woman built a first-rate department, although funds and facilities continued to lopsidedly favor the men. As recently as 1976, the women's bowling team had to iron the letters "OSWEGO" on their T-shirts to compete in national competition, while the men's varsity hockey team received both home and away-from-home uniforms. Lynn Meany, co-captain of the coed varsity fencing team, declared it was "high time" that some move be taken toward greater sex equality. However, John Glinski, director of men's intercollegiate athletics at that time, argued that equality does not mean equal funding, and that funding should depend on the need of the sport. "Fifty-fifty funding would cause our programs to go down the drain," he said.[4]

President Radley, who supports fairness for both sexes, set out to improve the situation for women—and did. One of her most important actions was to block the impending merger of the women's and men's departments, which a consultant had recommended. Almost universally, in instances in which a single department for both sexes exists, the men run the show and use most of the funds.

Over the years the women's plight would have been even worse had Oswego been involved in big-time athletics. Neither students nor faculty have ever supported such an emphasis. However, a minority favor it, partly on the grounds that it would enhance visibility of the college and support by alumni.

"With regard to curriculum," said Charles Davis, chair of Men's Health and Physical Education, "the single most important change in many years is the focus on wellness, the idea being to help students improve upon and maintain their health. Some people hesitate to endorse it, asking where it fits within a curriculum and who will implement it." Davis noted that "there is already a wellness center in connection with the Walker health facility." Davis believes it should become part of the general education program, and he is supported by Thomas Chapman, coordinator of counseling. "The physical education staff first became really interested in 1983," said Davis, "when the budget crisis threatened to reduce, or even eliminate, physical education. Now that the crisis is past, many have taken to sticking their heads back in the sand. The problem is that many of them are entrenched in their specialties and unwilling to tackle this area."

Reading education and educational administration are two departments with significant numbers of successful graduates. The number of graduates from "Ed Ad" who have become Principals and Superintendents of Schools is extraordinary.

Oswego's military science program, which has responsibility for the Army's Reserve Officers Training Corps (ROTC), is more controversial than any of the foregoing areas. The program consists of a basic course for freshmen and sophomores, with no obligation for future military service. Advanced courses are available to juniors and seniors and, upon completing military science studies and requirements for a baccalaureate degree, a cadet is commissioned a second lieutenant in the United States Army Reserve.

A cross-enrollment agreement was made in 1979–80 with Syracuse University's Army ROTC, and a military affairs committee was appointed to act as faculty sponsor for a joint program. Although academic credit was not to be awarded ROTC courses, the program would enable students to explore the possibility of pursuing Army careers while at the same time studying for their degrees.

Opposition to the ROTC, significant in Perdue's years, persisted on a lower key. In 1979 the Veterans' Club, which actively involved about 25 of the 250 to 300 veterans on campus, opposed it, believing its programs were not academic. They, and others, opposed giving academic credit for such courses, although Syracuse students can get such credit and transfer it to Oswego. Proponents of ROTC argued that the courses encourage free thought and questioning and that the difficulty of such courses was comparable to others on campus. The issue dragged on until, in May 1983, several departments agreed upon credit guidelines for selected ROTC courses.

Students may join the ROTC for varied reasons. John Duffy (1978) said, "I thought I could get a good deal of leadership experience, and my area is business." He didn't receive any "flack from other students, but did from some faculty members who believed that a military organization did not belong in a liberal arts college."[5] Kathleen Koehne, also a strong supporter of the ROTC, was chosen outstanding cadet by both the SUNY Oswego and Syracuse University cadet corps. As senior cadet, she carried the title of battalion commander, the leader of a five-member staff of cadet officers and the corps. Upon completing a course at Fort Benning, Georgia, during which she made five parachute jumps, Koehne earned an airborne badge. She said she planned to enter flight school. She noted, "I love my country and would defend it."[6]

The faculty strongly favor building bridges between the various disciplines discussed above. Ivan Brady, anthropology, deplores the "disciplinary mentality, and those who feel compelled to defend their own disciplines." He objects not to people being trained in particular disciplines but "to building a concrete wall between them." Perdue laments those who criticize colleagues who teach out of their field. "It's the mark of a scholar to get out of your field sometimes," said Perdue. Ronald Brown cautioned against attempting the interdisciplinary approach without a thorough grounding in the particular disciplines involved; however, Nicholas D'Innocenzo said "we can become too cautious—we should be able to dare."

The college has already developed a number of interdisciplinary programs combining two or more departments. These include mathematical economics (economics coordinator, U-Jin Jhun; and mathematics coordinator, Robert Deming), geochemistry (coordinators, Joseph Lipsig and Robert Maurer), linguistics (coordinator, Robert Carnes), management science (business administration coordinator, Lanny Karns; and mathematics coordinator, Paul Dussere), philosophy/psychology (coordinators, Rodney Byrne and Thomas Gooding), and public justice (coordinator, Luciano Iorizzo).

In addition, special interdisciplinary courses are sometimes offered. For example, in 1982–83, John Gannon, Donald Cox, Alfred Stamm, and Peter Weber offered a cross-disciplinary course in winter ecology for the "study of physical aspects of cold, snow and ice, and biological adaptation to the wintertime environment." They offered the course in a two-week long, all-day format at Oswego's Rice Creek Biological Station and at one of several suitable SUNY field stations in the Adirondacks. The students involved had a feeling of being real pioneers.

In effect, the overseas program is also interdisciplinary, since it combines the study of both the language and culture of each country involved. Among programs offered abroad are those in British literature in London; French language and culture in St. Malo and Paris; German language and culture in Bregenz, Austria; Spanish language and culture in Madrid, Spain; tropical biology in Discovery Bay in Jamaica; and International Broadcasting and Communications in London and other locations in England. There are also exchange programs between SUNY and the University of Puerto Rico, the University of Tsukuba in Japan, and the University of St. Etienne in France.

Area-studies programs focus on particular geographic regions including Latin America, the Middle East, Africa, Russia-Eastern Europe, and Asia. Interdisciplinary minors in this field include Afro-American Studies, Asian studies, Native American Studies, and Russian-Eastern European Studies.

Public justice, Oswego's most popular interdisciplinary program, became a department in 1980, with Luciano Iorizzo (chair) and Celia Sgroi, now the college's lawyer, its first full-time members. This career-oriented program prepares students for such fields as law enforcement, the courts, juvenile delinquents' probation, corrections, community-based rehabilitation programs, and pre-law. It is also concerned with delivering social services in those areas. The program focuses on the historical and contemporary, the scientific and the human, the intellectual and practical contributions to the service of justice. Originally, the program was practically oriented; now it is both practically and academically oriented. Governor Rockefeller had called for academic contributions to the administration of criminal justice as early as 1962, and this program plays an important role in fulfilling that function.

The program is distinctive in its methodology and organization. Certainly notable and distinctive were the lessons in law taught each week in the fall 1982 semester by Oswego County judge Frank Klinger to the public-justice class "Local and Municipal Courts"—lessons based on his courtroom experiences. "This program [public justice] is slowly but surely developing a name," said Associate Provost Wheeler. "Dr. Flack, one of our faculty members, took a leave to work in New York City on a funded project to reconfigure the city's prison system. The person for whom he worked while there was an Oswego alumnus who, two years earlier, had been one of Flack's students."

Turning now to special programs, beginning with the Honors Program, a college-within-the-college that was instituted in 1979—another reflection of President Radley's crusade for achieving excellence. This program has various distinctive features: close faculty mentoring, creative excursions and field trips, seminars and tutorials, and cross-fertilization of intellect among the students themselves. An honors dormitory and an honors lounge both serve their designated aims as "catalysts to excellence." The college received a $74,000 FIPSE grant in 1982, derived from a proposal written by Diana Balmori (history), Sara Varhus (English), and William Whipple (psychology) for the establishment of interdisciplinary seminars.

The Honors Program, composed of eighty students, with females outnumbering males two to one, is living up to its name. A study by psychologist Jacqueline Reihman showed that Honors College students do indeed constitute a highly select group. Essays these students wrote on five different issues of today, such as nuclear arms, the ERA, and the environment, surpassed comparison groups by a large margin. They also excelled over other students in their participation in cultural events on campus, including lectures and symposia.

The honors students themselves describe the program as highly effective. Cheryl Steiner (1983) said that "the opportunity to interact with professors and students in a smaller class is what attracted me to the Honors College and is something from which I profited a great deal. I especially enjoyed the many field trips because they provided the ideal setting for me to apply what I was learning. However, the biggest part of my education and growth occurred when students not in the program accused me of being elitist. I considered leaving the program for this reason. I spent many hours discussing this ethical issue with other students until I was able to reach conclusions which I found satisfactory. I think college students in general learn the most from these sometimes painful experiences or illuminating conversations which take place outside of the classroom. I did not include my 'solution' here because I think it is important for everyone to arrive at her or his own answer. In this case, process seems to be as important as the product."

The project *Quest*, an ongoing publication of symposia for sharing scholarly papers and research activities of students, faculty, and staff, is coupled with the Honors Convocation. In one convocation, fifty research papers covered topics ranging from "Hemifield Differences in the Perception of the

Poggendorf Illusion" to "Innovations in Chinese Woodblocks in the late Ming Period" and from "Historical Cryptanalysis" to "Mucoraleans Sporangiosprogensis."

Women's Studies, another special program, owes its origin to the women's movement itself, and to the recognition (by some people, at least) that studies of human behavior to date had been based mostly on male subjects, and that there had been a lopsided focus on males throughout the curriculum. Such programs began in 1970 at San Diego State University and numbered over three hundred by the early 1980s. Oswego's own program, launched in 1978 after several years of effort by Barbara Gerber, Christine Pierce, Blanche Judd, and Judith Wellman, and directed now by Karen Elias-Button and Bat-Ami Bar On, offers a minor. To date, all students pursuing minors in this area have been women, although men sometimes take individual courses. Two very well-received Women's Studies courses are taught by men, "Women in Politics" by Bruce Altschuler and "Women and Culture" by James LeFlore.

Since the mid-1960s, the disadvantaged have represented a population of concern, and most colleges have some kind of program for remedying their academic deficiencies. Developmental education specialists advise the following for helping disadvantaged students: use varied instructional techniques; relate content to their existing knowledge; treat them as individuals; give regular practice in writing; and provide "a rigorous, highly structured curriculum." This last may seem inadvisable, and teachers "may be tempted to handle unprepared students with kid gloves," but these specialists, without exception, say that such students "should be given regular assignments and tests, strict guidelines, and frequent feedback."

Oswego's own opportunity programs serve three to four hundred students in two categories: the economically disadvantaged; and students from Oswego who would not otherwise be accepted but are admitted by Oswego because a community college is lacking. These programs, funded by the state, are designed to provide help in basic learning and study skills that will enable students with the potential, but not the academic background, to earn a college degree.

Reactions to such programs are varied. Some critics believe an exorbitant waste of resources is involved—the attrition rate in Oswego's program is quite high. A better plan, suggested President Radley, would be to provide basic skills training. Others defend the program. "There are many nuggets out there, gems of individuals who've merely lacked opportunity," said Associate Provost Wheeler. When asked whether such students should simply receive a certificate of attendance rather than a college diploma, Wheeler replied: "If the program works, they should have a diploma." When asked if there was not a tremendous waste of money involved, he said, "After all, this is a state institution. We have an obligation to give people opportunities they would not otherwise have."

Widely approved continuing education programs involved over twenty-one million adults nationwide in 1982, an increase of 81.5 percent since 1978. About 60 percent of the programs' curricula related to jobs; the rest was highly varied.[7]

SUNY's Chancellor Wharton views this development as highly significant. He reminds us that universities were formerly cities of youth, populated by individuals ages eighteen to twenty-four.[8] Now, however, numbers in this age category are declining, while older cohorts born during baby-boom periods are on the increase. In addition, adults' perspectives on their own lives have changed. They want to keep growing and to make their lives meaningful. If older adults' college attendance continues to increase as it did in the 1970s, university enrollments will have doubled by the year 2000. Universities will be composed of parents, retirees, and business people who regard themselves as individuals and not primarily as students. The college clientele will represent growing diversity of thought, income, race, culture, age, and values. The result will be a more sophisticated and cosmopolitan campus.

Older and less traditional students will want programs tailored to their interests and needs in gaining new skills and dealing with a changing environment, noted Wharton. This influx of people from the community will help reduce the university's isolation, and they will also bring to the campus broad experiences they can share with younger students.

This growing tide of older students calls for greater flexibility, concluded the chancellor, such as courses held off campus, in the work place, and in evenings or on weekends. In this decade and beyond, he said, universities must "transform themselves from cities of youth into cities of the mind, open to men and women of every background and from every age group."

Oswego's continuing education embraces both degree and noncredit programs. At present there are eight master's and CAS (Certificate of Advanced Study) programs.

The college's main mission is undergraduate education, but the largest graduate program is the unified master's program in education, partly because of new requirements imposed to upgrade teachers' competency. Currently, individuals who wish to be permanently certified in New York State must earn a master's degree. Another graduate program, counseling and psychological services, is highly popular, and some students have had to be turned away despite being well qualified. The reading program is also well supplied with students.

Most of the graduate and continuing education programs are conducted in the summer sessions, directed by Dean Lewis (Pete) Popham. Formerly, these courses were mostly graduate, and mainly in education. Now they run the gamut; business courses are especially popular. "With regard to the age span involved," said Popham, "we may have set some sort of record. One semester, a child less than a year old was in our learn-to-swim program, and a man not quite ninety was taking an earth-science course."

The Oswego campus is especially attractive for summer activities because of its fine summer climate and location by the lake, two of the reasons the New York State Retired Teachers Association likes to meet here. Sometimes foreign students come, and they're not always familiar with our customs: "One day the campus police called," noted Popham, "saying that several nude bathers were on the lakefront by Onondaga Hall. They were Germans, perhaps accustomed to the Riviera and less puritanical places."

Also popular is the summer Elderhostel program, which offers varied noncredit courses to senior citizens, and conferences such as a Red Cross Divisional School and a Christian Youth Brethren program. Said Popham, "For summer activities, this campus, because of its cleanliness, beauty, and location, is practically unsurpassed in the East."

There are other assorted programs, generally quite successful. The Cooperative Education Program, established in fall 1975, offers students internships in businesses and corporations, among them IBM, General Electric, and Eastman Kodak. "The work assigned students and their academic courses are carefully coordinated," said Frances Koenigsberg, program coordinator. Another fine program is SURCO, the State University Research Center at Oswego, which helps obtain research grants and sponsors their implementation. Much of this money has been used to study environmental problems and issues relating to pollution and alternative energy sources.

Noncredit courses and institutes for general life enrichment have been highly successful also. Such studies include gymnastics, piano, underwater diving, beginning folk guitar, emergency medical technology, and a seminar on law in American society. Two quite successful institutes were held in summer 1982: the Methodology Institute for Foreign Language Teachers and the Sheldon Institute for gifted and talented children.

Another college feature, the Third Curriculum, has two main features: a lecture series and a student orientation–advisement program. Over the years, many notable and distinctive speakers have visited the campus. Members of the Black Panther Party spoke to a standing-room-only crowd in 1969. Congresswoman Shirley Chisholm and consumer advocate Ralph Nader were featured speakers on campus in 1974. During the 1977 "Radical Week," Oswego students heard experts on a variety of topics, including homosexuality, the revolutionary '60s, and the John Birch Society. Among the speakers were Jerry Rubin, a symbol of the flower children and free-speech era of the 1960s, the founder of a church in Rochester which serves gay Christians, and the head of the John Birch Society. In winter 1979, John Dean, former legal counsel to Richard Nixon, spoke at Oswego. He did not appear to be embarrassed about his role in Watergate, but said "if I stimulate one mind to explore this topic tonight it will be a success."[9] Two years later, when Muhammad Ali spoke here, he said he wouldn't fight a black man's war, a white man's war, or any man's war.[10]

An especially important area of Third Curriculum is the summer advisement orientation for new students. Groups of faculty and students travel to locations around the state, meeting with parents and advising prospective students. "The Road Show," explained Wheeler, "is an effort to orient, advise, and register entering freshmen at a time when it's easier to think about those things, rather than after they arrive, bag and baggage, on campus. This program continues after they arrive here in the fall—for example, by showing them where things are on campus." Freshmen also receive a small pamphlet called "You and Us," which outlines the Oswego curriculum.

Other types of advisement assume varied forms. Each department has its advisers, and almost every faculty member informally or formally advises many students who are not their assigned advisees. In addition, a mentoring program, managed by nonteaching professionals and by faculty volunteers, was instituted in 1978 for guiding undeclared majors. In short, all students have access to a wide range of people and programs prepared to assist them.

The foregoing programs are designed to elevate the level of students' interests and, to some extent, compensate for the recent lopsided preoccupation with career and purely personal goals. This turning inward, remarks David Riesman, is not a matter of complete personal isolation but involves finding similar individuals with whom to unite.[11] The world at large is sometimes viewed as "a lost cause."[11]

Students of the early 1970s expressed various societal concerns; however, by 1980 their main interest was economic. Nationwide, 1982 was the fourth consecutive year that business was the most popular area of college study, with the increase mainly among women. In 1973 only around 30 percent of women were studying business; in 1982, 56 percent were. Most students, especially women, were gravitating toward technological and higher paying fields and away from low-paying ones and the liberal arts. Interest in computer science had increased by 38.1 percent from 1975 to 1982.

Running like a thread through discussions of the curriculum has been the matter of majors. Many freshmen do not declare a major and rely on the student advisement center for assistance. Some double major, but receive only one degree. Many change their majors, some more than once. Kathy Johnson (1984), a communications studies major, first tried majoring in public justice and became interested in child abuse. While working in the Oswego sheriff's department, however, she found that she was inclined to bring home her problems. She had been in many plays while growing up, decided to go into communications, and is now working with WTOP, a totally student-run station.

The most popular majors at Oswego in the early 1980s were business administration, communications studies, computer science, elementary education, psychology, public justice and biology. The arts, industrial arts, meteorology programs had more majors than comparable ones in any of the other SUNY colleges. And more students were augmenting their classroom experience with internships and volunteer investment in local and national service projects. In spite of reduced economic resources, students continued to participate in overseas study programs. In the meantime, renewed interest was evident in English and foreign languages. It is clear that students' academic interests, locally and nationally, reflect the broader trends and concerns of society.

In recent years greater stress has been placed on gaining a broad general education than on the students' majors. As Associate Provost Richard Wheeler points out, "four out of five students change their majors at least once, and in the world of work, four out of five people pursue jobs unrelated to their college majors. Of course, there are certain disciplines where this observation is not true—if you want to be an engineer you must study engineering, but most jobs aren't that structured."

It becomes eminently apparent that Oswego's current curriculum is varied, complex, and ever-changing, and that its students have access to high-quality offerings in their respective fields. Moreover, even a brief comparison of the current curriculum with that of just a few decades ago will reveal a distinction as sharp as that between the Model T Ford and a recent Rolls Royce. Certainly, the college's basic curricular reforms are a dramatic demonstration of the changes in its mission.

13

Student Life in the 1980s

AMERICAN college students of the late 1970s were a "curious contradiction." They held "increasingly liberal views, yet, in contrast to students of the late 1960's and early 1970's, labeled themselves as middle-of-the-road and not liberal." Students' interest in "philosophies of life and idealistic values" had declined while increasing in "materialistic goals such as wealth and status." In the half decade, 1972 to 1977, cynicism had also increased.[1] In 1967, 79 percent of the men and 88 percent of the women defined, as a major life goal, developing a meaningful philosophy of life; only 61 percent felt committed to this goal in 1976. There was also a notable decline in political liberalism. In 1983, fewer freshmen endorsed altruistic goals, so popular in the late 1960s and 1970s, such as helping to promote racial understanding (30.7 percent compared with 35.8 percent in 1977) and helping others in difficulty (61.6 percent compared with 66 percent in 1975).[1]

A 1982 national survey revealed the following picture of college freshmen. About 72.1 percent indicated increased support for taxing the rich, while the number supporting legalization of marijuana dropped from 34 percent in 1981 to 29.4 percent in 1982. The ability to make a high salary was judged an important reason for going to college by 69.8 percent, compared with 49.9 percent in 1972. Those with the goal of helping to clean up the environment numbered 44.6 percent in 1972, 24.8 percent in 1981, and 22.9 percent in 1982. Developing a meaningful philosophy of life was cited by 82.9 percent of the freshmen in 1967, but only 46.7 percent in 1982.[2]

Not all writers portray current students as a large cut below the idealists of the late 1960s. They aren't the "self-centered, apathetic, spoiled brats—the gimme generation that some people think they are," writes Hoffman. "They don't go out to burn administration buildings and there's no reason that they should." "Today's students," notes Andee Hochman, editor of the *Yale Daily News*, "compared with those of the late 1960's, are more realistic. They realize that the world is complex and its issues not clear-cut."[3] In short, today's students are less liberal than those of six years ago. For example, just

30 percent think marijuana should be legalized, compared with 66 percent in 1976.[4]

Today's college students are not only different, but far more numerous. American college students numbered almost three million in 1965, almost eleven million in 1983. Also vastly increased are nontraditional students: the economically underprivileged, academic underachievers, ethnic minorities, and older students. The proportion of women students has increased, too. Males outnumbered female undergraduates in 1950 (1.7 million males to 726,000 females), whereas women outnumbered men in 1983 (5.5 females to 5 million males).[5]

There were 7,600 students at Oswego in 1980: 6,900 undergraduates and 700 graduate students. Most of the undergraduates were ages eighteen to twenty-five; 94 percent were attending full time; and 96 percent were studying toward a degree. Of the undergraduates, 3.5 percent were minority students, 3.5 percent veterans, and 50.4 percent women. Just over one-half of 1 percent were foreign, and 6 percent were in the Equal Opportunity Program. Of the 7 percent who were graduate students, the median age was twenty-nine, two-thirds were women, 85 percent were part-time students; and most were commuters. The most popular master's degree programs were education, reading education, and advanced study in educational administration.[6]

Almost all of Oswego's students were from New York state, just under a third from the metropolitan New York and Long Island areas and about one-quarter from the Oswego-Syracuse area. They were farther from home than most college students; the average freshman was 206 miles away from home compared to 59 miles for freshmen nationally and 108 miles for those in other SUNY colleges. For the most part their parents had always lived together, and one-half had had at least some college education, above the national average. The fathers were chiefly "businessmen, engineers, skilled workers or educators and less likely to be farmers, unskilled laborers or unemployed than the national average." Their median income was $31,000 compared to a national average of $26,000 and an overall SUNY college average of $29,000. The mothers were mostly homemakers, secretaries, educators, businesswomen, or nurses, and, in contrast to the national average, were more likely not to have worked full time. In terms of religion, one-half were Catholic, 13 percent Jewish, 22 percent Protestant, and the rest either "other" or "none." The number of Catholics had increased over six years from 40 to 50 percent, while the Jewish population had dropped from 18 to 13 percent.

Academically, Oswego students have been and are of high academic quality. The 1982–83 freshmen were the best entering class in seven years, with a high school average of over 85 percent and a composite SAT score of over 1,000. That same fall the college received over 2,200 more applications than any other SUNY four-year college of arts and science, and its acceptance rate was 54 percent, compared with 80 percent for most New York state colleges. Those accepted had somewhat stronger academic backgrounds than those at four-year public colleges nationally. "Overall," observed James Wassenaar, dean of students, "students are more sophisticated today than formerly. They have seen more, they have had television, and they live in an open society."

As freshmen, a majority declared a preference for career-oriented fields, such as business administration, computer science, public justice, industrial arts, teacher education, psychology, and communication studies. The initial choice was usually influenced by parental suggestion as well as perceived employment possibilities after graduation. However, 75 percent will not complete their major of first choice and can best be described as exploratory students.

Oswego's 1981 graduating class was a highly diverse lot, ranging in age from nineteen to sixty-three years, and they planned highly diverse careers, some with blue-chip corporations, such as IBM and Kodak. Other graduates included a husband–wife team entering the Peace Corps to teach industrial arts in Jamaica. Few graduates mentioned marriage as a part of their immediate future plans.

In terms of life-styles and religious affiliations, the student body is quite diversified; the largest religious category is Catholic. Overwhelmingly, students belong to the same church as their parents, although they are tied less to dogma. A very few are agnostic or atheist, and students generally respect others' right to differ. A significant development regarding religion has been the organization and growth of fundamentalist groups, both on and off campus. Throughout central New York, such churches have been growing, while more established denominations have been making only slight gains or even declining. An *Oswegonian* editorial called on students to do something about "the enemy," which "calls itself many things: the new right, the moral majority, the religious right. Whatever their name, they threaten the first amendment freedoms, women's and minority rights and the freedom to choose."[7]

Oswego's fundamentalist groups, whose members number about 350, are deeply dedicated to their faith and associate mostly with each other. They believe theirs is the only true faith and that they should seize every opportunity to save others. The gap between the campus life-style and their own is wide.

Another group, the gays, were formerly dismissed from campuses for homosexual practices, but no longer are they condemned to pathological concealment. Since the late 1960s, their rights have been protected, and many have come out of the closet.[8] Florida's Supreme Court ruled unconstitutional provisions that would have denied state funds to colleges and organizations that sanction sexual relationships between individuals not married to each other. Oklahoma's Supreme Court required that the University of Oklahoma grant recognition to the Gay Activists' Alliance.

In the meantime, homosexuals have organized on almost half of the campuses of all public and almost a fifth of all private institutions.[9] Oswego's GALA (Gay and Lesbian Alliance) is funded through student funds. Although there is some harassment on campus, officially their rights are protected.

Disabled students constitute an even smaller campus group; however, as required by the Rehabilitation Act of 1973 (discrimination on the basis of a handicap is forbidden at institutions receiving federal financial assistance), Oswego periodically assesses its status on this matter. One task is identifying the handicapped, of whom there are few at Oswego, possibly because of the harsh winter climate. However, in 1978 there were ten severely disabled or visually handicapped individuals on campus, including two professors.

Handicapped students have demonstrated remarkable courage and dedication in pursuit of their careers. Todd Hagans (1984), a paraplegic, propelled himself in his wheelchair up Route 104 to and from campus every day, even in the stormiest weather. He said he is a much stronger person than he was when he jumped off a railroad bridge into a pile of snow some years ago, accidentally injuring himself. Another remarkable student, Douglas Eckert, almost totally blind, fell down the Oswego River bank and drowned. Eckert enjoyed German songs and could often be heard singing as he strolled around. He was studying German through Braille and was thinking of studying abroad; he also wanted to attend law school. Guenther Gerlitzki, Eckert's German professor and friend, said that Eckert had developed his other senses and would often say, "I see." An award was made in Eckert's memory at the spring 1983 Honors Convocation and, the Douglas Eckert Award in Political Science has been given each year since at the spring Honors Convocation.

The number of black students on campus has increased five-fold since the 1960s. A 1982 *Black Students Guide* evaluated the ambiance on American campuses for these students through ratings made by five black students chosen by administrators at each of the colleges; Oswego was not one of those evaluated. A primary concern of New York state's policy is the matter of educational access for all students, including blacks, since minority group members do not earn degrees in this state in proportion to their numbers in the population.

There have been many articles by and about blacks in the *Oswegonian* since the mid-1960s. Ken Bush, president of the Black Student Union in 1978, believed that racism still existed on campus, mostly in subtle ways. He noted, for example, the poor attendance by the white majority at minority-oriented activities and a general lack of awareness of on-campus black culture.[10] Another 1978 *Oswegonian* editorial encouraged the administration to provide "programs for intercultural orientation, minority-oriented meals in the dining halls, and employment opportunities for minorities on all levels."[11]

Perhaps blacks have been the most conspicuous on-campus minority because they have outnumbered others and their cause has been in the national spotlight. In fall 1982 Oswego's black students numbered 127, Hispanics 67, Asian-Pacific Islanders 30, and Native Americans 11.

A 1979 Hart Hall survey gave a good profile of Oswego women. Almost all respondents, 68 of the 69, wanted to be career women following graduation: 65 wanted marriage, one was not sure; 65 would combine marriage and career, 3 were unsure; 62 wanted to have children, 4 said no, and 2 were unsure; 53 knew the type of career they wanted, 15 did not; 13 would choose a traditional marriage (wife works, cleans house, and tends children), 55 said no; 40 had mothers with careers outside the home, 28 did not.

The feminist movement persists here, as elsewhere, in a different form from earlier days. Most students, male and female, support the ERA but are far less militant and noisy than the earlier feminists. Many are uncomfortable with the feminist label, even when they clearly hold the views. Women have become actively participatory in campus leadership roles. The Women's Student Senate Caucus was organized in 1982, composed primarily of women student senators but welcoming all women to increase women's input on campus-wide issues.

In 1983, student body Vice President Sue Wray said she'd taken a really hard look at how far women had come on campus. "I've come to think more about women's issues than I ever have, and I'm proud to have made history with Sue (President Sue Castrigno). We opened up the doors, and we will do what we can to see that those doors stay open."

President Radley views the 1980s as the decade when women will begin "to mainstream in terms of jobs and careers." She perceives men as in the seat of power and not anxious to move over. Yet a young woman, "if she really wants to, can do what she wants to by standing up to peer pressure and not worrying too much about whether or not she is being loved."

Radley also advises that the woman in the business world learn to present herself "as a woman and a person," and stresses the importance of a firm handshake: "It should not be like that of a wet fish." Radley quotes Marjorie Downing Wagner, also a college president, who said, "Many women don't believe in themselves. One of the problems is helping the male faculty see their role as not paternalistic," which would increase women's confidence.

A much smaller, nevertheless significant, category, both here and elsewhere, is that of foreign students.[12] Nationwide, they numbered about 312,000 in 1981 and were predicted to exceed one million by the early 1990s. Many such students have financial problems and, in addition, the Immigration and Naturalization Service has not always dealt generously with them. As a result, some foreign students feel isolated and depend on one another for support. The Institute of International Education reports that few American colleges have thought through the issues associated with having foreign students on campus. The lack of a clear policy is an ambiguity higher education can ill afford, especially when foreign students are the majority in some graduate fields.

The forty-two foreign students on Oswego's campus in 1983–84 came from around the world, including Europe, Africa, Asia, and South America. The largest contingent, nine from Canada, included several ice hockey players. Ten were exchange students: six from Puerto Rico, two from Japan, and two from West Germany. At present, there are none from New Zealand or Australia.

Oswego's own program for foreign students has been carefully crafted. The International Students Association developed a guidebook in 1976–77 which provides information about such matters as transportation, how much spending money they should have, and to whom they may go for assistance. Also, they are urged to take maximum advantage of orientation programs existing for all students. Another service is the host family program, allowing them to spend holidays, weekends, or any time they wish in an Oswego home. In addition, the Foreign Student Affairs and Information Center provides foreign newspapers, a bulletin board for international current events, and a place to meet.

The foreign students themselves perform important services around campus; they are often invited to classes to act as resources in discussing customs, conditions, and events in other countries. Chris Mensah (1984), from Ghana, has been especially outstanding. Described as the college's most enthusiastic promoter of international exchange and communication between American and foreign colleges, he received an Outstanding Achievement Award in 1983 for his contributions to the college and the community.

The foreign students all testify to having been strongly affected by their Oswego experience. Chris Mensah said that "the only way we can come to understand each other in this world is for me to understand the guy sitting next to me and for him to understand me, but not for me to be him or for him to be me." Giovanni Baji (1984), from Bolivia, thinks that foreign students are treated pretty much like the others in large classes, although they might receive some special attention in smaller ones. Weber Debarros (1984), from Brazil, especially likes Oswego for its landscape, "and the freedom he has had to explore various areas of knowledge." Upon returning to his country, he believes he will have a definite advantage from having studied here.

Nationally, the most rapidly growing segment of the college population is older students, whose proportion to all students rose from 29 percent in 1972 to 35 percent in 1978, with 70 percent enrolled part-time.[13] There are several reasons for this rapid increase, one of which is that the whole population is aging. For another, leisure time is being used more for self-development than for simply time off from work. The adult learners of the early 1980s have these characteristics: they have gone beyond high school and are twice as likely to continue their education; they are better off financially, more likely to be employed, and more likely to be in professional or technical work than adults generally. They are also more likely to be single or divorced and slightly more likely to live in urban areas.

Oswego's older students may be categorized as graduate or undergraduate, full time or part time. Of the total student population of 7,423 in 1983, full-time graduate students numbered 80, and part-time 489. Of Oswego's total 1983 student population, full time and part time, 10 percent were age 30 and older, 15 percent age 23 and older, and about 70 percent age 25 and under.

Older students on campus make an important contribution to classes. Their observations are from a long-term, experienced perspective, and, to some extent, they diminish the age homogeneity on campus. Sue McNally (1984) said she met an older student on the bus one day "about the age of my grandmother. She explained that she was a student, and described her experiences in this role. She was quite an inspiration."

Older students experience their own special problems. Charlotte Briant (1985) said that her parents were somewhat old-fashioned and never encouraged her to return to school; however, she thought they had noticed in her a change for the better after she was in college a while. Briant's main problem was a certain hesitancy about "opening up" in class. John Cretaro (1980), age thirty-eight, found that school work occupied so much time he had little time for hobbies or for outside chores, especially household work. Donna Myers (1983), whose husband was also a student, believed it more difficult for the married: "Some students shy away when they learn you're married, but I've made some friends who're great."

To help these students with their problems, and to develop among them mutually supportive relationships, various resources are provided. The Nontraditional Student Union is the umbrella organization and provides advice, weekly bag lunches, and various social activities. A subsidiary group, Students and Mothers (SAMS), intends to change its name soon to include fathers.

Few, if any, older students care for the typical college life. Richard Blodgett (1980) said that older students weren't interested in beer blasts and rock concerts, and he recommended activities especially designed for older students.[14] Dennis White (1980) said, "I feel too old for the typical student and too young for most of the other married students. For me, Oswego has just one function, helping me receive my degree. My social activities are nonexistent, although I welcome the friends I have made here."

Practically without exception, older students have found their college experience rewarding. John Cretaro said when he finished high school, at age eighteen, he wouldn't have enjoyed his courses as he does now with "some of life's experiences behind me. I bring more to the classroom than I would have then." Sue Clemons, owner of a small business in Oswego, declared she was excited and pleased with what she had achieved. "My biggest problem was getting the courses I needed. I had to resort to all sorts of manipulations and survival techniques. I didn't feel 'out of it' because of my age, since I involved myself with the other students."

For students young and old, the 1980s brought changes in hairstyles but a less pronounced change in fashion. Men continued to wear faded, often ragged, jeans and T-shirts. Scott Fitzgerald (1986) described their appearance as "kind of laid back—jeans, cords, sportshirts. Once in a while they bust out in dress clothes." Others divided the men into two categories. Karen Zecchino (1985) said they're either "preppies or slobs," and James McKenna "the guys on the prowl, the wolves, dress to kill all the time. And there are the relaxed guys who rely on their own personalities." In general, males are reported to be "neater, more cleancut than a few years ago."

As for the women, here are observations made in 1983: "It's dress-for-survival with the weather up here. I wouldn't have been caught dead wearing my bright plastic raincoat back in the 12th grade. The styles are much more diverse here. Go preppy, dress up or dress down (my favorite), but anything goes is the rule. People don't seem to be so caught up in total conformity any more. About time, I'd say" (Linda Johanson, 1984). "In winter there are no clothing fads, because the weather is so severe. In the warmer months (fall and spring) you see a variety of clothing styles. This fall I was shocked at some of the wild outfits I saw—mini-skirts with tops matching, wild polka dots, etcetera. I felt like I was at a school in the city. I have noticed a big difference in the way students dress here compared to those in colleges on Long Island. Private schools compete in fashions regarding who has the most variety, but more importantly, who has the most status, or how many different designer names you display on different places on your body. It's much nicer here, where everyone is comfortable, and status isn't an important issue" (Marsha Wittenberg, 1981).

Just as each era dons a different mask, so do its students don short-lived fashions. Denise Morett (1983) mentioned "the ridiculous fad [1983] of wearing sweatshirts inside out." Mary Beth Butler (1983) noted several fads, such as girls dying a few strands of their hair a different color, perhaps bright cherry red or purple; girls wearing headbands of all sorts—thin, braided, beaded, with feathers—the "Olivia Newton-John style;" and "males shaving their heads, either totally or Mohawk style. Some are on the swimming team and claim that shaved heads allow them to swim faster."

Aside from clothes, the students' most important material items are cars and stereos, as these testimonials indicate: "Many students own stereos, and the object is to have the loudest one on your floor. Having a car on campus gives people the freedom to go where and when they want. Having any kind of car is envied by less fortunate students, but newer, sportier cars are looked at more favorably. Also important are clothes, mostly for girls, and having a nice dorm room, especially if you have a nice rug" (Roseann Esposito, 1981). "It seems that stereos and hi-fis were made for college life; and everyone I know has one. Cars are important, too, and choices are shifting from the big luxury ones to the better gas mileage, smaller, compact ones. Students who get cars usually do so by their junior or senior year because, by this time, many have moved to off-campus residences. Cars are preferred if they look good—like Corvettes, Camaros, and Firebirds, especially if they have stereos. People admire you more if you have a nice car rather than a beat-up old one. People think of your financial background by the car you drive" (Malcolm Streedy). Nevertheless, noted David Buck (1980), "the number of cars has decreased while that of bicycles has increased. Parking was a major problem before, but now there are always extra spots. I don't know whether this change represents altered priorities or the economy."

The increase in popularity of biking is just one aspect of Americans' current preoccupation with improving their health. Almost half of the population exercises in some way, compared with about one-quarter in 1960.[15] The practice of smoking has diminished by 28 percent among adult males and 13 percent among adult females since 1965. There is a big 'wellness' industry, and concern about health has invaded the campuses.

Dieting, mainly by women, is a perennial priority as an antidote to the typically high-calorie college menu. "The campus delivery of subs, pizzas, and beer has been a big hit," noted Doreen Blandino (1982). "Also, there's the ritual of hitting the vending machines; and when they're out of order, students have a fit and proceed to those at the next dorm."

Chris Nicolaidis (1984) called the problem of weight control "awesome. You've heard of the 'Freshman 10'. You spend your first year adding ten pounds and the next three trying to unload them. The cause is all the starchy foods and midnight pizzas." "Off-campus students," observed Janice Pacilio (1983), "eat a more balanced diet and less grease." These are traditional campus gripes. In fact, however, Oswego's talented Steven Hammond and his food service staff prepare fabulous salad bars for the students.

Measures taken to reduce weight are varied. Dawn Zuckman (1981) organized a campus chapter of Overeaters Anonymous after she had lost about thirty pounds as a member of a chapter at her home.[16] The college's chapter met on Fridays to help members get through the weekend, when pressures to eat and drink are greatest. Each new member, or "baby" as she was called, was assigned a sponsor, someone who had been with the group over twenty-five days. "Babies" had to call their sponsors every day to have their menus approved. For those who developed anorexia nervosa or bulimia, there were student support groups at the College Counseling Center. These eating-disorder support groups have been in existence since the early 1980s.

More recently, the focus has been on exercise, partly for weight control, mostly for maintaining optimum health. Michael Orlousky (1982) said that "all the girls in Onondaga are on diets and all the guys are lifting weights." Joanne Morelli (1983) added that "many floors in dorms have aerobic dancing classes; and Laker gym has swimming, racketball, and basketball courts. Students who don't have time for these sports may take stairs instead of elevators, walk to class instead of hopping the bus, or exercise on their own fifteen minutes a day." Deborah Quick joined the track team in her freshman year. She likes to jog but, unless forced to run, she "gets lazy about it." She "really wishes Oswego still had a track team."

Not every student is enthusiastic about the joggers. At least one student, Mark Chester (1979), protested joggers' inconsiderateness. Chester claimed they never yielded the right of way and monopolized sidewalks and roadways. He advised that "there's a big lake adjacent to the campus—go run on that!"[17]

The question arises: how do males view coeds with bulging muscles? Lorraine Schroeder (1983) said, "Right now, I'm in the weight-lifting club, and I really enjoy the pain for the gain. Now that I lift, I have more confidence in my personal safety, and I feel better about myself. One thing about it that I find quite amusing is that when guys ask me why I'm at the gym, and I tell them that I lift, their eyes open wide and all they can say is 'You do?'"

Although many individuals regularly exercise, the most important themes in students' lives are classes, study, dorm activities, and visits to hangouts. Paul Quigley (1982) said, "The typical day usually begins with a 10:10 or 11:00 A.M. class, with some time off later for lunch. Then there is at least one more class. After classes, students usually go back to the dorms to hang out, sleep, study, or go downtown. After dinner it's 'Miller time'."

Elizabeth Beerse (1984) spoke about her typical day. "I would wake up about an hour before my class, take a shower, pick up my room, and head out for class. Depending on my schedule I would go to lunch, do some work in the afternoon or finish up classes, if I had any left. Then when the nice weather came around we would jog about 4:00 every afternoon, come back, take another shower, and go to dinner about 6:00. Depending on what was going on, we would sit in the dining hall for a while, talk to people, look at the guys, and note who was with whom and gossip. After dinner, we would study, either in the suite or at the library. Around 11:00 we would all meet in the suite, make some popcorn, and talk about what was going on during the weekend, what was new, etcetera. Basically, there was a routine in students' social life. A lot of times you would buy some wine, beer, or whatever, sit around your room or, as in my case, suite, and then head downtown to the Ferris Wheel or Buckland's. On other nights there might be a concert or a party on or off campus. Sometimes the girls in my suite would make popcorn and stay home and watch 'Saturday Night Live' or a good movie, especially in the winter. When nice weather came, everyone would head out to Nunzi's or parties down by the lake. What I would do is go out Thursday night to Sereno's because Thursday nights were popular there. Then sometimes on Fridays we would stay in and take it easy, and on Saturday night 'do it up'."

"Sundays are days to relax," said Joanne Morelli (1983), "and days to do what must be done for Monday classes, and to do the odds and ends I never get done during the week. Weekdays mainly are filled with attending classes during the day, and trying to make it to the library in the afternoons. In a way, schedules revolve around dining hall hours. If you want to eat you have to be sure to get there before it closes, which means you find yourself eating when you're not hungry. Once Friday afternoon rolls around, forget it—I don't work on Fridays, unless I'm far behind. I also try to exercise at least once a week, but time flies by so fast that there's never enough to do the things I'd like."

Jeffrey McKelvey (1981) noted, "I go to the library some weeknights, shoot bull in between periods of studying, and then hit the tavern for a couple of nightcaps. However, sometimes I just have to be by myself, as I'm sure everyone does. Weekends wear me out, and by the time Monday rolls around, I'm ready to sit in class."

Campus life-styles are far more costly than formerly, and often students require financial aid.[18] The total cost of attending college in 1982–83 was 11 percent higher than the year before. The average basic expenses at public colleges in 1982–83 were about $4,388, compared with $7,475 at a private four-year institution. As a result, the average student at public colleges could not attend without some financial aid, and about a third who received such aid were otherwise self-supporting. About half of the federally aided students had family incomes below the poverty level, now set at $9,200 for a family of four. Not surprisingly, many students feel deeply concerned about the sacrifices their parents are making to send them to college.

One on-going college expense is for alcohol, the students' drug of choice, or "biggy," as one called it. According to a national survey made in 1983, 82.1 percent of all students drank, 86.4 percent of the men and 79.4 percent of the women. Almost 21 percent called themselves heavy drinkers, drinking six or more glasses at a sitting, at least once a week. When compared with a national sampling in 1974, the proportion of student drinkers was about the same. However, the proportion of women calling themselves heavy drinkers had risen sharply. In general, the lower a student's grade point average, the more he or she drank, and the more religious a student, the less he or she drank. More men than women drank. Students' alcohol consumption appeared to have stabilized, although cocaine use and drunkenness had increased.[19]

The correlates of alcohol abuse are serious indeed. Some colleges reported as much as 80 percent of campus vandalism to be alcohol related. Over 90 percents of deaths accompanying hazing were alcohol connected, and the main cause of death of young adults ages eighteen to twenty-four was traffic accidents: over half of traffic accidents are related to drunk driving.

In 1982, over two-thirds (68.5 percent) of the nation's colleges and universities had programs to educate students about the effects of alcohol, and 44.2 percent had programs to help abusers.[20] These programs were designed to encourage responsible drinking and focused on educating students about alcohol's negative effects. They involved providing alternative forms of recreation, counseling students with special problems, and intervening by confronting those with problems and being sure they obtained help. In addition, guidelines had been set up for on-campus social events requiring students to register parties in advance and requiring that a fraction of the money for a party be used for food and nonalcoholic beverages. Two-thirds of the institutions surveyed banned alcohol at athletic events.

Perhaps college students' main social activity was conversation, but they rarely dissected philosophies or debated world issues. In 1983, when asked what students talked about, several students replied this way: "We talk about sex, our future plans, politics, gossip—just about everything and anything that comes to mind" (female, age 20). "Daily problems—gives you someone to complain to. Also talk about your girlfriends" (male, age 21). "We talk about what we'll do after college, marriage, work, relationships" (female, age 20). "We talk about girls, sports, and then about girls some more. We also try to solve world problems occasionally" (male, age 20). "Talk is usually very casual, about school or everyday experiences. Talk is never on a heavy topic—politics, etcetera. It is on a more personal level. Talk is our main activity" (female, age 22). "We talk about sports, music (preferably rock) and traveling" (male, age 21). Dale Roberts (1983) asserted "I've been extremely aware this year that students are talking about only things relating to campus. We seem to get so caught up in our courses, our grades, people on campus, etcetera, that we don't see anything that goes on beyond the campus. If I change the subject to something worldwide, the conversation somehow gets steered right back to what some teacher has said and that teacher's course. It's a question of, is there life beyond college?"

Students' conversations are spiced with their own special and current lingo, which changes rapidly. These expressions bind them together; they're like passwords, opening doors to communication. Among the most popular at Oswego in 1983 were these: "blow-off," meaning not to do something, as "blow off class"; "mega," a lot ("mega homework"); "schlepper," "loser," "zero"—all meaning a person with no purpose in life; "psyches," makes you excited; "wing-ding," going out for as many chicken wings as you can eat; and "I'm scared of you" meaning "I'm impressed by you."

Also characteristic of students' communication is their use of nicknames for each other. "All my friends have nicknames," noted Luis Roca (1983). "Bobby is 'Boomer'; Chris is 'Henry'; Norm is 'Packer'; Fred is 'Little Guy'; Steve is 'Sluggo'; Rich is 'Rubble'; Bill is 'Elvira'; and I'm 'Harry.'" The origin of all these names has evolved over time as a result of personality and situation. Lisa Fuchs (1983) told of how certain nicknames on campus originated. These include "'Skins' (who was a very fat child), 'Happy Bottom' (her name was Gladys), 'J.O.' (this person once called O. J. Simpson J. O. Simpson), 'Skater' (a skate-board fanatic) and 'Rockhead' (for obvious reasons)." Denise Morett (1983) said that she never had a nickname until she came to college but since being here had been called "Hurricane-Proof-Head," "Peanut," and "Mary, the Cat."

After leaving behind a disliked nickname in high school, Lorraine Schroeder came to college where, she writes, "I was soon to be known as 'Schroeder'. Branded once again! As time went on I adopted several others, like 'Beamer' because I smile a lot, 'Quiche,' because my first name reminds people of food, and 'Rainy,' a shorter version of Lorraine. So I finally came to a conclusion: since your first name is hardly ever used, why have one, since nicknames do the job better!"

Details of campus life style vary somewhat from one dormitory to another, each of which is distinctive. The oldest dormitory complex, Lonis-Moreland, is somewhat "run-down and outdated," noted Philip Ferraro (1985). And Maryellen Heindl explained that "we are sort of isolated from the rest of the campus, but we are extremely close and often go out together. It's like having forty brothers and sisters." Nancy Colucci (1986) liked it, too, finding it "nice and cozy and we're all proud of it." Claire Conley (1986) noted some disadvantages of Lonis-Moreland, but mostly advantages. "It's near the NIMO steam plant noise, and the SAVAC ambulance goes by, but it's the closest dorm to town, has a good dining hall and many floor parties."

There are four dormitories by the lake: Scales, Waterbury, Riggs, and Johnson, in that order from west to east. "In Scales," observed Doug Daino (1985), "over 50 percent are underclassmen. The males live in one wing and females in the other; therefore, there is less intermingling than in other coed dorms. Of all the lakeside halls, it is noted for having the biggest parties."

Waterbury achieves a plus-rating from its residents, mainly because of its small size and location. "There's good interpersonal communication there," observed Kathleen Galvin (1986). "There's a hierarchy of discipline and respect, but small size and interaction make it less threatening. It's possible, too, to get to know all the two hundred residents, thus creating a warm, homelike atmosphere." Martin Salem (1985) liked the big lounge, fireplace, and homelike atmosphere. Diana Bruckner agreed, saying, "you get to know more people on a more intimate level." "Perhaps, partly for this reason," added Galvin, "we placed strong emphasis on academic excellence, and for the past nine years have had the highest cum on campus. Besides, Waterbury's central position makes it easy to reach the other buildings on campus, and our back yard is Lake Ontario." "The setting is perfect," according to Kathy Johnson (1985). "Living by the lake was quite an experience for someone who had never seen a body of water bigger than Oneida Lake."

Next comes Riggs, the only all-male dormitory. Students agree that its being a male dorm gives it a distinctive atmosphere. "At times it's very rowdy," recalled Jo Morelli (1983). "It can be a zoo at times." However, Larry McMindes (1986) thought it's becoming "a much better place to study. The worst disadvantage is the long, cold walk in winter to Johnson, the all-girls' dorm. Outsiders have sometimes referred to the residents there [Riggs] as 'Rigg's Pigs'." At least one male said, "We are all males, so we don't have to impress any girls—we are just ourselves."

Johnson Hall, next to Riggs, the only all-women's dormitory, has a very pleasant atmosphere and was very clean, observed Karen Gillett (1986). Just as mostly freshmen live in Riggs, so do they in Johnson. Susan Denecke (1984) added, "No matter how rowdy dorms get, Johnson is always quiet, friendly, and spotless. We were all very close, in the same boat. We visited Riggs quite often and were teased about it, especially by new campus people." Marybeth Furey (1986) said that "people put down all-girls' dorms, but as a freshman I was glad I was there." Susan Denecke noted that "half the girls go out all the time just to see civilization, and the other half never leave the floor."

The two dormitories at the center of the campus, Hart and Funnelle, are linked by Cooper Dining Hall. Most of the students like these dormitories for their convenience and find them "loads of fun." "Many younger students are there," said Tim Metallo (1986), "and there's much interaction between floors and between Hart and Funnelle. Everyone is close because of the way the buildings are set up."

In Hart's next door neighbor, Funnelle, noted Sandra Mielenhausen (1986), "there are many freshmen, and close relations among floor members and from floor to floor. People have fun and play pranks, not always funny, but a good time is had by all. The dorm is centrally located and provides easy access to other buildings." Eileen McCavanagh (1986) agreed that Funnelle is "very sociable. Floors develop family-type relations, and between floors, neighborlike relations." Another resident commented on the way Funnelle is set up: "Floors are separated, with guys at one end, girls at the other. However, both sexes spend time together in the TV lounge. Those who remain on the same floor at least a year ordinarily form cliques. In general, a whole floor hangs out together and goes in groups to dinner."

There are four dormitories on the west campus, and there is additional living space in the basement of the Pathfinder Dining Hall. Daniel Fink said these dorms are in a "great location, and nice looking." Kevin Weber (1985) called them "well kept;" and Barb Romano (1986) said they are "new, known for parties." Robbie Nicholson (1983) described his floor in Oneida as "a cohesive family unit. It's friendly there and easy to meet people." Its next door neighbor, Onondaga, said Maureen Baxter (1985), is inhabited "almost all by upperclassmen." And, added Henry Bottjer (1984), each living area is "set up like a small apartment, the type of place where I've always wanted to live." Added Paul Rowland (1983), "It's almost like living in your apartment off campus with two bedrooms, a living room, and bath in each suite. Mostly upperclassmen live there. The living style is more mature." Maureen Baxter (1985) observed that "students on particular floors stay mostly to themselves."

Next is Cayuga, which Maria Montalbano (1986) described as "one of the quieter dorms. Some people think it's too mellow." James McKenna called it a "clique of cliques." Christine Allen, though, (1986) saw it as democratic, calling it "a family-like setting—good to live in." Shari Staff (1985) liked it because you can "see the sunsets from your window."

At Cayuga, as in the other dorms, there are differences from one floor to another. For example, Maria Montalbano (1986) said that the third floor is "noisier than other floors." Christine Allen (1986) described the third floor as having two kinds of students: "Some are the mellow, studious type, while the majority are the partying type but very close." James McKenna (1987) said there are "some good eggs, some fireballs" on the fourth floor.

Seneca, the next dorm, has a reputation for being very lively. Holly Logan (1986) said that there's "much togetherness, and great sunsets on the lake." Terry Lehtonen (1986) called it a "party dorm," and Bryan Moroney (1986) referred to its "constant madness." "Anyhow," said Allen Woodin (1984), "it's a total living experience." Here, too, there are differences in floors. Holly Logan said the seventh floor is like a "big happy family. We think of floor members as brothers and sisters, and we go out a lot together." Virginia Borden (1986) called the tenth floor "mellow and friendly." Bryan Moroney said the sixth has the best softball team, and is noted for making up expressions."

The Pathfinder dormitory houses just twenty students and is distinctive from the others. "It's a quiet dorm, and students who live there have special interests in the arts, woodworking, photography, and so forth," explained

Eric Nygard (1984). "It's a form of special-interest housing, and students are interviewed to get a room there. Because of their shared interests, relationships are quite close."

Most students believe it is important to live in dorms, at least initially. William Bocchino (1983) said "they're great places to meet new friends." Lorraine Schroeder (1983) called the dorm "the place of experience and real honest-to-goodness soap opera living. You find people with all kinds of problems that involve family, girlfriend, boyfriend, or almost anything. It's where you meet people and find out how many different attitudes and kinds of people exist. You also find out what kind of person you are, such as neat, clean, good sense of humor or bad. You find out what kind of people you enjoy and how much you can tolerate things before losing your temper." Some dorm dwellers point out the pitfalls in off-campus living. There's "not enough time to cook meals—and one may not like to cook anyhow." Also there are the hassles for rides and occasional complaints about noise from townspeople.

Others cite the disadvantages of dorm life. It homogenizes its inmates; it's no place for a square peg. "One lacks privacy," said Bill Bocchino (1983). "If you don't get away from the dorm, it will stagnate you." One student simply "gets tired of saying hello to everyone who passes my room from 9 A.M. till midnight." Some find the dorm expensive and noisy, and they dislike having to eat at specific times.

Inevitably, some students seek in their own special ways to enliven dorm dwelling. "In 1982," recalled Jack Moore, "breeding mice as pets was popular on my floor. My friends would sit around chatting while their mouse, or mice, climbed on them or in their hair. One time all the guys went to the dining hall for dinner with their mice in their hair.

"One guy had a large boa constrictor in his room and once or twice a week would charge people a quarter to watch him feed a mouse to his snake. With the money he made, he would buy another mouse for the next week's feeding. This same individual also kept a pet ferret in his dorm room."

Those who move off campus are generally well satisfied with their decision. "It's definitely better for those who want to prove themselves and to become more self-reliant and responsible," said Janet Mandeville (1981). Cindy Rabert (1983) found the off-campus life style "a definite plus. I have a great time with my two housemates—we can come and go as we please and enjoy cooking our meals." Steven Specht (1982) found "it's much nicer to come home from class to a house than to a one-room habitat that's like a zoo." Sandy Schwertfager (1980) noted that "off-campus people stick together and hang out in the union. We dress differently and, perhaps because we're older, have a special group of 'old' friends with whom we party. Off-campus people accept living conditions that would be intolerable at any other time in life." Mary Ann Barbarino (1980) found off-campus life "quieter, pressureless from peers, more secure—in essence the optimum setting for the more introverted and studious student."

On weekends the campus looks like a deserted village—so where do students hang out? Dorm gatherings are commonly followed by sorties to bars that cater to students. With regard to other recreation in the Oswego area, Staci Rosenberg (1981) found the landscape somewhat bleak. "The only opportunities for me are ladies' night and free drinks, all you can drink for so much, etcetera. I've found a few scattered museums and two movie theaters offering last year's movies. Whatever happened to foreign films?" Others have had better luck, especially in sports. Ralph Suppes (1980) found more things to do on campus, such as movies, concerts, plays, racquetball, tennis, and swimming, than in town.

Certain hangouts, among them Buckland's, are perennial favorites. 'Buck's' is "where someone can pick up another person, and that's especially good for freshmen," noted Wendy Horawski. "Buck's is a pick-up joint," agreed Sue Gurley, "often so crowded you can't move and so hot you can't breathe." With a certain joyful masochism, they are scrambled together in a sort of collective embrace. In fall 1978, the second level of Buckland's, known as Dicken's pub, had been designed for couples and small groups of four, while the lower level was aimed at the rowdier, dateless students. Other old-time haunts, Sereno's and Nunzi's, said David Buck (1980) "remain packed, at least in the spring. I used to think students were fickle about hangouts, but these are eternal."

Different places appeal to different moods and serve varied functions. "To see a lot of people," recommended Joan Berkenblit (1983), "go to the Wheel, Barney's, Sereno's, or to the Cameo and the Patch for talks and more intimate nights." Steven Specht noted "the trend toward live music and mellowed-out establishments like the Ferris Wheel and the Cameo." Some males go to the Little While on Route 104 to shoot pool.

Linda Johanson (1984) noted that "a dumpy-looking little place on Bridge Street, the Clambar, remains my favorite late afternoon escape-way. Go ahead, relax. Leave your shoes at home; no one cares. Order a draft. Splurge—go for the grilled cheese or salt potatoes. Get both. Watch the TV or play a video game. Eat, drink, forget the time, enjoy yourself. Attracted to the Clambar are the easygoing sorts, individualistic folks. These are the people who are unafraid to voice their opinions or to be themselves, and they are the last to condemn anyone else for doing the same. They think, they speak, they philosophize. They find meaning in what others pass by as commonality. They live to live. Talk to them and let them enlighten your thoughts. The Clambar? A spot is only so special as the people there. It is indeed a very special and very classy place."

Several new student hangouts appeared on Water Street in 1977. The Matador on West First Street has a Spanish-oriented red-and-black decor, entertainment ranging from one-man bands to contemporary rock players, and a seven-foot TV screen for Monday-night football games.[21] Off the main drag, at East Ninth and Seneca Street, is The Railhead, designed by Oswego IA majors, and frequented mostly by off-campus students and upperclassmen. The closest bar to campus, The Odyssey, was trying out bands from hard rock to folk.

Water Street might be called Oswego's Greenwich Village. There, The Wheel, predecessor of the Ferris Wheel, was Oswego's dining and socializing center for over a century.[22] It began in the 1840s as a hotel restaurant called Ontario House and "provided housing and entertainment for various dignitaries, including Ulysses S. Grant, actors, and ship builders."[22]

Melanie Janowsky (1983) described three other Water Street hangouts.[23] There is the Low Life Caffe, with its special atmosphere, and a machine that makes over twenty kinds of coffee. It doesn't serve alcoholic beverages but has exotic foods and drinks such as "egg creams, pan gallacgic gargle and blasters (green lemonade and club soda). It's a place where people like to sit and talk, relax and listen."[23] At another Water Street establishment, the Old City Hall, the clientele is mostly older and from off campus. The bartender said that the stereotype of patron is one who has long hair, a bandana tied around torn Levis, and sings songs from The Grateful Dead with half-closed eyes. "But that isn't true," added Janowsky. "These people are just out for a good time." The music there is not commercial rock and roll but often includes folk and jazz bands. There is also the Market House Music Hall, a registered national historic landmark attached to the Low Life Caffe. This non-profit organization hosts both theatrical and musical shows, as well as the volunteer Ontario Center for Performing Arts.

The college's own Tavern continues to be popular, too, "a comfortable world where you can relax after an encounter with the FORTRAN monster at Culkin," noted Jack Olcott (1984). "It's hard to believe that this world exists in the lower reaches of Hewitt Union, just a flight of stairs down from the lobby." Said John Heesemann (1981), "This is no Buck's." The tavern's assistant manager in 1981 commented that "no one gets shoved or pushed. We've had maybe one fight here in three years, if that!" It's a mellow environment, where "the music is loud but not deafening. One hears a low buzz of . . . conversation. Yes, conversation! People actually carry on conversations at the Tavern, an unheard of feat in other such establishments."[24]

Historically, college life has been a time when otherwise bright young scholars sometimes do stupid things with enthusiasm, perhaps to offset the rigors of study or to enjoy a last fling before settling down as adults. Many episodes, such as the following, occur in the dorms. Deborah Quick told one story: "My roommate and I thought we'd pull a practical joke on the people in our wing. We tried the old 'vaseline on the doorknob' trick while everyone was at a dorm party. It was hilarious watching people come home and try to open their doors. It didn't take them long to figure out who had done it. Later on we found we had fallen victim to our own joke. When we went to open the bathroom door—vaseline! Our former victims had also greased the toilet seats with baby oil." Luis Roca (1983) related another story: "Take four ordinarily intelligent, conservative students and get them together, and it adds up to all four having their heads shaved. A month ago I did so along with three buddies. It was definitely out of character for me, not to mention the assortment of hats I had to buy to hide my baldness." Many episodes were harmless or unintentional, as when several students decided it would be nice to have some Canadian beer, so they hopped into a car and drove to Canada. Another time a student was roller skating down the hall and went through an open window, leaving her hanging half in and half out.

One rather strange event was a chicken-wing eating contest at the college's Tavern.[25] The team that managed to consume the most chicken meat from the wings, supplied by Sal's and the Cabaret, won beer and free dinners from the restaurant. The individual who ate the most wing meat, senior Robert O'Connor (1983), received a set of beer mugs and $25. "To make the contest livelier, hot mustard sauce was poured over each platter before the rounds began."[25]

For further insight into the undergraduate mind, one may read the *Oswegonian* personals:

> Beware—there's a turtle in 366 Scales.
> SSSsss—Python Patty, how's the snakin' in Onondaga?
> O Lord, what fools these mortals be. W. Shakespeare.
>
> Princess. The Secret of the Dragon is found—Come, take my hand and follow me to the Courts of Lavender, and be my Queen.
>
> Senator C—would you wash your face once in a while? The cute one.

Occasionally, students transcend the boundaries of such harmless emotional expression and commit infractions, mostly minor. In 1983, said James Wassenaar, dean of students, such behaviors fell in two main categories. "One might be called disruptive and the other damage to individuals or to property. Disruptive ones might involve such things as yelling, screaming, or not complying with someone's request to be quiet. Vandalism embraces a wide range of destructive acts."

A 1982 police report described the kinds of petty criminal acts in which students engaged.[26] In one case, someone called the Cayuga Hall desk continuously from midnight to 1:45 A.M. saying a bomb was going to go off in the building. Thefts around campus included a knapsack, a smudge pot, a telephone, and a coffee pot. In Funnelle Hall someone made a false report about pulling a fire-box alarm. A disorderly conduct charge was filed when a pedestrian was hit by a rubber band flung by a passenger in a passing vehicle. Other criminal activities included fireworks shot off in Scales Hall, arrest of a student for possession of a dangerous weapon, the breaking of a window in one dormitory and the throwing of a writing table out the window of another. Petty larceny reports included thefts of a battery, hub caps, a speaker, a Moneymatic card, bricks on the Cayuga grounds, and fire extinguishers.

The foregoing picture is modified by at least three factors: these behaviors involved only a very small minority; the trend is down; and Oswego's current record is the best in the SUNY system. Conduct hearings involving aggression due to alcohol abuse fell from forty in 1978 to four in 1980, and the cost of damage fell from $31,000 to $18,000. Another symptom of a "more serious and orderly college community appeared in the public safety report. For the second straight year the number of criminal incidents on campus decreased, a reduction of 20 percent over a three-year period."[27]

President Radley attributed the students' better behavior to four main factors: "decreased residence hall tripling, strict enforcement of regulations, an alcohol awareness and rehabilitation program, and a dormitory incentive program." According to this program, initiated in 1978, each dorm is allotted a certain amount of money for each student and, if this money isn't needed to repair damages in the dorm, it can be used to fix up residence halls. Many of the dorms have been quite successful with the program; for instance, Oneida used its extra money to build a new kitchen. In addition, a very effective student advisement center, staffed by sixty-four faculty and staff advisers, directed the advisement of seven-hundred lower division undeclared students. It appears, concluded Radley, "that the student body is, in general, more reflective and serious than those of the recent past, for there were 600,000 utilizations of Penfield Library last year."

Indeed, the vast majority of Oswego's students are a healthy, serious, dedicated lot, although here, as everywhere, some have emotional problems. In 1982, among sixteen colleges in Massachusetts, worry about finances was cited most often—by 40 percent of the students—as the cause of psychological problems. About 7 to 9 percent of the men and 4 percent of the women had psychological problems severe enough that these students could be called clinically ill.[28]

An antidote to such behaviors, and a theme since the 1960s, has been students' search for significant relationships between themselves and others, including faculty members and students.[29] This quest has meant dismantling old customs in favor of more natural, less hypocritical ones. Locally, it is widely agreed that healthy social relationships flourish, and visitors often comment on this campus's friendliness. The reactions of two students are typical. Joan Berkenblit (1983) said: "In my four years here I have made friends with many different kinds of people. In high school there were a few cliques, and no one crossed into a different one. In college I found these barriers broken, and people associated with anyone they wished." Said Linda Johnson (1976), "One of the best things about Oswego is its casual atmosphere." "It is so easy for even the most anti-social types to meet new people. And where else are you going to run into so many different people right in your same age group? Walking through a crowd, you recognize a hundred faces—you've probably talked to most of them at least once, some of them more—I find it most rewarding just seeing some of the people you once shared a class or an elevator ride with and knowing there are so many other faces you'll run into today. Easygoing, nonjudgmental attitudes prevail in relation to social life here."

There are exceptions to the foregoing among older commuting students, whose numbers continue to grow. Dennis White (1980), twenty-two years old when he enrolled, commuted from Auburn and spent almost no time socializing because he felt he "didn't quite fit in."

Although Oswego students are unusually democratic, certain factors seem to enhance one's status. These might include having plenty of spending money, dressing fashionably, being groomed properly, driving a fairly new car, having an expensive stereo, and always having some liquor around for entertainment. Andrew Burger (1980) believes that being attractive and active in organizations may contribute to popularity. However, insisted James Shaw (1983), "no students at Oswego need feel overshadowed or inferior. They all contribute socially on an equal basis by being themselves."

Despite occasional unfortunate episodes, relations between the sexes are healthier than ever before. Women and men are tired of using each other and seek companionship or emotional commitment, not merely physical involvement. As both sexes anticipate careers, they have become more supportive of each other. "In long-term relationships," noted Roger Grippe (1981), "much emphasis is given to the career orientation of both parties. If marriage is in the offing, the couple seldom expect to assume the traditional wife-childbearer-housekeeper and husband-breadwinner roles."

The following quotes aptly describe most male–female relations on campus. Janet Mandeville said, "There is a much more relaxed feeling about having guys as just friends or buddies. I feel very close to a few boys, without feeling as though I'm under any pressure to look at them as 'boyfriends'. It's fun just to go out with a group of friends (guys and girls) and to be able to enjoy yourself." Jacquelyn Bishop (1981) agreed: "There's no emphasis on girls' coming to school and finding a "rich, handsome young man" to marry. Many times, girls ask the guys out, without waiting for the guys to ask first. Although some relationships get serious, many people go out as just friends, without need for commitment."

Almost all students, perhaps 90 percent, approve premarital cohabitation of the sexes, although not always for themselves. Sex may be involved, but often, if not usually, women and men live together merely for reasons of companionship, convenience, and economics. "I live in an all-male house," said Andrew Burger (1980), "but sometimes I think having an additional female housemate would give our house a homey touch. Many cohabitants maintain a platonic, strong, brother–sister relationship."

Dating, another coed custom, has changed dramatically over recent years, and male–female relations on campus have become far less formalized, more casual. Students are generally agreed upon the status of such practices. Said Lucie de la Bruere (1981), "Most students develop sisterhood and brotherhood and, if dating develops, that's fine. If it doesn't that is no big deal. There is not the sense of pressure to date as was present in high schools."

Laurie Fields (1981) noted, "on this campus, dating in the traditional manner—flowers, dressing up, a nice place to go—is almost nonexistent. It's a lot easier to visit a friend on campus, and talk or whatever, than to go through the hassle of thinking of a place to go. Some popular alternatives are the movie and the union on Friday or the nearby one downtown, or maybe one of the shows in Tyler, but these alternatives aren't as popular as just plain visiting." A revolution has occurred not only in dating but sex relations in general: no longer are they exploitive but mutually respectful. In this area, as in others, Oswego students are a healthy lot and pretty typical of today's youths. And if we label their campus behavior immature and absurd, it's probably because we've forgotten our own youth! This same reminder is applicable to the other facets of Oswego's students to be highlighted in the next chapter.

14

More about Students of the 1980s

THE more informal aspects of student life in the 1980s lead inevitably to the students themselves within the context of their organizations. One of the most long-standing of student groups is the Greeks. By the 1980s, after having gone through a period of unpopularity, the Greeks revived and were emphasizing scholarship and service. Oswego's Greek Student Association, formed in 1979, set out to debunk the image of Greeks as "drunk and disorderly, cliquish and always partying," said Don Harrison (1968). In addition, a new state hazing law forbade "any stressful form of hazing or initiation into any organization." David Glick, dean of students, said he had never noted such hazing incidents at Oswego.

The concept of pledging had changed, too. While in the past the Greek sisters might have had pledges "roll eggs from here to there, today they are more likely to be put to work on the sorority house itself. The legendary hell nights are becoming less hellish, too, and physical and mental abuse have all but disappeared." "I pledged three years ago," said Colleen Toal (1981), "and it's cake." In the meantime, the status of Greeks on campus has dramatically changed. Non-Greeks were pretty much excluded from on-campus social and political life in the 1950s. As noted in an earlier chapter, the Greeks reached their lowest ebb in the 1960s and 1970s, then began slowly to revive. These days, Greek membership is simply an alternative life-style, carrying no higher status than others.

Elizabeth Pratt noted in the April 28, 1977 *Oswegonian* that one could find proof on almost any bathroom wall that Greeks were unpopular.[1] That same fall, the fraternities received more initiates than for some years; however, *Oswegonian* writer Patricia Szarek (1979) predicted that the Greeks would never be as popular as they once were, at least on state campuses: for most individuals, "it is more popular to be on your own than to belong to a . . . cliquish social fraternity or sorority from the 1950's."[2] "Compared to other campuses," concluded Beth Carroll (1982), "Oswego students attach much less importance to brotherhood and sisterhood, and popularity does not depend on being a member." Marianne Plante (1983) noted "a rise [in

1981] in membership, and the pledge classes have been growing ever since. I don't believe Greek life will ever be that of the majority on campus, but there are more now than there were four or five years ago. One thing that really hasn't changed much is the attitude of non-Greeks about Greeks. Some people still look on Greeks at Oswego as cliques and put them down. I don't think this will ever change. Greek life is not for everyone. If it were, the Greeks would not have the special feeling that comes from being a Greek. But what I have to say to the people who put Greeks down is, 'It might not be for you, that's O.K., but why knock something you have never tried?' "

Other Greeks also find their affiliation quite rewarding. Beth Marola is one example: "My feelings about Greek organizations are very special. I have been in Oswego for only two years but have been a sister of Alpha Delta Eta for that entire time. I am pinned to a Sigma Tau Chi brother. My sorority sisters and the fraternity brothers have proved to be the best friends I have made in Oswego. But the most special part of being a Greek is the fact that I know (as an alumna) that I'll always have a home to come back to. Greek alumni are always welcomed back to their respective houses with open arms, and from my experiences, Greeks seem to be a majority of visiting alumni."

"Pledging a fraternity in my freshman year", said John Shoemaker (1979), "and rising through the frat to be elected its president, I've seen what Greek organizations have done for people, including myself. I've seen shy, insecure people, through the brotherhood's support and caring and the experience Greek life offers, become confident persons. I've seen some of the worst critics of fraternities and sororities come by just once and see what we're like, and their whole perception would be reversed by the time they left. You come in contact with many different types of people and, through this mutual bond, you get to know them in a way that you would not usually. You see and spend time with every type of person you could meet on campus. I lived in a dorm for two years, and in a frat house for two years, and to me there is no comparison. You come out a more well-rounded person by being a part of Greek life."

In recent years, the Greeks have stressed service to the campus and community: they sponsor the Dance Marathon for Muscular Dystrophy; sell daffodils for Youth Against Cancer; extend to Oswego's students various open social gatherings every fall, including picnics and parties and; every year, clean up the college shoreline.

One fraternity, Delta Kappa Kappa (DKK), sustained a major blow on January 9, 1983, when its house was destroyed by fire. The five residents of the house, which was not insured, escaped unharmed. Arson was suspected but never proved; the culprit could also have been defective wiring. The fraternity hoped to have a new "party-proofed" house in September. Many organizations gave financial assistance, including the Red Cross, the Salvation Army, and DKK alumni, and the Lake City Police Club sponsored a benefit hockey game.

The Greeks had made a comeback by 1983, numbering eleven fraternities and sororities governed by the Greek Student Organization. Yet non-Greeks felt no lower status for not belonging and vastly outnumbered those who did. Attacks against the Greeks in the 1970s had diminished, replaced by relative indifference.

The various student-run media have a significant impact on campus life, such as WOCR, the campus radio station. This was begun in the late 1960s by a group of students, including John Krauss (1971), who is now WRVO's assistant manager. Often advised and encouraged by professors from the college's broadcasting department, seventy-five students were involved in the station's operation by 1982. That same year, United Press International presented to WOCR its Most Outstanding News Service Award for a Small Market, the first college station ever to receive this award. WTOP, Channel 1, the campus television station, is also owned and operated by the students. Topics aired in 1982 included "Dorm Dating Games," a nightly news show, Oswego Lakers hockey games, and "From the Press Box."

The *Oswegonian*, the major college newspaper, has won many awards over the years. It was awarded first place in 1983 by the American Scholastic Press Association. In receiving this award, the paper received 945 points out of a possible 1000. First place was given papers scoring 850 points or better. "The students who produce our paper work very hard," said *Oswegonian* Editor-in-Chief Melanie Janowsky (1983). "It's nice to know that our work is deemed outstanding by professional journalists." The letter which accompanied the award observed that "this is a very fine publication. It has all the makings of a very professional scholastic newspaper."

Ever since the 1940s, when *Oswegonian* faculty advisor Mildred Larson stubbornly insisted on freedom of the press for its writers, the campus newspapers have been quite independent. In 1979, an *Oswegonian* editor noted that some people had suggested more faculty advisers for campus organizations, but freedom of the press might suffer if "this potential adviser became a reality."[3] Freedom from censorship would "be impossible if . . . a watchdog were imposed, to growl down the necks of the *Oswegonian* staff."[3]

The *Pendulum* and *Great Lakes Review* also are quality productions. The *Pendulum* is issue oriented and contains features, news, opinion, and creative writing. The *Great Lakes Review*, devoted to the arts, was begun in 1974 and, during 1982–83, was edited by Melora Turco (1983), daughter of Professor Lewis Turco.

Dormitory newspapers, highly varied and often short-lived, recently included *The Johnson News*, *Para FUNNELLEia*, Riggs's *The Toilet Paper*, Tyler's *What's the Buzz*, and Waterbury's *Rainbow Resort Review*. Riggs's *The*

Toilet Paper received its name because it was distributed to the bathroom stalls. Resident profiles, stories about dorm-council activities, original poetry, and personals were the staples of most of these publications. The Scales paper, called *As The Scales Tip,* had a feature called "Drink of the Week." *The Johnson News* featured puzzles and cartoons. Both the Scales and Riggs papers had "Quotes of the Week," ranging from Riggs's ex-wrestlers commenting on female wrestlers to a Scales resident who remarked, "Today is the tomorrow you worried about yesterday." *What's the Buzz* published a list of what the dorm residents would give up for Lent. Items included Buck's, Barry Manilow, dorm council, quiet hours, General Hospital, and finally, Lent. Their rendition of " 'Twas the Night Before Buckland's" is already a cult classic. The Waterbury and Scales newspapers also carried advice to the lovelorn. "Dear Abby the 2nd" and "Dear Barry" dealt with love lives, roommate problems and, in one letter, a "guy allergic to girls."[4]

Student government, a considerably more formal activity nationally, has become increasingly stronger and better organized. The National Student Lobby (NSL) and the National Student Association (NSA) merged in 1978, becoming the United States Student Association (USSA). SUNY students are represented by the Student Association of the State University (SASU), which is a member organization. Issues of immediate concern to SASU in 1978 were student participation in campus governance, the funding of higher education, women's issues, including rape laws and ratification of ERA, and student rights.

One statewide organization, the New York State Public Interest Research Group (NYPIRG) produced considerable controversy at Oswego. Directed and funded by college students in New York State, the program is designed to inform the public and gain its support in such fields as energy, health, consumer protection, the environment, government and corporate accountability, and economic and social justice. Since these problems are approached through research, college students are accorded the necessary resources, including labs, computer facilities, and libraries. However, as of 1984, the Student Senate had not yet endorsed the establishment of a chapter on campus.

The spring 1983 student government elections made history when for the first time a woman, Sue Castrigno (1980), was elected president. To add to the drama, another woman, Sue Wray, was elected vice president. Unusual also was the defeat of two Mikes (Murray [1984] and Vottis) by the two Sues. The two winners later observed that their families were very proud of them. Wray recalled that, "My Mom went all out. She sent me a balloon telegram, a thing that looks like a plant with balloons instead of blossoms, with sticks in a basket and little fake ferns about the bottom."

Castrigno said, "We told the students that we needed their help in the problems we faced. We had an organization meeting and over 300 students showed up, although we'd expected twenty to fifty at the most." She added, "I attend many meetings and find myself time after time sitting with ten men to discuss what we are going to do. It's nice to have Wray as my vice president—someone who's intelligent, bright, poised and female, a good companion who works well with me. There's always a certain strain, I think, when men and women become close in a working situation."

Turning to sports, women athletes have had their share of controversy. The women's softball team had the second best record (9 to 1) in the state in 1979 but was not chosen for the championship. Their only loss was to Cortland (7 to 6) in one game of twin ball. Again, after the women's ice hockey team was invited to participate in a "prestigious tournament" at St. Lawrence University, the administration rejected the bid "with the cynical excuse that two unused playing jerseys were missing," said Denise LePine (1983). "We were given the ultimatum of either finding the jerseys or raising $100 to compensate for the missing items within eighteen hours. The team members located one jersey and raised enough money within twenty-four hours; hence, expected reversal of the decision, but it was denied."[5] At least one respected source contended that this story was "a bit doctored."

Women's sports teams not only have performed well collectively but have possessed a very respectable quota of stars. Laurie Irving (1983) won New York state's three-meter diving championship in 1980 and was praised by Coach Grace Mowatt for consistency and ability to handle pressure. Irving later qualified for the nationals by consistently finishing either first or second at various meets. Gretchen Byrne (1982) stole headlines in spring 1981 by becoming the first woman to qualify for the men's golf team. Also in 1981, the women's softball team, coached by Alice Struzinsky and with a 15 to 4 record, qualified for the regional tournament.

The next year, 1981–82, also proved to be a banner year for women athletic stars. Hockey goalie Shirleen Dubuque (1985) was selected for the New York All-State Field Hockey team in fall 1982. 'Dube' was surprised, but her coach, Shirley Hodge, was not at all. Also in 1982, Nancy Lobb (1983), of the Great Laker softball team, hit .500 in the first eleven games. She once hit a liner to third base so hard that, even though the third baseman caught it, she was knocked off her feet in the process. In high school, 'Lobber' had become the first woman in New York State to receive five varsity letters in basketball. Robin Wiggins (1982) was voted the female athlete of the year, barely winning—five to four—over Laurie Irving. Wiggins was the all-time leading scorer in women's basketball and Irving, then a junior, was the all-American diver.

The year 1982–83 saw still other women stars emerge. In the preliminaries of a swimming meet in Canton, Ohio, Kathy Bloom (1986), a computer science major, set a national record and won third place and all-American status in the finals. Bloom, who had only hoped to be in the top twelve, was "shocked" to receive such honors.[6] That same year, Oswego's co-captain of basketball, Eileen Sommers (1983) set two records in Laker history: 1,058 career points and a record 684 rebounds. Sommers believed that women players have the same dedication as men and protested the lesser publicity accorded them. Nevertheless, largely because of President Radley's insistence on equality of opportunity for the sexes, women athletes have fared better at Oswego than in colleges nationwide.

Sport by sport, the performance record of Oswego's men athletes is equally impressive. In swimming, Peter Rosenkranz, a student from West Germany, was ranked first in 1977 in the NCAA division III and the 200-yard butterfly event, a college and SUNYAC conference record. Rosenkranz had been West Germany's national champion in two free-style swimming events; he did not lose an individual event for the Lakers all season. He placed seventeenth in one swimming event in the 1972 Munich Olympic Games and eighteenth in another.

The performance of the college's hockey team has been especially outstanding. In the 1978 ECAC Division II West Playoffs, Oswego's Greg Preston (1978) became SUNY's second all-American hockey player; the first, in 1971, was Peter Sears (1971). The Lakers's hockey team had the best nationwide record in 1980–81, finishing second in the ECAC Division II West and posting a 26-3-1 season, the best winning percentage in the nation. Richard Pratt (1982), the team's high-scoring hockey forward, also received an all-American award. The team earned a berth in the fall 1981 championship tournament and became the only nonscholarship institution to defeat the eventual national champion. David Lair received notice that he had been named to the 1983 NCAA Division Coaches' all-American Team. He was also named the ECAC player of the year for the second year in a row, as well as making the ECAC all-star hockey team for the fourth time in as many years. By this time he had become the most prolific scorer in NCAA modern-day annals. His coach, Donald Unger, said, "He's definitely the best Division II player in the nation, and I would guess that, if he were in Division I, he would be one of the best offensive players in the country."

The basketball team had also performed well. Nicknamed "The Cardiac Kids" in 1981, the team's twelve-to-four record brought it an invitation to participate in the ECAC's spring 1982 post-season tournament. In that same spring, Walter Nitardy's young baseball team had an eighteen-game winning streak, outdoing the former record of thirteen.

Meanwhile, Coach James Howard's grapplers were winning headlines. Paul Corley (1979) won the state's 1979 167-pound mat title, and the 1980–81 wrestlers' thirteen-to-two record was Oswego's best in eighteen years, placing the team among the nation's top ten. Wrestler David Parisi (1982) was named all-American in the NCAA Division I tournament and, by 1983, the Great Laker team ranked third in the nation.

Coach Thomas Brennan's golf team also produced stellar performers. The Lakers reached the NCAA championships fourteen consecutive years. Oswego student Wayne Levi was a national champion in 1972, earning all-American status, and he was a top money winner in the 1982 PGA tour, finishing ninth in the money.

The year 1981–82 was Oswego's best sports year ever. In addition to the feats already mentioned, diver Donald Potter (1983) was named all-American; the lacrosse team placed fifth in the SUNY conference; and Michael Deegnan (1976) was named all-conference goalie. The golf team placed fourth in its own invitational tournament, and the baseball team finished the season with twenty-five wins, seven losses. Walter Nitardy was named SUNY coach of the year, Michael Charles (1983) all-conference infielder, and Barry Dillon (1986) all-conference pitcher with an eight-to-one record. In the meantime, the softball team posted a twelve-to-five record and placed ninth out of ninety-eight teams in Division III and was seeded third in New York State. David Lair, the hockey team's "scoring wizard," was again named male athlete of the year, edging out the national wrestling champ, David Parisi, four votes to three.

Despite the foregoing accomplishments, Oswego can hardly be called a sports-oriented school. "There's not much support or school spirit for the teams," remarked Roseann Esposito (1981). Thomas Shambo (1981) concluded that "sports here are just for the players and not the spectators. Most people don't bother to follow them." Jackie Bishop (1981) added that spectators at men's basketball games hardly filled a single row of bleachers, and Donna Roberts (1978) noted the student body's apathy toward varsity sports and the lack of prestige accorded athletes. It seems that hockey is the only varsity sport given any significant attention, and it is hardly overwhelming.

At least two sports had already fallen victim to the budget crunch. In 1977 the Student Senate decided not to fund the men's football program because it was such an expensive sport. Such ideas as alumni funding or selling buttons and banners had not worked in the past to help fund football and, it was believed, would not work in the future. Two years later, in 1979, fencing also fell victim to the senate axe.

The disinterest in varsity sports is commonly blamed on budgetary factors. Athletic budgets on SUNY campuses are controlled by student governments, paid primarily with student activity fees, and students are reluctant to pay high fees for athletic programs. For this reason, teams on the SUNY campuses compete in Division III of the NCAA, the lowest level of intercollegiate competition. In addition, athletic scholarships are not available to students in institutions within that division. To assess this situation and student life in general, Chancellor Wharton created "The Task Force on Improving the Quality of Student Life Within the University" in 1982. Composed of administrators and faculty, the study of sports within the sixty-four units of the SUNY System constitutes the first phase of "a comprehensive review of all aspects of student life." The study is expected to continue for several years.[7]

Contrary to the relatively lukewarm interest in varsity sports, students are firmly supportive of a broad range of services for themselves. One of these, the Peer Advisement Center in Seneca Hall, was begun in fall 1980 to help Seneca residents deal with general education requirements. Reorganized in fall 1981 by Mitchell Rosenthal (1984), psychology senior and assistant dorm director, the center was expanded to help people from all across campus with academic matters and such topics as birth control, drug-related problems, and personal concerns. The eighteen staff members received their training in the Student Advisement and Counseling Centers in Rich Hall.

Several services have been designed mainly for women students. The all-women Johnson Hall has a mentoring program, two mentors assigned to each of Johnson Hall's six wings. The mentors are volunteers who hold professional positions on campus and act as role models, friends, and academic advisers. The Women's Center was established in 1971, located in the old Mental Health Center across from Sheldon. When that building was torn down, the center moved to a house on Bridge Street; it returned to the campus in 1979, first to Rich Hall, later to Johnson Hall. The center's services include walk-in and over-the-phone counseling, consciousness-raising, and advice on personal safety. In particular, the Women's Center strives to deal effectively with sexist practices and harassment on campus. The center also publishes a newspaper called *Arise*, and it arranges informal workshops which provide opportunities to discuss the various concerns of women. The Matilda J. Gage Library, a feature of the center, contains over nine hundred books, as well as feminist periodicals the Penfield Library does not receive.

This center has been the subject of considerable controversy. In 1980, upon learning that the Student Association budget council recommended $2,190 for the Women's Center instead of the $3,875 it had requested, the center's representatives Nancy Perlin (1981), Lisa Korwin (1981), and Rosemary Calderalo (1981) stood up to declare the Senate defunct, reading a list of demands. In the meantime, eleven other women tried to prevent anyone's leaving the room; eight of them locked arms and blocked the door. This action was taken because they believed they were not being taken seriously. The episode precipitated considerable debate; some people supported the action, others denounced it.

In a 1983 letter to the editor of the *Oswegonian*, three students objected to harassment of the Women's Center. Attention was called to a poster placed on the bulletin board to advertise an open house at the center—the word "feminists" had been crossed out and the word "dykes" scrawled over it. One group in support of the Women's Center was "Women for a New World."[8]

A related facility, the Rape Crisis Center, opened in September 1980, with a trained staff always on duty. This center was "a community-based operation designed to care for all victims of rape and sexual assault with the cooperation of local medical, legal, social and law enforcement agencies." Also it conducted a full-time training program for both sexes for study of related matters.[9]

Because of a number of sexual assaults on campus, the Student Evening Escort Patrol (SEEP) was organized in 1982 for walking women anywhere on campus between 9:00 P.M. and 1:00 A.M. Sunday through Thursday. These escorts, all screened by campus police, always walked in pairs and used walkie-talkies and flashlights. They had ID cards and were required to wear red-and-white SEEP hats. However, the women made very little use of this service. In a letter to *The Oswegonian,* Philip Zampino (1983) noted that "scare techniques" to promote use of SEEP were manifestations of clutching at threads to save an unnecessary organization. "It is upsetting," he said, "to see someone . . . trying to spread a feeling of paranoia—one that need not exist to save this organization."[10]

Students have been extremely helpful in campus improvement projects, whether painting a mural or designing a "rec" room or making decisions about what functions they are going to serve. Student volunteers also help with the annual Open House, and when 2,000 students and their families visited the college in 1982, students served as tour guides and policed the campus, ridding it of debris. It should be added that the campus is spacious and beautifully kept, perhaps unequaled—and certainly not surpassed—by the other SUNY campuses.

Other services are supervised mainly by the administration. Since over a third of the students live off campus, an Off-Campus Association and a Non-Traditional Student Union were established in 1980–81. That same year a special bar bus was added on Friday and Saturday nights for the late returnees to the campus. Other organizations were a re-enlivened veterans' club and a more accessible student advisement center, which became an important part of the college's mentoring program. In addition, the Mary Walker Health Center made contraceptive and gynecological care available to students, including two contraceptive clinics each week and a clinic devoted primarily to gynecological care. Other student services are in the areas of counseling, orientation, judicial conduct review, residence life, and assistance for disabled students.

The above services relate to life on campus. Off campus, as in all college communities, there is a measure of town–gown conflict. In September 1978, students protested townspeoples' efforts to inspect students' dwellings and to limit the number who might live in each house in zoned areas. Later that fall Oswego officials abandoned plans to license group residential quarters but chose instead to work within existing ordinances in dealing with multifamily dwellings. However, this conflict continued to simmer.

Another persistent problem is the assumption by many in the community that the college is responsible for whatever students do off campus. However, the official jurisdiction of the college is limited to the campus itself. The following telephone exchanges, examples of complaints, took place in early morning hours. Caller, on a very early 1978 Saturday morning: "Dr. Radley, a student threw a tire on my porch. What are you going to do about it?" Answer: "Sir, if I were you I would pick it up and throw it around his neck. But inasmuch as I'm not you, why don't you call the police?" And, from a 2:00 A.M. caller in 1980: "Dr. Radley, my sleep is disturbed, so I am disturbing yours. There's a noisy party next to me and I need my rest." Answer: "Have you called the police?" Caller: "What good would that do? It's your responsibility to take care of these students." Answer: "I'm not going down there, but you can come up here. It's quiet and peaceful here. Then we can both get some sleep."[11] Radley said that she can well understand the outrage of citizens under such circumstances, but responsibility must be clearly defined.

Because of such conflicts, the college, both administration and students, conducts an ongoing program for maintaining good community relations. As part of a National Youth Sports Program, volunteers operate camps for economically disadvantaged Oswego county youth. In this program, teenagers are taught lifelong sports skills and health practices. By skipping a meal in the dining halls, students raised almost $2,500 for Oswego County's 1980 United Way Drive. Two years later, in 1982, the Big Brothers–Big Sisters of Oswego, a volunteer organization whose members work on a one-to-one basis with children who need role models and friends, held a picnic at Fort Ontario. The day's finale was a long game of "duck, duck goose," in which children, their big brothers and sisters, and many student Greeks participated. Also in 1982, students supported the Oswego Red Cross Blood Drive, contributing more than half of the blood drawn annually in Oswego County. The next year's dance marathon, a two-day event, raised $21,000, or $16,000 after expenses. Proceeds were given to Services-to-Aid Families in Oswego County, the American Heart Association, and the Farnham Youth Development Center. And, through the Adopt-a-Grandparent program, students visit with residents of nearby nursing homes.

Students also help with services for the larger world community. In 1979, 2,043 students, out of a possible 4,100, voted to miss a meal for the benefit of Cambodian relief. On the much larger SUNY Binghamton campus, just 1,351 students participated in a similar program. In the next year, 1980, students in Edward Frey's "Critical Health Issues" course collected funds for cancer research, bringing the total collected in recent semesters to almost $5,000.

With regard to activism concerning more controversial issues nationally and internationally, the student mood had cooled. Students were seeking meaning in their lives in the later 1960s and insisted on the right to "do their thing," but sometimes their behaviors got out of hand. Nationwide, between 1969 and 1978, freshmen of the far left had declined from 4.5 to 1.8 percent, and middle-of-the-roaders had increased by almost half, from 42 to 58 percent. By the later 1970s, students had become more concerned about particular issues than overall social reform. Broad-scale political activism waned in the summer of 1970. Nor were students especially interested in academic reform. Their activism was more of the "trade union variety: no increase in tuition, better counseling, and so forth."[12] They had less respect for rules and regulations: there was increased defaulting on loans, more vandalism and cheating. They were more confident than formerly about their own personal futures but less hopeful about the world.

One observer described the students of the 1970s as able to laugh at themselves and as aware of their own frailties. Riots and uprisings of the late 1960s seemed as "remote and hard to believe as, say, the Boer War or the Whiskey Rebellion." Students of today had come face-to-face with reality. Many had gone home on spring vacation and found their fathers out of work. Older siblings had graduated with college degrees and "wound up pushing hacks on the night shift, if they were lucky."[13]

There was intermittent comment about student apathy in *Oswegonians* of the late 1970s. Halette Torby in her article "Students Don't Give a Damn," argued that most students are extremely apathetic and that this apathy "does not only run skin deep. On this campus it takes every form and shape imaginable."[14] She even believed that many professors were also apathetic and complained about tenured professors who remain on campus regardless of the quality of their teaching. In addition, there was a mood of less tolerance for extremes and experimentation on campus. Instead of taking risks, students strove for grades which would look good on their transcripts.

Joel Lee (1980) said in his senior year that most students seemed "extremely selfish and self-oriented." In 1982, though, James Shaw (1983) insisted that students' moods "varied from one to another. I see apathy, concern, people who know where they are going and people who have no clue. I see the total mood as one of people who want success but are not sure how they are going to attain it. Many have direction, but a large fraction are just moving with the tide."

Such activism as has existed in recent years has mainly concerned issues hung over from the early 1970s. Throughout the 1970s, the *Oswegonian* carried articles, mostly in opposition, about arming the campus night police with guns. The Student Advisory Committee suggested various alternatives, among them a student escort program, lighting, campus police patrols in pairs, and radio-equipped patrol cars. The officers themselves insisted that, wearing firearms, they would be better able to "prevent or terminate incidents of first-degree arson or burglary, forceable rape or sodomy."

Certainly, the officers could cite ample evidence to support their request. One police officer, Leo Boland, upon observing a pickup truck traveling at high speed, radioed for help. After the truck blew a tire and overturned in a ditch, Boland apprehended the driver, pretending his flashlight was a gun. The driver later said he would have killed Boland, had he known the officer was unarmed. In another incident, the student director of Hewitt Union was threatened with a knife and called for police assistance; the officer, who was unarmed, was slashed on the hand.

In a 1979 letter to Chancellor Wharton, Radley cited other incidents. In one case, a student was assaulted at four in the morning and subjected to attempted rape. A security guard chased and apprehended the man, and found a loaded gun on the seat beside him. In other cases, one staff member was robbed at knife point, another was robbed of a wallet and stabbed in the arm. Because of such incidents, Radley seriously considered arming campus security when they were on night patrol. She knew that the student body had a strong "emotional set" against it, but she felt a responsibility, not just to the students but also to the officers.

Ultimately, President Radley felt compelled by such events to approve arming officers on the 11:00 P.M. to 7:00 A.M. shift, a decision which outraged Student Association President Michael Flores (1980). In September 1979, two hundred students held an afternoon rally, and five hundred attended an evening student senate meeting opposing the measure. Although only 10 to 15 percent of the students were against security officers' carrying guns, the Student Association spokesman claimed that most of the students were against that policy. In the meantime, a *Palladium Times* editorial supported Radley's decision that the police be allowed to carry guns. The editor felt that "equipping police cars, charged with protection of lives and property, only with night sticks, makes as much sense as the United States signing an arms race agreement with the papal guards."[15]

Nuclear power has been another persistent issue. As one *Oswegonian* editorial pointed out, "At the Fitzpatrick plant [near Oswego] there were nine evacuations of personnel last year because of radiation leaks." This editor called the people of Oswego "blind. They want the jobs; they want a better economy for their county; and they want to die of radiation cancer and have birth-defective children." The writer concluded by warning: "Don't let nuclear power increase in the county or the country. Don't trust the Nuclear Regulatory Commission; they've already sold you out."[16]

The protests were not limited to words. In 1978, the Community Energy Alliance sponsored Sun Day activities, and a huge sun image was painted on the academic square between Lanigan and Mahar Halls to commemorate that event. In May of that year, faculty members and students participated in an antinuclear rally in East Park as part of a statewide protest. In November 1982, the Student Senate passed a resolution urging "the Public Service

Commission of the Nuclear Regulatory Commission to re-evaluate the need for nuclear power. . . ." Copies of the resolution were sent to President Ronald Reagan, the United States Senate, the New York State Senate Assembly, and Oswego's president, Virginia L. Radley.

The most vigorous protests of recent years have involved pocketbook issues. Students in the 1970s were concerned about being drafted and losing their lives in Vietnam; their current concern became economic survival. In 1978 students from Oswego, Oneonta, Cortland, and Binghamton picketed the Commission on Independent Colleges and Universities to stress the need for unity among the public and private sectors in higher education through a mutually beneficial tuition assistance program. In the following spring, SUNY college students went to Albany to protest the proposed tuition hike. They marched with a police escort through the streets chanting, "SUNY, CUNY must unite, same struggle, same fight."

In January 1980 ten students and thirty faculty members went to Albany to represent SUNY in a rally protesting proposed cuts in the 1980–81 budget. Later that year SUNY students, including Oswego's, established a tent city on the front lawn of SUNY's central administration building to protest the new policy of making dorms self-sufficient by raising rents. Three years later, in 1983, the SUNY Board of Trustees recommended increasing undergraduate tuition by $300 a year and, after many battles with the governor and board of trustees, raised it by $150 a year.

A majority of SUNY students had supported Cuomo for governor in 1982 and were incensed at his proposed budget cuts for SUNY; hence, they launched a series of budget battles. In a February 1983 letter-writing campaign protesting the 1983–84 SUNY budget, Oswego students produced about six hundred letters, and about two hundred students (four busloads) went to Albany, where lobbying workshops were held. In the next month, March, along with a "pep band, hand-painted banners and an array of chants and cheers, over 3,000 students and three hundred faculty members from all across the SUNY system" converged on the convention center in Albany.[17] They were attempting to convince the legislature to oppose Cuomo's proposed SUNY cuts. All through the corridors echoed chants of "When they cut back, we say fight back." Mike Vottis, an Oswego student senator, said, "We lobbied this afternoon and talked with a lot of legislators. It really went well." Said student Jill Lacey (1984), "It was very inspiring. I'm glad to see that everybody came." However, at least two Oswego students thought that lack of experience in lobbying hampered many of them. Peter Sawyer said there was a high-spirited atmosphere, yet it seemed very unorganized.[17]

Other issues were of concern mainly to particular segments of the student body, such as the Gay Rights Movement. Letters to *Oswegonian* editors carried emotionally charged pro and con opinions, and name-calling.[18] One gay man received a threatening phone call in response to a letter he had written to the editor.[19] Opposition to the Gay Rights Movement has lessened in the intervening years, although it cannot yet be called a dormant issue.

Military registration was a topic of somewhat broader concern. Student Association President Michael Flores (1980) was among the three hundred student leaders from schools across the nation invited to Washington by President Carter in 1980. After Carter defended his call for military registration, Flores asked a White House official why registration was necessary since there were already two million active troops. The aide replied that only registration was planned and not a draft. In 1982, when male college students who failed to register for the draft were declared ineligible for federal financial aid, President Radley observed that the college lacked enough support services to assume the function of such regulation.

Some students have opposed President Reagan on a variety of topics, mainly on his effort to beef up defense. The May 1982 Peace Day march began with twenty walkers chanting, "Ronald Reagan, he's no good; send him back to Hollywood." Later the number grew to forty, and then came a speak-out in front of Hewitt Union, beginning with Meteorology Professor Peter Caplan. The speeches dealt with budget cuts, feminism, mutually assured destruction (MAD), military theory, and nuclear weapons. Workshops were held on environmental issues and racism.

Again in 1980, a number of SUNY students went to Albany to protest SUNY's investments in South Africa, because of the country's racist policies. Some students decried the selling of baby formula in third-world countries. It was argued that many infants had died because their mothers had been convinced by such companies as Nestlé and Libby that formula feeding was better than breast feeding. The formulas lacked immunological and other benefits of breast milk, and the mothers could not afford to buy the formulas for long. In response, William Tucker, director of auxiliary services, stated that Nestlé hot chocolate would no longer be found in the dining halls or snack bar in Hewitt Union.

On a vastly different matter, students expressed displeasure at the American boycott of the winter 1980 Olympic games in Moscow because of Russia's military occupation of Afghanistan. Students believed the games were one way of bringing countries together; instead, athletes were being punished.

Still other issues related strictly to the local campus. Recent students, as well as many alumni, have protested the closing of Sheldon Hall, dictated by the prohibitive expense of keeping it open. A Save-Sheldon-Hall committee launched a petition drive to ensure that the closing would not be permanent. On a quite different campus issue, George Edwards (1983) objected to the college's alcohol policy limiting the amount of beer allowed at a party. Said George, "My reasoning is thus: students should remain in the dorm where it's safer than going on the road for further drinks and constituting a potential hazard."

On purely political matters, few students became actively involved in campaigns, nor did many talk much about them. There was a Student-for-Carter campaign on campus in 1976; twenty students were involved, but only seven attended the third meeting. This group distributed Carter-Mondale stickers and buttons around the campus; an organized campaign in support of Gerald Ford was not evident. Students usually know whom they support, although often not in depth.

Nationwide and at Oswego, many students supported Republican presidential candidate John Anderson in 1980. In a poll that fall, before the election, 44 percent of Oswego's students supported John Anderson, 29 percent Jimmy Carter, 14 percent Ronald Reagan, and nine other votes were scattered. Following the election, senators of the Student Association defeated a resolution to send Ronald Reagan a telegram congratulating him upon his election.[20] In 1982 an *Oswegonian* editor complained about James Watt, Secretary of the Interior, for "taking his axe and chopping away at the national parks and the environment."[21]

These types of activities are often spontaneous, mainly temporary. Others, nonpolitical, are more formalized or traditional. Among the latter, the annual Open House offers visitors an opportunity to learn more about the campus. Academic departments set up booths in the Hewitt Union Ballroom to provide exhibits as well as information about their programs. In addition, tours are provided. Visitors find the dormitories especially interesting, and every dormitory has an open house. Throughout the day, tours are conducted through academic buildings, the library, and the biological field station, where taxidermy demonstrations are given.

On Honors Day, another special occasion, students are recognized for outstanding achievement, academic and otherwise. Jeffrey Carr (1984) and Peter Tassini (1983) received awards in 1983 for exceptional accomplishments outside the classroom. Carr was recognized for his efforts to improve all aspects of the student television station, WTOP, and Tassini for persistent efforts to improve the effectiveness of the Student Association's Supreme Court.

Springfest, among the less serious local customs and occasions, celebrates the arrival of spring; students enjoy bands and beer all day at Reagan's Silver Lake. The first major snowfall is the precursor of another special occasion: the annual snowball fight. "You can't graduate from Oswego without participating in this activity at least once," said Hope Rosenhaus (1983). "It's new campus versus old campus, and the idea is to see who can take over the bridge which crosses the lagoon. It's a great time, but watch out—those snowballs come flying. One time, new campus chased old campus all the way back to their dorms and broke many windows. Disregarding the violence, it was a riot."

Of course, students also enjoy national holidays, and they can usually tell you just how long it is until the next one. On St. Patrick's Day, drinking begins for some students at 8:00 A.M. at Buckland's; for others, any time is appropriate to indulge. Buck's offers five-cent green beers at 8:00 A.M., and every half hour the price rises five or ten cents. "On Halloween," noted Mary Jean Krolik (1984), "college students dress in costumes and go from one house party to another to drink beer. A common practice is to go to the Salvation Army to find something to wear. Some students wear masks and don't let their identity be known all evening."

Perhaps the most far-out behaviors occur at spring break, when students from many colleges, including Oswego, make the pilgrimage to Florida, most often to Fort Lauderdale. The trek triggers a sort of craziness, the college-student brand of spring fever. About this pilgrimage, Hope Rosenhaus said, "At spring break more than a half of the school population heads to Florida, which is crazy, wild, and fantastic at this time. Last year I had the time of my life. I've never seen so many kids at one place at one time before. You relax all day and party all night. There are many sponsored activities, so you are never bored. You meet people from all over the country, people with different values, morals, and accents." And this from Luis Roca (1983): "For many students spring break means Florida and getting a tan. Those who are fortunate enough stay for a week and enjoy the opportunity to go crazy, releasing the winter tension and frustrations, along with thousands of other students. It's a party so filled with having 100 percent fun that it becomes almost perverse. And for many, the rest and relaxation you were looking for are never found. Rather, endless days of sunning and nights of partying all contribute to making you more tired when you come back than when you left!"

The big winter snowstorms are among the most notable, though unplanned, Oswego events. In his *Tonight* show in 1977, and again in 1978, Johnny Carson commented on the small town in upstate New York covered with snow. His 1977 commentary was on Oswego's snowfall of fifty-eight inches in seven days. In 1978, Oswego had 221 inches of snow by February 9. David Morford (1983) said, "In the winter of 1982 we had an ice storm followed by extremely high (over 70 m.p.h.) winds. Well, at the corner of Seneca (nicknamed "The Wind Tunnel"), nobody could make it through. People gathered in the north lounges of Seneca and looked down on the poor people trying to make it across the ice. The only successful crossings were made by people who sat down and slid across, or by people who slid down to the tennis courts and held onto the fence there. Finally, maintenance came and spread sand and salt and made the path easier to walk, ruining the entertainment for the people in Seneca."

Said Daniel Smith (1986), "I remember one snowstorm very well. It happened in February last year [1982]. The snow was blowing around so hard that it was hard to see six feet in front of you. People were slipping on the pavement and getting blown down by the wind. People were clinging to trees, buildings, other people, or anything they could get their hands on. I remember seeing one girl, her arms wrapped around a tree, calling for someone to help her. It looked funny, so I turned to my friend to point her out to him, but he was no longer near me. I looked on the ground and saw him sprawled out like he was swimming."

Now and then these activities are punctuated by visits to, or from, parents or relatives, some of whom hold Oswego degrees; Both of Howard Hooper's (1983) sisters came to visit, as did Aaron Wood's. Gary Dievendorf's (1984) great aunt and grandmother have Oswego degrees, and his father was working on his Oswego degree when Gary was a junior.

Students have an easier time when their parents are supportive. "My parents reminisce about their college years," said Julie Wright, "and that helps me realize I can enjoy mine." Sue McNally (1984) believed that "my parents' backing has helped me understand my college experience better." John De Francisco (1983) noted that "my mother is particularly proud to see me in college, as I am the first in the family to go beyond a two-year degree. She is also proud of the way I have worked and saved to put myself through college."

Students are always interested in their parents' reactions to the college. Timothy Cochrane (1983) says that "my father's first and last trip to Oswego was in January 1982, during one of our notorious whiteouts. After that he has always referred to Oswego as 'where the Eskimos live'."

It's always interesting to get the parents' perceptions of Oswego. One parent, Dominic Gangi, described his experience. "When I sent my son here, with him came all my anxieties, all my concerns, all my wishes for him to be a successful and productive individual. If I can be melodramatic, I passed the buck to you at Oswego. All those complex things that parents want for their children, I expected the faculty here to do, to complete what I had started in a manner I thought was appropriate."

When asked about Parents' Day, Gange said, "I must be honest with you. When I first became a student's parent, I thought the event was a total waste of time, but it proved not to be because I had a chance to see my son in the college environment and had the privilege of meeting some of the faculty. Besides, I have talked to many of the other parents on this occasion. On such occasions Dr. Radley does a very important thing: she makes the parents proud that their children are here. That is an invaluable feeling to pass on to parents because they leave feeling that 'this is the place for my children'."

The college released its first *Parents' Handbook* in 1983. "We do not yet have a formalized parents' group," said Dean of Students James Wassenaar, "but we have some feelers out about how to go about it. Parents contacted during the Road Show or on Parents' Weekend have been canvassed to determine their views on how to keep up with the college on a continuing basis."

As noted earlier, some students choose a college because parents or relatives attended. Two-thirds of all entrants, nationwide, give easy accessibility as the most common reason.[22] In fall 1982 the chief reason for choosing Oswego was its "good academic reputation." Oswego's low tuition was the second most important reason, an important criterion for freshmen nationally. And these tuition concerns are greater now than they were six years ago. Individual reasons for selecting Oswego were varied. Mark "Hippo" Taylor said, "I came to Oswego because it's a good school academically. The campus is beautiful, and there are a lot of fine people here. So far there's a lot of work, but I guess it will all pay off in the end." Cathy Mediatore (1987) said she came to Oswego "so my father would stop hassling me. I like quaint little towns, and hicks are cool." Katherine Craine (1986) said, "I came to Oswego for computer programming. Oswego's the only state college with a strong program in computer science, as well as an extensive earth science program." Said Wendell Pope, "I wanted a less urban setting, and I like the large campus. I like the people. The classes are difficult, but in a challenging way."[23]

Other students in the Class of 1983 expressed their reasons for coming here. Cindy Rabert said, "I really liked the campus when I came for visitation. Two advisers at Cobleskill had recommended Oswego to me and had spoken highly of its business program. Oswego's standards for being admitted into this program are higher than at most other colleges." Anita Soovajian (1983) came to Oswego because of its friendly atmosphere and warmth. "I came to Oswego," said Debbie Cruppenink (1983), "because of what it has to offer. It has good business administration, computer, and psychology departments. The professors teach their own courses, which is great; there are no substitutes. I also like the academic record of Oswego; it rates very highly in state colleges and is affordable. The campus is very well planned, and I also enjoy being right on Lake Ontario. It makes me feel like I'm close to the ocean."

Students are less certain about the college's history. In spring 1981 a class of juniors and seniors was asked questions about the college's roots. Almost all knew that Oswego is well known for its contributions to industrial arts and teacher education. A few more than a third (37 percent) knew that Sheldon was the founder, and about the same number had some idea of who he was, but the others had either no idea or a wrong one. He was conjectured variously to have been mayor of Oswego, to have built the first high school here, to have built Dr. Radley's house, and to be buried under Sheldon Hall. Almost no one knew anything about the people for whom the campus buildings were named. A few students said that Mary V. Lee, for whom Lee Hall is named, was a famous athlete, and one thought she had died while playing a game of field hockey for Oswego. Actually, she was a scientist, a brilliant physician, and a physical educator on Sheldon's faculty. The remainder of Sheldon's outstanding faculty had become anonymous to these students. When first asked if they would like to know more about the historical roots of the college, including answers to the above questions, about a third said yes, a fourth were uncertain, and the rest said no. However, after being told the highlights of Oswego's achievements, the erstwhile disinterested students changed their minds.[24]

Students are quick to proclaim Oswego's virtues today. Overwhelmingly, they are proud of the college. Perhaps its best-known attributes are its friendliness, location, and academic reputation. "The appearance of the college and its location on the lake makes you proud to spread by word of mouth how much you like it," said Student Association Vice President Sue Wray. "We rank here with the best." Nancy Steigauf (1983) commented on the friendly atmosphere, one of Oswego's best known trademarks. "At many other colleges," said Steigauf, "the competition is so fierce that no one is willing to share knowledge with others. Here, as a computer science major, I've found that we're all willing to help each other, and all one has to do is ask." Dale Roberts (1983) especially liked the democratic atmosphere. "One thing I've noticed over and over," she said, "is the difference in the college atmosphere compared to that of my high school. In high school people evaluated each other in terms of social status—if you hung out with the 'in group' or 'upper clique' or the 'middle' or 'lower' cliques—all in terms of popularity. At college people don't judge you by who your friends are, but who you are as a person. There's no social ladder, everyone is equal. You can talk to whomever you like and usually get a good response, whereas in high school there were some people you just didn't talk to."

Barbara Replogle (1980) declared that "Oswego State has a special mystique which most people find difficult to pinpoint. The entire college environment has a magnetic quality that draws you further and further into the Oswego experience. I'm not sure whether it's the closeness of the people, the size of the town, or a number of elements mixed together that make it unique."

Graduation exercises are still held on the hockey rink in Romney Field House. Only the hockey fans in the audience realize that the platform dignitaries and guests are seated in the penalty box area, which is transformed with flowers in the college colors, carpeting, drapes, and a huge replica of the college seal. In present-day graduation exercises a quartet of trumpeters alerts the audience that the ceremony is about to begin. Such trumpetry dates from medieval times when trumpeters in watch towers signaled the arrival of visiting dignitaries. Although most universities confer degrees en masse, or by areas of specialty, Oswego to date has preserved its tradition of individual recognition. At the ceremony's close, the seniors and faculty emerge from Romney Field House to the tune of another trumpet fanfare. The entire ceremony is carefully timed so that it will be completed within a maximum time of two hours.

These days, as in years past, the Torchlight Ceremony is held on graduation evening. Prior to the 1981 ceremony, alumna Ann Robson (1977), then president of the Heritage Foundation, formally dedicated a plaque designating Sheldon Hall an historic landmark. She also dedicated a bronze tablet donated by the Oswego Alumni Association detailing the Hall's National Register listing. Both plaques hang in the main lobby of the building.

Oswego graduates generally evaluate their college experience very positively. Some credit it with having helped them to grow as people. Mary K. Gibbons said, "I wouldn't trade these last two years of college for anything in the world. I have grown so much as a person, learned to be myself, and to trust the way I feel." "I came here a scared, insecure child," said Mary Ann Barbarino (1980). "Now I feel more confident of who I am and where I'm going. I have met many people, and this has contributed greatly to my maturity. I am no longer 'judged' as *not* being a cheerleader or any of the other titles that confer popularity. I am myself, and people accept me for what I am."

Other people place special value on what they learned while at Oswego. Kathleen Bishop (1984) said that "college has had a great impact on me. I've learned many important things such as managing money, responsibility, independence, and the value of friendships. I also feel good about myself, and I have a sense of direction in life. If I had to do it all over again, I would!"

A major factor in accounting for the alumni's satisfaction with their Oswego experience has been President Radley's unrelenting efforts to provide an on-campus ambiance conducive to maximum development of students' potential. An analysis of the creative innovations and improved services developed (and developing) during her presidency bears witness to her dedication and genius in this essential administrative area.

Surveys have shown that most students anticipate that their college diplomas will be passports to successful careers. A 1983 national survey showed that college students in general were career-oriented; consciousness of grades and credentials was still on the rise; orientation toward liberal learning, interest in contemporary affairs, and public activism were on the wane; and use of alcoholic beverages was increasing. At the same time, conscientious work, general academic achievement, and participation in extracurricular activities were gaining.

Perhaps because of pressures from their students/consumers, most major universities were focusing on preparing students for a job as well as educating them. Syracuse University students, for example, "didn't want to make a

$25,000 to $40,000 investment in a four-year degree and end up using their sheepskin as a ticket to pump gas."

In 1981, Oswego's students also overwhelmingly preferred career-oriented programs by which to set their compasses toward reducing the feeling of 'setting out on uncharted seas' upon graduation. Overall, concluded Professor Barbara Shineman, elementary education, students were less radical and more serious about the role of education in obtaining employment, and more realistic regarding competitiveness in the job market.

Whatever their career choices, Oswego's graduates are forevermore connected to the college as alumni. Living members, for whom the Alumni Association has addresses, number about 30,000. The then oldest of these in 1976 later died at the age of 104.

As of fall 1981, SUNY alumni numbered about 800,000 and included two U.S. congressmen, four mayors, two New York State senators, at least two university presidents, a cosmetics firm president, an Emmy and Academy-Award winning producer/director, and a renowned botanist. Currently, there are eleven active alumni groups, with locations in Buffalo, Mohawk Valley, Long Island, Florida, Washington, D.C., Rochester, the Capital District, Finger Lakes, North Country, and New York City. Many individuals remain active, faithfully returning to homecoming celebrations and paying alumni dues.

Oswego's Alumni Association has been especially fortunate in recent years in the quality of its leadership. Patricia Ruppert (1972) became alumni director in 1980, followed by Peg Lowery (1974) in 1983. Both demonstrated unusual loyalty, vigor, vision, and effectiveness. In her brief tenure, Lowery, along with her assistant and volunteers, increased active alumni branches from three to eleven, including the reactivation of the Capital District unit in Albany. The local operation won four awards from the SUNY Confederation of Alumni Associations in a single year, 1984, for excellence in fund raising (topping all other SUNY units), off-campus alumni programs, growth of alumni chapters, and excellence in the field of communications. The *Alumni Bulletin* (Denise Harrigan, editor) was called by the judges "a truly class publication." Dorothy Brown Clark (1936), President of the Association from 1969 to 1984, brought about a dramatic increase in the Sheldon Associates membership. Sheldon Associates is composed of members of the Oswego college community and friends of the college, each of whom contributes a minimum of $250 annually. The Century Club also is composed of alumni and friends of the college; members contribute $100 or more a year to the annual fund. The 10-to-25 Club recognizes alumni who have contributed $25 or more to the annual fund in each of the preceding ten years.

The Alumni Association conducts a phonathon every year. Student and faculty volunteers bait the verbal hook in calls to alumni in seeking donations. The money is used to fund scholarships and such special events as student receptions, the Honors Convocation, graduation ceremony, Homecoming, and the *Alumni Bulletin*. In addition, various individuals have made sizable contributions. Patti M. Peterson, former Oswego vice president and now president of Wells College, and Diana Balmori, former director of the Honors Program, have contributed money for scholarships. Alumni annual contributions are up from $25,000 in 1975 to $339,000 in 1986.

Homecoming Weekend is the alumni event of the year, the time when nostalgic alumni make a pilgrimage to their alma mater. This event ordinarily includes tours of the campus, a banquet, and various arrangements to welcome alumni home and to help them greet old, and make new, friends. Recipients of Distinguished Alumni Awards at the 1981 Banquet included the first alumni couple to be honored: Darwin Schley Ricketson, Jr. (1966), now chief of the Research and Analysis Division of the Army Safety Center, and Maria Kimmel Ricketson (1965), outstanding educator and former president of the Associated Women Students, president of a dormitory council, and president of the Vega Honor Society. Recipients of the award in 1984 were George Allen (1934), Joseph Barnes (1959), Casimir Kowalski (1965), Frank Maraviglia (1958), and Stanley Mattson (1959).

Other alumni achievements are also outstanding. Joseph Long, Oswego chemistry alumnus, now at Broome Community College, received the SUNY Chancellor's Award for Excellence in Teaching in 1982. And Alice McDermott (1975) returned in 1982 to give readings from her first novel, *A Bigamist's Daughter*, which had received an excellent review in the *New York Times*.

Director Peg Lowery detects among the alumni two main categories: graduates before and after the Rockefeller years, the latter during which the college vastly expanded and became a multipurpose institution. Some of the earlier alumni, she said, feel less identity with the college because "it has gone liberal arts," others because it has become so large "they've lost any feeling of closeness." She has resolved to bridge the gap between them.

15

Beyond the Horizon

HIGHER education, as it exists today, earns low marks for anticipating the future. Nationwide, it is vast and diverse but not vibrantly healthy and dynamic. It consists of over 3,000 institutions, private and public, large and small, single-purpose and complex, traditional and experimental.[1] As few as 250 have attempted true reform. College students at present are relatively self-seeking and vocationally oriented, with little concern for society or campus welfare. Overall, concluded one observer, the average university is a "lumbering mastodon" that can barely be convinced to change direction without a lead time of three years.[2]

Historically, most institutions have not anticipated change but have simply reacted to it. They have been entrenched bureaucracies, absorbed in perennial battles with budgets. Their focus has been on the present, not the future. "This is a period of transition for higher education," said Provost Ralph Spencer. "The question is: Transition to what?"

Increasingly, colleges are being admonished to anticipate and plan for what may lie ahead. Looking to the future, warns the Carnegie Council, is not just being curious, but is essential for proper adaptation.[3] It is a matter of trying to direct the future, and not simply to react to what comes along. Chancellor Wharton suggests that "all too many [of our educators] appear not to have noticed."[4] Forecasting is indeed a precarious but essential task; it is not a mere journey into fantasy, but a defense against the myopia of preoccupation with the present.

Others, too, believe that the time has come to get our universities on the right track, considering their important social role. An editorial in the *Washington Post* declared that "taken together, the universities are probably the strongest of all institutional influences on the American culture."[5] Also, they are, or should be, the country's pioneers for successive new stages of culture.

Oswego's Rosemary Nesbitt endorses such assessments. "These kinds of renewals should take place every little while in the history of any great organization. The major universities of the world should get together to take stock. We ought to look at the university, where it has been, where it is, where it is going. Universities are the greatest institutions in the world, except perhaps for religious institutions. Yet we go about our task in a catch-as-catch-can manner—let's just wait and see what happens tomorrow."

SUNY itself, poised on the threshold of the future, has formidable potential. It annually educates more students (381,000) than comparable institutions anywhere on the globe. Currently, its main contributions are superb teaching and research facilities and an extensive network for public service. With regard for its future, Chancellor Wharton appointed a fourteen-member blue-ribbon commission in 1984 to make recommendations regarding SUNY's accountability and academic quality.[6] A major recommendation, a course long advocated by President Radley, is that individual colleges should be granted more autonomy.

There have been conjectures for some time about SUNY's future. Chancellor Wharton predicts that not all of its colleges will march in tandem, affected alike. As a result of falling enrollments, he observed, many "policy makers are acting as if the projected declines, like St. Matthew's rain, will fall on the just and unjust alike. However, over the decade, some campuses may wilt or even wither, just as a hardy few may flourish in a climate too severe for others."[7] Wharton also recommends that each SUNY college develop its special strengths to avoid wasteful duplication.

Each university unit already has considerable autonomy in defining its mission which, nevertheless, evolves over time. For about a century, Oswego's one mission was the preparation of superior teachers; then liberal arts became the main focus. Recently, both President Radley and Provost Spencer have suggested that teacher education might regain at least some of its former luster. "We might again become a center for teacher education," reflected President Radley. "Much work has to be done, but we have that reputation, and had it over a century. There is nothing more important today than educating teachers well for all levels—elementary school, secondary school, and college. The colleges have done a terrible job of educating teachers for the professoriate. I can't imagine anything that equals it except taking a year-old baby and throwing it into the swimming pool, and seeing whether it sinks or swims." Radley added, "Oswego might also become something of a center, at least in State University, for language teaching, but we have to educate our faculty to the need for advising students to take foreign languages." Oswego might also assume a leading role in the instructional training of professors, as in future planning for higher education.

Others prefer upgrading what is already being done to effect dramatic change. "To the extent that we do something better than other places," observed Associate Provost Wheeler, "even if it's something other places do, to me that is uniqueness." Oswego psychologist Edward Lonky suggested that what we need "is a renewed commitment to the concept of quality in liberal arts education. Oswego should continue to do what it does best: prepare an educated citizenry for the future through a presentation of state-of-the-art knowledge in the arts and sciences. Collectively, such views tend to foreshadow the shape of things to come. As such, we must not let our curriculum be ruled by a shortsighted Bureau of Labor Statistics mentality. The past several years have seen a broad expansion of undergraduate programs in business and computer science, based in large part on short-term job forecasts indicating that there will be jobs in these fields (as if an English major could not get a job in business)."

One aspect of defining a mission is identifying categories of students to be served. Should Oswego be two-tiered, serving both well-qualified students from across the state and from within the community? Should larger numbers of foreign and older students be encouraged to attend? To what extent should we admit students with deficiencies in languages and numerical skills, which may be dispelled with remedial courses? Despite some attention to all of these categories, Oswego's main focus in recent years has been on students of high academic achievement from across the state. "Quality attracts quality" declared Dr. Radley, a statement Oswego's recent record proves.

The increasing diversity of students, along with the growing fragmentation of society, does pose a challenge. Course content and the total college experience must be structured to produce greater intercultural and subgroup understanding. Specific needs must be identified and met. For example, how can women acquire leadership roles on a coed campus? How can a campus capitalize on the presence of older and foreign students?

Both President Radley and Chancellor Wharton underscore the importance of extending the SUNY experience to minorities. However, warns Chancellor Wharton, shrinking budgets threaten SUNY's ability to provide access to all categories of students and "cast a lengthening shadow across the State University's very reason for existence."[10]

The "older student" category is of growing importance. In the early 1970s even the most traditional colleges began special degree programs and services for such students, a trend expected to continue. It is anticipated that by 1990 older students will constitute 47 percent of the total enrollment, compared with 38 percent in 1980. For one thing, as more people have high school and college diplomas, more will want to continue their education, for learning is "addictive."[9] The changing role of women is another stimulus. Between 1969 and 1975, the number of adult women learners increased by 45 percent, while the number of adult men learners increased by 18 percent. A third factor is the labor market and the competition for more desirable jobs. People may want a mid-life career change, or they might want simply to upgrade present skills. Education was once intended for the young, work intended for the middle-aged, and enforced leisure for the elderly. Now, however, there is a blended life plan in which work, education, and leisure proceed concurrently throughout life. Finally, there is a growing concern about "investment in self" and, as a result, a concern for continuing education.

In general, continuing education has been viewed as "somehow superimposed" on a university's "real or legitimate center."[8] However, the current mood is to create programs appropriate for the needs of the people involved; courses might be offered in homes for the elderly, more often in the evening.

With regard to all students, whatever their category, the question arises: What kinds of people can best adapt to what lies ahead? Such individuals must have appropriate thinking modes, be able to think globally and analytically, and exhibit flexibility while maintaining stability. They can perceive the linkages and patterns in intricate relationships. They can conceptualize and deal with things in both mega- and micro-terms. They keep up with, and capitalize on, new and revolutionary discoveries and ideas. They are widely traveled and fluent in one or more foreign languages. They are not solely privatistic [sic], but concerned about, and ready to assume, their share of responsibility for others' welfare. They "are sufficiently competent and articulate to have the wisdom to govern the universe," declared Professor Jacqueline Reihman.

Properly prepared graduates also know how to effectively engineer their own lives in the context of a technological age. They possess technological literacy and skills and use them for developing an effective life-style. They possess up-to-date knowledge about the entire life-span. They possess sound health habits and effective living skills—economic, social, and recreational. They have quality ethics and values and can deal realistically with issues posed by a high-tech society. They are open to new ideas and dedicated to continual personal growth, coupled with a sense of perspective and humor.

To produce such individuals, what kind of curriculum is most effective? Most authorities would agree with President Radley that everyone needs, in addition to calculators, "basic computational skills, language and interpersonal skills, and a general background in history." Radley also stresses the integrity of the curriculum, which eroded in the 1960s. "We remedied this situation," she said, "by adding general education, reviewing all major programs, and tightening the curriculum." However, because of diminishing resources, she sees fewer electives in the future.

There is a wide difference of opinion regarding the relative emphasis which should be placed on the past, present, and future in the curriculum. Certainly, it would be a colossal error not to tap the reservoirs of wisdom stored in the archives of the past. Professor Rosemary Nesbitt said that "people need to read the past, because the past is the window of the future. Everything is cyclical and will come again. It will come in different forms, but the essence is the same. The four horsemen of the apocalypse will continue to ride and always will."

President Radley believes students should know the past but keep abreast with the present. "The past has been terribly neglected by contemporary educators. Students are more interested in computer technology, and sending people to the moon, than they are in reading the great books. However, most students don't really keep up with current events. They don't read the daily papers. True, our student leaders are pretty well informed—maybe that is why they are student leaders—but our general population should read much more than it does."

Chancellor Wharton reviews SUNY's past to gain clearer perspective on its future. The country had just crossed the boundary between industrial and post-industrial societies when SUNY was established in 1948. Knowledge replaced physical capital and labor "as the central engine of economic growth and social progress." Now we stand "at the gateway to another age. . . . We can discern at least part of its outline. It will be a society in which knowledge plays even more of a role, not less than before. It will be a culture in which change is relentless, and the ability to deal with change will be indispensable. It will be a society in which ideas will literally be the most important commodity, in which education is quite identical with enfranchisement."[11] Moreover, as nations become increasingly industrialized, there will be a great need for technological and scientific literacy, continues Wharton. In the meantime, the major problems and issues will be increasingly "complex and competitive, demanding the analytical and synthesizing skills of the humanist." For instance, Congress has had before it a United Nations treaty regarding disposition of rights on the moon, including "settlement rights, natural resource rights, everything . . . yet how many discussions of this issue have you seen in the humanistic forums: historical, philosophical, legal, or otherwise?"[12]

To achieve such broad goals, noted Oswego's Professor John Fisher, universities have linked with the larger society to provide auxiliary educational facilities.[13] Examples are Genesee Brewing Company's "preserved village" near Rochester and Oswego's restoration of its historic downtown area. Also noted is the increased patronage of the traditional arts (opera, ballet) as in Syracuse's Landmark Theater and Oswego's Opera Theatre, which may help offset the current tendency by youths to ignore their cultural heritage. Meanwhile, colleges are becoming cultural centers for their areas, diffusing the university into the community through cable TV and cooperative arrangements.

The dawn of a new era of university–industry relationships is a related development. Joint ventures are undertaken in research, telecommunications, and engineering. Students, including those at Oswego, conduct their apprenticeships in various corporations such as Eastman Kodak in Rochester and Miller Brewing Company in Fulton.

In growing numbers, agencies other than universities, such as corporations, museums, and military organizations, are launching educational ventures wholly on their own, often on the graduate level. The question arises: To what extent may traditional functions of universities be assumed by "educational minisystems" initiated by large corporations? AT&T has a nationwide training program with no college collaboration; and the AETNA insurance company created its AETNA Institute, or mini-university, to train over 20,000 employees each year.[14] In varying degree, all such developments reflect the failure of traditional universities to meet corporate needs.

Global emphasis is another high-priority curricular concern. Chancellor Wharton observes that "everything around us tells us that the next century will be more global, requiring knowledge of historical trends, cultures, religions, traditions and languages of non-Western as well as western nations."[15] Moreover, he adds, the economic and political realities through the world intermesh, and the network is becoming increasingly complex. This world view, in turn, demands also that we not limit our foreign language offerings to French, Spanish, and Italian as is commonly done, but acknowledge the significance of the third world, China, the African states, the Soviet Union, and Eastern Europe. Yet only a small number of colleges provide language learning of Japanese, Chinese, Arabic, or Russian. Foreign area studies in general should receive greater attention. Few Americans are acquainted with non-Western cultures; this ignorance is reflected in "our balance of trade, our diplomacy and foreign policy, and our relations with other countries."[16]

Sue Fines, a member of Oswego's foreign language department, warned in 1975 that the Helsinki Commission faulted the United States on its lack of formal training in foreign languages and cultures. In 1978, only six Americans in the Embassy in Iran knew Farsi, and most of those were in the secretarial pool. In 1980, the rise of Solidarity in Poland caught many "experts" by surprise. Such situations, and there are many, not only diminish this country's reputation and stature, but also put us at risk. Our government must know the attitudes and current concerns of people around the world if it is to act wisely in the international arena. Especially needed are well-trained experts knowledgeable in specific geographic areas. Fines suggested that "Oswego could very well become a leader in training teachers and other specialists in a global perspective. One fact of the second half of the twentieth century is that the cultural and linguistic isolation of the United States has had negative results which must be dealt with if we are to remain on an equal footing, politically and economically, with the rest of the world. Oswego already has a strong foreign language department and an education department with a history of creative innovation. Drawing primarily on those two strengths and adding to them the international expertise of other departments, there is no reason this college could not make a major contribution in the area of global understanding."

Special attention should be given discussion of global ethical/social issues. A panel of 135 scholars projected an era of persistent turbulence in the next quarter century, one component being competing values and ideologies, or "values in collision." Furthermore, "the world in 2000 will be more crowded, more polluted, less stable ecologically, and more vulnerable to disruption than the world we live in now."[17] Another source of turbulence will be the "electronic assault on human reason made by the media, and spearheaded by television."[17] Also hanging over the world is the danger of super-sophisticated weapons and the prospect of colossal nuclear accidents. As a result "our country is becoming a pressure-group democracy," said Oswego's Professor Fisher, "and these issues should be discussed."

This concern for the larger world should not obscure the need to attend to students' immediate environment, the campus. Yet universities have largely ignored the possibilities for upgrading the quality of students' lives outside the classroom. "At the end of classes there is a sort of 'click' and academic life ends," observed Professor Nicholas D'Innocenzo. "Then there's the life outside, whether it's at Buckland's, or wherever." Associate Dean Thomas Gooding said that current films have made college life seem "frivolous, but it's significant." Students themselves say college life is far more important than their classroom experience to their overall development. The question arises: Can campus life be made more meaningful? Creative thinking may bring about a quality of total environment, inside and outside the classroom. Perhaps such a program should become a unique part of Oswego's mission.

Some basic principles should guide a college's plan for the future. One calls for a broadly based core of general studies. As James Perdue said, "Specialization ought to be more like building a pile of sand than digging a hole, and the higher you build a peak on a pile of sand the bigger the base has to be." George Pitluga agrees, and recalled reading about the education of a prince compared with that of the commoner: "The prince had to know much in addition to the three R's—diplomacy and some psychology, geography and finance. He had to be a man of the world. In America we have traditionally stressed the three R's, and recently the basics, and certainly we need expertise there. However, in a democracy the common man needs to know as much as the prince, hence must be stimulated to go on learning after he leaves school."

Beyond this general core, colleges must determine the relative emphasis to be placed on professional studies and liberal arts. Graduates with non-technical liberal arts training in the 1970s had less favorable job prospects than those with medical and professional training. As a result, many students shifted their areas of concentration from the less favorable academic majors, especially in the humanities, into professional fields.

Chancellor Wharton, whose overall views on this topic are strongly endorsed by President Radley, takes a somewhat different view. The new ethic in higher education, he writes, seems to be that students attend college chiefly to learn job skills, better still a particular job skill. As a result, degrees in accounting, marketing, and business have attained "very nearly the status of a blue chip tax-exempt bond."[18] In the meantime, social science, liberal arts, and humanities courses are perceived by students and their perspective employers as irrelevant. Yet, notes Wharton, college graduates have always experienced less unemployment than other workers. It is also a myth that liberal arts students are the least vocationally successful. Recruiters often look for people with specific skills. However, some executives value more highly employees who can adapt to unusual or unpredictable situations. This dual point of view is one reason the State University encourages students to pursue particular fields as well as the liberal arts, humanities, and social sciences.

Oswego's Anthropologist Ivan Brady suggests a more moderate position. "We should continue to stress liberal arts. In conjectures about the future we shouldn't just count heads but be concerned about what's in those heads. We should be aware of the backwash from a pragmatic emphasis. On the other hand, career objectives cannot be ignored. For example, larger numbers of workers will be required in professional and managerial occupations than persons specializing in scientific and engineering skills."

Much attention is also focused on future technology and the sciences. When the first global conference on the future brought together leaders in many fields from fifty nations, the question was asked: Is higher education preparing citizens to live and work effectively in the next century—the world in which today's students will spend the majority of their lives? Much of the world's crisis, observes Chancellor Wharton, relates to science and technology, since few college-educated lay individuals understand their basics. A century ago adults were in touch with their dominant technology, which involved shoeing horses, plowing fields, or repairing buggies. In contrast, few of today's students have even a rudimentary understanding of the currently dominant technologies "of laser communications, nuclear power generation, and genetic engineering."[19]

Nevertheless, cautions Wharton, in these times when computer technology extends into every crack and cranny of modern life, computer illiteracy is the rule. Increasing numbers of people are using modern technologies without understanding them; hence, they are conceding control over their lives to specialists and technicians. They are becoming "technopeasants: modern day serfs, nominally free, but disenfranchised by ignorance—and fear—of prevailing technologies." Also of significance is that technical innovations have widespread implications. For example, the labor relations expert must know something of robotics.[20]

However, Oswego's Jacqueline Reihman advises that "we must not overreact to an as yet unknown mandate. The college must not, in short-sighted manner, put all its eggs in a technologically based computer basket. To do so would be reductionistic, and the role of a faculty member would become no more than that of technical supervisor. This is not to say that the college should ignore the tremendous effect technology will play in our lives. Rather, it must be viewed as a challenge to integrate new knowledge content with the role of the college—which is and must continue to be the education of the mind."

The more traditional subjects are also assuming a new look, appropriate for a new age. Scientists currently stress basic survival concepts; humans may be arriving at the limits of the planet's "carrying capacity." In the life sciences, in biology and related fields, "scholars repeatedly stress the need to recognize ingenuity in producing new life forms, as giving to humans awesome powers that may well exceed our judgment in using them."[21] Another goal is to help students appreciate the unity of the basic laws of nature. It simply isn't enough to understand its constituent parts, a concept which recalls the whole child emphasis by the progressive educators in the 1930s.

In chemistry, physics, and geology, students must appreciate that humans are significant environmental "change agents," and must exercise great caution when "exploiting their planet." To date, in what "amounts to uncontrolled experiments," humans have become "powerful geological agents, capable of changing rates of erosion, influencing climate, and altering the natural functions of energy."[22]

Biology, in particular, is predicted to become to the twenty-first century what chemistry and physics have been to the twentieth century. The next twenty years will be the age of biology in the manner that the last two decades have been the age of microelectronics. Other areas of opportunity ahead are "alternative energy resources and conservation products, robotics and seabed mining."[23]

New courses have been proposed for implementing these broader objectives. Oswego psychologist Edward Lonky suggests the development of some "complex issues which continue to define the human condition, now and in the future. They might concern the roles of men and women, energy, poverty, freedom, and justice, all approached from an interdisciplinary perspective and forming the core of a general education curriculum." Chancellor Wharton recommends a foundation course in world history and culture, "a serious and ethnocentric version of the old western civilization requirement." Such a course would help students to acquire some comprehension of the historical underpinnings of present-day international relations, as well as "a genuine exposure to non-Western humanities, arts, literatures and philosophies."[24] Other courses might relate to travel abroad, consumer technology, life-styles, religion from a sociocultural standpoint, and the cultural revolution in music, literature, and art. Compact minicourses of a highly varied nature might also be offered.

Psychology chair Norman Gordon sees a need for a human-information science major that would combine efforts of the best people in psychology, philosophy, computer science, math, and English to encourage literacy and understanding of problems of processing information. He also believes that "we should get into studying more deeply the nature of intelligence and the nature of humanity that makes us unique. Is there a sharp distinction between humans and animals? Students should also be asking such questions as: 'Am I just a part of nature, or am I some special being destined to exploit it and just walk off with its fruits?'"

The professional areas also will require mega-modifications, especially in teacher education. "Edward Austin Sheldon was a marvelous man, the founder of our college," reflected President Radley, "but he is dead, and he has been for a long time. So we have to move forward in that [academic] area."

Varied suggestions have been made for upgrading programs in teacher education. Professor of Physics Ronald Brown believes that students in education might double-major to prepare for their careers because "often a teacher will have to teach perhaps general science and biology." In addition, advised Radley, all teachers should know a language other than English.

The industrial arts and computer fields must also take a hard look at changing needs. Jobs for computer specialists are expected to increase by almost 90 percent and about 40 percent for engineers in general. For engineers in aeronautics and space specialties, an increase of about 70 percent is projected.[25] In general, employment for professional and technical workers is expected to increase almost twice as fast as for all occupations combined.

Physical educators should remain abreast of the dramatic new discoveries about health and body. "The whole psychomotor area is significant," observed Dean Barbara Gerber. "Where the body is concerned, they don't give out spares." There will also be a greater demand for fitness education and for better health services on campuses, especially as the number of older students increases.

Perhaps the most commonly suggested organizational change is to work toward the dilution of rigid departmental boundaries. "Oswego can and should take a lead in developing a curriculum which recognizes that knowledge cannot be neatly divided into disciplinary cubby-holes," observed psychologist Edward Lonky. "Students needing to cope with the complex technologies, problems, and social issues of the future will require a curriculum which [fosters] an interdisciplinary understanding of these issues. The interrelatedness of knowledge [should become the] core conceptual focus."

This recommendation, that studies not be rigidly dissected by discipline, may be realized in various ways. An international panel of distinguished scholars noted that cross-disciplinary and interdisciplinary linkages have been growing rapidly, as reflected in such labels as "Department of Psychobiology" or "Professor of BioPhysics," and by scholars with joint appointments such as professor of history and geography.[26]

Professor Lonky thinks that interdisciplinary courses may become part of general education. "Instead of students' selecting six, nine, or twelve hours of 'approved courses' in discipline-specific areas such as social and behavioral sciences, humanities, and natural sciences, problem-focused courses, with an interdisciplinary perspective, would be required." However, Oswego physicist Ronald Brown warns that such interconnectedness becomes shallow and meaningless unless the instructors and students are properly prepared in the basic disciplines concerned.

An additional advantage of such interdisciplinary programs, observed psychologist William Whipple, is "the discovery of colleagues with complementary interests, which in my case proved a source of incredulous delight." The Fund for the Improvement of Post-Secondary Education (FIPSE) Interdisciplinary Studies program and the Honors College have been encouraging "transdisciplinary lines of communication," added Whipple, "but the same goal can be sought in other ways as well. Even as simple a thing as a faculty club might help."

In all of the foregoing areas, anticipatory planning hinges on the quality of an institution's administrators, especially of its president. Many presidents lack the qualities needed: courage, enterprise, commitment. Some lack real authority or strong support. All serve a median term of five years, and some avoid coping with long-term problems by offering temporary, expedient solutions. In contrast, the Carnegie Council suggests a minimum tenure of ten years. Entrenched old-line administrators manage to stifle new ideas and refuse actively to support innovation. Another obstacle is the inordinate amount of time often required to make administrative decisions because of the many constituencies and endless red tape involved. Many of the more scholarly individuals dislike confrontations and nit-picking and tend to withdraw, leaving decisions to less able people. In the meantime, limited financial resources tend to pit segments of the college community against each other, each striving to get its share of resources: department against department, academic against vocational areas, nontenured against tenured faculty members, administrators and councils against faculties and students. Thus, shrinking budgets limit opportunities for innovation.

Various suggestions have been made for the improved administration of colleges. "Administrators should allow faculty members the initiative and the opportunity to fall flat on their faces," said Professor Nicholas D'Innocenzo. "And we should have networks, not hierarchies in the faculty, representing a natural, egalitarian, spontaneous formation of groups among like-minded people."

Administrators and their faculties might also engineer some changes in the traditional organization of curricula. Education critic Harold Shane predicts that this decade will see great strides in lifelong learning, and that secondary and higher education will overlap, so that each will lose much of its identity. Great communiversities will combine the flexibility and variety of community college offerings with the academic offerings of state and private liberal arts colleges.[27] Similarly, Chancellor Wharton warns that "the explosion of knowledge . . . indicates that we should more urgently than ever rethink the traditional time frame of higher education."[28] The depth and breadth of knowledge needed by educated people and productive employees will require more than four years of advanced learning. The question then arises: How realistic is a four-year degree? Is the baccalaureate meaningful any more?

At least temporary approval of new courses, without undue delay, would be a step forward. Course offerings are often delayed because they must be approved by many committees and administrators and might, through lack of proved academic quality, risk the accreditation process. Such reservations derive from the presumption that "present realities" will endure forever.[29] Also, a clearer distinction might be made between programs in the academic core and other parts of a university's offerings. Universities must respect students' "diversity and needs, but not whims." President Radley affirms the growing need for even more efficient management, "and the legitimacy of that need"; however, "management systems must not take precedence over the quintessence of it all, namely the individual human being." Perhaps the best answer lies in a reasonable balance of programs, respecting but not surrendering to student choice, better informed consumers, and "fair competition among institutions based on the quality of their services."

The success of even the best future planning hinges on the quality of the general faculty. "In these times of dual-spouse employment," warned Professor of Psychology Herbert Van Schaack, "when youth are guided mainly by their peers and the electronic media, faculty members should be fully aware of their responsibilities as role models and sources of guidance." For greatest effectiveness they must also be "prepared to take on the unexpected," noted D'Innocenzo. "In addition," said former President Perdue, "they must know how their respective disciplines relate to each other. Knowledge is a seamless garment." Psychologist Jacqueline Reihman agreed: "The faculty will need to engage in more generalist activities and will have to 'retool' their skills in order to meet the challenges offered by a changing world. As models for their students, they will need to focus on the importance of examining issues and problems from many perspectives. Students with narrow and undisciplined minds will be the consequence of our failure to respond to this new challenge."

Expanding on this concept, Reihman said that "the responsibility for dealing with the tension created by new technology must lie with a faculty willing to go beyond what has traditionally been required of them. The faculty can no longer be expert in a solely unidimensional sense. To do so denies the very complexity and interrelatedness of knowledge that the new technology is creating. A faculty which is narrow and one-dimensional in focus will produce students ill-equipped to grapple with the issues posed by the technological age. . . . Faculty resources outside of one's own discipline must be shared and used to the fullest. . . . One need only consider one of the myriad controversial issues to understand the limited perspective any single discipline can offer. Genetic engineering serves well as an exemplar issue: an infant industry now, it promises to become a major employer in the future. To future biologists, chemists, and pharmaceutical engineers, the future must indeed seem rosy; but genetic engineering has already spawned controversy. . . . Indeed, the moral/ethical questions raised by genetic engineering are staggering and must involve considered attention from multiple disciplines. In order to succeed in addressing the issues raised by a new technology, the philosopher or the psychologist must be able to communicate with the scientist and this [dictum] requires a reciprocal interaction which has been previously unnecessary."[30]

One must also account for the realities of faculty employment. Overall, faculties have been projected to decline by 10 percent during the 1980s, but a great resurgence will occur later, as those hired during the boom period of the 1960s retire.[31] Even now there is a faculty shortage in some areas, such as adult education, biology, and some foreign languages, due to changing needs. As Professor Sue Fines pointed out, "the demand for specialists in numerous fields, who are also trained in at least one foreign language area, will be high. . . . [By the year 2000] we will need well-qualified teachers of various foreign languages and cultures—teachers who have had some experience in living in the specific culture—as well as teachers of international politics, foreign governmental systems, international trade, business and banking, and experts in sociology, psychology, history, environmental studies, etc., who have also been trained in a foreign language and culture."[32]

Future demands also call for more effective use of faculties. Colleges should identify and capitalize upon individuals' area of expertise, including auxiliary ones. And they might also avail themselves of the talents of retired faculty members living in the area. A corollary to the above is the need to continuously preserve and upgrade faculty morale. Constructive, cooperative networks should be developed and means instituted for meeting individual faculty members' needs. Excellence in whatever valid form should be recognized and rewarded, and current modes of evaluation reexamined. Most instruments take little account of the significant factors of individuality, class size, or long-term impact on students.

Certainly, the future should see radical changes in prevalent antiquated instructional methods—anachronisms in a technological age. Former President James Perdue warned that "if we don't change, we are in serious trouble. If we can't lower the cost of instruction, we must find new modes, as by computers. However, that would be unfortunate, since people learn best by following models. Just watch a child playing with computers. With ordinary toys, children have an attention span of perhaps three or four minutes, but they'll stay with computers much longer." Educator Harold Shane goes further, suggesting that the most interesting instructional "technovations" will be the "use of calculators and computers, and the application of holographic science to the projection of almost perfect images—literally surrounding learners with a meticulously contrived electronic environment."[33]

Others believe machines can never displace professors, who serve as role models and who manage somehow, said Psychologist Mark Morey, to articulate the pieces of education that students receive. Professors must also be sensitive to students' "level of conceptual understanding of knowledge; and they must become aware of developmental differences in how students view knowledge and the world. . . . Teaching style, course content and structure, and even examinations, should be presented in ways that both match students current conceptual understandings and stimulate more sophisticated thinking on their part. For many faculty the future may require fundamental changes in the way they teach and view their own disciplines; and such must be the case as they lead their students into the twenty-first century."[34]

Other suggestions include assessing alternative methods and using a variety of approaches; keeping abreast of learning research; requiring students to become adept in using knowledge centers and data retrieval systems; and developing creative, more attractive learning environments. The Carnegie Council suggests increased autonomy of the colleges, greater diversity, new initiatives, the cooperative use of facilities, "intrastate consortia," and scholarships based on need.[35] In the meantime, academic requirements should be elevated and tightened. "With regard to having some sort of comprehensive test at the end of the four years," reflected Dr. Radley, "I went to a college from which you did not graduate without passing comprehensives in your senior year. I'm all for that—that is essential." Radley especially favors careful appraisal of students' basic literacy and computational skills. She refuses to let Oswego's standards become tinged with the aura of either complacency or mediocrity.

From his perspective as a retired faculty member, Robert Sykes suggests, for the future, acknowledgment of significant faculty problems; abandonment of certain "dinosauric programs and tactics"; "revitalization" or "aggressive reconceptualizations"; and "continuous readaptation to the transformation from the industrial era to the next communications, information, or whatever era."

Still others suggest what may be required for effective implementation of the future's approach. "The road ahead won't be easy," cautions education critic David Henry. "As we seek to deal with current problems and ambiguities in higher education, we may feel that we are living in the worst of times. However, the history of higher education has been one of frequent crises, continuing struggles, uncertainties and ups and downs. Nor can we anticipate straight-line developments in years to come. Technological innovation—indeed, all innovation—'weaves and bobs and lurches and sputters'."[36]

We should be prepared, therefore, to reset our curricular compasses when unforeseen developments occur. A single event or new product can set into motion a chain reaction throughout society. Consider the development of the birth control pill: it produced a revolution in life-styles, reduced taboos against premarital sex, and brought about a sexual revolution, including extramarital cohabitation. "The time between eras is uncertain," contends John Naisbitt, "but it is a great and yeasty time filled with opportunity. If we can learn to make uncertainty our friend, we can achieve much more than in stable eras."[37] The secret lies in possessing the resources that allow readiness for whatever happens.

Chancellor Wharton warns that the approach to the future is an ongoing process. Universities must add "complementary activities of updating, revision and, if you will, knowledge-servicing or educational maintenance. Like your automobile, your personal word processor or your video disk player, your undergraduate education is going to need periodic overhauls to keep it viable."[38]

Former President Perdue cautioned against expecting miracles overnight. "Universities aren't an instantaneous development. A university must grow—it grows through a childhood—and I think we've been through that in State University. If I had to identify its developmental stage, I would say SUNY is in its adolescence."

When universities grow up, including SUNY, what will they be like? Already the climate has grown unfavorable for "overweight pachyderms; agility and adaptability are keys to survival and they will grow in importance in the years ahead." In general, the universities of the year 2000 will differ as much from those of the 1950s as those did from the institutions of the Middle Ages. Their walls will become "increasingly porous," but they will still maintain their "distance from everyday involvement—a distance that permits contemplation of one's own morality, shape and meaning."[39]

We cannot even assume that future universities will look much like those of today; nor will they be confined to campuses. Already there has been considerable experimentation with extramural efforts, including outreach programs in high schools and libraries, and cable TV instruction for disabled and senior citizens and for all those who cannot come to campus at the usual hours.

Stephen J. Trachtenberg sums up his "vision of higher education" for the year 2000 as follows: "The flagship schools—including Harvard, Chicago, and Stanford—will be attended by the brilliant and the rich. Those of lesser status will serve less gifted students."[40] The tax-supported schools will at first endure decaying facilities, excessively large classes, and outmoded equipment, and they will serve those students who simply can't afford the independent colleges. Even they must be increasingly selective because they cannot pay for all. In short, there will be a growing stratification and differentiation of status among colleges and universities, with a consequent increasing stratification in society itself. Thus, despite the strides taken during the past several decades toward equality, inequality in universities is on the increase.

Some institutions are assuming the approach of the future far more rapidly than are others. The larger schools have led the way, notably the College of the University of California at Santa Cruz. Oswego took its first formal step on February 28, 1984, when the Faculty Assembly created a Futures Task Force to envision a prototype of the Oswego of tomorrow. Specifically, it was charged with identifying and assessing issues likely to be of academic concern in the 1990s.[41] The extent of involvement is uncertain. "You can't get everybody concerned and involved," writes Naisbitt. "You will have a meeting about something important and fifteen people will show up. That is the way it has always been. These few will talk and the word will get out. The other five hundred will not have anything to say anyway. The world doesn't run as a total democracy, and leaders emerge no matter where you are."[42]

Who will become involved in the college's programs? Those like Ivan Brady who always like to deal with fuzzy horizons instead of those where there is closure. Or those like Jacqueline Reihman, who recognizes the importance of the Futures Task Force. Writes Reihman, "To examine the role that history has had in shaping the present is important, to understand how present actions will shape the future is imperative. Futures courses and symposia should be routine and should draw on multiple disciplines."

Real obstacles to progress exist, but the rewards can be rich. These are exciting times when successive breakthroughs tread on each other. The bell tolls in the tower, marking progress toward the inevitable tomorrow. Oswego's Sheldon tradition, its more recent traditions, and its traditions-in-the-making, demand that Oswego be in the vanguard of those colleges resolved to create fuller lives and richer environments for those who will live in the next century. And President Radley is resolved that the founder's fame will not cast the shadow of his prestige over future years, but will instead serve as a beacon lighting the way.

Appendix

STATE UNIVERSITY'S FIRST FAMILY

THE significance of SUNY's chancellor, Dr. Clifton R. Wharton, Jr., can hardly be overestimated for the total university enterprise or for its constituent units. Just as SUNY Oswego's historic achievements and trends have always reflected the skills of its current administrator, so does the chancellor play the key role in SUNY's overall destiny.

Wharton, the seventh educator to be designated as chief administrative officer of State University in its twenty-nine year history, wasn't sure he was interested in the post when the trustees' search committee first discussed the chancellorship with him. However, after reflecting, he was swayed to acceptance by what he felt was the "tremendous potential" of a system which he described as "already outstanding."

While Wharton "had been very happy as president of Michigan State University," a post he had held since 1970, his view that "State University has the greatest potential for further growth towards academic excellence of any system in the United States" was a key factor in his decision to accept the SUNY chancellorship. He said he was particularly interested in the fact that State University has a sense of mission which relates to providing a meaningful response, in all aspects, to the educational needs of the State.

Prior to 1970, Wharton was an official of the Cultural Development Council and the American International Association for Economic and Social Development, helping developing nations in Asia and Latin America, particularly in agriculture.

Born in Boston in 1926, he attended Boston Latin School, America's first public school, and entered Harvard College at age 16. While an undergraduate student at Harvard, he was a founder and national secretary of the U.S. National Student Association; he received a B.A. in history from Harvard in 1947. Wharton was the first black to be admitted to Johns Hopkins University School of Advanced International Studies, receiving his M.A. in international studies in 1948. The University of Chicago awarded him an M.A. in economics in 1956 and a Ph.D. in 1958.

Wharton is a director or trustee of the Rockefeller Foundation; the Carnegie Foundation for the Advancement of Teaching; the Equitable Life Assurance Society; Ford Motor Company; and the Burroughs Corporation. In 1976 he was appointed by President Gerald Ford to chair the Board for International Food and Agricultural Development, USAID, and the U.S. Department of State, and he served as chair of the Food Advisory Panel for the Office of Technology Assessment in the U.S. Congress.

He also served as a member of the Governor's Economic Expansion Council (Michigan) and as a member of the Governor's Economic Action Council (Michigan). He is a fellow of the American Academy of Education and the National Academy of Public Administration. He has been active in the field of U.S. foreign policy: he was a member of the Advisory Panel on East Asian and Pacific Affairs of the U.S. Department of State (1966–69). President Johnson's Task Force on Agriculture in Vietnam (1966); and Governor Nelson Rockefeller's Presidential Mission to Latin America (1969). He is a member of the Commission on U.S. Latin American Relations and a director of the Asia Society, the Agricultural Development Council, and the Overseas Development Council.

Wharton has written extensively on the problems of development and is editor of the book, *Subsistence Agriculture and Economic Development* and co-author of *Patterns for Lifelong Learning*, and he has been a contributor to many professional journals.

SUNY's entire first family, including Clifton's wife, Dolores, and his sons, Clifton III and Bruce, are an asset to the university, both in providing the chancellor important support and assisting with many functions. Dolores Wharton is a very distinguished person in her own right. During an interview once she said: "I hope I've had a career that is more than just being the wife of . . ." (*Albany Times Union*, January 3, 1982).

"Mrs. Wharton and I have always operated as a team." In this way did Chancellor Wharton introduce his wife, the former Dolores Duncan of Danbury, Connecticut, to Albany media representatives. He explained that while she had special interests in her own right, in the arts and the corporate field, they worked together well and often.

Dolores Wharton is a writer and advocate of the arts, a member of the National Council on the Arts, and a director of such organizations as the Museum of Modern Art, the Detroit Institute of Arts, and the China Medical Board. In addition to her interest in the arts, she is extensively involved in the business corporation world, as a director of the Kellogg Company, Phillips Petroleum Company, Michigan Bell Telephone Company, and the Michigan National Bank.

Dolores Wharton studied at the Little Red Schoolhouse and later attended Danbury High School (Connecticut). She holds a B.A. degree in fine arts from Chicago State University.

Chancellor and Mrs. Wharton, who were married in 1950, have traveled extensively throughout the world, particularly in Asia. They resided in Malaysia for a period of six years (1958 to 1964) during which Dolores Wharton was active in the arts. She served as a judge on various art panels and for art competitions. In 1966 and 1968 she conducted a survey on the artists of Malaysia which was published in 1972 as a book, *Contemporary Artists of Malaysia: A Biographic Survey*, by the Asia Society of New York.

Since coming to Albany in 1978, Chancellor Wharton has performed brilliantly despite a particularly difficult financial situation, marked by an ongoing recession and federal cuts to education. In the meantime, he rejected making SUNY a partisan political institution because he believes the university is designed to serve all people. Although caught in the cross fire between the state budget crunch and rising costs, he has managed to deploy the university's resources effectively. Despite budget cuts, he has not weakened in his resolve to maintain the quality of education. Rather, he has done much to create a climate for academic excellence, recognizing that the quality of higher education is closely tied to the effectiveness of leadership in the country.

Wharton has strongly encouraged on all campuses opportunities for women, minorities, and the economically disadvantaged. He recognizes knowledge as the ultimate weapon against poverty and discrimination. If the State University is truly to represent the interests of New York's highly diverse population, it must serve the needs of its disadvantaged as well as its more favored groups.

Another key element of Wharton's plan, of which he has been the skilled architect, is a reinvigorated, leaner organization. He has reorganized the university, making it a true system and not simply an aggregate of individual units that form overlapping services and squander resources through unnecessary duplication.

He is an open-ended thinker and planner, careful and deliberate. In the face of unprecedented challenges to higher education, he beats no timid retreat into the safe and secure. Instead, he recognizes the rapidity of change and keeps State University poised on the threshold of the future.

Against such a backdrop, it is hardly surprising to learn that the Whartons have received national recognition. They were included, for example, in a continuing Florida State University research study which tracks by computer the career moves of about 6,000 of the country's most successful people. Certainly, any astute observer would note that the Whartons have brought to SUNY what they were said to have brought to Michigan State University, a genuine touch of class. They have both managed to develop a well-organized, multidimensional life-style with a combination of effectiveness and flair.

Notes

Preface

1. Karen J. Winkler, "Public Relations or Scholarship: Writing College Histories," *Chronicle of Higher Education*, March 30, 1983, pp. 31–32.
2. Ibid.
3. Ibid.

1–Building a Proud Tradition

1. Alan Tobin, Judy Wellman, "More Than a Blast From the Past," *Oswegonian*, March 21, 1974, p. 6.
2. Lillie (Babcock) Herrick, *My Yesterdays*, Watertown, New York: Robinson's Bookstore, 1949.
3. Ibid.
4. Richard Piez, "Recollections of the Oswego Normal School," Oswego: *Palladium-Times*, January 13, 1943, p. 8.
5. Uldrick Thompson, "Recollections," unpublished, 1881.
6. Herrick, op. cit.
7. Ralph L. Spencer, "Edward Austin Sheldon," unpublished, 1982.
8. E. Alexander Powell, *Gone Are the Days*, Boston: Little, Brown, 1938, p. 14.
9. Powell, op. cit.
10. Ellen Sivers, "Times of Change: Life in Oswego Town at the Close of the Nineteenth Century." 26th Publication of the Oswego County Society, 1963, pp. 23–27.
11. *History of the First Half Century of the Oswego State Normal and Training School*, Oswego, New York: Radcliffe Press, 1911.
12. "Rules for Teachers Posted in 1872," *Alumni Bulletin*, p. 8.
13. Thompson, op. cit.
14. Letter from E. J. Deupree to Dorothy Rogers, May 27, 1982.
15. Alexander Beattie, "Oswegonians' Involvement in Nineteenth Century Latin America Teacher Education: A Summary of Preliminary Research," unpublished.
16. Beattie, Oswego college librarian, for several years has been researching the influence of Oswego alumni on Midwestern and Latin American education. When completed, this fascinating addition to Oswego's early history will be available in the college archives.
17. Hideo Murayama, "A Study of the Oswego Movement," Tokyo, Japan: *Kazamashobo*, 1978.
18. Saisuke Ieno (trans.), "Pioneer of Modern Japanese Education. 60th Anniversary of the Founding of the Tokyo Higher Normal School," *Encyclopedia of Modern Education History of Japan*.

19. *History of the First Half Century of the Oswego State Normal and Training School*, op. cit.
20. Minutes of the board, March 31, 1908.
21. *History of the First Half Century of the Oswego State Normal and Training School*, op. cit.
22. Muriel Allerton, "It Used to Be the Normal School," *Oswego County Messenger*, September 3, 1981.
23. Letter from Ella Walrath (Class of 1905) to Dorothy Rogers, received 1959, "Phillipines and Oswego," *Alumni Bulletin*, Spring 1962, p. 13.
24. Calvin B. T. Lee, *The Campus Scene, 1900–1970*, New York: McKay, 1970.

2–The Darkest Years

1. David D. Henry, *Challenges Past, Challenges Present: An Analysis of American Higher Education Since 1930*, San Francisco: Jossey-Bass, 1975.
2. Calvin B. T. Lee, *The Campus Scene, 1900–1970*, New York: McKay, 1970.
3. Ibid.
4. Ibid., p. 13.
5. *Ontarian*, 1927, p. 31.
6. "Torchlight Ceremony," *Alumni Bulletin*, spring 1978, p. 19.
7. Lee, op. cit.

3–Years of Transition

1. *Three Thousand Futures: The Next Twenty Years for Higher Education*, San Francisco: Jossey-Bass, 1981.
2. Ibid., p. 44.
3. Ibid.
4. L. R. Veysey, "Stability and Experiment in the American Undergraduate Curriculum," in C. Kayser (ed.) *Content and Context*, New York: McGraw-Hill, 1973, pp. 1–63.
5. Calvin B. T. Lee, *The Campus Scene, 1900–1970*, New York: McKay, 1970.
6. Ibid., p. 46.
7. Lee, op. cit.
8. Editorial, "Dress or Not to Dress," *Oswegonian*, October 30, 1964, p. 2.
9. "Freshman Rules Revisited," *Oswegonian*, September 9, 1977, p. 6.
10. Editorial, "Women Demand Majority Rules," *Oswegonian*, February 26, 1965, p. 2.
11. Paul Woodring, "Higher Education in This Decade," *Higher Education*, December 1970, pp. 20–25.
12. "Lack of Ice and Snow Frustrates Skiers," *Oswegonian*, February 29, 1965, p. 8.
13. Eva Mahoney, "Exploding the Great Greek Myth," *Oswegonian*, March 1, 1973, p. 12.
14. Editorial, "Christmas Present," *Oswegonian*, February 11, 1962, p. 2.
15. "Campus, '65," *Newsweek*, March 22, 1965, p. 47.
16. Ibid.
17. Bob Rein, "Fallout Shelters a Moral Issue?" *Oswegonian*, December 13, 1961, p. 3.

4–The Curtain Rises on a New Era

1. Harold Rubenstein, "Richard Nixon: Non-President," *Oswegonian*, November 15, 1968.
2. Ellen K. Coughlin, "From the Great Society to the Me Decade: A Minority View of the '60s and '70s." (A review of Peter Clecak's *America's Quest for the Ideal Self: Dissent and Fulfillment in the '60s and '70s*, New York: Oxford University Press, 1983.) *Chronicle of Higher Education*, June 1, 1983, pp. 29–30.

3. Editorial, "Healthy Trend at SUCO," *Oswegonian*, August 11, 1973, p. 2.
4. Peter Clecak quoted in Coughlin, op. cit., p. 29.
5. Ibid.
6. Editorial, "Jim Perdue: College Friend," *Oswegonian*, November 6, 1965, p. 2.
7. Donald Mathieu, "Academic Implications," *Oswegonian*, February 1, 1973, p. 12.
8. Scott Stafford, "State Evaluates Oswego's Master Plan," *Oswegonian*, November 11, 1976, p. 3.
9. "Dean's Summary Report," 1968–1971.
10. From 17th Century Harvard Administration Requirements. Quoted in Howard Greene and Robert Minton, *Scaling the Ivy Wall*, 1975.
11. Editorial, "Three Important Changes," *Oswegonian*, April 26, 1973, p. 2.
12. *Carnegie Council Surveys*, 1978. Cited in *Three Thousand Futures: The Next Twenty Years for Higher Education*, San Francisco: Jossey-Bass, 1981, p. 13.
13. Calvin B. T. Lee, *The Campus Scene, 1900–1970*, New York: McKay, 1970.
14. David D. Henry, *Challenges Past, Challenges Present: An Analysis of American Higher Education Since 1930*, San Francisco: Jossey-Bass, 1975, p. 140.
15. Editorial, "Sheer Disbelief," *Oswegonian*, August 1, 1974, p. 2.
16. Alan Tobin, "The Master Plan: Emerging Goals," *Oswegonian*, March 6, 1975.
17. Ibid.
18. Paul Woodring, "Higher Education in This Decade," *Higher Education*, December 1970, pp. 20–25.
19. Editorial, "Opening Channels," *Oswegonian*, March 30, 1976, p. 2.
20. Coughlin, op. cit., p. 30.
21. Editorial, *Oswegonian*, May 3, 1973, p. 2.
22. Editorial, "Mishandled Activism," *Oswegonian*, October 2, 1975, p. 2.
23. Editorial, "Indecision," *Oswegonian*, May 3, 1968, p. 2.
24. Ibid.
25. James E. Perdue to Chancellor Gould, September 1, 1969.

5—Dramatic Changes in Faculty and Curriculum

1. Everett C. Ladd and S. M. Lipsitt, "How Professors Spend Their Time," *Oswegonian*, October 23, 1975, p. 10.
2. Patricia Bird, "Faculty Birdmen Claw the Issue," *Oswegonian*, February 23, 1969, p. 2.
3. R. L. and Lester Jacobson, *Chronicle of Higher Education*, March 30, 1983, p. 1.
4. Paul Woodring, "Higher Education in this Decade," *Higher Education*, December 1970, pp. 20–25.
5. Steven Austin, "To the Point," *Oswegonian*, December 12, 1969, p. 4.
6. Laurie Bennett, "Unsurping Students' Rights," *Oswegonian*, December 18, 1975, p. 3.
7. Ron Dygert, "Oswego State Strike Revisited," *Oswegonian*, February 13, 1975, p. 3.
8. "Dean's Summary Report," 1968–71, pp. 68–71.
9. "State of the College Message to the Faculty Assembly, April 1973," *Oswegonian*, April 5, 1973, p. 15.
10. David Leonard, "Mandatory P.E. Abolished Statewide," *Oswegonian*, August 11, 1973.
11. "Dean's Summary Report," op. cit.

6—A Turbulent Era of Student Activists

1. Calvin B. T. Lee, *The Campus Scene, 1900–1970*, New York: McKay, 1970.
2. Loyal D. Rue, "While Most of the World Prepares for Less, a Generation of U.S. Students Wants More," *Chronicle of Higher Education*, September 8, 1982, p. 25.

3. "Universities in Ferment," *Newsweek*, June 15, 1970, p. 66.
4. Rue, op. cit., p. 25.
5. "National Poll of College Editors," *Oswegonian*, May 3, 1973.
6. "Campus '65," *Newsweek*, March 22, 1965, pp. 43–48.
7. "Supplement Concerning Draft," *Oswegonian*, March 15, 1968.
8. Editorial, "Sisters!" *Oswegonian*, February 22, 1973, p. 15.
9. "Supplement Concerning Draft," op. cit.
10. Editorial, "PDQ Draft Females," *Oswegonian*, September 15, 1967, p. 2.
11. Ellen Bialo, "Silly Jungle War—Really?" *Oswegonian*, September 22, 1967, p. 12.
12. Editorial, "To the Faculty," *Oswegonian*, October 3, 1969, p. 3.
13. Ron Dygert, "Oswego State Strike Revisited," *Oswegonian*, February 13, 1975, p. 9.
14. Editorial, "E-day," *Oswegonian*, April 17, 1970, p. 2.
15. Gloria Greenfield, "An Interesting Discrepancy: $67,088," *Oswegonian*, December 7, 1972.
16. Sandy Wallace and Kay Kemp, "Letter to *Oswegonian*, Women Hoopsters Claim Discrimination," April 26, 1973, p. 4.
17. Laurie Bennet, "Common Toilet Law Flushed Down the Drain," *Oswegonian*, November 13, 1975.
18. Teri H. Rourke, Letter to the Editor, *Oswegonian*, November 20, 1975, p. 3.
19. Editorial, "Abortion Law Under Attack," *Oswegonian*, May 12, 1972, p. 12.
20. Editorial, "Call for an End to Curfews," *Oswegonian*, September 29, 1967, p. 2.
21. Editorial, "Is our Parentis Loco?" *Oswegonian*, November 8, 1968, p. 2.
22. Editorial, "Should Security Bear Arms?" *Oswegonian*, September 20, 1973, p. 2.
23. Russell Tarby, "Eight Arrested Protesting Marine Recruitment," *Oswegonian*, March 1, 1973, p. 1.
24. Letter to the Editor, from Moreland E-3, "Men of Moreland Like Long Hair," *Oswegonian*, December 10, 1965, pp. 3–4.
25. B. C. Smith, "Students Should Aid in Course Selection and Prof Evaluation," *Oswegonian*, September 29, 1967, p. 19.
26. Letter to the Editor, Burt Naznitsky, "Time to Assert Student Rights," *Oswegonian*, April 19, 1968. p. 5.
27. Steve Austin, "To the Point," *Oswegonian*, January 9, 1970, p. 14.
28. Editorial, "Student Rights," *Oswegonian*, January 9, 1970, p. 2.
29. Editorial, *Oswegonian*, September 18, 1975, p. 2.
30. Letter to the Editor, Bob Tompkins and Paul Dupont, *Oswegonian*, October 2, 1975, p. 3.
31. Paul Church, "Boyer Besieged by Demonstrators," *Oswegonian*, March 6, 1975.
32. Megan Singer, "Students Demonstrate on Housing Issue," *Oswegonian*, April 11, 1975, p. 1.
33. Sue Bilan, "Survey of Littlepage Estimates Discontent," *Oswegonian*, November 15, 1973, PP. 1;10.
34. Editorial, *Oswegonian*, March 3, 1967.
35. Letters to the Editor, *Oswegonian*, November 1, 1973.
36. *Oswegonian*, December 12, 1969, p. 12.
37. *Oswegonian*, March 20, 1970.

7–Campus Life

1. *Presidential Review, 1973–1974*.
2. "Campus '65," *Newsweek*, March 22, 1965, pp. 43–48.
3. Elynn Lambert, "Style-Conscious," *Oswegonian*, September 22, 1967, p. 12.

4. "Goodbye to Long Hair," quote from *National Review; Oswegonian*, October 9, 1975, p. 17.
5. Marilyn Whitney, "Co-ed Residence Complexes Planned," *Oswegonian*, February 9, 1968, p. 5.
6. Scott Stafford, "Perdue Vetoes Coed Dorms," *Oswegonian*, May 1, 1975, p. 1.
7. Steve Flesser, "Such is SUCO," *Oswegonian*, March 3, 1967, p. 2.
8. Stephanie Stamp, "Loft Controversy in Riggs," *Oswegonian*, September 11, 1975, p. 9.
9. Patricia Intini, "Off-campus Alternative Ideal for Some," *Oswegonian*, March 17, 1977, p. 13.
10. Patricia Intini, "So You Want to be an RA?" *Oswegonian*, November 18, 1976, p. 5.
11. Luke T. Bush, "Shoreline Tavern Grows with College," *Oswegonian*, May 5, 1975, p. 8.
12. Editorial, "God Save the King," *Oswegonian*, February 14, 1974, p. 2.
13. John Spring, "Stickmen Rescue Woman in Fire," *Oswegonian*, April 25, 1974.
14. Eva Mahoney, "Perdue Calls Referendum One-sided," *Oswegonian*, November 29, 1973, p. 1.
15. Letter to the Editor, "Busted," *Oswegonian*, October 17, 1974, p. 3.
16. "Results of Marijuana Survey," *Oswegonian*, February 20, 1975, p. 16.
17. Letter to the Editor, "Busted," *Oswegonian*, October 17, 1974, p. 3.
18. Arthur Suntag, "Throw Away the Key to Pushers," *Oswegonian*, September 6, 1973, p. 2.
19. Ellen Tracy and Sandy Shear, "Normal Day for SUCO Coed," *Oswegonian*, September 29, 1967, p. 16.
20. George Dummit, "The Waterfront," *Oswegonian*, April 25, 1967, p. 3.
21. Calvin B. T. Lee, *The Campus Scene, 1900–1970*, New York: McKay, 1970, p. 159.
22. Editorial, "Spring Fever," *Oswegonian*, April 10, 1970, p. 2.
23. "Jayne Mansfield, Actress, Visited Hillcrest," *Oswegonian*, May 6, 1966.
24. John Berninger, Letter to the Editor, *Oswegonian*, May 17, 1968.
25. Sam Waggoner, "Observations of our Greek Way of Life," *Oswegonian*, April 5, 1968, pp. 6;22.
26. Joseph Alff, Letter to the Editor, *Oswegonian*, April 22, 1966, p. 3.
27. Laurie Bennett, "Older Undergrads: Active, Diverse," *Oswegonian*, January 27, 1977, p. 6.
28. Editorial, "Dr. Peterson, Affirmative Action Officer," *Oswegonian*, January 18, 1973, p. 12.
29. Uhuru Sasu, "Black Messiah," *Oswegonian*, April 5, 1973, p. 22.
30. Op. cit., *Oswegonian*, October 5, 1973.
31. "Black Students Make Progress at SUCO," *Oswegonian*, October 18, 1973, p. 11.
32. Winsome Tulloch, "Sister to Head Black Student Union," *Oswegonian*, February 14, 1974, p. 18.
33. Elise M. Reinish, "Acceptance Doesn't Come Easy to Oswego Gays," *Oswegonian*, October 21, 1976, p. 17.
34. Richard Galloway, "Hippies and Causes Shut Out in Cold," *Oswegonian*, November 16, 1958.
35. Megan Dunning, "SAVAC," *Oswegonian*, February 7, 1974, p. 8.
36. Editorial, Paul Murphy, *Oswegonian*, December 7, 1972, p. 4.
37. Bill Zystyniak, "Student Government at the Crossroads," *Oswegonian*, January 25, 1973, p. 3.
38. David Leonard, "The $64 Question," *Oswegonian*, April 5, 1973.
39. Peter Bernhardt, "The Pendulum 'Cult'," *Oswegonian*, December 7, 1972, p. 3.
40. John Antonucci, "Recent Oswego Hearing Critical of Students," *Oswegonian*, April 23, 1976, pp. 1;6.
41. Sammang Soeur, "Why Students Come to Oswego," *Oswegonian*, May 2, 1974.
42. Greta Petry, "Oswego Campus Rich in Folklore," *Oswegonian*, September 27, 1973, p. 8.
43. "Universities in Ferment," *Newsweek*, June 15, 1976, pp. 66–68.

44. Abigail Zugar, "Acrophobia in the Ivory Tower," *Harper's*, October 1975, pp. 4–5.
45. "Fewer Jobs for the Class of '70," *U.S. News and World Report*, March 9, 1970, pp. 38–40.
46. Letter to the *Alumni Bulletin*, spring 1978, p. 18.

8–A New Mission

1. John Naisbitt, *Megatrends*, New York: Warner Books, 1982.
2. Ellen K. Coughlin, "From the Great Society to the Me Decade: A Minority View of the '60s and '70s." (A review of Peter Clecak's *America's Quest for the Ideal Self: Dissent and Fulfillment in the '60s and '70s*, New York: Oxford University Press, 1983). *Chronicle of Higher Education*, June 1, 1983, pp. 29–30.
3. Naisbitt, op. cit.
4. *Three Thousand Futures: The Next Twenty Years for Higher Education*. San Francisco: Jossey-Bass, 1981, p. 80.
5. Clifton R. Wharton, Jr., "Making do with More," *The News*, October/November, 1982, p. 3.
6. David Riesman, *On Higher Education*, San Francisco: Jossey-Bass, 1980, p. 21.
7. Suzanne Perry, "Finding the Right College President Means Looking First at the College," *Chronicle of Higher Education*, February 2, 1983, p. 21.
8. Suzanne Perry, "Women Administrators Say They Still Battle to Win Acceptance from Male Colleagues," *Chronicle of Higher Education*, 1982, pp. 27;30.
9. Ibid.
10. Clifton R. Wharton, Jr., "Enrollment: Higher Education's Window of Vulnerability," *The News*, March/April, 1983, pp. 3;8.
11. Ben Brodinsky, "Something Happened: Education in the '70s," *Phi Delta Kappan*, December 1979, pp. 238–241.
12. "Everywoman's Guide to Colleges and Universities," *Feminist Press*, 1982.
13. Charles S. Farrell, "They Took My Chair Away: Effects of Layoffs on Tenured Professors," *Chronicle of Higher Education*, Decenber 8, 1962, p. 23.
14. Robert O'Connor, "Letter to Virginia Strangelove," *Oswegonian*, October 20, 1977, p. 11.
15. Timothy Dickinson, "Diminished Faculties," *Harper's*, October 1975, pp. 8–9.
16. Tongue-in-Cheek Suggestions Concerning Graduation," *Alumni Bulletin*, Summer 1981.
17. Robert L. Jacobson, "Reagan Budget Would Cut Student Aid, Arts and Humanities Funds by a Third," *Chronicle of Higher Education*, February 17, 1983, pp. 15–17.
18. Mike Grogan, "SUCO Faculty Talk of Saving Jobs," *Syracuse Post-Standard*, February 3, 1983, p. 81.
19. "SUCO Faculty Weigh Strategies to Fight Cut," *Syracuse Post-Standard*, February 11, 1983.
20. Letter from President Radley to Chancellor Wharton, August 10, 1979.
21. Dan Keefer, "Foster Excellence—Out of Blood to Tears," *Oswegonian*, November 1, 1979, p. 2.
22. Louis Harris, "On Higher Education," *The News*, summer 1981, pp. 5–6.
23. *Three Thousand Futures: The Next Twenty Years for Higher Education*, op. cit., p. 100.
24. "SAT Verbal, Math Scores up the First Time in 19 Years," *Chronicle of Higher Education*, July 29, 1982, p. 1.
25. "Frosh Scores 1010," *Alumni Bulletin*, fall 1982.

9–A Faculty of Distinction

1. Ronald Brown (physics); Robert Carnes (philosophy); Nicholas D'Innocenzo, Michael Fox, Thomas Seawell (art); Irwin Flack, Thomas Judd, Thomas Powell (history); George Koenig

(German); Paul Roodin, Herbert Van Schaack, Paul Wilbur (psychology); Kenneth Sipser (education); Sue Ann Steck-Turner (music); Sanford Sternlicht (theater); Norman Weiner (sociology).
2. *Carnegie Council on Policy Studies in Higher Education, the Next Twenty Years for Higher Education*, San Francisco: Jossey Bass, 1980, p. 376.
3. *Three Thousand Futures: The Next Twenty Years for Higher Education*, San Francisco: Jossey-Bass, 1981.
4. *National Research Council*, 1979. Appendix C in *Carnegie Council*, op. cit., p. 376.
5. David Riesman, *On Higher Education*, San Francisco: Jossey-Bass, 1980.
5. David Riesman, *On Higher Education*, San Francisco: Jossey-Bass, 1980.
6. Fred Bartle, '56 (political science); Richard Benjamin, '59 (experience-based education); Nevart Boghosian, '56, Constance Bond, '55, Raymond Bridgers, '58, Alvin Westcott, '59 (education); Joseph Braco, '57, William Hanks, '57, Richard Pfund, '57, Charles Phallen, '58, Charles Shoemaker, '56, William Todd, '55 (industrial arts); John Fisher, '57 (English); John Glinski, '58, Joan Huff, '58, Ernest Luongo, '57, Walter Nitardy, '58 (physical education); Paul Hutko, '59, Owen Pittenger, '55, Frederick Ratzeburg, Herbert Van Schaack, '56 (psychology); Pearle Monroe, '58 (chemistry); Richard Wheeler, '57 (associate provost).
7. Willard Allen, Vincent Barone, Betty Bartkowiak, Leonard Becker, Joseph Braco, Paul Briand, John Cooper, Peter Diez del Rio, Robert Harrison, Richard Hyse, Saisuke Ieono, Rosalind Kimmich, Albert Leighton, Ernest Luongo, Georges Markow-Totevy, Thomas Marshall, Pearle Monroe, Richard Pfund, Lewis Popham, Thomas Putnam, Dorothy Rogers, Aline Rudd, Socrates Sampson, Charles Shoemaker, George Stark, William Todd, Obele Van Dyke, Richard Walker, Richard Wheeler.
8. Vice president, Sherwood Dunham, 1955–1977; Charles Coward, 1954–1977; administration, Frank Robinson (1948–1982), White Warner (1952–1977); audiovisual services, Theodore Beers (1949–1981); industrial arts, Carl Gerbracht, (1954–1981), James Hastings (1946–1978), Charles Phallen (1959–1983); music, Sylvia Irwin (1958–1978); education, Theodore Moss (1958–1971; science, Harold Powers (1948–1978); Robert Stirling (1948–1980); English, Vernon Rank (1946–1977); mathematics, John Schleup (1959–1980); history, Norman Whitten (1948–1978); reading education, Robert Canfield (1951–1983); physics, Rufus Moore (1962–1983); earth sciences, Paul Shaver (1960–1983).
9. Jean Evangelauf, "Colleges Must Hire 500,000 Professors in the Next 25 Years, New Study Finds," *Chronicle of Higher Education*, 1984, 29 (11), 1:p. 29.
10. Richard R. Renner, "Comparing Professors: How Student Ratings Contribute to the Decline in Quality of Higher Education," *Phi Delta Kappan*, October 1981, pp. 128–130.
11. Jean Shepherd, "Today's Students," *Harper's*, October 1975, p. 7.
12. Ibid.
13. Editorial, "Students Screwed Again," *Oswegonian*. October 23, 1975.
14. Riesman, op. cit.

10–The Roles Faculty Members Play

1. "Put Education at the Top of Your Agenda, 51 Leaders Urge," *Chronicle of Higher Education*, April 13, 1983, pp. 1;6.
2. David Riesman, *On Higher Education*, San Francisco: Jossey-Bass, 1980, p. 13.
3. Ellen K. Coughlin, "Recording the Great Performances of Teachers Who Made a Difference," *Chronicle of Higher Education*, May 4, 1981, p. 17/

11–Crafting a Curriculum

1. Jack Magarell, "American Students Seek Survival Skills, Not Social Conscience, Interview Showed," *Chronicle of Higher Education*, April 7, 1982, p. 11.

2. *Three Thousand Futures: The Next Twenty Years for Higher Education*. San Francisco: Jossey-Bass, 1981.
3. Peter Drucker, *Managing in Turbulent Times*, New York: Harper and Row, 1980, cited in John Naisbitt, *Megatrends*, New York: Warner Books, 1982, p. 256.
4. Naisbitt, op. cit.
5. *Three Thousand Futures: The Next Twenty Years for Higher Education*, op. cit.
6. *Naisbitt*, op. cit.
7. Clifton R. Wharton, Jr., "General Education: Stopping the Pendulum—Can We Get Off?" *The News*, April/May, 1982, p. 3.
8. Ibid., p. 7.
9. Ibid., p. 3.
10. Naisbitt, op. cit., p. 33.
11. Edward B. Fiske, "A University in Transition," *The News*, September 1981, pp. F1:F4.
12. Lynn Breslawski, "Tyler Hall: A Cosmopolitan World of Creativity," *Oswegonian*, March 1, 1979, p. 13.
13. John Breves, Steven Flesser and Elaine Re, "The Symphonic Choir at Expo '67," *Oswegonian*, May 12, 1967, pp. 6–7.
14. Eva T. H. Braun, *Defending Return to the Classics in U.S. Colleges*, Chicago: University of Chicago Press, 1979.
15. Ronald W. Labuz, "Philosophers have an Image Problem," *The News*, March/April, 1983, p. F1.
16. Richard Rorty, *Philosophy and the Mirror of Culture*, Princeton: Princeton University Press, 1981.
17. Naisbitt, op. cit.
18. Jack Magarell, "Microcomputers Proliferate on College Campuses," *Chronicle of Higher Education*, April 6, 1983, p. 9.
19. Harold G. Shane, "A Curriculum for the New Century," *Phi Delta Kappan*, January 1981, pp. 351–355.
20. James Rutherford, "The Dangerous Decline in U.S. Education," *Chronicle of Higher Education*, April 13, 1983, p. 64.
21. Shane, op. cit.
22. Ibid.
23. Karen J. Winkler, "A History that Pulls Things Together," *Chronicle of Higher Education*, July 7, 1983, p. 3.

12–Professional Studies and Special Programs

1. "An Open Letter to the American People: A Nation at Risk: The Imperative for Educational Reform," *Education Week*, April 27, 1983, pp. 12–16.
2. "Higher Education," *Chronicle of Higher Education*, March 2, 1983, p. 4.
3. N. Scott Vance, "Half of Women's Teams Coached by Men, Study Finds," *Chronicle of Higher Education*, March 30, 1983, pp. 21;24.
4. Don Slater, "How Equal is Equal?" *Alumni Bulletin*, October 1976, p. 11.
5. Lou Oritz, "ROTC: A New Area of Interest?" *Oswegonian*, April 3, 1978, p. 8.
6. Marion Godey, "Kate Koehne," *Oswegonian*, October 28, 1982.
7. Beverly T. Watkins, "Twenty-one Adults Found Taking Part in Continuing Education Programs," *Chronicle of Higher Education*, May 5, 1982, p. 10.
8. Clifton R. Wharton, Jr., "Farewell to the City of Youth," *The News*, summer 1981, pp. 3;7.
9. *Oswegonian*, November 29, 1979, p. 6.
10. *Alumni Bulletin*, fall 1981.
11. David Riesman, *On Higher Education*, San Francisco: Jossey-Bass, 1980, p. 291.

13–Student Life in the 1980s

1. Charles Gonzales, "Today's Students—Moderately Liberal," *Oswegonian*, December 8, 1977, p. 13.
2. Jack Magarell, "Freshmen Aim to Make Money, but Shift Slightly to Left," *Chronicle of Higher Education*, January 26, 1983, p. 10.
3. Andee Hochman, *Chronicle of Higher Education*, January 1983, p. 5.
4. "Freshmen Surveyed," *Palladium-Times*, March 3, 1983.
5. Hank Whittimore, "Why Today's College Students May Be the Smartest Ever," *Parade Magazine*, February 20, 1983, pp. 4–8.
6. Linda Michaels, Office of Institutional Research, "Profile of the Fall 1979 Student Body," *Annual Report*, 1979–1980.
7. Editorial, "Enemy Moral Majority," *Oswegonian*, October 18, 1981.
8. "Florida Law Denying Funds to Campus Homosexuals Overturned," *Chronicle of Higher Education*, February 17, 1982, p. 9.
9. Lawrence Biemuller, "Homosexual Academics: A Coming Out Would Jeopardize Careers," *Chronicle of Higher Education*, October 20, 1982, p. 9.
10. Scott Stafford, "Controversy Over Racism Surfaces on Campus," *Oswegonian*, March 30, 1978.
11. Editorial, "Racism," *Oswegonian*, March 30, 1978, p. 2.
12. Malcolm G. Scully, "One Million Foreign Students at U.S. Colleges: Triple Present Number Seen Likely by 1980," *Chronicle of Higher Education*, October 21, 1981, p. 1.
13. Alan W. Ostar, "Part-time Students: The New Majority for the 1980s," *Chronicle of Higher Education*, October 7, 1981, p. 56.
14. Richard Blodgett, "Older Students," Letter to the Editor, *Oswegonian*, October 12, 1978, p. 12.
15. "Americans Shift Their Habits, Surgeon General Finds," *Washington Post*, December 6, 1980, reported in Naisbitt, 1982, p. 260.
16. "Overeaters Anonymous Helps Slaves to Food," *Oswegonian*, February 15, 1979, p. 7.
17. Mark Chester, "Students Born to Job," *Oswegonian*, September 8, 1978, p. 13.
18. "Cost of Going to College Rises 11% in 12 Months, College Board Finds," *Chronicle of Higher Education*, September 1, 1982.
19. Zoe Ingalls, "Although Drinking is Widespread, Student Abuse of Alcohol is Not Rising, Study Finds," *Chronicle of Higher Education*, January 19, 1983, p. 9.
20. Ibid.
21. Marie Marcoccia, "New Bars Offer Choice of Atmosphere," *Oswegonian*, October 27, 1977, p. 9.
22. Howard Maurer, "Local Tavern Keeps Century-Old Tradition Alive," *Oswegonian*, February 23, 1978, p. 15.
23. Melanie Janowsky, "The Greenwich Village of Oswego," *Oswegonian*, October 22, 1981, pp. 12–13.
24. Jack Olcott, "The Tavern," *Oswego News*, October 8, 1981.
25. John Marini, "Hungry Students Dig in on Smokin' Chicken Wings," *Syracuse Post-Standard*, October 2, 1982, p. 8–11.
26. Jeannine McPartlin, "Police Report," *Oswegonian*, October 14, 1982.
27. "Better Behavior: Why?" *Annual Report, 1981–82*.
28. Zoe Ingalls, "40% of Students in Survey Say They Worry about Finances," *Chronicle of Higher Education*, November 17, 1982, pp. 1;7.
29. Calvin B. T. Lee, *The Campus Scene, 1900–1970*, New York: McKay, 1970.

14—More About Students of the 1980s

1. Elizabeth Pratt, "A Great Greek Myth Challenged," *Oswegonian*, April 28, 1977, p. 14.
2. Patricia Svarek, "SUNY Frats and Sororities Slowly Join Nationals," *Oswegonian*, December 9, 1976.
3. Editorial, "Autonomy Essential," *Oswegonian*, May 10, 1979, p. 12.
4. Joseph Bua, "Dorm Papers: Fun to Read," *Oswegonian*, March 12, 1981, p. 5.
5. Denise LePine, "Disheartened by Sexism," *Oswegonian*, March 18, 1982, p. 8.
6. Scott Clark, "It's Come a Long Ways," *Oswegonian*, March 4, 1982.
7. "Wharton Forms a SUNY-wide Evaluation Team," *The News*, December 2, 1982, p. 17.
8. Maria Cristina, Carolyn Cason, Mary Jo Stenson, "Women Upset Over Abuse," *Oswegonian*, March 5, 1983, p. 11.
9. Sharon DeFren, "Crisis Center Opens Doors," *Oswegonian*, September 18, 1980, p. 11.
10. Philip Zampino, Letter to the Editor, *Oswegonian*, March 3, 1983.
11. Virginia L. Radley, "Freedom, Responsibility Go Hand in Hand," *Palladium-Times*, May 12, 1982.
12. *Three Thousand Futures: The Next Twenty Years for Higher Education*, San Francisco: Jossey-Bass, 1981, pp. 28–29.
13. Jean Shepherd, "Today's Students," *Harper's*, October 1975, p. 7.
14. Halette Torby, "Students Don't Give A Damn," *Oswegonian*, October 12, 1978, p. 13.
15. Editorial, *Palladium-Times*, September 20, 1979, p. 2.
16. Editorial, "Say No to Nukes," *Oswegonian*, October 6, 1977, p. 10.
17. Dan Williams, "SUNY Students Fight the Hike in Albany Rally," *Oswegonian*, March 3, 1983.
18. E. Kevan Rowlee, Letter to the Editor, "Gay or Sad," *Oswegonian*, October 6, 1977, pp. 10–22.
19. Gladys Henderson, "Concerned Member of the Gay Alliance," Letter to the Editor, *Oswegonian*, October 6, 1977, pp. 10–11.
20. "Campus Gives its Vote to Anderson," *Oswegonian*, October 30, 1980, p. 15.
21. Editorial, "Heckling Watt," *Oswegonian*, November 19, 1981, p. 10.
22. David Riesman, *On Higher Education*, San Francisco: Jossey-Bass, 1980, p. 2.
23. "So Why Didn't You Decide to Come to Oswego?" *Oswegonian*, September 9, 1932.
24. Dorothy Rogers, Founder's Day Address, *Alumni Bulletin*, fall 1981, p. 9.

15—Beyond the Horizon

1. David D. Henry, *Challenges Past, Challenges Present: An Analysis of American Higher Education Since 1930*, San Francisco: Jossey-Bass, 1975.
2. Stephen H. Trachtenberg, "What Universities Will be Like in the Year 2000," *Phi Delta Kappan*, January 1983, pp. 327–330.
3. *Three Thousand Futures: The Next Twenty Years for Higher Education*, San Francisco: Jossey-Bass, 1981.
4. Clifton R. Wharton, Jr., "Curriculum 2001: Education for the 21st Century," *The News* September 1981, pp. 3;8.
5. Editorial, *Washington Post*, December 21, 1977.
6. Clifton R. Wharton, Jr., "Facing the Crossroads," *The News*, February 1984, p. 3.
7. Clifton R. Wharton, Jr., "Enrollment: Higher Education's Window of Vulnerability," *The News*, March 1983, pp. 3;8.
8. Fred Best and Barry Stern, *Lifetime Distribution of Education, Work and Leisure*, Washington, D.C.: Institute for Educational Leadership. Postsecondary Convening Authority, 1976.

9. Trachtenberg, op. cit.
10. Clifton R. Wharton, Jr., "SUNY Budget 1982: The Issue of Access," *The News*, February 1982, pp. 3;7.
11. Wharton, "Curriculum 2001: Education for the 21st Century," op. cit.
12. Ibid.
13. Paper by John Fisher, 1984, unpublished.
14. Trachtenberg, op. cit., p. 329.
15. Wharton, "Curriculum 2001: Education for the 21st Century," op. cit.
16. Jack Magarell, "U.S. Forecast: 10% Decline in College Teaching Jobs by 1990," *Chronicle of Higher Education*, October 21, 1981.
17. Harold G. Shane, "A Curriculum for the New Century," *Phi Delta Kappan*, January 1981, pp. 351–355.
18. Wharton, "Curriculum 2001: Education for the 21st Century," op. cit.
19. Ibid.
20. Ibid.
21. John Naisbitt, *Megatrends*, New York: Warner Books, 1982, pp. 73–74.
22. Ibid.
23. Naisbitt, op. cit.
24. Edward Lonkey, "Conjectures About SUCO's Future," unpublished.
25. Wharton, "Curriculum 2001: Education for the 21st Century," op. cit.
26. Shane, op. cit.
27. Harold G. Shane, "Education in Transformation: Major Developments of the Uneasy '80s (in Retrospect)," *Phi Delta Kappan*, December 1979, pp. 241–243.
28. Wharton, "Curriculum 2001: Education for the 21st Century," op. cit.
29. Trachtenberg, op. cit.
30. Paper by Jacqueline Reihman, 1984, unpublished.
31. Magarell, op. cit.
32. Paper by Sue Fines, 1984, unpublished.
33. Shane, "Education in Transformation: Major Developments of the Uneasy '80s (in Retrospect)," op. cit., p. 243.
34. Paper by Edward Lonkey, 1984, unpublished.
35. *Three Thousand Futures: The Next Twenty Years for Higher Education*, op. cit.
36. Henry, op. cit.
37. Ibid.
38. Wharton, "Curriculum 2001: Education for the 21st Century," op. cit., p. 3.
39. Trachtenberg, op. cit., p. 329.
40. Ibid.
41. Oswego's Task Force to Assess Future Needs: Robert Carter, Sue Fines, John Fisher, Joan Fitzgibbons, DeWight Middleton, Harry Nash, Raymond Schneider, Ronald Scrudato, Marilyn Smiley, Ralph Spencer, Larry Spizman, John Sullivan, Herbert Van Schaack, and Vernon Tryon (chair).
42. Naisbitt, op. cit.

Index

Note: Titles are set in *italics;* n refers to footnotes

"Abnormal Psychology" (course), 200
Abortion, 112, 136
Academic Fair, 163–64
Adams, Marion Steele, 47
Adams, Mignon, 165, 171, 195
Admission standards, 56, 76–77, 168–69
Adopt-a-Grandparent Program, 137, 270
Adult students. *See* Older students
Advisement, 237
Affirmative action, 158, 192
African and Afro-American Studies, 221
Afro-American Studies, 233, 232
Alcan Aluminum, 79
Alcohol, 61, 63, 115, 117, 126–27, 249–50, 258, 274–75
Alcohol Beverage Committee, 126
Alessia, Joseph, 201
Alff, Joseph, 129, 130
Alford, Harold, 36, 38, 41, 53, 54
Alfred P. Sloan Foundation, 207
Ali, Muhammed, 237
Allen, Catherine. *See* Poucher, Catherine Allen
Allen, Christine, 253
Allen, Fred, 92
Allen, George, 282
Allen, Willard, 226, 309n8
Alliance of Women Against Repressive Education, 111
Alpha Delta, 40, 65
Alpha Delta Eta, 262
Alpha Kappa Phi, 65
Alpha Sigma Alpha, 65
Altschuler, Bruce, 234
Alumni, 12–16, 33–34, 68–69, 141–43, 212, 262, 281, 303n16; faculty, 171–72; SUNY, 281. *See Also* specific names
Alumni Association. *See* Oswego Alumni Association
Alumni Bulletin, 68, 142–43, 184, 281, 282
Alumni Day, 68
American Association of Colleges for Teacher Education, 57, 225
American Federation of Teachers, 160, 161
American Revolution, 1–2
American Studies program, 223
Ames, Herbert, 34
Ames, Richard, 124
Anderson, John, 275
Andrews, Eugene P., 13
Angel, Marian, 54
Animal House, 130
Anthropology department, 220–21
Archaeological expedition, 57
Area Studies programs, 232
Arethusa, 40
Armeson, Robert, 193
Argentina, 15–16
Arise, 268
Armstrong, Clara, 15–16
Armstrong, Frances, 15
Art department, 209–10
Arthur Hauler Memorial Resource Center, 227
Asimov, Isaac, 102
Associated Women Students, 61, 63, 112–13, 282
As the Scales Tip, 264
Auleta, Betsy, 86, 93, 94, 106, 112, 113, 118

INDEX

Auleta, Kenneth, 142
Austin, Steve, 94, 115
"Automobiles" (course), 226
Awad, Ed, 200, 216
AWARE. *See* Alliance of Women Against Repressive Education
AWS. *See* Associated Women Students
Aylward, John, 47

Babcock, John, 13
Bagley, William C., 20
Bailyn, Bernard (cited), 222
Baird, Bill, 112
Baji, Giovanni, 244
Baker, Steve, 200
Balmori, Diana, 173, 223, 333, 282
Barach, Daniel, 210
Barbarino, Mary Ann, 254–55, 280
Barclay, Dorothy, 47
Barclay, Douglas, 151
Barnes, Earl, 7
Barnes, Joseph, 282
Barnes, Mary Sheldon, 7, 12
Barnes, Randall, 200
Barney's, 255
Bar On, Bat-Ami, 196, 202, 234
Barone, Vincent, 199–200, 309n8
Bartkowiak, Elizabeth (Betty), 196, 201, 309n8
Bartle, Fred, 221, 309n7
Batungbacal, José, 22
Baxter, Maureen, 253
Beaman, Wilma, 196
Beamon, Elijah, 133
Beattie, Alexander, 15, 303n16
Becker, Leonard, 309n8
Beerse, Elizabeth, 248
Beers, Theodore, 309n9
Belt, John, 194, 201
Benedict, Katherine, 155
Benjamin, Richard, 309n7
Bennett, Laurie, 97
Berkenblit, Joan, 255, 258–59
Bernhart, Peter, 136
Berninger, John, 129
Berson, Thomas, 127
Beta Tau Epsilon, 40, 65, 130
Bethany, James, 114
Bieling, Robert, 169
A Bigamist's Daughter (McDermott), 142, 282

Billings, Jeffrey A., 212
Biology department, 219
"Biology of Sex" (course), 200
Bishop, Charles, 193, 220
Bishop, Jacquelyn, 259, 267
Bishop, Kathleen, 280
Black and Puerto Rican Student Union, 86
Black Panthers, 108, 236
Black students, 132–33, 242–43
Black Student Union, 132–33, 223, 242; photo, center section
Black Student Union's Excellence in Teaching Award, 223
Blair-Parker, Charlotte, 13
Blanding, Sarah Gibson, 146
Blandino, Doreen, 247
Block, Joel, 69
Blodgett, Richard, 245
Bloom, Kathy, 265–66
Boardway, Ed, 47
Bocchino, William, 254
Boghosian, Nevart, 309n7
Bohall, Hilda Guy, 68, 141
Boland, Leo, 272
Bond, Constance, 194, 309n7
Bonn, Hank 137
Borden, Virginia, 253
Boston Girls' High School of Practical Arts, 12–13
Boswell, Lyn, 66
Botjer, Henry, 253
Boyd, Maurice, 54, 95, 210
Boyer, Ernest, 82, 100, 116
Braco, Joseph, 309n7, 309n8
Brady, Ivan, 193, 194, 198, 231, 290, 298
Branigan, James, 200
Braun, Eva, 212
Bremmer, Allen, 93
Breneman Window Shade, 79
Brennan, Thomas, 202, 267
Briand, Paul, Jr., 92, 142, 193, 309n8; photo, center section
Briant, Charlotte, 245
Bridgers, Raymond, 199, 309n7
Brindle, Elizabeth, 216
Brine, John Francis, 18
Brown, Darcy, 201
Brownell, Clifford Lee, 33
Brown, Foster S., 41, 45–69; buildings, 48–49; curriculum, 53, 56–58; faculty, 52–55, 58; photo, center section
Brown, Leyden, 150, 155

INDEX 317

Brown, Ronald, 194, 204, 215, 231, 292, 293, 308–9n1
Bruckner, Diana, 252
Bruere, Lucie de la, 260
Buck, David, 247, 255
Buckland's, 40, 62, 64, 123, 126, 130, 214, 249, 255, 276
Buckley, Helen, 54. *See also* Simkewicz, Helen Buckley
Buckley, William F., Jr., 67, 102
Buildings, 48–49, 79–81. *See also* specific names
Burchell, Earl, 21
Burger, Andrew, 259, 260
Buritt, Hugh, 210
Burling, James, 84
Burns, John, 34
Business administration department, 229
Butler, Mary Beth, 226, 246
Butler, Nicholas Murray, 146
Button, Jay, 195
Byrne, Gretchen, 265
Byrne, Rodney, 232

Cahill Fish Market, 79
Calderalo, Rosemary, 268
Cameo, 255
Camp Shady Shore, 28; photo, center section
Campus police, 76, 114, 129, 169, 181, 271–72
Campus School, 25, 27, 38, 53, 56, 81; closing, 8, 159, 166–67, 225
Canale's, 62
Canfield, David, 197
Canfield, Robert, 58, 309n9
Cangemi, Joseph P., 69
Capen, Samuel, 24
Caplan, Peter, 274
Carapetyan, Leon, 211
Carillon bells, 49
Carnegie Council on Higher Education, 78, 167–68, 172, 174, 204, 283, 296
Carnes, Robert, 232, 308–9n1
Carr, Jeffrey, 275
Carroll, Beth, 202, 261
Carter, Jimmy, 274, 275
Carter, Robert, 172
Castaldo, Samuel, 47
Castigno, Sue, 188, 243, 264–65
Cayuga Hall, 121, 127, 129, 139, 253, 257

Centennial celebration, 51–52, 66
Centennial history. *See Oswego: Fountainhead of Teacher Education*
Center of International Research in Historical Cryptanalysis, 222
Century Club, 281
Century of Opportunity (Deupree), 14
Chamber Raiders, 211
Chamber Singing Group, 210
Champlain, Samuel de, 1
Chancellor's Award for Excellence in Teaching, 171, 192, 223, 282, 308–9n1
Chapel, 29, 40, 43, 62
Chapman, Thomas, 200, 230
Charles, Michael, 267
Charlton, Harry, 49–50
Chemistry department, 217–18
CHE/MSA. *See* Commission on Higher Education of the Middle States Association of College Schools
Chernov, Randi, 122
Chester, Mark, 248
Chewins, Michael, 197, 229
Children: migrant workers', 157; retarded, 28
Chisolm, Shirley, 102, 236
Christensen, Lawrence O. (cited), x
Chumney, James R. (cited), x
Civil rights, 60, 66, 68, 70, 106
Clambar, 255
Clark, Antoine, 183, 184
Clark, Dorothy Brown, 172, 281
Clark, Frederick, 20
Clecak, Peter (cited), 71–72
Clemons, Sue, 163, 246
Clio, 32, 40
Coast Guard Reserve Training School, 58
Cochrane, Timothy, 197, 277
"Code Breaking and History" (course), 222
Cody, Buffalo Bill, 2
Cody, Cecil, 222
Coed dorms, 114, 115, 121
Coeducation, 2–3
COGS. *See* Committee on Governance and Scholarship
Collective bargaining, 84, 160, 168
College Community Orchestra, 211
College Council, 47, 50, 52, 150, 154–55, 181
College Counseling Center, 248
College Development Office, 157
College histories, x

College presidents, 146–48, 182–83
Collins, Richard, 141
Colucci, Nancy, 251
Commencement. *See* Graduation exercises
Commerton, Anne, 195
Commission on Higher Education of the Middle States Association of Colleges and Schools, 164
Committee on Alcohol Use, 126
Committee on Education Beyond the High School, 46
Committee on Government and Scholarship, 87
Communication Studies department, 211–12
Community Energy Alliance, 272
Community Service headquarters, 101
Comploier, Linda, 197, 200
Computers, 92
Computer science department, 216
Conant, Mildred, 23
Conley, Claire, 251
Continuing education, 74, 101, 235, 286
Conzone's, 40
Coon, Mr., 19
Cooperative Education Program, 157, 236
Cooper Dining Hall, 78, 252
Cooper, Hermann, 35, 37, 51
Cooper, Johnson, 56, 195, 225, 309n8
Cooper, Matilda, 6–7, 20
Corcoran, Mr., 21
Coreas, Edmundo, 16
Corley, Paul, 266
Coughlin, Ellen K. (cited), 71
Counseling and psychology services. *See* Department of Counseling and Psychology Services
Country Inn, 62
Coward, Charles (Bud), 49–50, 309n9
Cox, Donald, 219, 232
Crain, Anthony, 92, 211
Craine, Katherine, 278
Crawford, Edward, 112
Crawford, John, 142
Cretaro, John, 245, 246
Cribben, Leo, 36, 54
"Critical Health Issues" (course), 270
Crozier, Gerald, 33
Crime, 129. *See also* Campus police
Cruppenink, Debbie, 278
Culkin, Francis D., 81
Culkin Hall, 79, 81, 108–9

Cullinan, P.W., 20
Cuomo, Mario, 154, 155, 165, 273
Cuppernull, George, 210
Curriculum, 286–94, 297; Brown, 53, 56–58; faculty attitudes, 204–6; Perdue, 95–102, 204, 205; Poucher, 21; Radley, 203–38; Rice, 41–42; Riggs, 28–29; Sheldon, 8; Swetman, 35, 37–38
Cutler, Diane, 200
Cyclotherm, 79

Daily, Harriet, 14
Daily Times, 20
Daino, Doug, 251
Daly, Helen, 194, 195, 196, 200
D'Amato, Frances, 69
D'Ambrosio, Vincent, 195
Danahar, David, 223
Dane, Frank, 172
Dashley, Emily, 52
A Daughter of the Sky (Briand), 193
Daughters of the Wilted Wallet, 41
Davis, Charles, 200, 229, 230
Dean, John, 236–37
Dearing, Bruce, 183, 186, 189
"Death and Dying" (course), 221
Debandi, Brenda, 229
Debarros, Weber, 244
DeBaun, Ella, 15
Deegnan, Michael, 267
DeFrancisco, John, 201, 277
De La Vergne, Louis, 33
Del Pino, E. Ahumada de, 16
Delta Kappa Kappa, 32, 40, 210, 262–63
Delucia, Lawrence, 84
Demidowicz, John, 213
Deming, Robert, 232
Denecke, Susan, 252
Department of Counseling and Psychological Services, 194, 235
Department of Foreign Languages and Literature, 198. *See also* Foreign Language and Literature program
Department of School Psychology, 228
Department of Technology, 226–28. *See also* Industrial Arts
Depression of 1930's, 30, 34
Deupree, Joseph E., 14
De Vore, Paul, 53
Dewey, John, 21, 38
Dewey, Thomas E., 42

INDEX 319

Dicken's pub, 255
Dievendorf, Gary, 201, 277
Diez del Rio, Peter, 309n8
Dillon, Barry, 267
D'Innocenzo, Nicholas, 156, 194, 198, 209, 231, 289, 294, 308–9n1
DiPasquale, Dominic, 72, 194
Disabled students, 242
Disadvantaged students, 234
Distinguished Alumni Awards, 68, 69, 282
Division of Continuing Education, 101. *See also* Continuing education
Division of Elementary and Secondary Education, 225–26
Dodd, Joseph, 201
Dogs, 117
Doll, William, 194, 225
Donnellon, Karen, 197
Dormitories. *See* Housing, specific names
Dormitory newspapers, 263–64
Downum, Philip, 192
Draft. *See* Military draft
Draper, Commissioner, 19
Drazek, Stanley J., 163
Drinking. *See* Alcohol
Drucker, Peter (cited), 203
Drugs, 61, 106, 118, 125–27, 136. *See also* Alcohol
Dubuque, Shirleen, 265
Duffy, John, 231
Dummit, George, 212
Duncan, Dolores. *See* Wharton, Dolores Duncan
Dunham, Sherwood: about, 53, 195, 309n9; cited, 46, 54, 56, 57, 74, 78, 175, 205, 225
Dupont, Paul, 116
Dussere, Paul, 232
Dygert, Ronald, 98

Eaker, Charles, 181
Earhart, Amelia, 193
Earth sciences department, 219–20
Echelbarger, Charles, 215
Eckersley, Thomas, 209
Eckert, Douglas, 242
Ecology Action, 138
Economic Opportunity Program, 77, 101
Economics department, 223
Educational administration department, 230

Edwards, George, 274–75
Elderhostel program, 236
Electron microscope, 219
Elias-Button, Karen, 194, 196, 234
Elk's Lodge, 139
Emerson, David, 131
Enders, John, 33–34
Enders, Richard S., 69
Endicott, Douglas, 65
Energy alternatives, 156
English department, 98, 212–13
Environmental concerns, 106, 110–11, 138
Epstein, Joseph, 198
Equal opportunity programs, 157–58
Equal Rights Amendment, 112
Erie Canal, 2
Erwin, Gail, 173
Escuela Normal Clara J. Armstrong, 16
Esposito, Roseann, 247, 267
Essex, Gene, 54
Estabrooks, George, 58
Eurich, Alvin C., 42
Everett, Ruth, 193
Everywoman's Guide to Colleges and Universities, 158
Exline, Jerry, 201, 211
Experience-Based Education, 194
Extension programs, 56–57

Faculty, 294–96; attitudes toward curriculum, 204–6; Brown, 52–55, 58; department chairs, 180–81, 192; evaluation by students, 94–95, 176; mandatory retirement, 175; Perdue, 78, 79, 83–85, 89–95; Poucher, 20; Radley, 159–60, 171–82, 191–202; relationship with students, 40, 55, 94, 178–80, 197, 258; Rice, 41; Riggs, 26–28; Sheldon, 6–8; Swetman, 35–38; union, 83–85, 152, 160–62
Faculty Assembly, 56, 77, 83–85, 86, 97, 107, 181–2, 298
Faculty Council, 42, 56
Faculty Senate. *See* SUNY; Faculty Senate
Fair Haven Bay, 49
Fallbrook Farm, 49, 166; photo, center section
Farnham, Amos W., 27, 51
Farnham Hall, 51
Farnham Youth Development Center, 136, 270

Farrell, Elizabeth, 12
The February Revolution: Petrograd, 1917 (Hasegawa), 193
Feminist movement, 243. *See also* Women's liberation movement, Women's suffrage
Ferraro, Philip, 251
Ferris State College, 14
Ferris Wheel, 126, 214, 249, 255, 256
Ferris, W.N., 14
Festival Chorus, 211
Festival of the Arts, 51, 57, 66
Fields, Laurie, 260
Filburn, Eleanor, 195
Fillmore, Millard, 79, 156
Fines, Sue, 214, 288, 295
Fink, Daniel, 253
Finnegan, Thomas E., 19
FIPSE. *See* Fund for the Improvement of Post-Secondary Education
First Half Century: State Normal and Training School, Oswego, N.Y., 19
Fischer, Frederic, 216
Fisher, John, 195, 287, 289, 309n7
Fitz, George, 12
Fitzgerald, Scott, 246
Fitzgibbons, Joan, 155
Flack, Irwin, 223, 233, 308–9n1
Flores, Michael, 272, 274
Folk Dance Association, 134
Fonda, Jane, 110
Food, 117, 247
Forbes, Geraldine, 193, 195, 223
Foreign exchange programs, 214–15, 232
Foreign Language and Literature program, 213–14, 288. *See also* Department of Foreign Languages and Literature
Foreign Student Affairs and Information Center, 244
Foreign students, 22, 214–15, 236, 243–44, 285
Foreign Studies Center, 99, 198
Fort Ontario Refugee Project, 54
Fort Oswego, 1
Founder's Day, 19, 51, 57, 170
Fox, James, 21
Fox, Michael, 308–9n1
Frankel, Charles, 115
Fraternities. *See* Greek organizations, specific names
"Freedom and Responsibility on Campus"; 110
Freedsen, Professor, 197

Freimanis, Walter, 210, 211
French and Indian War, 1
Frey, Edward, 270
Friendship: How to Give It, How to Get It (Block), 69
Froebel, Friedrich, 21
Fuchs, Lisa, 251
Fund for the Improvement of Post-Secondary Education, 293
Funk, Richard, 221
Funnelle, Amanda, 20, 81
Funnelle Hall, 81, 122, 129, 252–53, 257, 263
Furey, Marybeth, 252
Furrer, Harry, 65
Fur trade, 1
Futures Task Force, 298

GALA. *See* Gay and Lesbian Alliance
Galloway, Richard, 134
Galvin, Kathleen, 251–52
Gangi, Dominic, 183, 277
Gannon, John, 232
Garsiele, Charles, 52
Garzone, Tullio, 200, 225–26
Gay and Lesbian Alliance, 242
Gay Brothers and Sisters of Oswego, 134
Gay Rights Movement, 273–74
General Organization, 33
"General Shop" (course), 226
George, Carol, 93
George, William, 197
Gerber, Barbara: about, 158, 173, 191, 194, 196, 197, 204–5, 234; cited, 152, 154, 174, 178, 179, 192, 228, 292
Gerbracht, Carlton, 54, 309n9
Gerlitzki, Guenther, 242
Gibbons, Mary K., 280
Gibbs, David, 20
Gifted and Talented Institute, 189
Gillett, Karen, 252
Girolamo, Marcia, 124
Glenn, John, 228, 229
Glick, David, 147, 191, 261; photo, center section
Glimmerglass Lagoon, 49, 139; photo, center section
Glinski, John, 125, 230, 309n7
GO. *See* General Organization
Goldman, Debra, 142
Goldwater, Barry, 67, 68

Good, Carter (cited), 16–17
Good-Bye, My Fancy, 41
Gooding, Thomas: about, 193, 194, 195, 232; cited, 91, 96, 108, 109–10, 172, 175, 179, 199, 289
Goodman, Paul, 78, 93
Gordon, Norman, 91, 177–78, 180, 192, 220, 292
Goslin, Jean, 123
Gould, Samuel B., 50, 72, 74
Gould, Wayne, 138
Graduate programs, 42, 48, 56–57, 95, 102, 235
Graduation exercises, 51, 52, 141, 162–63, 195, 279–80, 282
Grafitti, 139
Grant, James F., 155
Grant, Joseph, 157
Great Laker Inn, 214
Great Lakes Review, 136, 263
Greek organizations; 32, 40–41, 60, 62, 65–66, 130–31, 139, 261–63. *See also* specific names of fraternities, sororities
Greek Student Association, 261, 263
Greenberg, Jeffrey, 138
Greene, E. Milton, 14–15
Greenfield, Gloria, 111, 142
Green, William H., 155
Greer, Arthur, 54
Gregory, Dick, 102
Griffin, Clifford S. (cited), x
Griffin, Mary, 92–93
Guevara, E. (cited), 15
Grippe, Roger, 259
Guide to the Best, Most Popular and Most Exciting Colleges (Barron's), 169
Guile, Ronald, 114
Gurley, Sue, 255
Guttendorfer, Hildegarde (Babette), 201

Hadley, Charles, 228
Hagans, Todd, 242
Hagger, Helen, 36, 44, 95, 113
Hall, Melissa, 127
Hamilton, Hiram, 15
Hamilton, Thomas Hale, 51
Hammermill Paper, 79
Hammill, Terrence, 194, 200
Hammond, Herb, 125
Hammond, Steve, 247
Handicapped students. *See* Disabled students

Hanks, William, 199, 309n7
Harper, William, 146
Harrigan, Denise, 142, 184, 281
Harriman, Averill, 49
Harrington, Estelle, 21
Harrington, Patricia, 61, 64
Harris, Emmy Lou, 102
Harrison, Donald, 93, 106, 112, 128, 141, 194, 261
Harrison, Robert, 309n8
Hart Hall, 54, 81, 122, 127, 243, 252
Hart, Isabel Kingsbury, 26, 36, 54, 81
Harvey, Norman, 65
Hasegawa, Tsuyoshi, 193, 200
Hastings, James, 95, 309n9
Hauler, Arthur, 28, 53, 227
Haviland, Alice, 12
Hawkins, Harry, 194
Hayden, Sabra, 23
Hayden, Tom, 110
Hazing, 40, 62–63, 65, 261
Healey, Ruth, 186
Health and physical education departments, 229–30
Health Services, 136–37. *See also* Mary Walker Health Center
Heesemann, John, 256
Heindl, Maryellen, 251
Helmke, Margaret Garno, 61, 62, 66
Helsby, Robert, 53, 141, 163
Hemink, Lynn, 155–56, 166, 177, 191
Henderson, Bernie, 171, 192
Henry, David, 297
Herbartianism, 4, 17, 21
Herman, John, 93
Herrick, Lillie, 5–6, 7, 12
Hewitt, Hazel, 81
Hewitt, Jesse Merle, 81
Hewitt Student Union, 79, 81, 116, 123, 256, 275; photos, center section
Hickey, David, 132
Hicks, Helen, 132
Higher education, 2–3, 24, 34, 35, 45–46, 145–48, 170, 283–98; equal opportunity, 157; finances, 164–67; New York State, 42, 48, 153; 1960's, 81–83
Highways Across the Horizon (Rogers), vii
Hillcrest Hall, 129
Hill, David, 193, 194, 212
Hillick, J. Sheridan, 155
Historical Dictionary of Argentina, 15
History department, 222

"History of Ideas and Concepts of Physics" (course), 218
"The History of Organized Crime" (course), 142
Hitching corner, 64
Hoboken Academy, 13
Hochman, Andee, 239
Hodge, Shirley, 194, 201, 265
Hoffman, Abby, 118
Hoight, Arthur, 13–14
Homecoming, 66, 282
Homespun (Blair-Parker), 13
Homosexuals, 241–42
Honors College, 169–70, 188, 191, 233, 293
Honors Convocation, 57, 163–64, 188, 233–34, 242, 282
Honors Day, 275
Honors Program, 233, 282
Hooper, Howard, 197, 200, 277
Horawski, Wendy, 255
Houdini, Harry, 2
Housing, 10, 21–22, 34, 42, 43, 68, 116, 121–23, 251–55
Howard, James, 162–63, 194, 202, 266
Huang, Mab, 196; photo, center section
Huff, Joan, 201, 309n7
Hulme, Francis (Frank), 90–91, 93–94, 178
Humphreys, Claire, 221
Hurlbutt, Robert, 200
Hurley, Audrey, 157–58
Huss, William, 22
Hutko, Paul, 309n7
Hyde, Kenneth, 193, 218
Hynch, Grace, 26
Hyse, Richard, 229, 309n8

Ieono, Saisuke, 195, 309n8
Immigrants, 2
Industrial arts, 9, 25, 32, 37, 53, 100, 226; curriculum, 28–29, 37, 42, 56–57; women, 32, 227. *See also* Department of Technology
Influenza epidemics: 1918, 25; 1962, 50, 66
Initiations. *See* Hazing
Interdisciplinary programs, 100–101, 231–33, 293
"Intermission" (sculpture), 156
International Education Center, 101
International Relations Club: photo, center section

International Students Association, 244
Internship programs, 212, 215, 221–22, 223, 227, 236
"Introduction to Theatre" (course), 211
Iorizzo, Luciano, 142, 193, 195, 210–11, 232
Iota Clio, 65
Iroquois Indians, 1
Irving, Laurie, 198, 265
Irwin, Sylvia, 309n9
Izzett, Richard, 193, 194, 220

Jackim, Halas, 95, 200
Jacobson, Robert L. (cited), 92
Jakeway's, 30
Janowsky, Melanie, 256, 263
Japan, 16, 50, 79, 146, 164, 215
JEOL Company, 219
Jeopardy and a Jeep (Rogers), vii, 54
Jhun, U-Jin, 223, 232
Johanson, Linda, 246, 255
John Birch Society, 236
Johnson Hall, 137, 139, 158, 251, 252, 263, 268
Johnson, Harold, 37
Johnson, Kathy, 131, 237–38, 252
Johnson, Linda, 259
Johnson, Lyndon B., 68, 107
The Johnson News, 263, 264
Johnston, June Vescio, 194
Jones, Margaret E.M., 4, 6, 7
Judd, Blanche, 194, 195, 234
Judd, C. H., 28
Judd, Thomas, 93, 193, 200, 222, 223, 308–9n1
Judo tournament, 50
Julian, Joseph, 105

Kappa Kappa Kappa, 32
Karate Club, 134
Karcher, Harry, 33, 54
Karns, Lanny, 232
Karr, Grant, 20
Kemp, Kathryn, 111
Kennedy, John F., 67, 99
Kennedy, Robert, 58
Kent State, 70, 86, 105
Kidder, W. H., 18
Kimmich, Rosalind, 309n8
Kindergarten, 17

King, Carol, 54
King, David, 93, 191–92, 195, 223
King Hall, 54
King, Martin Luther, 79
Kingsford Starch, 24
Kingston, John, 13
King, William, 156
Klinger, Frank, 232–33
Knapp, John, 193
Know Your Car (Allen), 226
Koehne, Kathleen, 170, 231
Koenig, George, 308–9n1
Koenigsberg, Frances, 157, 194, 221, 228, 236
Koller, Kathrine, 184, 186
Kon, Gregory, 218
Korean War, 67
Korwin, Lisa, 268
Kowalski, Casimir, 282
Krauss, John, 263
Krolik, Mary Jean, 276
Krusi, Hermann, Jr., 6, 14, 81
Kurasarva, Takashi, 50

Labruz, Ronald, 215
Lacey, Jill, 273
Lackey, James, 201
Laing, Mary E. (cited), 5, 18
Lair, David, 266, 267
Lake Ontario, 110–11, 140
Laker Hall, 79
Lakeside, 149
Lakeside Dining Hall, 51
Lambda Chi Delta, 131
Lanigan Hall: photo, center section
Lanigan, James, 47, 50, 52
Lapinski, Frances, 86, 199
Larson, Mildred, 95, 263
Latin Student Union, 132
Lauria, Diana, 185, 187
Lawrence, Isabel, 7, 19
League for Emancipation of Girls' Skirts, 121
Learning Resources Center, 92
LeBouef, Jack, 69
Lee, Calvin B. T., 30
Lee Hall, 65, 81
Lee, Joel, 271
Lee, Mary V., 7, 81, 193, 201, 279
LeFlore, James, 200, 234
LEGS. *See* League for Emancipation of Girls' Skirts
Lehtonen, Terry, 253
Leighton, Albert, 193, 222–23, 309n8
Leighton, Clarence, 47
LeMoyne, Simon, 1
Leonard, David, 100, 135
LePine, Denise, 265
Lester, Bruce, 192, 228
Lester, Ordelia (Ardie), 8
Levi, Wayne, 267
Libby, Ransom, 32
Liberal arts, 57, 73, 284–85, 290
Liebenauer, Paul, 195
"Light and Color" (course), 218
Linguistic Institute, 99
Linn, Charles, 226
Lipsig, Joseph, 232
The Little Lady Who Wore Pants (Snyder), 54
Littlepage Dining Hall, 79
Little While, 255
Little, Wanda, 122
Liu, Cheng, 195
Lobb, Nancy, 265
"Local and Municipal Courts" (course), 233
Local traditions, 139
Loder, Richard, 220, 221
Logan, Holly, 253
London Home and Colonial School, 3, 4, 6
Long, Joseph, 282
Lonis Hall, 122, 251
Lonky, Edward, 195, 202, 284–85, 291, 292–93
Loonan, Liz, 123
Loper, Orla, 55, 56
Louis XV, 1
Loveridge-Sanbonmatsu, Joan, 193, 196, 212
Lowery, Margaret (Peg), 93, 105, 118, 130, 136, 141, 172, 199, 281, 282; photo, center section
Low Life Caffe, 256
Ludwig, Coy, 194, 209
Luiggi, Alice H., 15
Lundy, William, 197
Luongo, Ernest, 194, 309n7, 309n8
Luyster, Julia, 221
Lydon, Terry, 122

McCavanagh, Eileen, 252
McCullough, Anderson, 211

McDermott, Alice, 142, 282
Macey, Kathleen, 211
McGarvey, William, 56, 201
McGovern, Eleanor, 102
McKelvey, Jeffrey, 249
McKenna, James, 246, 253
Mackin, Hoover, 34
Mackin, Marian, 47
McLaughlin, Carol, 38
McManus, Robert, 225
MacMillan, Mary, 15–16
McMindes, Larry, 252
McNally, Sue, 226, 245, 277
Madore, David, 214
Maestras de Catamarca, 16
Magnarelli, Armand, 43
Maguire, Alice, 212
Mahar Hall, 54, 79, 81
Mahar, Marian, 36, 54, 81
Makeovers (Schrader), 69
Male sexism, 130
Mandeville, Janet, 254, 259
Mangel, Gordon, 47
Manhattan Tribune, 142
Mann, Horace, 17
Mansfield, Jayne, 129
Manual training, 8, 9, 17, 19, 21
Maraviglia, Frank, 282
Market House Music Hall, 256
Markow-Totevy, George, 195, 309n8
Marola, Beth, 262
Marron, Edward, 214
Marshall, Thomas, 309n8
Marsh, Leland (Lee), 195, 199
Martin, Kathryn, 219
Marty, Sherri, 200, 226
Mary Walker Health Center, 81, 136, 230, 269
Master plans, 48, 74–75
Masterson, Donald, 194, 195
Masters: Portraits of Great Teachers (Epstein), 198
Master's program in education, 235
Matador, 255–56
Mathematics department, 215–16
"Math for the Math-Anxious" (course), 216
Mathieu, Donald: about, 158, 191, 195, 223; cited, 74, 85, 96, 159, 166, 167, 180, 206, 209, 213, 219, 221, 222
Matilda J. Gage Library, 137, 268
Mattson, Stanley, 282
Maurer, Robert, 232

Max Ziel Classic, 124
Mayo, A. B., 14
Mazzoli, Frank, 169
Meadows, JoAnn, 201
Meany, Lynn, 230
Mediatore, Cathy, 278
Medieval studies program, 223
Mena, Manuel, 195
Mengel, Gordon, 93
Mensah, Chris, 244
Mental Health Center, 268
Mental Hygiene in Elementary Education (Rogers), 54
Mentoring program, 137, 158, 268
Messere, Frank, 195
Metallo, Tim, 252
Meteorology program, 220
Methodology Institute for Foreign Language Teachers, 189, 236
Mexico, 14–15
Mexico City Normal School, 14
Middleton, DeWight, 193
Mielenhausen, Sandra, 252
Military draft, 106–7, 118, 274
Military science program, 230–31
Miller, Gerritt, 18
Miller, Jean, 142
Miller, Thomas, 34, 35, 41
Milo, Edith, 24, 27, 31
Mincher, John, 170, 211
Minorities, 173–74, 243
"Modern Jamaica" (course), 221
Molinari, James, 197, 200
Mollison, Gilbert, 81
Mondale, Walter, 102
Mongeon's Dungeon, 37
Mongiello, Paul, 122
Monroe, Pearle, 309n7, 309n8
Montagu, Ashley, 102
Montalbano, Maria, 253
Moody, Elizabeth, 191–92, 197–98, 200, 225, 226
Moore, Jack, 254
Moore, Marcia, 192, 212
Moore, Robert, 195
Moore, Rufus, 309n9
Moreland, James, 37, 41
Moreland Hall, 121–22, 251
Morelli, Joanne, 248, 249, 252
Morett, Denise, 246, 251
Morey, Mark, 195, 197, 216, 220, 296
Morford, David, 276

Morgan, Allison, 201
Mormon, Paul, 195
Moroney, Bryan, 253
Morrow, Alcinda, 15
Morse, Thomas, 212
Moss, Theodore, 95, 225, 309n9
Mott, Dorothy, 44
Moving-up Day, 66
Mowatt, Grace, 194, 198, 201, 265
Mueller, Paul, 210
Murayama, Hideo, 79
Murphy, Paul, 135
Murray, Mike, 264
Music department, 210–11
Mustico, Thomas, 195
Myers, Donna, 245

Nader, Ralph, 236
Naisbitt, John (cited), 216, 297, 298
Narkier, Shep, 138
National Commission on the Accreditation of Teacher Education, 164
National Education Association, 161
National Protest Movement, 87
National Student Association, 264
National Student Lobby, 264
National Youth Sports Program, 157, 270
Nation, Margaret, 99
Native American Brotherhood, 132
Native American Studies program, 221, 232
Naznitsky, Burt, 115
NCATE. *See* National Commission on the Accreditation of Teacher Education
Neary, Nancy, 201
Nelson, Sigurd, 219
Nesbitt, Rosemary: about, 164, 171, 192, 193, 197; cited, 146, 150, 170, 175, 179, 203, 205, 211–12, 283–84, 286
New campus: photos, center section
Newman, Edwin, 102
New Principles of Education (Takamine), 16
New York State Public Interest Research Group, 264
New York State Retired Teachers Association, 236
Niagara Mohawk, 79, 110
Nicholson, Robbie, 253
Nicolaidis, Chris, 247
Nielsen, Helen, 27, 31, 32
Nitardy, Walter, 201–2, 266, 267, 309n7
Noncredit courses, 236

Non-traditional Student Union, 245, 269
Nordby, Edward, 99, 213, 214
Normalians, 33
Northrup, Kent, 33
Norton, Lucy, 27
NSA. *See* National Student Lobby
Nuclear power, 110, 272–73
Nuclear war, 68, 110
Nunzi's, 64, 123, 249, 255
Nygard, Eric, 254
NYPIRG. *See* New York State Public Interest Research Group

Object teaching, 4, 8–9, 17
Observatory, 49
O'Connell, George, 194
O'Connor, Peter, 85
O'Connor, Robert, 162, 257
Odell, Marietta, 36, 41
O'Donnell, Lewis, 195
O'Dwyer, John, 192, 218
Oertel, Thomas, 142
Off-Campus Association, 269
Office of Employee Relations, 162
Office of Research and Sponsored Programs, 157, 169
Office of Special Programs, 216
O'Grady, Lois, 27, 31, 32
"Oh, Blue Ontario's Waters," 27
Olcott, Jack, 256
Old City Hall, 256
Older students, 83, 131–32, 235, 245–46, 285–86, 292
Old Main, 51
Oneida Hall, 121, 138, 253
Onondaga Hall, 79, 253
Ontarians, 33
Ontario Center for Performing Arts, 256
Ontario House, 256
Ontario Park, 32
Open-air school, 28
Open House, 269, 275
Operation Attic, 79
Oppenheimer, Mary Ann, 187
Orientation, 237
Orlousky, Michael, 248
Orphan and Free School Association, 3
Osborne, James, 214
Osborne, Nancy, 193, 195, 196
Oshwakee, 25
Ostberg, Louise, 44, 52, 201, 230

Oswego Alumni Association, 14, 16, 42, 44, 53, 68, 141, 210, 280, 281–82
Oswego Boys Club (New York City), 16, 44, 68
Oswego Candy Companies, 79
Oswego Chamber of Commerce, 192
Oswego, City of: history, 1–2, 24; name, 2; 125th birthday, 79; relations with college, 138, 269–70
Oswego: Fountainhead of Teacher Education, A Century in the Sheldon Tradition (Rogers), ix, 14, 52, 54
Oswego Historical Society, 1, 36
Oswego Housing Authority, 47
Oswego Industrial Arts Curriculum Library, 227
Oswegonian, 66, 95, 135–36, 142, 148, 263; personals, 257. Also cited throughout
Oswego Normal School, 3–38; alumni, 12–16; educational philosophy, 21; fire, 34; founding, 3–4; new site, 18–19
Oswego Normal School Alumni Association, 16
Oswego Opera Theatre, 211
Oswego Port Authority, 128
Oswego Red Cross Blood Drive, 270
Oswego Seminary, 3
Oswego State Normal and Training School, 4, 25
Oswego Switch Canal, 2
Oswego Women's Center. *See* Women's Center
Overseas study programs, 98, 99, 214–15, 232, 238

Pacilio, Janice, 247
Palladiu, 20
Palladium Times, 47, 81, 128, 272
Panty raids, 129–30
Para FUNNELLEia, 263
Parents' Day, 277
Parents' Handbook, 277
Parents' Weekend, 50, 163–64, 210, 278
Parisi, David, 266, 267
Packer, Francis, 17
Park Hall, 42
Park, Joseph C., 21, 27–18, 37
Parkside Drive-In, 123
Patch, 255
Pathfinder Dining Hall, 127, 253
Pathfinder Dormitory, 253–54

Peace Corps, 67
Peer Advisement Center, 268
The Pendulum, 136, 263
Penfield Library, 36, 79, 156, 258, 268
Penfield, Lida, 36
Penney, George, 47
Penney, Sherry, 205
Perdue, James E., 50, 70–143, 151–52, 181, 186, 231, 289, 294, 296, 297; acting Provost, 164; background, 72–73; buildings, 79–81; curriculum, 95–102, 204, 205; faculty, 78, 79, 83–85, 89–95; photos, center section
Perez, José, 195
Perlin, Nancy, 268
Persephone Press, 142
Perticore, Eugene, 228
Pestalozzi: His Life Works and Influence (Krusi), 14
Pestalozzianism, 3–4, 6, 16, 17, 21
Peterson, Patricia, 201, 229
Peterson, Patti McGill, 77, 133, 137, 173, 187, 192, 197, 282; photo, center section
Pfund, Richard, 100, 309n7, 309n8
Phallen, Charles, 309n7, 309n9
Phi Delta Kappan, 176, 217
Phillips, Thomas, 134
Phillips, Walter P., 49
Philosophy department, 215
Phi Omicron Xi, 139
Phi Sigma Epsilon, 65
Phi Sigma Phi, 65, 130
Phoenix, Lydia, 22
"Photography" (course), 226
Physical education, 100. *See also* Health and physical education departments
Physics department, 218–19
Pierce, Christine, 194, 215, 234
Piez Hall, 51, 100
Piez, Richard, 9, 18, 20, 21, 26, 192
Pillar of Pepper (Knapp), 193
Pitluga, George: about, 49, 99, 178; cited, 34, 35, 50, 55, 60, 73, 75, 84, 90, 91, 92, 94, 98, 175, 289
Pittenger, Owen, 195, 228, 309n7
Piucci, Virginio, 53
Plante, Marianne, 261–62
Plunkett, Mr., 21
Political science department, 221–22
Politics, 67–68
"Politics and Education" (course), 73

Pollution, 110–11. *See also* Environmental concerns
Pope, Wendell, 278
Popham, Lewis, 74, 101, 147, 170, 191, 192, 197, 227, 235–36, 309n8
Potter, Donald, 267
Poucher, Catherine Allen, 20
Poucher Hall, 81
Poucher, Isaac, 6, 18–23, 81; curriculum, 21; death, 25; faculty, 20; photo, center section
Poucher, Matilda Cooper, 20. *See also* Cooper, Matilda
Powell, Thomas: about, 193, 223, 308–9n1; cited, 75–76, 78, 85, 88, 89, 90, 91, 96, 98, 100–101, 102, 110, 168, 180, 181
Powers, Harold (Hop), 56, 178, 309n9
Practice teaching, 8, 28
Pratt, Elizabeth, 261
Pratt, Peter, 57
Pratt, Richard, 266
Pratt, Virginia, 93, 199, 223
Pregnancy, 136–37
Preston, Greg, 266
Professional studies, 96, 100
Professor Recognition Day, 163–64
Project Intervene, 157
Psi Phi, 32, 40
Psychological Counseling and Consultation Center, 136
Psychology department, 58, 220
Public Ceremonies Committee, 163
Public justice, 232–33
Putnam, Thomas, 309n8

Quest, 233
Quest '80, 169
Quick, Deborah, 248, 256–57
Quigley, Paul, 248

Rabert, Cindy, 278
Racism, 105, 106
Radin, Leslie, 197
Radley, Virginia L., 5, 74, 144–298; background, 147, 182–90; campus police, 272; controversies, 148–49; curriculum, 203–38, 286–87, 290; English department, 212–13; faculty, 159–60, 171–82, 191–202; health and physical education departments, 230, 266; inauguration, 162; photos, center section; Provost, 75, 85, 102–3; role model for women, 158–59; Shady shore, 148–49; Sheldon Hall, 149; student behavior, 258, 270; teacher education, 284; women, 243
Rainbow Resort Review, 263
Rank, Vernon, 212, 309n9
Ransom, George B., 8
Rape Crisis Center, 137, 268–69
Ratzeburg, Fred, 108, 109, 183, 200, 228, 309n7
Reading Center, 58
Reading education department, 230, 235
Reagan, Ronald, 164, 274, 275
Reagan's Silver Lake, 275
"Realm of Physics" (course), 218
Refugee Children's Council, 54
Regents Scholarship Examination Scores, 60
Reihman, Jacqueline, 195, 202, 233, 286, 291, 294–95, 298
Religion, 134, 241
Renner, Richard, 176
Replogle, Barbara, 279
Reserve Officer Training Corps. *See* ROTC
Resident assistants, 122
Retired Senior Volunteer Program of Oswego, 157
Reynolds, William, 54
Rice, Anna. *See* Roberts, Anna Rice
Rice Creek Biological Filed Station, 79–80, 219, 232
Rice, Dorothy, 41
Rice, Harvey Mitchell, 41–44; curriculum, 41–42; faculty; 41; photo, center section
Richardson, Harold, 54
Richardson, Margaret Mansfield, 47, 155
Rich Hall, 107, 114, 268
Richmond, David, 195, 201
Ricketson, Darwin Schley, 282
Ricketson, Maria Kimmel, 61, 62, 282
Riesman, David (cited), 90, 158, 173, 179, 198, 212, 237
Riggs Hall, 139, 251, 252, 263–64
Riggs, James, 24–34; 81; curriculum, 26, 28–29; faculty, 26–28; photo, center section
Ripp, Joan, 142
Ripp, Victor, 142
Robbins, John, 122
Robert, Cindy, 254

Roberts, Anna Rice, 15
Roberts, Dale, 250, 279
Roberts, Donna, 267
Roberts, George, 15
Robinson, Frank, 54, 174, 309n9
Robson, Ann, 132, 280
Roca, Luis, 251, 257, 276
Rockefeller, Nelson, 48, 78–79, 127, 151, 152, 232, 282
Rock, Robert, 100, 113, 114, 117, 135
Roe, Debbie (cited), 94, 110, 113–14, 118, 121, 125, 128, 130, 136, 140, 200, 201
Rogers, Dorothy, vii, 36, 42, 44, 52, 54, 81, 171, 174, 195, 196, 309n8
Rogers, Paul, 210
Romano, Barb, 253
Rombach, Richard, 142
Romney, Golden, 35, 36, 41, 48
Romney Field House, 48–49, 51, 163, 279
Roosevelt, Franklin D., 25
Roodin, Paul, 193, 308–9n1
Rorty, Richard, 215
Rosenberg, Harold, 75
Rosenberg, Staci, 255
Rosenhaus, Hope, 275, 276
Rosenkranz, Peter, 266
Rosenthal, Mitchell, 268
Rosovky Plan, 207
ROTC, 101, 105, 114, 230–31
Roth, Francine Israelton, 143
Rourke, Theresa H., 112
Rowland, Paul, 253
Rubber stamps, 56
Rubin, Jerry, 118, 236
Rudd, Aline, 309n8
Rudolph, Jay, 54
Ruppert, Patricia, 141, 281
Rushwood Hall, 149
Russian department, 99
Russian-Eastern European studies, 232
Russian exchange program, 99, 214
Rutherford, James (cited), 217

St. Onge, Edward, 66
St. Patrick's Day, 276
Salander, Cary, 49
Salem, Martin, 252
Salisbury, Robert, 200
Salisbury, Seward, 93, 95
Sampson, Socrates, 194, 309n8
SAMS. *See* Students and Mothers

SANE. *See* Students Against Nuclear Energy
Sanford, Nevitt (cited), 114–15
Sarmiento's Daughters, (Coreas), 15–16
SASU. *See* Student Association of State University
Saunders, Aulus, 95, 209
SAVAC. *See* Student Association Volunteer Ambulance Corps
Savage, Leslie, 27
Sawyer, Peter, 273
Scales, Caroline L.G., 20, 26, 27; photo, center section
Scales Hall, 122, 251, 258, 264
Schattle, Amy, 229
Schell, Michael, 155
Schell, Robert, 138, 194, 195
Scheuerman, William, 152, 153, 161, 176, 181, 197, 204, 222
Schleup, John, 309n9
Schneider, Frank, 26, 30, 55
Schoenbaum, David, 58
Schoenfelt, Joseph, 55, 72, 194
School psychology and counseling department, 228
Schrader, Constance Del Bourgo, 69
Schroeder, Lorraine, 248, 251, 254
Schwab, Suzanne, 219
Schwertfager, Sandy, 254
Science department, 99–100, 217
SDS. *See* Students for a Democratic Society
Seago, James, 219
Sears, Cynthia Lovelace, 184, 187–88
Sears, Peter, 266
Seawell, Thomas, 194, 308–9n1
SEEP. *See* Student Evening Escort Patrol
Senate Professional Association, 161
Seneca Hall, 114, 121, 139, 253, 268, 276
Sereno's, 249, 255
Services to Aid Families in Oswego County, 270
Severance, Lena H., 12
Sgroi, Celia, 172, 197, 201, 202, 232
Shady Shore, 3, 6, 72, 148–49; photos, center section
Shallit, Jonathan, 210
Shambo, Thomas, 267
Shane, Harold (cited), 217, 221, 294, 296
Shanker, Albert, 160
Shapiro, Steven, 216–17
Shaver, Paul, 55, 309n9

INDEX

Shaw, James, 259, 271
Shear, Sandy, 127
Sheldon Associates, 281
Sheldon, Charles, 18, 20, 24–25
Sheldon, Edward Austin, 3–6, 8, 16–18, 186; curriculum, 8; death, 5; disciplinarian, 5; elementary education, 16–17; faculty, 6–8; founding of Oswego Normal School, 3–4; furniture, 156; physical appearance, 5; photos, center section; statue, 18, 64, 128, 136, 139, center section; teacher training, 17
Sheldon Forum, 41
Sheldon, Frances Stiles, 3
Sheldon Hall, 14, 24, 42, 51, 64, 149, 280; closing, 149, 274; photo, center section
Sheldon Institute, 189, 236
Sheldon, Mary. *See* Barnes, Mary Sheldon
Shimada, Keiji, 164
Shineman, Barbara, 197, 281
Shoemaker, Charles, 40, 47, 154, 173, 197, 227–28, 309n7, 309n8
Shoemaker, John, 262
Shore Acres Park, 49
Un Siglo de Educación en Catamarca (Del Pino), 16
Sigman, Nancy, 201
Sigma Phi Rho, 41
Siugma Tau Chi, 65
Silveira, Augustine, 171, 192, 193, 217, 218
Simkewicz, Helen Buckley, 158, 193, 197. *See also* Buckley, Helen
Simmonds, Tom, 201
Sinnamon, Caroline, 26, 27
Sipser, Kenneth, 100, 308–9n1
65 Valiants (Luiggi), 15
Skidmore, Owings and Merrill, 48, 80
Slater, Dawn, 198
Sloan, Robert, 56
Smernoff, Richard, 192, 213
Smernoff, Susan, 214
Smiley, Marilynn, 171, 173, 196, 210
Smith, B.C., 115
Smith, Daniel, 277
Smith, James, 193
Smith, M. Estellie, 193, 200, 220, 221
Smith, Pearl, 30, 33
Smoking, 117
Snakepit, 40
Snow, Frances, 14–15
Snowstorms, 50, 78, 125, 276–77
Snyder, Charles, 54, 79, 156, 222

Snygg, Donald, 81
Snygg Hall, 79, 81, 100
Sociology department, 221
Solid State, 210
Soluri, James, 210, 211
Sommers, Eileen, 266
Sons of Sam, 210
Sons of Soluri, 210
Sons of the Wilted Wallet, 41
Soovajian, Anita, 278
Sorensen, Hilda, 210
Sorensen, Ronald L., 197
Sororities. *See* Greek organizations, specific names
SOS Rock Band, 210
"Sound of Music" (course), 218–19
Specht, Steven, 254
Spector, Charles, 229
Spector, Sherman, 187
Spencer, Ralph: about, 164, 171, 191; cited, 18, 146, 150, 162, 167, 168, 170, 175, 178, 205–6, 209, 225, 228, 283, 284
Splinter Village, 42, 48, 81
Sports, 23, 33, 43–44, 64–65, 123–25, 266–68; women, 23, 124–25, 229–30, 265–66
Spring break, 276
Springfest, 275
Stamm, Alfred, 232
Stamm, James, 229
Stark, George, 194, 209, 309n8
Stata, William, 130
State Singers, 210
State University Atmospheric Sciences Research Center, 57
State University Federation of Teachers, 161
State University of New York. *See* SUNY
State University Research Center at Oswego, 236
State University Senate Governance Committee, 85
Steck-Turner, Sue Ann, 308–9n1
Steignuf, Nancy, 279
Steiner, Cheryl, 233
Steinkraus, Warren, 92
Sternlicht, Sanford, 90, 172, 193, 195, 211, 308–9n1
Stevens, Jeannette, 15
Stiles, Frances. *See* Sheldon, Frances Stiles
Stirling, Robert, 309n9

Stoller, Josh, 172
Stolwell, Mr., 19
Straight, Emma Dickerman, 16
Straight, Henry, 7-8
Streedy, Malcolm, 247
Strickland, Marian, 44
Struzinsky, Alice, 201, 265
Student activity fees, 115-116
Student Advisement and Counseling Centers, 268
Student Advisement Center, 188
Student Advisory Committee, 271
Student Association, 115, 117, 125, 126, 134-35, 158, 268, 275
Student Association of State University, 116, 135, 264
Student Association Volunteer Ambulance Corps, 135
Student Evening Escort Patrol, 269
Student government, 33, 264-65
Student Handbook: 1941-42, 39-40; 1961-62, 60-61; 1963-64, 63
Student Industrial Arts Association, 209
Student League of Women Voters, 31-32
Student protests, 70, 104-19; 1920's, 24; 1930's, 38-39; 1950's and 1960's, 62; 1970, 86-87; strike, 108-10
Students, 202, 203, 237; 1800's, 9-12; 1900's, 21-23; 1920's, 29-33; 1930's, 38-39; 1940's, 39-41, 43; 1950's and 1960's, 58-68; 1965-1976, 120-43; 1970's, 86-88, 97, 104-19; 1980's, 239-82; activities, 11, 22-23, 29, 32, 40, 44; dress, 9-10, 21, 29, 31, 39, 43, 60-61, 105, 112-13, 120-21, 246; evaluation of faculty, 94-95, 176; expenses, 10-11, 31, 61-62, 68, 123, 249; food, 117, 247; housing, 10, 21-22, 34, 42, 43, 68, 116, 121-23, 251-55; relationship with faculty, 40, 55, 94, 178-80, 197, 258; religion, 134, 241. *See also* Black students, Disabled students, Disadvantaged students, Homosexuals, Older students, Women, Veterans
Students Against Nuclear Energy, 110
Students and Mothers, 245
Students for a Democratic society, 86-87
Students' Oracle, 95
Sucher, Steve, 141
Sullivan, John T., 155
Summer sessions, 28, 48, 57, 235-36
Sunsets, 140

SUNY, 47, 82-85, 91, 150-54, 284, 287, 297; admissions, 168-69; competition with private education, 88; creation, 42; curriculum, 205-6, 208; faculties, 160-62; Faculty Senate, 85; finances; 82, 165-67, 273; Greek organizations, 65; investments in South Africa, 274; master plans, 48, 74-75; sports, 267-68; 25th anniversary, 79, 102
SUNY Association of Council Members and College Trustees, 155
Suppes, Ralph, 255
SURCO. *See* State University Research Center at Oswego
Svec, Melvina, 54, 95
Sweeney, Robert, 141
Swetman, Ralph Waldo, 34-41, 81; curriculum, 35, 37-38; death, 54; faculty, 35-38; photo, center section; portrait destroyed, 42-43
Swift, Nathan, 179-80, 194
Sykes, Robert, 55, 57-58, 178, 193, 220, 296-97
Syrell, Linda, 171, 192
Szarek, Patricia, 261

Takamine, Hideo, 16, 50, 81
"The Task Force on Improving the Quality of Student Life Within the University", 267-68
Tassini, Peter, 275
Tavern, 256, 257
Taylor, Eliza, 12
Taylor Law, 83, 84
Taylor, Mark, 278
Teacher education, 16-18, 19, 46, 56, 57, 73, 100, 224-25, 284, 292; influence of Oswego alumni, 17-18
10-to-25 Club, 281
Tasoriero, Sam, 123
Tevendale, William, 130
Theater department, 211-12
Third Curriculum, 102, 236-37
Thole, Robert, 65
Thomas, David, 219
Thomas, M. Carey, 146
Thompson, Uldrick, 7, 12, 13
Thorndike, Edward, 28
Timberlake, Constance H., 155
Toal, Colleen, 261
"Today's Technology" (course), 226

Todd, William, 309n7, 309n8
The Toilet Paper, 263–64
Tokyo Normal School, 16
Tompkins, Robert, 116
Torby, Halette, 271
Torchlight Ceremony, 35, 163, 170, 280
Tracey, Ellen, 127
Trachtenberg, Stephen L. (cited), 298
Travis, Diane, 214
Tryon, Vernon, 40, 47, 55, 58, 154, 172, 173, 192, 226, 227
Tucker, William, 274
Tulloch, Winsome, 133
Turco, Lewis, 193, 213, 263
Turco, Melora, 263
Turcotte, Alice, 200
Turner, Charles S., 45, 48, 50, 52, 53
Tyler Art Gallery, 194; photo, center section
Tyler Chamber Readers, 209
Tyler Hall, 79, 81, 156, 209

"Uhuru Sasu", 132–33
"Unchained", 142
Understanding American Industries (Gerbracht), 54
Unger, Donald, 266
United States Hotel, 4, 24
United States Student Association, 264
United Student Social Workers, 116
United University Professions, 83–85, 152, 160, 181
University of the State of New York, 42
USSA. *See* United States Student Association
UUP. *See* United University Professions

Vaillencourt, Ronnie, 200
Vandalism, 169
Van Dyke, Obele, 309n8
Van Dot, Benjamin, 68
Vanouse, Donald, 165
Van Schaack, Herbert, 166, 182, 192, 195, 199, 294, 308–9n1, 309n7
Varhus, Sara, 195, 233
Vega Honor Society, 282
Vendango, 99
Vermilye, Jon, 212
Veterans, 34, 39, 42, 43, 46, 134, 231
Veterans' Affairs Office, 134

Veterans Club, 231
Vietnam War, 67–68, 70, 71, 92, 105, 107–8, 118, 220
Vocational technical education department, 228–29
The Vocationist, 34
Vona's, 62
Vottis, Mike, 264, 273

Wager, Michael, 200
Waggoner, Sam, 130
Wagner, Marjorie Downing, 243
Wahl, Ellen, 157
Walker Health Center. *See* Mary Walker Health Center
Walker, Mary E., Dr., 7, 23, 54, 81
Walker, Richard, 309n8
Walker, Ursula, 198
Wallace, Sandra, 111
Walters, James, 83
Warner, White, 54, 309n9
War of 1812, 2
Wassenaar, James, 121–22, 156, 178–79, 191, 241, 257, 277–78
Waterbury, Edwin, 81
Waterbury Hall, 81, 251–52, 263–64
Waterfront Studio, 72
"Watergate and the Presidency" (course), 100
"Watergate: Discretionary Justice" (course), 100
Waterman, Charlotte, 27, 81
Waterman Theatre, 81, 156, 211
Watt, James, 275
Way Down East (Blair-Parker), 13
Weber, Kevin, 253
Weber, Peter, 232
Weber, Sue, 196
Weeks, Charles, 122
Weeks, John, 55, 94
Weiner, Norman, 201, 308–9n1
Welland Hotel, 10, 21–22, 25, 27, 30, 31, 149
Wellman, Judith, 79, 192, 194, 196, 223, 234
Wells, Charles, 54, 95
Wells, Lillian, 49
Westcott, Alvin, 309n7
Wharton, Clifton R., Jr.: about, 154, 299–301; cited, 151, 152, 153, 158, 167, 177, 206–8, 235, 267, 283, 284, 285, 287,

288, 290, 291–92, 294, 297
Wharton, Dolores Duncan, 154, 300–301
What's the Buzz, 263, 264
The Wheel, 256
Wheeler House, 31
Wheeler, Richard: about, 53, 191, 309n7, 309n8; cited, 46, 52, 86, 108–9, 151, 154, 167, 168, 175, 204, 205, 216, 217–18, 233, 234–35, 237, 238, 284
Whipple, William, 202, 233, 293
White, Dennis, 245–46, 259
Whitten, Norman, 54, 309n9
Widrick, Glendon, 124
Wiecha, Joseph, 171, 193, 198–99, 214
Wiggins, Robin, 265
Wilber, Gordon, 22, 37, 41, 53, 55
Wilbur, H.B., 4
Wilbur, Paul, 166, 195, 308–9n1
Williams, Helen, 12
Wing, Lucy, 194, 228
Winter Weekend, 66
Wise, Ernest, 55
Witney, Marilyn, 121
Wittenberg, Marsha, 246
WOCR, 263
Wolfe, Barbara, 122
Wolniak, Steve, 219
Women, 38, 39–40, 51, 60, 62, 67, 77, 111–13, 138, 240, 243; alcohol, 250; business majors, 237; curfew, 21, 63, 113–14, 115; dress, 7, 10, 21, 23, 31, 43, 61, 112–13, 246; faculty, 26, 173; Industrial Arts, 32, 227; married, 132; mentoring program, 137, 158, 268; older, 83, 130–31; pregnancy, 136–37; relationship with men, 259–60; restrictions, 10–11, 21–22, 23, 30, 31, 43, 63–64; rights, 106; role in higher education, 147–48, 158; sports, 23, 124–25, 229–30, 265–66
"Women and Culture" (course), 200, 234
Women for a New World, 142, 268
"Women in Management" (course), 205
"Women in Politics" (course), 234
Women's Caucus, 158, 196
Women's Center, 137, 142, 268
Women's Crisis Center, 134, 136, 137
Women's liberation movement, 158. *See also* Feminist movement, Women's suffrage
Women's Student Senate Caucus, 243
Women's studies, 158, 194, 196, 202, 223, 234
Women's suffrage, 22, 29–30
Wood, Aaron, 277
Woodin, Allen, 253
Woodring, Paul, 84, 94
World War I, 25, 29, 81
World War II, 34, 37–38, 39, 45–46, 48, 56, 81
Wray, Andy, 197
Wray, Sue, 243, 264, 279
Wright, Fanny, 2
Wright, Julie, 277
Wrinkles, How to Prevent Them (Schrader), 69
Writing Institute, 188–89
WRVO, 142, 263
WTOP, 263, 275

Yager, Charles, 55, 99, 178
Yamaki, Yoshizo, 164
Yearbooks, 25
Yeo, James, 2
Yockey, Wilbur Dean, 140
Young, Alfred, 221, 223
Young Americans for Freedom, 67
Young, Charles, 30

Zampino, Philip, 269
Zecchino, Karen, 246
Zeller, Gerhard, 93, 201
Zeta Rho, 65
Ziel, Max, 32, 43, 55, 58, 124, 193
Zoology department, 219
Zuckman, Dawn, 247
Zystynaik, Bill, 135

SUNY College at Oswego:
Its Second Century Unfolds
was set in 10/12 Caledonia, with display type set in Caslon italic,
on a Linotron 202 by Coghill Book Typesetting Co., Inc.;
printed by sheetfed offset on 50-pound, acid free Glatfelter
B-16 Natural Hi-Bulk, Smyth sewn and bound over binder's boards
in Holliston Roxite C, with dust jackets printed in two colors
by Braun-Brumfield, Inc.;
and designed by Will Underwood